Applying GAA[

2019–20

A Practical Guide to
Financial Reporting

Applying GAAP
2019–20

A Practical Guide to Financial Reporting

Michelle Roberts ACA

Croner-i

HR · Tax · H&S · Audit & Accounting

© 2019 Croner-i Ltd

Croner-i Ltd
240 Blackfriars Road
London SE1 8NW
United Kingdom
Telephone: 0800 231 5199
E-mail: client.experience@croneri.co.uk
Website: croneri.co.uk

ISBN 978-1-78887-283-6

British Library Cataloguing-in-Publication Data

A catalogue record for this book is available from the British Library.

Typeset by Innodata Inc., India.

Printed and bound by L.E.G.O. S.p.A. – Italy

Contents

Contents

Contents

Contents

Contents

Contents

Contents

About the author

Michelle Roberts ACA is a senior technical writer for audit and accountancy at Croner-i where she focuses on UK GAAP commentary products, audit tools and Croner-i eCPD.

Before joining Croner-i, Michelle spent 11 years in KPMG's audit department gaining experience across a wide range of industries including business services, construction and utilities. Michelle also has experience of authoring and delivering technical training material to meet the needs of KPMG's UK audit staff.

Preface

Just as the UK financial reporting regime seemed to be settling down, 1 January 2019 signals a period of yet more change as the amendments to FRS 102 *The Financial Reporting Standard applicable in the UK and the Republic of Ireland,* arising from the FRC's triennial review of the UK financial reporting framework, take effect. While the impact on disclosure and presentation is relatively minimal, some significant changes to recognition and measurement may result in accounting policy changes and the need to restate comparative figures. The FRC published updated editions of FRSs 100–105 in March 2018 which incorporate the changes arising from the triennial review.

Further down the line, the FRC is expected to consult on how to implement the requirements of IFRS 9 *Financial Instruments* (in respect of impairment), IFRS 15 *Revenue from Contracts with Customers* and IFRS 16 *Leases* into FRS 102. The FRC has not yet indicated when this consultation may take place, but it appears unlikely that any proposed amendments relating to IFRS 9, 15 or 16 will take effect in UK GAAP until at least 2023 and possibly later.

Applying GAAP 2019–20 covers both the requirements of FRS 102 and of FRS 105 *The Financial Reporting Standard applicable to the Micro-entities Regime* for periods beginning on or after 1 January 2019. The guide is based on the March 2018 editions of these standards so includes the amendments which arose from the triennial review. Key differences in the requirements for micro-entities under FRS 105 for each relevant topic are highlighted in a grey tinted box.

This guide addresses the accounting principles, policies and procedures in FRS 102 and FRS 105. Commentary on disclosures is provided where relevant but a comprehensive list of disclosure requirements is not included here; further detail and checklists on disclosures are available in *Preparing FRS 102 Company Accounts* and *Preparing Small and Micro Company Accounts.* Interactive Disclosure Checklists and Model Accounts are also available on the *Croner-i Tax and Accounting* platform.

Michelle Roberts ACA

May 2019

1 Scope and purpose of Applying GAAP

1.1 Purpose of this guide and how to use it

This guide provides a detailed in-depth commentary on what is required by FRS 102 *The Financial Reporting Standard applicable in the UK and the Republic of Ireland* and how to apply those requirements in practice. It is applicable for entities of all sizes, including small entities applying the reduced disclosure regime set out in Section 1A (as the recognition and measurement requirements of FRS 102 apply equally to small entities).

Applying GAAP 2019–20 reflects all amendments made to, and versions of, FRS 102 up to April 2019. As such, it is based on the standard published in March 2018 (referred to in this guide as FRS 102 or FRS 102 (2018) where needed). This is effective for periods beginning on or after 1 January 2019 but is available for early adoption. FRS 102 (2018) includes the amendments to FRS 102 arising from the Financial Reporting Council's (FRC's) triennial review of the framework.

The guide also contains commentary on applying FRS 105, the Financial Reporting Standard applicable to micro-entities, again based on the version dated March 2018. Where the requirements in FRS 105 differ from those in FRS 102, they are set out and explained in a tinted box in the relevant section.

The guide is divided into themed sections which address FRS 102's 36 sections. The guide sets out the comparable standard in IFRS, discusses the detailed application of the FRS 102 requirements and provides notes on disclosure requirements and on any transitional provisions that apply in that area.

The primary focus of this product is on application of the recognition and measurement requirements of FRS 102 and disclosures are therefore not addressed in detail; for further guidance on presenting and disclosing information under FRS 102 or FRS 105, please refer to *Preparing FRS 102 Accounts* or *Preparing Small and Micro Company Accounts*, as relevant.

1.2   The UK financial reporting framework

1.2.1   The financial reporting standards

In addition to EU-endorsed IFRS, the UK financial reporting regime consists of the following six standards:

- FRS 100 *Application of Financial Reporting Requirements* sets out the overall framework for financial reporting, explaining which standards apply to various types of entity, when an entity can apply the reduced disclosure framework available through FRS 101, and when an entity should also make reference to a SORP.

- FRS 101 *Reduced Disclosure Framework* sets out a reduced disclosure framework, available to qualifying entities which otherwise apply the recognition, measurement and disclosure requirements of IFRS as adopted by the EU. Such entities – which include subsidiaries and parent entities which meet certain criteria – can elect to apply this reduced disclosure framework when preparing their individual financial statements. Many listed groups have taken advantage of the reduced disclosure framework for the preparation of the individual financial statements of their UK subsidiaries and the separate financial statements of the parent company.

- FRS 102 *The Financial Reporting Standard applicable in the UK and Republic of Ireland* contains all the detailed accounting requirements for those entities not applying EU-adopted IFRS, FRS 101 or FRS 105. It also includes specific provisions for small entities, including a new Section 1A setting out disclosure exemptions.

- FRS 103 *Insurance Contracts* is relevant to entities applying FRS 102 that issue insurance contracts and may be relevant to some entities other than insurers.

- FRS 104 *Interim Financial Reporting* applies to FRS 102 preparers presenting interim financial information and is based on IAS 34.

- FRS 105 *The Financial Reporting Standard applicable to the Micro-entities Regime* offers a considerably simplified set of requirements for companies that qualify as micro-entities.

Non-small (i.e. medium/large) entities were required to adopt FRS 102 (unless opting for IFRS or FRS 101) for accounting periods commencing on or after 1 January 2015. Reduced disclosures for qualifying entities (broadly, companies within a group which prepares publicly available consolidated accounts) are also available under FRS 102. Small companies were required to adopt FRS 102, with the optional Section 1A dealing with reduced disclosure and presentation requirements, for accounting periods commencing on or after 1 January 2016.

Micro-entities qualifying for and wishing to adopt the micro-regime must use FRS 105 for accounting periods commencing on or after 1 January 2016. Previously, the rules for micros were contained within the FRSSE, which was withdrawn at the end of 2015.

For companies, the requirements in financial reporting standards are underpinned by company law, in the form of the *Companies Act* 2006 (CA 2006) and related regulations, primarily the *Small Companies and Groups (Accounts and Directors' Report) Regulations* 2008 (SI 2008/409) and the *Large and Medium-sized Companies and Groups (Accounts and Reports) Regulations* 2008 (SI 2008/410), both as amended by the *Companies, Partnerships and Groups (Accounts and Reports) Regulations* 2015 (SI 2015/980).

1.2.2   Who applies which standard?

Any UK company may choose to apply EU-adopted IFRS and listed companies are required to apply EU-adopted IFRS in their consolidated accounts. Qualifying companies within a group can choose to apply FRS 101. Unlisted large and medium-sized companies can apply 'full' FRS 102, while small companies can apply FRS 102 with the optional Section 1A which offers reduced disclosure. Micro-entities can apply FRS 105, the simplest standard. **Table 1.1** sets out the various options depending on the type of company.

Table 1.1	*Financial Reporting Framework as set out in FRS 100*					
	EU-IFRS	Reduced disclosures (FRS 101)	FRS 102	FRS 102 with Section 1A	Reduced disclosures (FRS 102)	FRS 105
Micro-entities						
Group consolidated	✓	✗	✓	✓	✗	✗[1]
Parent or subsidiary[2]	✓	✓	✓	✓	✓	Possibly[3]
Standalone entity	✓	✗	✓	✓	✗	✓
Small unlisted entities (not micro)						
Group consolidated	✓	✗	✓	✓	✗	✗
Parent or subsidiary	✓	✓	✓	✓	✓	✗
Standalone entity	✓	✗	✓	✓	✗	✗

Large or medium-sized unlisted entities						
Group consolidated	✓	✗	✓	✗	✗	✗
Parent or subsidiary	✓	✓	✓	✗	✓	✗
Standalone entity	✓	✗	✓	✗	✗	✗
Listed entities						
Group consolidated	✓	✗	✗	✗	✗	✗
Parent or subsidiary	✓	✓	✓	✗	✓	✗
Standalone entity	✓	✗	✓	✗	✗	✗

[1] *The micro-regime cannot be applied to consolidated accounts.*

[2] *A qualifying entity is a member of a group that prepares publicly available consolidated financial statements, which are intended to give a true and fair view, in which that member is consolidated.*

[3] *The micro-regime can only be applied to entities that do not prepare and are not included in consolidated accounts, so FRS 105 would only be available if the group is exempt from preparing consolidated accounts (i.e. because the group is small).*

1.2.3   Qualifying for the small and micro-regimes

Under CA 2006, a company is treated as micro, small or medium-sized if it does not exceed more than one of the following criteria for two consecutive years:

Table 1.2 Size criteria for the small and micro regimes		
	Micro	Small
Turnover	£632,000	£10.2m
Balance sheet total	£316,000	£5.1m
Average number of employees (on a monthly basis)	10	50

The following companies cannot use the small companies regime:

(a) public companies (i.e. any UK incorporated public limited company, whether its securities are traded on a market or privately held);

(b) authorised insurance companies, banking companies, e-money issuers, MiFID investment firms or UCITS management companies;

(c) companies carrying on insurance market activity (as defined by the *Financial Services and Markets Act* 2000, s. 316(3), 'insurance market activity' means a regulated activity relating to contracts of insurance written at Lloyd's); or

(d) members of an ineligible group.

Such companies are excluded from the small companies regime, regardless of their size.

A group is ineligible if any one or more of its members is:

(a) a traded company (note that this used to be a public company prior to the implementation of SI 2015/980);

(b) a body corporate (other than a company) whose shares are admitted to trading on a regulated market in an EEA State;

(c) a person (other than a small company) who has permission under the *Financial Services and Markets Act* 2000, Pt. 4 to carry on a regulated activity;

(d) an e-money issuer;

(e) a small company that is an authorised insurance company, a banking company, a MiFID investment firm or a UCITS management company; or

(f) a person who carries on insurance market activity.

A group is defined in CA 2006, s. 474 as 'a parent undertaking and its subsidiary undertakings', as defined in CA 2006, s. 1162. A company is generally a subsidiary if more than 50% of its voting shares are held by another (parent) company.

A traded company is defined in CA 2006, s. 474 as a company any of whose transferable securities are admitted to trading on a regulated market. The definition of a regulated market is set out in the EU's Markets in Financial Instruments Directive (CA 2006, s. 1173). Not all European markets are regulated and it is necessary to check whether the specific market is regulated or not. This can be done via the European Securities and Markets Authority (ESMA) website: https://registers.esma.europa.eu/publication.

In determining whether a company is part of an ineligible group, it is necessary to look at all companies within the largest group of which the company is part. This means that not only the subsidiaries of the company in question are assessed, but also any companies that sit above – or either side – of it. All companies in the group, including overseas companies, are taken into consideration.

For a company to qualify as a micro-entity, the company must first qualify as small (and not be excluded from the small companies regime).

After the 'small' test, a company is excluded from the micro-entities regime if it is:

- an investment undertaking (as defined in art. 2(14) of Directive 2013/34/EU of 26 June 2013 on the annual financial statements, etc. of certain types of undertakings);
- a financial holding undertaking (as defined in art. 2(15) of that Directive);
- a credit institution (as defined in art. 4 of Directive 2006/48/EC of the European Parliament and of the Council of 14 June 2006 relating to the taking up and pursuit of the business of credit institutions, other than one referred to in art. 2 of that Directive);
- an insurance undertaking (as defined in art. 2(1) of Council Directive 91/674/EEC of 19 December 1991 on the annual accounts of insurance undertakings); or
- a charity.

A company within a group cannot qualify as a micro-entity if any of the following apply:

- the company is a parent company and the group headed by the company does not qualify as a small group;
- the company is a parent company which prepares group accounts for that year; or
- the company is not a parent company but its accounts are included in consolidated group accounts for that year.

1.3   Current status of FRS 102

Since FRS 102 was first published in 2013, several sets of amendments have been issued. These, together with their effective dates, are as follows:

Table 1.3 Summary of amendments made to FRS 102		
Date issued	**Amendment**	**Effective for periods commencing on/ after**
July 2014	Basic financial instruments and hedge accounting	1 January 2015
February 2015	Pension obligations	1 January 2015
July 2016	Small entities and other minor amendments	1 January 2016
March 2016	Amendments to fair value hierarchy disclosures	1 January 2017
December 2016	Removal of requirement for qualifying entities to notify shareholders	1 January 2016
December 2017	Amendments resulting from the FRC's triennial review of FRS 102	1 January 2019

There have also been other minor editorial amendments and clarification statements. All amendments to date have been included in the March 2018 edition of FRS 102.

1.4   Amendments to FRS 102 and FRS 105 – the triennial review

In December 2017, the FRC issued *Amendments to FRS 102 – Triennial Review 2017: Incremental Improvements and Clarifications*. Although the title only refers to FRS 102, the amendments have some consequential effects on the other UK standards and introduce two disclosure requirements into FRS 105 for micro-entities.

The amendments take effect for periods beginning on or after 1 January 2019. Early application of the amendments is permitted as long as all amendments are applied early, with the exception that certain amendments to Section 11 *Basic Financial Instruments* and Section 29 *Income Tax* can be applied early without having to apply the others. These are the small entity directors' loans exemption (which was introduced into FRS 102 as an interim measure in May 2017) and the requirements for the treatment of the tax effect of Gift Aid for charitable subsidiary companies.

1.4.1   Key changes

Table 1.4 summarises the key changes to FRS 102 arising from the triennial review amendments; these changes are discussed throughout the guide in more detail. An asterisk (*) indicates that this change also affects FRS 105.

Table 1.4 Summary of key measurement changes in FRS 102 arising from the triennial review (effective for periods commencing on/after 1 January 2019 with early adoption available)	
FRS 102	**Amendments**
Section 1A *Small Entities*	Introduce additional guidance and requirements for small entities in the Republic of Ireland following publication of the *Companies (Accounting) Act 2017* (see *Preparing Small and Micro Company Accounts*).
Section 7 *Statement of Cash Flows*	Introduce requirement to provide a reconciliation of net debt (similar to that in old UK GAAP).

Section 11 *Basic Financial Instruments*	Add a new principles-based definition of a debt instrument. Even if an instrument breaches one or more of the rules in Section 11, it could still be basic as long as it falls within that definition.
	Introduce an exemption allowing small entities to use the transaction price (or 'face' value) when accounting for loans from director-shareholders or close family of the director-shareholders (rather than imputing a market rate of interest). Only available for loans from directors who are natural persons (small LLPs should read 'members' for 'directors'). Does not extend to intragroup or other related party borrowings. Note that this exemption was introduced as an interim measure in Section 1 of FRS 102 in May 2017; on adoption of this amendment, the interim measure is deleted.
	Amend the reference to non-convertible preference shares and non-puttable ordinary or preference shares to refer instead to 'non-derivative equity instruments of the issuer'. This means that investments in shares will only be accounted for at fair value in the accounts of the holder if they meet the definition of equity for the issuer, or if they are non-basic. If they are basic and meet the definition of liabilities for the issuer, they can be accounted for as any other basic debt instrument by the holder, i.e. at amortised cost.
Section 12 *Other Financial Instruments Issues*	Allow entities to apply the macro-hedging provisions of IAS 39 but otherwise apply the recognition and measurement requirements of FRS 102.
Section 16 *Investment Property*	Remove the 'undue cost or effort' exception, meaning that investment property will need to be held at fair value through profit or loss. The only exception is for property let out to another group member, where the amendments introduce an accounting policy choice between cost and fair value.

Section 18 *Intangible Assets other than Goodwill*	Introduce an accounting policy choice for intangibles acquired as part of a business combination:
	(a) separate out only if the asset both:
	    (i) arises from legal/contractual rights; and
	    (ii) is separable; or
	(b) separate all intangible assets that are reliably measurable and have a probable chance of future economic benefits.

Section 22 *Liabilities and Equity**	Clarify that where equity is issued to extinguish debt (a 'debt for equity' swap) with a party under common control or who is a direct or indirect shareholder, no gain or loss arises and there is no profit or loss impact.
Section 23 *Revenue**	Include additional guidance in identifying whether an entity is acting as agent or principal.
Section 29 *Income Tax**	Introduce requirements stating that the tax effect of a Gift Aid payment by a charitable subsidiary is recognised at the reporting date where: (a) the charitable subsidiary is wholly owned; (b) it is probable that a Gift Aid payment will be made within the group within nine months of the reporting date; and (c) the payment will qualify to be set against taxable profits.
Glossary to FRS 102	Extend the definition of a group reconstruction to include transfer of a business (i.e. trade and assets) from one entity to another where the entities are under common control. Amend definition of a financial institution so that it no longer says 'any other entity whose principal activity is to generate wealth or manage risk through financial instruments'. Instead, the focus is on entities with similar activities to those in the list. Remove retirement benefit schemes from definition of a financial institution.

In addition to the changes asterisked above, FRS 105 is amended to introduce two disclosure requirements into Section 6 *Notes to the Financial Statements*. These reflect requirements in the *Companies Act* 2006 (CA 2006, s. 410A and 411):

'FRS 105.6A.1 If in any reporting period a micro-entity is or has been party to arrangements that are not reflected in its statement of financial position and at the reporting date the risks or benefits arising from those arrangements are material, the nature and business purpose of the arrangements must be given in the notes to the financial statements to the extent necessary for enabling the financial position of the micro-entity to be assessed. (Section 410A of the Act)

FRS 105.6A.2 The notes to a micro-entity's financial statements must disclose the average number of persons employed by the micro-entity in the financial year. (Section 411 of the Act)'

These requirements were extended in law to micro-entities by SI 2015/980 and have therefore been required in micro-entity accounts for all periods beginning on or after 1 January 2016. Although the FRC's amendments are effective for periods beginning on or after 1 January 2019, these particular amendments can (and should) be applied with immediate effect since they are required by law. The FRC acknowledges this by an amendment to Section 1 of FRS 105 which states 'Section 6 reflects legal requirements that are applicable in the UK for accounting periods beginning on or after 1 January 2016.'

FRS 105 is also amended to extend the micro-entity regime to the Republic of Ireland, following the implementation of the EU Accounting Directive into Irish law. The Irish micro-entity regime is available retrospectively for periods beginning on or after 1 January 2015. Accordingly, all amendments that relate to the implementation of the regime for Irish micro-entities can be applied immediately, provided that the relevant Irish law is applied at the same time.

1.4.2 Areas of no change

When the FRC first consulted in 2016 on the approach to the triennial review, it asked for views on whether or not certain areas should be amended in line with IFRSs. In particular, it suggested that the control model should be updated to bring in the approach taken in IFRS 10 *Consolidated Financial Statements* which looks at the power to control and direct activities, and that the fair value model should be amended in line with IFRS 13 *Fair Value Measurement*.

Respondents to the consultation disagreed with both of these suggestions. In relation to IFRS 10, it was pointed out that most entities would end up with the same situation as they have under the current control model, but would need to go through a lengthy and potentially expensive exercise to establish this, so the cost of implementing it would far outweigh the benefits. In respect of IFRS 13, the feedback was that implementing it could have unintended consequences and may be difficult for those who have only just grown used to the current fair value requirements.

The FRC, therefore, decided not to amend these two areas for the time being, but it has added some additional disclosure requirements about unconsolidated structured entities to make sure users have enough information in this area. However, it has not ruled out making these changes in future.

It also considered amendments in the following areas, but decided not to make any amendments at this time.

- Leases: the FRC suggested enhancing lease disclosures in anticipation of revisions based on IFRS 16, but decided it would have been difficult for entities to provide more information about obligations arising from operating leases without first deciding on how to update FRS 102 for IFRS 16.

- Share-based payments: the FRC asked for feedback on the cost-effectiveness of applying these requirements for private companies, and received mixed responses. Overall, it concluded that no significant changes will be made in this area under the triennial review.

1.4.3   Effect on other FRSs

As a result of the triennial review on FRS 102 there are consequential amendments to the other standards, as well as added clarity.

FRS 100 now contains the effective date of these amendments, which will be 1 January 2019, and instructions on early adoption. FRS 101 reflects the changes to the financial institution definition, but also contains some amendments to make it clear that additional disclosure may be necessary in some areas – for example, discontinued operations – to comply with UK company law. FRS 103 and 104 have only a handful of minor amendments.

1.5   Future developments

Originally, the December 2017 amendments were intended to be the first of two stages of the triennial review; the FRC had planned a second consultation towards the end of 2017 to propose more substantial amendments to FRS 102, incorporating new and amended IFRSs including IFRS 15 *Revenue from Contracts with Customers*, IFRS 16 *Leases* and the impairment requirements of IFRS 9 *Financial Instruments*. However, in response to stakeholder feedback, the FRC decided to postpone this consultation, noting that further evidence-gathering and analysis needs to be undertaken and more IFRS implementation experience would be helpful. At the time of writing, the FRC has not indicated when this further consultation may take place. Had the consultation gone ahead as planned, these more significant amendments would not have taken effect until 1 January 2022; accordingly, it appears unlikely that any proposed amendments relating to IFRS 9, 15 or 16 will take effect in the UK until at least 2023 and possibly later.

IFRS 17 *Insurance Contracts* was published by the IASB in 2017; the FRC has currently set no date for any changes to FRS 102 or FRS 103 in relation to IFRS 17 and is not expected to make any such changes until more IFRS implementation experience is available.

In 2019, the FRC is consulting on changes to FRS 102 to improve the accounting regime for defined benefit pensions, as well as amendments to FRS 101 to take into account IFRS 17 *Insurance Contracts* (FRED 70 – see *Preparing FRS 101 Accounts*).

1 Scope and purpose of Applying GAAP

The FRC exposure draft, FRED 71 *Draft amendments to FRS 102 – Multi-employer defined benefit plans (January 2019)*, proposes new requirements in FRS 102 for presenting the impact of transition from defined contribution accounting to defined benefit accounting for affected pensions.

The decision to amend the rules on accounting for multi-employer defined benefit plans is the result of reporting issues with the current framework under FRS 102, with reporters expressing concerns about a lack of clarity over how to report the pension plans, particularly with a view to longer term impacts.

2   Concepts, principles and policies

2.1   Scope of this section

This section examines the concepts underlying financial statements prepared in accordance with FRS 102, as set out in Section 2 *Concepts and pervasive principles*. This leads naturally to a discussion of how accounting policies should be chosen, developed, and where appropriate, changed, based on the requirements in Section 10 *Accounting policies, estimates and errors*.

In IFRS, the concepts underlying financial reporting are set out in the *Conceptual Framework,* and guidance on determining accounting policies is in IAS 8 *Accounting policies, changes in accounting estimates and errors*.

Sections 2 and 10 apply to the financial statements of all entities within the scope of FRS 102.

> **Application to micro-entities:** The basic concepts and principles set out in Section 2 of FRS 105 are similar to those in Section 2 of FRS 102, although the only measurement basis permitted is cost. Assets and liabilities are measured initially at cost and subsequently at cost or amortised cost. Alternative measurement bases such as current cost or fair value are not permitted. FRS 105 also does not contain the ten qualitative characteristics set out at **2.2.1**, although it does highlight the importance of prudence in recognising items in the accounts.

2.2   Applying the requirements

FRS 102 operates from the following critical assumption about the objective of financial statements:

'To provide information about the financial position, performance and cash flows of the entity that is useful for economic decision-making by a broad range of users who are not in a position to demand reports tailored to meet their particular information needs. [2.2]'

So, the financial statements are produced not just for the benefit of shareholders, but for a wider range of stakeholders which might include employees, suppliers, customers, government bodies, and others. This can influence the types of disclosures that are required in order to give a true and fair view, and places significant responsibility on the shoulders of directors who need to ensure that their accounts meet the needs of the business's stakeholders. The standard also refers in paragraph 2.3 to how the financial statements can be used to help in assessing the quality of stewardship by management.

2.2.1   Qualitative characteristics

Section 2 sets out ten qualitative characteristics of information in financial statements:

- understandability;
- relevance;
- materiality;
- reliability;
- substance over form;
- prudence;
- completeness;
- comparability;
- timeliness;
- balance between benefit and cost.

The term 'qualitative characteristics' is an unwieldy one, and does not necessarily communicate the purpose of this list. It might be better named 'features to be considered', 'qualities to be balanced' or even 'desirable properties of financial information', although the most accurate name of all could be 'wish list' – the most informative set of financial statements will be one that has all of these characteristics, adequately weighted so that none is achieved at the expense of the others. Taking this to extremes, a set of financial statements produced and sent to shareholders within two weeks of the year-end would be achieving excellent timeliness, but would be unlikely to be complete (in respect, for instance, of accruals, and post balance sheet events). On the other hand, a set with very detailed analysis of sensitivities on all judgmental disclosures, and multiple pages of information for each line item, might be very complete, but would be unlikely to provide enough benefits to justify the high cost of producing such detail, and might also fail the materiality and relevance tests.

The characteristics themselves, though, are in most cases fairly self-explanatory.

The standard subtly allows for the idea of an item's being *material* even if it does not have a numerical value which is significant to the accounts as a whole. This is done by referring to 'the size and nature of the omission or misstatement judged in the surrounding circumstances' [2.6].

Example 2.1

A company makes disclosures about its loans receivable, but does not specify the interest rate, which is zero. It also does not state that the counterparty is married to one of the directors.

The zero-interest income would clearly not exceed any size threshold for quantitative materiality in disclosures, but is still likely to be of great qualitative interest to users, particularly when combined with the information on the identity of the counterparty.

The section on materiality then goes on to comment that:

'... it is inappropriate to make, or leave uncorrected, immaterial departures from this FRS to achieve a particular presentation of an entity's financial position, financial performance or cash flows [2.6].'

In other words, it is not acceptable to calculate a materiality threshold and then make adjustments of a value below that threshold simply to achieve a better-looking result or position. This is a very valid prohibition although it is hard to see how it would be possible in practice to detect that a company had done this, and hard to see how auditors could insist on changes to accounts where the misstatements noted are not material.

The *comparability* requirement applies both to enabling users to compare the entity's results with its previous and future results and to giving them the means to compare the entity to others. There are many challenges associated with this requirement, not least in attempting to establish comparability with a diverse range of peers. It should perhaps best be seen as a reminder to be careful with the selection of accounting policies, particularly when considering changing them, as it is very easy to cloud the true picture by readjusting policies too often.

The *cost-benefit* requirement is another challenging one to assess, as both elements involve considerable subjectivity in their measurement. As paragraph 2.13 says, 'the costs are not necessarily borne by those users who enjoy the benefits', so any judgment on whether benefits justify costs will have to take into account the relative weight apportioned by the management to each user group's needs.

In practice, the cost-benefit argument is one most often put forward by preparers hoping to avoid an onerous disclosure requirement or the obligation to pay to have items independently valued, such as share-based payment arrangements or financial instruments. For example,

Section 26 on share-based payments has a slight relaxation compared with IFRS. While equity settled share-based payments are required to be measured at the fair value of goods or services received or, where this is not available, at the fair value of the instruments, the valuation hierarchy does not require use of an option pricing model (as IFRS 2 Appendix B does), but rather gives this as one example method of determining fair value.

FRS 102 (2018) removed all specific 'undue cost or effort' exemptions due to difficulties in applying them in practice. Instead, the standard identifies areas where the cost would clearly outweigh the benefit and provide alternative accounting requirements, thus minimising the level of judgment required by preparers. This does not undermine the pervasive cost-benefit principle but rather attempts to provide clarification about how it should be used.

For example, the standard states that investment property let out to other group members can be measured at depreciated cost but all other such property must be held at fair value. Previously, it was permitted to revert to depreciated cost if the fair value could not be measured reliably without undue cost or effort.

2.2.2   Financial position and performance

An entity's financial position is summarised in its assets, liabilities and equity at the reporting date. The three key definitions should be familiar.

(1) An asset is a resource controlled by the entity as a result of past events and from which future economic benefits are expected to flow to the entity.

(2) A liability is a present obligation of the entity arising from past events, the settlement of which is expected to result in an outflow from the entity of resources embodying economic benefits.

(3) Equity is the residual interest in the assets of the entity after deducting all its liabilities.

'Future economic benefits' as referred to in both asset and liability definitions effectively means access to cash, whether directly (for instance where a customer is expected to settle an outstanding balance) or indirectly (where the use of a piece of plant will enable the manufacture of stocks which will be sold). The definitions are therefore (necessarily) broader than those of financial assets and liabilities, which refer to contractual inflows or outflows of cash.

Section 2 is brief in its coverage of these definitions, though it does helpfully point out that ownership is not a condition to meet the definition of an asset – a lessee in a finance lease will include the leased asset on their balance sheet despite the fact that the lessor is the legal owner, by virtue of the control the lessee has over the use to which the asset is put and the benefits to which it gives rise.

Looking at equity, paragraph 2.2 makes explicit the possibility of further subdividing the category of equity in the statement of financial position: it gives examples of funds contributed by shareholders, retained earnings and gains or losses recognised directly in equity. This is not controversial, as it is merely permitting the introduction of extra line items that add to a total, but is nonetheless crucial for UK companies complying with the requirements of the relevant part of UK company law, being the *Companies Act* 2006 and either the *Large and Medium-sized Companies and Groups (Accounts and Reports) Regulations* 2008 (SI 2008/410) or the *Small Companies (Accounts and Directors' Report) Regulations* 2008 (SI 2008/409), both as amended by the *Companies, Partnerships and Groups (Accounts and Reports) Regulations* 2015 (SI 2015/980). All UK companies must show called up share capital, share premium and revaluation reserves as distinct line items on the face of their balance sheets, and some will face the additional challenge of dealing with items that are legally shares but are not, in accounting terms, classified as equity. This is discussed further in **7.2.2**.

Moving on from the definitions of assets, liabilities and equity as components of the statement of financial position, the definitions of income and expenses are built on these earlier concepts. Paragraph 2.23 defines income and expenses as follows:

> 'Income is increases in economic benefits during the reporting period in the form of inflows or enhancements of assets or decreases of liabilities that result in increases in equity other than those relating to contributions from equity investors.
>
> Expenses are decreases in economic benefits during the reporting period in the form of outflows or depletions of assets or incurrences of liabilities that result in decreases in equity, other than those in relation to distributions to equity investors.'

Income is then explained as including both revenue and gains. Revenue is a term with a broader meaning than it has in its use in everyday language, including as it does not only turnover (income from sales of goods or services) but also interest income, dividends, royalties, rent receivable and so on – broadly, virtually any item that would give rise to a credit (not a reduction of a debit) in the income statement, or the top part of it if a single statement approach is taken (see **3.4**). Gains, then, are items that would appear in other comprehensive income, with probably the most common being revaluation gains on property, plant and equipment.

A standard example of a receipt that would fail the test to be classified as revenue or a gain is when a capital contribution is received from a shareholder, perhaps through a direct injection of cash (with no shares or commitment to repay received in return) or perhaps by a sale of an asset to the company at undervalue. This is particularly common within groups, where a parent might sell a valuable property to a subsidiary for a nominal amount, and the accounting which best represents the transaction involves recording the transferred property in the recipient's books at its fair value, with the balancing credit recognised in equity. This type of transaction will itself have complicated repercussions when it comes to establishing distributable profits, but nonetheless serves as a useful example of amounts received which are not classified as gains.

The subdivision in the category of 'expenses' is slightly less clearly worded, in that one group is also called 'expenses' and the other 'losses', but they are simply the converse of the items included in income. Again, to review an example of an item which would give a debit but not be an expense or a loss, distributions to owners are a direct reduction in equity whether they are typically structured as dividends on shares, or as more complex situations involving, for instance, excess payments for assets and off-market intragroup loans.

2.2.3   Recognition and measurement

2.2.3.1   Recognition

Recognition refers to the process of bringing an asset or liability onto the balance sheet or item of income or expense into the statement of comprehensive income. The criteria for recognition of an item are set out in paragraph 2.27:

> '(a)   it is probable that any future economic benefit associated with the item will flow to or from the entity, and
>
> (b)   the item has a cost or value that can be measured reliably.'

Although these conditions are mainly self-explanatory, it is interesting to note the points that the standard-writers chose to emphasise. With reference to the probability of a flow of economic benefits, it is noted that the assessment must be made by looking at conditions that are in place as at the reporting date (rather than considering events which happen subsequently, even if they do lead, for instance, to income from a transaction which was initiated before the year-end). Then looking at the reliability condition, paragraph 2.30 points out that this does not preclude the use of estimates, which 'is an essential part of the preparation of financial statements'. Since this section of the standard is brief, there is no explanation of how to determine whether an estimate is 'reasonable': this will be a matter of judgment for directors, to be discussed with their auditors.

Section 2 does, however, go into more detail on how to apply the basic recognition criteria to each of the types of financial statement items.

For assets, the guidance in paragraph 2.37 effectively just repeats the earlier defining features of an asset, although paragraph 2.38 supplements this with a confirmation of the point that contingent assets are not recognised on the balance sheet (this is then repeated in paragraph 21.13 in the section on provisions and contingencies, with a disclosure requirement added too).

For liabilities, the guidance will be familiar as it refers to the conditions usually applied for recognising provisions, requiring a reliably measurable probable future cash outflow relating to a past event: again this is repeated and expanded upon in Section 21 of FRS 102, and is followed in Section 2 by a brief commentary on contingent liabilities, which in this guide are discussed in detail in **9.2.4**.

The guidance on income and expenses is then brief, relying mainly on the observation that income and expenses are inextricably linked to assets and liabilities.

The subsections on recognition, then, appear in the main to be very intuitive and unlikely to give rise to general issues; where more detailed guidance is needed, the standard tends to provide it within the relevant sections, and this subsection is therefore more about providing support for the theory behind the more detailed rules, and giving general principles for preparers who need to account for transactions that are not covered in the standard.

2.2.3.2 Measurement

The subsection on measurement has a little more substance to it, although again the detailed guidance in Section 11 onwards is crucial for fleshing this out for application to most common situations and transactions.

For both assets and liabilities, initial measurement is usually at historic cost, except for particular items which are explicitly required to be initially measured at fair value (2.46). Subsequent measurement is more complex, and depends on the nature of the asset or liability:

- property, plant and equipment is measured using the cost model or the revaluation model (discussed in **5.2.3**);

- inventories are measured at the lower of cost and selling price less costs to complete and sell (see **6.2.1**);

- impairment losses are recognised where appropriate for non-financial assets (see **5.2.4**);

- some financial instruments are measured at amortised cost less impairment, and some at fair value (see **7.3.4**).

None of these measurement bases are discussed in detail in Section 2 of FRS 102 – the list seems to have been produced mainly to give readers an impression of the range of available measurement bases. This is then further elaborated upon in paragraph 2.50 which gives two examples of non-financial assets that may or must be held at fair value, being investment property and some biological assets and agricultural produce.

FRS 102 (2018) contains guidance on establishing fair value in an Appendix to Section 2 (previously the fair value guidance was contained in Section 11). This appears logical, since fair value is a relevant concept outside the complex sphere of financial instruments. The FRC emphasises that the guidance constitutes a methodology for approaching fair value measurement, rather than a definition of what constitutes fair value. As mentioned in **1.4.2**, the FRC is not currently planning to introduce any of the content of IFRS 13 *Fair Value Measurement*, although this has not been ruled out for the future.

2.2.4   Other areas covered in Section 2 of FRS 102

In general, the standard prohibits offsetting of assets and liabilities, unless detailed conditions in some of the individual sections are met. Paragraph 2.52 helpfully clarifies two situations which are not treated as the offset of assets and liabilities, and so are permissible: measuring assets net of valuation allowances (for example, bad debt provisions, or stock provisions), and offsetting the proceeds of a fixed asset disposal against its previous carrying amount as part of the calculation of the gain or loss on disposal to be reported in the income statement.

2.3   Accounting policies

FRS 102, in paragraph 10.2, defines accounting policies as:

> '...the specific principles, bases, conventions, rules and practices applied by an entity in preparing and presenting financial statements.'

Application to micro-entities: Although the definition of an accounting policy set out in Section 8 of FRS 105 is the same, micro-entities do not have any choice in which accounting policies they can apply. If FRS 105 does not specifically address a transaction, Section 8 states that an appropriate policy should be developed that represents the transaction faithfully and reflects its substance, is neutral and prudent. However, there are some specific places in FRS 105 where prepares are referred to the requirements of FRS 102. For example, micro-entities with foreign branches are told to look to Section 30 of FRS 102 and apply the requirements therein.

> The other requirements around consistency of accounting policies and changes to accounting policies are similar to those in FRS 102. Micro-entities are not required to make any disclosure about accounting policies or changes thereto.

2.3.1   Specified accounting policies

The simplest situation, and the one where no decision needs to be made, is where an accounting policy is specified within FRS 102 and relates to a matter that is clearly material to the reporting entity. In this case an entity has no choice but to adopt the policy specified. Such policies are dealt with in other Sections in relation to the specific subject matter of the policy.

Strictly, FRS 102 mentions a requirement to apply any FRS that specifically addresses a transaction, other event or condition, rather than just FRS 102 alone. This is most relevant in the case of entities with insurance contracts, who will need to apply FRS 103 alongside FRS 102, and those choosing or required to prepare interim financial statements, which must comply with FRS 104.

FRS 102 (2018) only refers to an 'FRS' rather than an 'FRS or FRC Abstract' suggesting that any future amendments to accounting standards will be made within the relevant standard rather than as a separate Abstract.

In addition, a small number of entities within the scope of FRS 102 will also have to comply with the accounting policies set out in IAS 33 *Earnings per Share,* IFRS 8 *Operating Segments* or IFRS 6 *Exploration for and Evaluation of Mineral Resources,* in each case in the version adopted in the EU.

All entities within the scope of FRS 102 have the choice of adopting IAS 39 or IFRS 9 in place of the requirements of Sections 11 and 12 of FRS 102. Any entity that does so will then have to follow the recognition and measurement provisions set out in that standard while retaining the disclosure requirements of FRS 102.

The requirement to apply specified policies is restricted to those policies which have a material effect. Paragraph 10.3 of FRS 102 notes:

> 'However, the entity need not follow a requirement in an FRS if the effect of doing so would not be **material**.'

'Material' is itself defined, in the Glossary:

> 'Omissions or misstatements of items are material if they could, individually or collectively, influence the economic decisions of users taken on the basis of the **financial statements**. Materiality depends on the size and nature of the omission or misstatement judged in the surrounding circumstances. The size or nature of the item, or a combination of both, could be the determining factor.'

The emphasis on the effect on the economic decisions of users, and on the need to consider the particular issue in context, means that the determination of whether the application (or non-application) of a policy has a material effect is always going to be a matter of judgment. While the amounts involved will always be a relevant factor, the definition makes clear that it is not the only factor. Consideration must always be given to the nature of the item under consideration and not just its absolute amount. This means that it is entirely consistent with FRS 102 to have two situations with a very similar financial effect, yet in one case, this is deemed to be material and in the other it is not. There has always been a tendency to associate materiality with large numbers (relative to a relevant comparator). While there is obviously a connection, the definition in FRS 102, like those in many other reporting frameworks, is intended to make clear that this is an oversimplification. It is the effect or potential effect on users of financial statements that must lie at the heart of all decisions involving materiality.

Example 2.2

Situation 1

A group prepares financial statements using sterling as its presentation currency. Sterling is also the functional currency of the parent and of all bar one of the subsidiaries within the group. The other subsidiary has a functional currency of US dollars.

The subsidiary with the US dollar as its functional currency accounts for less than 2% of the revenues, profits, gross assets and net assets of the group. In the year in question, the exchange difference arising from the difference between the entity's functional currency and the group's presentation currency is less than 0.1% of the group's reported profit.

Section 30 of FRS 102, and 30.18 in particular, require that exchange differences arising from the translation of the dollar operations into sterling be recognised in other comprehensive income.

The group in fact includes these exchange differences with all other exchange differences that arise, and reports the total figure within profit or loss.

Whilst this accounting policy does not comply with that specified within FRS 102, such a treatment may nonetheless be acceptable. The effect of adopting the policy the group in fact applies is not material, since it is extremely unlikely that the non-compliance could affect the economic decisions of users based on the financial statements.

Situation 2

The situation is the same as in situation 1 except that:

- the subsidiary which has a functional currency of the US dollar accounts for between 40% and 50% of each of the revenues, profits, gross assets and net assets of the group; but

---

- in the particular year in question, the exchange difference arising from the difference between the entity's functional currency and the group's presentation currency is slightly less than 2% of the group's reported profit.

This is a slightly more complicated situation. The amount involved is much larger than in the original situation, but nonetheless might not be considered to be material if considered in isolation.

In this case, most people would be likely to consider that the group would need to apply the accounting policy specified in FRS 102, and could not deal with all exchange differences in profit or loss.

The difference here is that, even though the specific amount involved might not be considered material as a pure amount, the context differs from that in the first situation. The group clearly does have a significant potential exchange exposure as a result of having operations with a different functional currency. In any particular year, it is always possible that the effect of such exposure may be relatively small, but that may change from year to year. The very fact that the amount is relatively small in one year could also be argued to be directly relevant to the views that might be taken, and therefore the economic decisions that might be made, by a user of financial statements. That in itself makes the issue material. It would also be inappropriate to treat exchange differences differently from year to year just on the basis that in some years the amounts may be somewhat larger than in others.

Situation 3

The situation is exactly the same as in situation 1. However, in addition, the parent company has terminated the employment contract of a director just prior to the end of the accounting period. The terms of the agreement are that the company will continue to pay the director's salary for twelve months, but that during that period the director will not be required to provide any services to the company. The amount involved is almost exactly the same as the exchange difference arising on the retranslation of the subsidiary with a functional currency of the US dollar.

The group (and parent company) accounts do not reflect the terms of the agreement reached with the directors, in that no provision has been created, and it is intended that the amounts be charged as salary in the next accounting period.

The policy that the group and company are intending to apply is not in accordance with the requirements in relation to termination benefits set out in Section 28 of FRS 102.

In this case, most people would consider that the amount is material, and that provision should be made. This applies even though the amount is the same as for the exchange differences which were not considered material. This is on the basis that the amount is in connection with a related party, specifically a director.

Again, some might take a slightly different view. It would be highly unlikely that anyone would consider the amounts not to be material. What they might consider adequate would be disclosure of the details of the arrangement. (In considering whether disclosure would be required, reference could not just be made to FRS 102. The requirement to disclose compensation to directors for loss of office is specifically set out in para. 4 of Sch. 5 to SI 2008/410 for large and medium-size companies and para. 2 of Sch. 3 to SI 2008/409 for small companies.) This approach would be based on the view that the fact and amount of the arrangement is material, since it could have an effect on users of the financial statements. At the same time, where the amount is only a relatively small percentage of, say, profits and net assets then whether or not it is actually reflected in the primary statements is not going to affect users, and is therefore not material.

It is the oldest of accounting chestnuts that no amount of disclosure can make up for an inappropriate accounting policy. Paragraph 2.28 of FRS 102 makes specific reference to that fact that failure to recognise an item that meets the recognition criteria set out in the standard cannot be rectified by disclosure of the accounting policy that has actually been adopted or by inclusion of information in the notes to the financial statements or other explanatory material. Despite this comment, it does not really help very much in a situation where it is arguable that, on the basis of quantum, it is the fact of disclosure that is crucial and the accounting policy applied that is secondary.

There is also some discussion of materiality in Section 2 of FRS 102, in paragraph 2.6:

'Information is material—and therefore has relevance—if its omission or misstatement, individually or collectively, could influence the economic decisions of users taken on the basis of the financial statements. Materiality depends on the size and nature of the omission or misstatement judged in the surrounding circumstances. The size or nature of the item, or a combination of both, could be the determining factor. However, it is inappropriate to make, or leave uncorrected, immaterial departures from this FRS to achieve a particular presentation of an entity's financial position, financial performance or cash flows.'

While much of this discussion is similar to the way in which materiality is defined in the Glossary, it does add the idea that items should be considered to be material where an accounting decision has been prompted by the desire to present a specific picture of the entity. This may be relevant to the determination of whether an accounting policy set out in FRS 102 needs to be applied if there is an indication that a proposed departure from the requirements has not been based on a neutral assessment of its materiality, but on a wish to show the entity's position or performance in a particular light.

2.3.2   *Determining other accounting policies – general principles*

FRS 102 specifies accounting policies for many matters. Most entities within the scope of FRS 102 will find that the standard provides accounting policies for all, or at least nearly all, of the accounting issues that they face.

Nonetheless, it does not cover all of the situations for which an accounting policy may be required. Where an entity is required to determine an accounting policy for an area that is not covered by FRS 102 this may be a fairly complex task, as deal with below, but it is worth stressing that this situation will not be one that entities will face all the time.

Because the accounting policies included within FRS 102 are not necessarily complete, the standard provides guidance on the factors that should be taken into account in developing a policy where the matter is not covered in the standard, or in future in other standards and guidance.

The basic rule is set out in paragraph 10.4:

'If an FRS does not specifically address a transaction, other event or condition, an entity's management shall use its judgment in developing and applying an accounting policy that results in information that is:

(a)   relevant to the economic decision-making needs of users; and

(b)   reliable, in that the financial statements:

    (i)   represent faithfully the **financial position**, financial **performance** and **cash flows** of the entity;

    (ii)   reflect the economic substance of transactions, other events and conditions, and not merely the legal form;

    (iii)   are neutral, ie free from bias;

    (iv)   are prudent; and

    (v)   are complete in all material respects.'

In interpreting and applying these requirements, reference needs to be made to Section 2 of FRS 102 *Concepts and Pervasive Principles,* where many of the terms that are used are defined or discussed.

2.3.2.1   *Relevance*

Relevance is explained in the following terms in paragraph 2.5:

'The information provided in financial statements must be relevant to the decision-making needs of users. Information has the quality of **relevance** when it is capable of influencing the economic decisions of users by helping them evaluate past, present or future events or confirming, or correcting, their past evaluations.'

This could be summarised, in the context of accounting policies, by saying that the policies adopted must result in information that is actually useful. FRS 102 does not contain any extended discussion of what it means for information to be useful or relevant, but does make it clear that preparers of financial statements must put themselves in the shoes of users in deciding upon accounting policies where the standard is silent. The preparer must think about what a user would need to know in order to make an economic decision.

There is also a definition of relevance provided in the Glossary, but this differs little from the discussion in paragraph 2.5.

2.3.2.2   Reliability

FRS 102 also provides some guidance on the concept of reliability, in paragraph 2.7:

'The information provided in financial statements must be reliable. Information is reliable when it is free from material **error** and bias and represents faithfully that which it either purports to represent or could reasonably be expected to represent. Financial statements are not free from bias (ie not neutral) if, by the selection or presentation of information, they are intended to influence the making of a decision or judgment in order to achieve a predetermined result or outcome.'

This mentions some of the matters that are included in paragraph 10.4, although it could not be considered an extended discussion. Again, the Glossary contains a definition of reliability which is similar, although it does not make reference to the potential effects of bias.

Despite there being a definition in the Glossary and a discussion in Section 2, paragraph 10.4 introduces further factors into the meaning of reliability where this needs to be considered in the determination of an accounting policy.

2.3.2.3   Faithful representation

Faithful representation forms part of the definition of reliability in the Glossary.

In practice, it is not a straightforward concept to apply in the determination of appropriate accounting policies. FRS 102 includes within the definition of reliability, as set out above, that it represents faithfully that which it either purports to represent or could reasonably be expected to represent. In determining an accounting policy to be applied this can become rather circular, as what it purports to represent will depend on the accounting policy that is adopted.

2.3.2.4 Substance over form

In developing accounting policies, entities must have regard to the economic substance of the event or situation, and should not be guided solely by the legal form.

FRS 102 makes reference throughout to the requirement that the accounting for a transaction reflect the substance of that transaction. Despite this, it remains the case that the requirement to apply substance over form will continue to be relevant in only a small minority of cases. In the substantial majority of cases, there is no relevant difference between the economic and the legal implications of an event or transaction and therefore the principle of substance over form has no role to play. It is relevant only in the comparatively rare cases where the legal position would not provide a fair reflection of the commercial substance of the transaction or of the position in which the entity finds itself.

This means that in setting accounting policies, substance over form will often need to be considered after consideration of the other potentially relevant factors, and as a check on the policies that would have been applied without such reference. In effect, does the policy that is proposed properly reflect the commercial position? It is interesting that FRS 102 treats substance over form as a component of reliability, when an argument could be advanced that it has more to do with the relevance of the policy than its reliability. An accounting policy that failed to reflect the commercial position might be considered to be reliable, but of little or no relevance.

2.3.2.5 Neutrality

Neutrality, or freedom from bias, is an important part of reliability. An accounting policy cannot provide reliable information if the policy has been chosen with the intention of providing a particular picture of the entity's performance or position. As the discussion of reliability in paragraph 2.7 (as quoted above) makes clear, accounting practices, including accounting policies, should not attempt to influence the making of a decision or judgment in a particular direction.

2.3.2.6 Prudence

Accounting policies are also required to be prudent. Most of the discussion of prudence in paragraph 2.9 refers specifically to the judgments that need to be made in preparing financial statements:

'The uncertainties that inevitably surround many events and circumstances are acknowledged by the disclosure of their nature and extent and by the exercise of prudence in the preparation of the financial statements. Prudence is the inclusion of a degree of caution in the exercise of the judgements needed in making the estimates required under conditions of uncertainty, such that assets or income are not overstated and liabilities or expenses are not understated. However, the exercise of prudence does not allow the deliberate understatement of assets or income, or the deliberate overstatement of liabilities or expenses. In short, prudence does not permit bias.'

Nonetheless, the same considerations apply in the determination of accounting policies.

Accounting policies should be determined in such a way that they deal with matters of uncertainty in a reasonably cautious manner, so that they will not lead to assets or income being recorded at amounts that are in excess of reasonable amounts, nor lead to the understatement of liabilities and expenses. For example, if an accounting policy needs to be determined in order to decide whether a potential asset falls to be recognised, then it must fully reflect any uncertainties associated with that asset.

At the same time, FRS 102 cautions against the excessive use of prudence. As the standard makes clear, prudence cannot be used as a justification for deliberately understating assets or income, or overstating liabilities or expenses. Such a treatment would not be prudent, it would simply be biased. In framing an accounting policy, preparers therefore need to ensure that the policy reflects reasonable caution in dealing with any uncertainties to which the matter is subject, but that it does not reflect a hyper-cautious approach.

2.3.2.7   Completeness

The discussion of completeness in FRS 102 relates to the information that should be included in financial statements. It points out that information should be complete, within reasonable bounds of materiality and cost.

In relation to accounting policies, the inclusion of completeness in the list of factors that should be considered in establishing policies has two main implications:

- that the accounting policy selected should itself take account of all relevant matters affecting the items with which it deals; and

- that the policy adopted should lead to recognition of all relevant items.

2.3.2.8   Balancing the factors

FRS 102 simply lists the various factors that must be considered in developing an accounting policy where no policy is specified in the standard. It does not deal with any potential conflicts that might arise between those factors.

In practice, the factors may tend in different directions. The most likely conflict is where one possible policy provides information that is probably more relevant, but somewhat less reliable, than the alternative being considered.

In this case, the best approach would be to consider the guidance in FRS 102 that deals with voluntary changes in accounting policy. This is discussed at greater length below, but in summary, FRS 102 allows a voluntary change in accounting policy only where the new policy is reliable and more relevant. Applying the same principle to a situation where an entity has to determine an accounting policy in the absence of the matter being addressed specifically in FRS 102, this implies that:

- reliability should be treated as a threshold criterion. No accounting policy should be adopted if it results in an accounting treatment that is not reliable; but

- once that threshold has been reached, the policy adopted should be that which is most relevant, that is, would provide the most useful information for decision-making purposes to users of the financial statements.

2.3.3   Determining other accounting policies – the hierarchy

FRS 102 does not just set out general principles that should be applied in developing accounting policies for matters on which the standard is silent.

10.5 also provides a specific hierarchy that should be applied:

'In making the judgment described in paragraph 10.4, management shall refer to and consider the applicability of the following sources in descending order:

(a)   the requirements and guidance in an FRS dealing with similar and related issues;

(b)   where an entity's financial statements are within the scope of a **Statement of Recommended Practice** (SORP) the requirements and guidance in that SORP dealing with similar and related issues; and

(c)   the definitions, recognition criteria and measurement concepts for assets, liabilities, income and expenses and the pervasive principles in Section 2 *Concepts and Pervasive Principles*.'

These requirements run in parallel with the considerations mentioned in 10.4 and in practice may often make their application simpler than would be the case in the absence of this additional guidance.

The first requirement is sometimes referred to as the 'analogy' principle. An entity may need to decide on an accounting policy on a matter which is not specifically covered in FRS 102, but where FRS 102 deals with a matter that is similar in principle. Where this applies, then the same logic that underpins the accounting policy that is specified in the standard should be applied to arrive at an accounting policy in the analogous area.

This requirement should not be interpreted too narrowly. Whilst the standard refers to 'similar and related issues', it is often the case that an accounting issue may raise very similar issues of principle, even where there is a substantial superficial difference between the subject matters.

The second requirement is broadly the same as the first, except that it makes reference to SORPs rather than to standards. However, there are two relevant differences:

- the fact that this is second in the list, and that the requirement states the sources must be considered in descending order, matters. An analogy based on the requirements in a SORP should not be applied where an analogy can be developed based on the requirements in a standard. This simply reflects the fact that standards must always take precedence over SORPs; and

- the section specifically refers to the fact that this applies where an entity is within the scope of a SORP. This means that an entity which does not fall within the scope of a SORP should not normally base an accounting policy on a similar issue that is dealt with in a SORP. Whilst not stated explicitly, this should also be taken to mean that even where a SORP in fact deals specifically with the issue that the entity has it should not necessarily apply the same policy. This is not to say that in such a case the SORP should be ignored. If the accounting policy it includes, directly or by analogy, is in fact appropriate based on all other criteria, then there is no reason why it should not be applied. But it does mean that a great deal of caution needs to be adopted. SORPs normally deal with particular types of entity and some of the accounting problems that may arise in applying a general purpose accounting framework (such as FRS 102) in a situation for which they were not specifically developed. Some of the requirements they contain may therefore be appropriate in the particular context for which they were developed, but may not be appropriate where that context is absent. It cannot simply be assumed that the same policies should be applied without consideration of why they were developed.

The final requirement refers back to the most basic elements of FRS 102, its concepts, pervasive principles and its various definitions of the elements of financial statements. Where no analogy can be found, preparers must go back to the principles that underpin FRS 102, and which are themselves ultimately based on the IASB's *Framework for the Preparation and Presentation of Financial Statements*. (As a footnote to 2.35 of FRS 102 notes, that Framework has itself been superseded, but remains relevant to the IFRS for SMEs and therefore to FRS 102, which is based on that standard.) This means, for example, that no entity could develop an accounting policy which gave rise to the recognition of assets which would not meet the definition of, or recognition criteria for, assets under FRS 102.

As well as the requirements, FRS 102 also includes an option. Under paragraph 10.6:

'In making the judgment described in paragraph 10.4, management may also consider the requirements and guidance in EU-adopted IFRS dealing with similar and related issues ...'

FRS 102 allows entities to consider the requirements set out in full IFRS in relation to any matters that are not covered. So where there is no specific policy (or choice of specified policies) set out in FRS 102, entities can consider the policies for the same issue set out in whichever IFRS deals with the issue. Entities will often be allowed, but not required, to adopt the policy in the full IFRS.

The policy in the full IFRS could not be adopted where this would involve a breach of the hierarchy in FRS 102 itself. The most likely situation is where a policy is not covered in FRS 102, but there is a clearly analogous issue that is covered. If the policy required by the full IFRS were inconsistent with the analogy that would be derived from FRS 102 itself, then it could not be adopted.

It is also worth pointing out that, with one exception, entities may not follow the accounting policies set out in full IFRS where the matters with which they deal are covered in FRS 102. The exception is in relation to financial instruments, where entities have the option of adopting IAS 39 or IFRS 9 rather than Sections 11 and 12 of FRS 102.

One matter that is not mentioned in the hierarchy within FRS 102 is whether an entity can take account of another national GAAP or, most relevantly in practice, the policies set out in a previous national GAAP. For instance, if FRS 102 does not include an accounting policy in an area but there was a policy under previous UK GAAP, can that be applied? There is nothing in FRS 102 to prohibit account being taken of other GAAPs, or previous GAAPs, but this must be undertaken in accordance with the standard itself. Carrying over policies without consideration of whether the same policy could be determined in accordance with the hierarchy for setting policies within the standard itself will not be acceptable, and 'old UK GAAP' does not have any authority under the current framework.

2.3.4   Consistency of accounting policies

Whether an accounting policy is specified in FRS 102, or has been developed by the entity itself, it should be applied consistently. Similarly, the accounting policies selected should, as far as is possible, be consistent with each other.

Paragraph 10.7 requires that:

'An entity shall select and apply its accounting policies consistently for similar transactions, other events and conditions, unless an FRS specifically requires or permits categorisation of items for which different policies may be appropriate. If an FRS requires or permits such categorisation, an appropriate accounting policy shall be selected and applied consistently to each category.'

This paragraph is pointing out that there are a few cases in FRS 102 where the standard allows different policies to be applied. One example of this is in relation to property, plant and equipment. FRS 102 allows both a cost and a revaluation model to be applied to property, plant and equipment. It requires whichever policy is adopted to be applied consistently to a class of property, plant and equipment, described as items having a similar nature, function or use in the business. It does not require a single policy to be applied consistently to property, plant and equipment as a whole. So, for example, an entity could state all interests in real estate on a revaluation basis whilst carrying all motor vehicles on a cost basis.

2.3.5   Changing accounting policies

Consistency of accounting policies is desirable since regular changes in policy would be unhelpful to users of financial statements. At the same time, standards themselves develop and change and sometimes an entity may determine that a different accounting policy, where there is a choice, might be more appropriate.

As a result, paragraph 10.8 states that:

'An entity shall change an accounting policy only if the change:

(a)   is required by an FRS; or

(b)   results in the financial statements providing reliable and more relevant information about the effects of transactions, other events or conditions on the entity's financial position, financial performance or cash flows.'

The first deals with situations where the standard setter makes a deliberate decision to change an accounting policy from that which had previously been specified or to mandate a particular policy where standards had previously been silent and entities had had some flexibility in the determination of an accounting policy.

When this happens, then entities will be required to adopt the policy stated. (This will, of course, be subject to the considerations set out above as to whether an accounting policy is material to the entity, so in some cases, an entity may not have to change or adopt an accounting policy set out in a revised standard where doing so would have no material effect on the decisions that would be made by users of financial statements.)

The second deals with voluntary changes in accounting policies, those that have not been prompted by any action on the part of the standard setter. Such a change is allowed only where it would provide information that is ' ... reliable and more relevant ...'. This can be summarised as stating that the accounting policy must be 'better' than that which it replaces. As mentioned above in relation to selection of accounting policies, reliability is treated as a threshold condition in order for an accounting policy to be acceptable at all. Once this threshold has been met, then an accounting policy change can be made only if the information that would result from application of that policy is 'more relevant' than the information provided under the current policy.

One of the implications of this is that entities may have less choice when changing their policies than they might have had when setting their policies initially since the change must represent an improvement. In particular, in many cases it could be argued that information about the fair value of assets provides more relevant information about those assets than information about their cost.

There are a number of areas where FRS 102 allows entities to use either a cost or a revaluation/fair value model. Therefore, if an entity acquires such assets for the first time, it will be allowed to adopt either model. However, if it has initially adopted the fair value model, then it would be very difficult to argue that a change to a cost model would provide 'more relevant' information. (This assumes that fair value continues to be reliably measurable – if this ceases to apply then a reversion to cost would be considered appropriate, but would not be just a voluntary change in accounting policy and is specifically covered in paragraph 10.9 as set out below.) Where an entity initially adopted a cost model but later decided to adopt a fair value model, then it would be far easier to argue that this provides more relevant information and that the change may therefore be made. (Again, this assumes that the information to allow the use of fair value has always been available, even if previously unused, and has not recently become available.)

For the avoidance of doubt, FRS 102, in paragraph 10.10, does make clear that a change in accounting policy does include those changes which are between accounting policies which are specified in the standard but where a choice is allowed:

'If an FRS allows a choice of accounting treatment (including the measurement basis) for a specified transaction or other event or condition and an entity changes its previous choice, that is a change in accounting policy'

(Implicitly, this must mean that the standard setter accepts that within the accounting policies allowed by FRS 102, in areas where a choice is provided, some must provide more relevant information than others.)

FRS 102 also distinguishes between changes in accounting policy and additions to accounting policies, or perhaps refinement of existing policies. In practice, the dividing line between changes in accounting policies and additions to those policies is not always clear, so it is useful that FRS 102 provides at least some guidance.

Paragraph 10.9 states:

'The following are not changes in accounting policies:

(a) the application of an accounting policy for transactions, other events or conditions that differ in substance from those previously occurring;

(b) the application of a new accounting policy for transactions, other events or conditions that did not occur previously or were not material; and

(c) a change to the cost model when a reliable measure of fair value is no longer available (or vice versa) for an asset that an FRS would otherwise require or permit to be measured at fair value.'

The first two clarifications deal with the issue of the borderline between a change in accounting policy and the determination of an accounting policy for a new situation.

The second is the most straightforward. If an entity has a transaction, event or condition for the first time and needs to determine the appropriate accounting policy to apply then this is not a change in accounting policy. The same applies where the situation is not novel, but where the scale has changed such that an immaterial issue has become a material one.

Example 2.3

A service company has always had two income streams, but one of them has accounted for 97% of revenues. Whilst an appropriate accounting policy has always been adopted for accounting for the primary income stream, the policy adopted for revenue recognition for the other income stream has always been based on completed contracts, even though it clearly falls within the requirement for the use of the percentage of completion method. Given the number and duration of the contracts, the impact on the financial statements has always been estimated as clearly immaterial.

In the current year, the balance of the business has changed and the secondary income stream now accounts for over 10% of revenues, and is likely to take an increasing share of total revenue in future years.

In this situation, the company should adopt a revenue recognition policy that is in accordance with Section 23 of FRS 102, and 23.14 to 23.16 in particular. Such a policy will be based on the percentage of completion method.

This should not be treated as a change in accounting policy, as it is the application of an accounting policy to a previously immaterial area.

The first clarification is a little more complex, since it makes reference to there being a change in the substance. This is not as clear as a new type of transaction, or where a transaction is not of a new type but was previously immaterial. Many situations that look like they might be a change in substance could probably also be described as new or changed situations. However, since FRS 102 makes clear that in neither case is there a change in accounting policy the distinction between them is of limited relevance.

The third clarification does not deal with a voluntary change, and simply covers the situation where:

- an entity has a policy of valuation, but there is no longer a reliable measure of fair value available; or

- an entity would previously had applied fair value, but could not do so due to the absence of a reliable fair value measure, and a fair measure become available.

In both cases the information available has changed, due to external factors, and not the policy preference of the entity.

2.3.6   Applying changes in accounting policies

The default rule in FRS 102 for changes in accounting policies is that they should be applied retrospectively, which basically means that they should be applied as far as possible as if they had always been applied.

The default rule is not applied where:

- a change in accounting policy is made as a result of a change in an FRS. In this case, the transitional provisions set out in that standard should be followed. If there are no transitional provisions, then the default treatment of FRS 102 will apply and the requirements should be applied retrospectively;

- a change in accounting policy has been made as a result of a change to another standard which FRS 102 allows or requires the entity to follow. Again, in this, case the transitional provisions included in that other standard should be followed, and if the standard is silent then the change should be made retrospectively. The standards that may be relevant for this purpose are:

  - IAS 39 *Financial Instruments: Recognition and Measurement*;

  - IFRS 9 *Financial Instruments*;

  - IAS 33 *Earnings per Share*;

  - IFRS 8 *Operating Segments*; and

  - IFRS 6 *Exploration for and Evaluation of Mineral Resources*.

FRS 102 is very clear that the second exemption applies only where it is the requirements of the relevant standards that have changed. Where these standards allow a choice of accounting policy and an entity changes its choice (in a manner that is consistent with the FRS 102 requirements allowing a voluntary change in accounting policy) then this is like any other voluntary change in accounting policy and must be dealt with retrospectively.

There is also an exception where an entity decides to adopt a revaluation policy for property, plant and equipment or intangible assets having previously adopted a cost policy. Whilst FRS 102 acknowledges that this is a change in accounting policy, it is not dealt with in accordance with the normal rules. Instead, it is treated as a revaluation in its own right. This means that an initial valuation will reflect the cumulative change in value from the date of acquisition to the date of revaluation and not the change in the value in the accounting period in which the change is made (assuming the date of acquisition is not in the same period).

As noted above, where none of the exceptions applies the default rule in FRS 102 is that changes in accounting policies should be applied retrospectively. This means that, as far as possible, the policy should be applied to all previous periods, including the opening position for the earliest period presented, as though that policy had always been applied.

The problem is how far this is possible. There is an exemption in paragraph 10.12 where it is impracticable to make the change retrospectively in the way normally required by FRS 102:

> 'When it is **impracticable** to determine the individual-period effects of a change in accounting policy on comparative information for one or more prior periods presented, the entity shall apply the new accounting policy to the **carrying amounts** of assets and liabilities as at the beginning of the earliest period for which **retrospective application** is practicable, which may be the current period, and shall make a corresponding adjustment to the opening balance of each affected component of **equity** for that period.'

Under FRS 102 something is considered to be impracticable as follows:

> 'Applying a requirement is impracticable when the entity cannot apply it after making every reasonable effort to do so.'

This is intended to be a very high hurdle, and entities are not allowed to give up too easily. Something is not impracticable simply because the entity would be required to expend time, effort or cash in obtaining the information that is required.

The educational material produced by the IASB in relation to the IFRS for SMEs, the standard on which FRS 102 is based, states that:

'For a particular prior period, it is impracticable to apply a change in an accounting policy retrospectively if:

(a)   the effects of the retrospective application are not determinable;

(b)   the retrospective application requires assumptions about what management's intention would have been in that period; or

(c)   the retrospective application requires significant estimates of amounts and it is impossible to distinguish objectively information about those estimates that:

   (i)   provides evidence of circumstances that existed on the date(s) as at which those amounts are to be recognised, measured or disclosed; and

   (ii)   would have been available when the financial statements for that prior period were authorised for issue from other information.'

Given the background to FRS 102, and in particular that this is not one of the requirements that the FRC has changed from the IFRS for SMEs in its development, this would appear to be a reasonable interpretation of the requirement in FRS 102.

2.3.7   Changing policies on moving to FRS 102

While FRS 102 has many transitional provisions that deal with how particular policies might change on moving to the new standard, it has only one generic requirement, set out in paragraph 35.8:

'The accounting policies that an entity uses in its opening statement of financial position under this FRS may differ from those that it used for the same date using its previous financial reporting framework. The resulting adjustments arise from transactions, other events or conditions before the date of transition to this FRS. Therefore, an entity shall recognise those adjustments directly in retained earnings (or, if appropriate, another category of equity) at the date of transition to this FRS.'

It would seem consistent with the basic approach of FRS 102 that, except where the standard states otherwise, entities have a free choice of accounting policies amongst those which are allowed by (or consistent with) the standard on first-time adoption. This could be described broadly as a tabula rasa approach.

It seems reasonable to assume that most companies will continue with their previous accounting policy on transition. Some companies may reconsider their policies and decide to change to the policy that is generally considered more relevant. The oddity arises if a company chooses to change its policy from the more relevant to the less relevant. In general, this change would be prohibited under FRS 102 except on first-time adoption of the standard.

2.3.8   Disclosing changes in accounting policies

Whether required by a change in standard or voluntary, the disclosures required on a change in accounting policy need only be provided in the year in which the change in policy is made. So there is no requirement to provide comparatives where a change in accounting policy was made in the previous financial year, or years prior to that.

Where a change is required by a standard, the financial statements must disclose:

- the nature of the change in accounting policy;
- for the current period and each prior period, the amount of the adjustment for each financial statement line item affected, to the extent that this is practicable;
- the amount of the adjustment relating to periods before those presented, to the extent that this is practicable; and
- an explanation where any of the information required above in relation to previous periods has not been provided on the grounds that to do so is impracticable.

There may also be additional disclosures required. These will be set out in the standard in relation to the change.

The requirements are fairly similar where the change is voluntary, although in this case, there is an additional requirement for an explanation. The disclosure then becomes:

- the nature of the change in accounting policy;
- the reasons why applying the new accounting policy provides reliable and more relevant information;
- the amount of the adjustment for each financial statement line item affected, to the extent that this is practicable, showing separately:
  - the effect for the current period;
  - the effect for each prior period;
  - the effect in aggregate for periods prior to those presented; and
- an explanation where any of the information required above in relation to previous periods has not been provided on the grounds that to do so is impracticable.

The disclosure requirements for small entities applying Section 1A are broadly similar, although set out in a less detailed manner [1AC.7–9].

Example 2.4

Extract from statement of income and retained earnings:

	20X1	20X0
...	...	...
Profit on ordinary activities after taxation	120,000	130,000
Retained earnings at the beginning of the year	330,000	200,000
– As previously stated	360,000	220,000
– Effect of change in accounting policy	(30,000)	(20,000)
Retained earnings at the end of the year	450,000	330,000

Note

The company has changed its accounting policy for […]. The previous accounting policy was to […]. The new accounting policy is to […]. In the opinion of the directors, the new policy provides reliable information and is more relevant than the policy it replaces because […].

The change in accounting policy has been applied retrospectively, and comparative information has been restated accordingly. The effect of the change is to reduce reported profits for 20X0 by £10,000, and to reduce the opening balance of retained earnings by £20,000. The effect in the current year is estimated at a reduction in profit of £5,000.

2.4 Accounting estimates

2.4.1 Changes in accounting estimates

Changes in accounting estimates need to be distinguished from both changes in accounting policies and errors.

A change in accounting policy is where, whether through choice or as a result of a new or amended standard, an entity changes the approach that it takes to accounting for a particular transaction, even or circumstances.

An error is where financial statements, at the time they were prepared, did not reflect the information that they should have reflected.

A change in accounting estimate is where the quantification of an item (in accordance with an accounting policy) has changed due to changes in the information on which that estimate is based.

For example, depreciating items of property, plant and equipment is an accounting policy. The period over which property, plant and equipment should be depreciated, the useful economic life, is an estimate. Not depreciating property, plant and equipment with a limited useful economic life is (subject to materiality) an error.

FRS 102 deals, in paragraphs 10.16 and 10.17, with the basic treatment of changes in accounting estimates:

> 'An entity shall recognise the effect of a change in an accounting estimate, other than a change to which [the following] paragraph … applies, prospectively by including it in profit or loss in:
>
> (a) the period of the change, if the change affects that period only; or
>
> (b) the period of the change and future periods, if the change affects both.
>
> To the extent that a change in an accounting estimate gives rise to changes in assets and liabilities, or relates to an item of equity, the entity shall recognise it by adjusting the carrying amount of the related asset, liability or equity item in the period of the change.'

The treatment is therefore very different from that for a change in accounting policy. As a change in accounting estimate is based on new information, it is applied to the current period (and future periods if relevant) and the current value of assets, liabilities and equity. It has no effect on any amounts that may previously have been reported.

> **Application to micro-entities:** The definition of and approach to changes in accounting estimates is the same under FRS 105 as under FRS 102. Micro-entities are not required to make any disclosure about changes in accounting estimates.

Example 2.5

A company acquires an item of plant in 20X1 for £10,000. The plant is expected to have no residual value, and to have a useful economic life of ten years. Usage over the life is expected to be broadly even, so straight line depreciation is considered appropriate.

In 20X3, it becomes clear that the item will not last as long as had previously been estimated, and that the total life is now expected to be eight years, giving a remaining useful economic life of just six years. The other assumptions are unchanged.

So long as the original estimate of ten years was reasonable at the time it was made, this would be treated as a change in estimate. After two years, the plant will have been depreciated by £2,000 and have a carrying value of £8,000. The carrying value will now be depreciated over the remaining useful life of six years, giving a depreciation charge per annum of £1,333.

Comparatives and balances brought forward are not amended.

Other typical examples of changes in accounting estimates which would simply be dealt with as they arise would include:

- adjustments to allowance accounts for irrecoverable receivables;

- adjustments to the provisions made for taxation;

- minor omissions of accruals and prepayments in prior periods;

- revenue recognised in the year which relates to a prior year, but which was not recorded in that prior year as it did not meet the necessary recognition criteria;

- bad debts recovered which had been written off in previous periods; and

- changes to the estimated profit arising over the life of a contract.

2.4.2   Disclosing changes in accounting estimates

FRS 102 requires disclosure of the impact of material changes in accounting estimates. As paragraph 10.18 states:

'An entity shall disclose the nature of any change in an accounting estimate and the effect of the change on assets, liabilities, income and expense for the current period. If it is practicable for the entity to estimate the effect of the change in one or more future periods, the entity shall disclose those estimates.'

It is worth pointing out that in some cases, the information required may already be provided as a result of other disclosure requirements. For example, where there have been movements in a provision, this may arise as a result of changes in the estimates that underlie that provision. The disclosure of movements in the provision, as required by paragraph 21.14 of FRS 102, would also satisfy the requirements to disclose the effect of changes in accounting estimates if sufficient description were provided.

Small entities are not required to make disclosures about changes in accounting estimates in particular, although disclosure might be necessary to give a true and fair view.

2.5   Prior period errors

2.5.1   Correcting prior period errors

FRS 102 goes to some lengths to make clear the distinction between an error and an estimate.

In paragraph 10.19:

'Prior period errors are omissions from, and misstatements in, an entity's financial statements for one or more prior periods arising from a failure to use, or misuse of, reliable information that:

(a) was available when financial statements for those periods were authorised for issue;

and

(b) could reasonably be expected to have been obtained and taken into account in the preparation and presentation of those financial statements.'

In effect, the standard does not set unrealistic expectations about how accurate (with the benefit of hindsight) it is possible for a set of financial statements to be.

Something is only an error where the information to enable it to have been stated correctly was available at the time that the previous financial statements were actually prepared and where it is reasonable that the information could have been obtained and reflected. The information also needs to have met the criterion of reliability at the time. This means, for example, that it is not an error to have omitted to record a liability in previous periods if at the time the financial statements were prepared it was not possible to have come up with a sufficiently reliable estimate even though it may have been clear that a liability existed. Therefore if the amount becomes known with certainty, or sufficient reliability, in the current accounting period this is treated as a current year item and there is no correction of a prior period error.

This does not mean that estimates cannot give rise to errors; while an estimate can never be expected to be precisely accurate there can still be an unreasonable estimate. For example, if an entity has previously been depreciating assets over five years, when it should always have been obvious that they would have a useful economic life of at least ten, then this is an error. If material, this would be corrected by way of prior period adjustment and not by changing the period to be applied prospectively. At the same time, the requirements in relation to errors should not be applied where an assessment was made previously, on the basis of all the information that was available at the time, which subsequently proves to have been incorrect. For example, a company develops software for its own use. All the indications are that the software is effective and likely to operate efficiently. At the end of the year, the company concludes that the costs meet the recognition criteria for an intangible asset. An amortisation period of four years is decided upon, which is consistent with the period the company has usually been able to use developed software before requiring a major upgrade. After a further six months, it becomes clear that the software is not working as expected. The software will need substantial rewriting to continue to be useable, and the asset is clearly impaired. The impairment charge should be taken in the current year. Whilst the assessment made at the end of the previous period now looks to have been unreasonable, it was not unreasonable at the time that it was made.

The standard notes, in paragraph 10.20, that:

'Such errors include the effects of mathematical mistakes, mistakes in applying accounting policies, oversights or misinterpretations of facts, and fraud.'

Under FRS 102, any error that has a material effect on the financial statements must be corrected retrospectively. This is consistent with IFRS.

Where a material prior period error is identified the correction should be dealt with by:

- adjusting the comparative period or periods in the financial statements so that they include the correct amounts, if the error affects a period which is presented;

- adjusting the opening balances for the earliest prior period presented, where the error dates back to prior to the start of the period.

The correction of some errors may involve a combination of both, for example where a depreciable asset was recorded at an incorrect acquisition cost in a prior period, so that both the initial recording and the subsequent depreciation will require correction.

In some cases, it may be impossible to determine the effect that an error had on a particular accounting period. Where this applies, the correction should be made at the earliest date were this is possible. As the standard notes, this may mean in the current accounting period.

> **Application to micro-entities:** The definition of and approach to prior period errors is the same under FRS 105 as under FRS 102. Micro-entities are not required to make any disclosure about prior period errors.

2.5.2   Disclosing prior period errors

FRS 102 requires the following disclosures where the entity has corrected a material prior period error:

- the nature of the prior period error;

- for each prior period presented, the amount of the correction for each financial statement line item which has been affected;

- the amount of any correction at the beginning of the earliest prior period presented.

For the quantification, the standard makes clear that this information need be given only to the extent that it is practicable to do so. Where it is not practicable to provide some of this information then the financial statements must provide an explanation of why it is not practicable to provide such information.

The disclosure of prior period errors is required only in the financial statements of the year in which the error has been corrected. So, where a prior period adjustment was identified and corrected in last year's financial statements, and full disclosure provided at that time, the disclosure is not repeated in the current year.

The form in which prior period errors are disclosed is very similar to that for a change in accounting policy as set out above. The disclosure requirements for small entities applying Section 1A are broadly similar, although set out in a less detailed manner [1AC.7–9].

3 Financial statement presentation

3.1 Scope of this section

This chapter covers all of the sections of FRS 102 that directly relate to the presentation of financial statements, namely:

- Section 3 *Financial Statement Presentation* (see **3.2**);

- Section 4 *Statement of Financial Position* (see **3.3**);

- Section 5 *Statement of Comprehensive Income and Income Statement* (see **3.4**);

- Section 6 *Statement of Changes in Equity and Statement of Income and Retained Earnings* (see **3.5**);

- Section 7 *Statement of Cash Flows* (see **3.6**); and

- Section 8 *Notes to the Financial Statements* (see **3.7**).

The final paragraph of Section 3 clarifies that the presentation of interim reports is not covered by FRS 102, so a preparer preparing an interim report will need to use an appropriate basis of preparation, and describe this basis within the document. FRS 104 is the appropriate standard to apply in this case.

The comparable requirements in IFRS are IAS 1 *Presentation of Financial Statements (revised 2007)* and IAS 7 *Statement of Cash Flows.*

Small entities applying Section 1A of the standard are exempted from some paragraphs of Section 3 and the whole of Sections 4–8. This has the effect of drastically limiting the requirements of small entities – the differences are highlighted throughout this section (and through all other sections where relevant).

Application to micro-entities: The equivalent sections in FRS 105 are Section 3 *Financial Statement Presentation*, Section 4 *Statement of Financial Position*, Section 5 *Income Statement* and Section 6 *Notes to the Financial Statements*. Micro-entities are not required to prepare any of the other statements set out above, so a complete set of micro-entity accounts contains only a statement of financial position and income statement (note that the profit and loss account must be prepared for members but does not need to be filed).

The formats for the statement of financial position (balance sheet) and income statement (profit and loss account) for a micro-entity are set out in company law (SI 2008/409, Sch. 1). There is no choice as to the layout and terminology of the profit and loss account, and only two different formats are available for the balance sheet. The form and content of the micro-entity accounts is therefore simply a profit and loss account and balance sheet, laid out as prescribed in the formats and reproduced in Sections 4 and 5 of FRS 105.

The notes to the accounts required for a micro-entity are extremely limited and are presented at the foot of the balance sheet rather than in a separate section of the accounts. They derive from company law and are reproduced in Section 6 of FRS 105. More detail on the requirements for preparing micro-entity accounts can be found in *Preparing Small and Micro Company Accounts*.

3.2   General points on presentation

3.2.1   Contents of financial statements

The central requirement of financial statements prepared under FRS 102 is that they 'present fairly the financial position, financial performance and cash flows of an entity' [3.2]. While this is a phrase imported from IFRS, it does not exempt preparers from the requirement of the *Companies Act* 2006, s. 393, which states that the directors must not approve accounts 'unless they are satisfied that they give a true and fair view of the assets, liabilities, financial position and profit or loss' of the company or group.

Section 3 specifies the contents of a complete set of financial statements, being:

- a statement of financial position (balance sheet);
- a single statement of comprehensive income, or an income statement accompanied by a shorter statement of comprehensive income;
- a statement of changes in equity;
- a statement of cash flows;
- accompanying notes.

In addition, there is an option in certain cases to combine the statement of changes in equity with the statement of comprehensive income, discussed more fully at **3.4**.

Certain minimum information must be included somewhere in the accounts, none of which is controversial: this information includes the reporting entity's name, a statement on whether the accounts are for a company or group, the dates covered by the accounts, the presentation currency, and the level of rounding used.

Accounts must be presented at least annually, with an explanation if the length of the reporting period changes. Presentation and classification should be consistent between years unless a change is necessary for a more appropriate presentation – the conditions are as for changing accounting policies, discussed in **2.3.5** of this guide.

Note again that company law continues to apply to companies preparing accounts under FRS 102. This includes all of the requirements about changing accounting reference dates and shortening or lengthening accounting periods.

3.2.1.1 Statement of compliance

Large and medium-sized entities applying FRS 102 need to include 'an explicit and unreserved statement of compliance' [3.3] in the accounts. Small entities are encouraged but not required to include this statement in the accounts.

If, for any reason, there are departures from the requirements of the standard, or from the requirements of applicable legislation (including company law where relevant), three disclosures are needed:

(1) the fact that management has concluded that the accounts give a fair presentation (the implication being that typically departure from the FRS would suggest departure from fair presentation, so there is an onus on management to state that this is not the case);

(2) the fact that the accounts comply with FRS or applicable legislation in all other respects;

(3) a description of the nature and effect of the departure, including an explanation of what the treatment should have been under the FRS or legislation, and a reason why that treatment was considered too misleading to use.

Small entities only need to give the last of these three disclosures, unless more are necessary to give a true and fair view.

It is clear that a decision to depart from the requirements should not be taken lightly and needs to be properly explained in the accounts.

3.2.1.2 Comparatives

Paragraph 3.14 includes a general requirement to present comparatives for all amounts in the financial statements including, where relevant, narrative and descriptive information, except where there is a specific contradictory requirement elsewhere in the standard. This adds a few requirements in places that could be surprising, for instance the need to show a fixed asset movement table for both the current and previous years.

3.2.1.3   Going concern

An assessment of an entity's going concern status must be made as part of the financial statement preparation process. Paragraph 3.8 states that an entity is a going concern unless:

> '... management either intends to liquidate the entity or to cease trading, or has no realistic alternative but to do so ... '

This assessment must look at least 12 months forward from the date that the financial statements are authorised, although it can look further if necessary, perhaps if there are clear cash flow forecasts showing longer-range problems, or if the entity knows of a forthcoming regulatory change which will effectively put it out of business.

There are no requirements for a positive statement on going concern, unless there are material uncertainties, in which case these should be described.

Example 3.1

Company F has prepared a five-year cash-flow forecast which shows it can continue trading, but this is dependent on the (assumed) successful outcome of a court case in progress.

Assuming the directors have confidence in the case's outcome, the accounts could still be prepared on a going concern basis but the material uncertainty would be disclosed and explained, and probably also cross-referenced to the provisions/contingent liabilities note.

Where an entity is not a going concern, no accounting guidance is given, although it is common to construct an accounting policy that reclassifies non-current liabilities as current and measures assets based on their immediate (rather than best) resale price, ignoring any alternative future use potential. The basis chosen should be fully explained, together with the reasons that the going concern basis has been deemed inappropriate.

3.2.2   Materiality and aggregation

Paragraphs 3.15–3.16 give very high-level guidance in this area. They require separate presentation of each material class of similar items, and allow aggregation of non-material items. They also clarify that specific disclosure requirements within the standard do not apply if the information in question is not material. This is supplemented by the statement in the Glossary that:

> 'Omissions or misstatements of items are material if they could, individually or collectively, influence the economic decisions of users taken on the basis of the financial statements. Materiality depends on the size and nature of the omission or misstatement judged in the surrounding circumstances. The size or nature of the item, or a combination of both, could be the determining factors.'

Most preparers do not, in practice, find it hard to develop a sense of materiality; however, care is needed in areas where the driver is qualitative, such as the disclosure of sensitive related party transactions; where an entity is only marginally profitable or loss-making, so that a small adjustment could change the picture; and where the existence of a zero or low-value balance is in itself a fact of interest.

FRS 102 (2018) includes the following paragraph 3.16A in Section 3, to add clarity to the existing requirements:

'When applying this FRS an entity shall decide, taking into consideration all relevant facts and circumstances, how it aggregates information in the financial statements, which includes the notes. An entity shall not reduce the understandability of its financial statements by obscuring material information with immaterial information or by aggregating material items that have different natures or functions.'

The standard also notes that company law requires certain disclosures to be made, regardless of materiality (e.g. loans made to directors, employee numbers).

3.2.3 Small entities

The contents of a complete set of financial statements for a small entity are briefer than those of one that is not small, comprising:

(a) a statement of financial position;

(b) an income statement;

(c) notes.

Small entities are permitted to 'abridge' the statement of financial position and income statement. This allows them to show fewer line items on the face of the balance sheet and profit and loss account. It is important to note that abridged accounts are not a separate set of accounts for filing, but rather a replacement to the full accounts that members would otherwise receive. This means that abridged accounts, despite having a number of exemptions from a disclosure and presentation point of view, are still required to give a true and fair view. The requirements for preparing abridged accounts are dealt with in detail in *Preparing Small and Micro Company Accounts*.

Certain other primary statements are 'encouraged' but not required. Where a small entity recognises gains or losses in other comprehensive income, it is 'encouraged' to present a statement of total comprehensive income, and where it has transactions with equity holders, it is 'encouraged' to present a statement of changes in equity or a statement of income and retained earnings. The cash flow statement is not required.

As for all other entities, small entities may use other titles for their primary statements, so long as these are not misleading; they are also required to present comparatives for the preceding period in all cases except where the standard explicitly permits or requires otherwise.

The contents of notes to the accounts are discussed very briefly at **3.7**, but the key point is that small entities are exempt from the disclosure requirements of Sections 8–35 of the standard, unless required to give a true and fair view.

3.3   Statement of financial position

Section 4 of FRS 102 addresses the requirement to present a statement of financial position, or balance sheet (since this is its name under the Companies Act, FRS 102 cannot prohibit its use, and it is widely used in this publication for both familiarity and convenience).

3.3.1   Company law formats

The formats available for the balance sheet are those set out in the Accounting Regulations, even for entities that are not in the scope of the Companies Act. These are not reproduced in the standard, so preparers must look to the relevant part of the regulations.

Four sets of requirements are available: those in Sch. 1 (companies that are not banks or insurance companies), 2 (banking companies) or 3 (insurance companies) to the Accounting Regulations, or those in Sch. 1 to the LLP Regulations. For a group, the relevant references are Sch. 6 to the Accounting Regulations or Sch. 3 to the LLP Regulations.

Schedule 1, the schedule which will apply to most preparers, then offers two balance sheet formats.

The most commonly used is format 1, although format 2 is also reproduced here for reference:

Format 1

(A) Called up share capital not paid

(B) Fixed assets

    (I)   Intangible assets

        (1) Development costs

        (2) Concessions, patents, licences, trademarks and similar rights and assets

        (3) Goodwill

        (4) Payments on account

    (II) Tangible assets
- (1) Land and buildings
- (2) Plant and machinery
- (3) Fixtures, fittings, tools and equipment
- (4) Payments on account and assets in course of construction

    (III) Investments
- (1) Shares in group undertakings
- (2) Loans to group undertakings
- (3) Participating interests
- (4) Loans to undertakings in which the company has a participating interest
- (5) Other investments other than loans
- (6) Other loans
- (7) Own shares

(C) Current assets

    (I) Stocks
- (1) Raw materials and consumables
- (2) Work in progress
- (3) Finished goods and goods for resale
- (4) Payments on account

    (II) Debtors
- (1) Trade debtors
- (2) Amounts owed by group undertakings
- (3) Amounts owed by undertakings in which the company has a participating interest
- (4) Other debtors
- (5) Called up share capital not paid
- (6) Prepayments and accrued income

    (III) Investments
- (1) Shares in group undertakings
- (2) Own shares
- (3) Other investments

    (IV) Cash at bank and in hand

(D) Prepayments and accrued income

(E) Creditors: amounts falling due within one year
- (1) Debenture loans
- (2) Bank loans and overdrafts

   (3) Payments received on account

   (4) Trade creditors

   (5) Bills of exchange payable

   (6) Amounts owed to group undertakings

   (7) Amounts owed to undertakings in which the company has a participating interest

   (8) Other creditors including taxation and social security

   (9) Accruals and deferred income

(F) Net current assets (liabilities)

(G) Total assets less current liabilities

(H) Creditors: amounts falling due after more than one year

   (1) Debenture loans

   (2) Bank loans and overdrafts

   (3) Payments received on account

   (4) Trade creditors

   (5) Bills of exchange payable

   (6) Amounts owed to group undertakings

   (7) Amounts owed to undertakings in which the company has a participating interest

   (8) Other creditors including taxation and social security

   (9) Accruals and deferred income

(I) Provisions for liabilities

   (1) Pensions and similar obligations

   (2) Taxation, including deferred taxation

   (3) Other provisions

(J) Accruals and deferred income

(K) Capital and reserves

   (I) Called up share capital

   (II) Share premium account

   (III) Revaluation reserve

   (IV) Other reserves

      (1) Capital redemption reserve

      (2) Reserve for own shares

      (3) Reserves provided for by the articles of association

      (4) Other reserves

   (V) Profit and loss account

Format 2

Assets

(A) Called up share capital not paid

(B) Fixed assets

    (I) Intangible assets

        (1) Development costs

        (2) Concessions, patents, licences, trade marks and similar rights and assets

        (3) Goodwill

        (4) Payments on account

    (II) Tangible assets

        (1) Land and buildings

        (2) Plant and machinery

        (3) Fixtures, fittings, tools and equipment

        (4) Payments on account and assets in course of construction

    (III) Investments

        (1) Shares in group undertakings

        (2) Loans to group undertakings

        (3) Participating interests

        (4) Loans to undertakings in which the company has a participating interest

        (5) Other investments other than loans

        (6) Other loans

        (7) Own shares

(C) Current assets

    (I) Stocks

        (1) Raw materials and consumables

        (2) Work in progress

        (3) Finished goods and goods for resale

        (4) Payments on account

    (II) Debtors

        (1) Trade debtors

        (2) Amounts owed by group undertakings

        (3) Amounts owed by undertakings in which the company has a participating interest

        (4) Other debtors

        (5) Called up share capital not paid

        (6) Prepayments and accrued income

    (III) Investments

        (1) Shares in group undertakings

        (2) Own shares

        (3) Other investments

    (IV) Cash at bank and in hand

(D) Prepayments and accrued income

Liabilities

(I) Capital and reserves

    (I)   Called up share capital

    (II)   Share premium account

    (III) Revaluation reserve

    (IV) Other reserves

        (1) Capital redemption reserve

        (2) Reserve for own shares

        (3) Reserves provided for by the articles of association

        (4) Other reserves

    (V) Profit and loss account

(II) Provisions for liabilities

    (1) Pensions and similar obligations

    (2) Taxation, including deferred taxation

    (3) Other provisions

(III) Creditors

    (1) Debenture loans

    (2) Bank loans and overdrafts

    (3) Payments received on account

    (4) Trade creditors

    (5) Bills of exchange payable

    (6) Amounts owed to group undertakings

    (7) Amounts owed to undertakings in which the company has a participating interest

    (8) Other creditors including taxation and social security

    (9) Accruals and deferred income

(IV) Accruals and deferred income

In both formats, the headings with letters and Roman numerals are compulsory (unless the balance is zero in both years), and must appear in the order specified; the headings with Arabic numerals must appear but also must be adapted (in their names or order) if in the directors' view this would give a more appropriate presentation.

Section 4 only gives a very small amount of additional guidance on the use of these formats. Paragraph 4.3 mandates the use of additional line items, headings or subtotals where necessary, and paragraph 4.4A requires entities to show debtors due after more than one year separately on the face of the balance sheet if this is necessary to prevent misinterpretation of the financial statements.

There is also a clarification about how creditors are split between amounts falling due within and after more than one year. A balance is classified as due within one year if 'the entity does not have an unconditional right, at the end of the reporting period, to defer settlement of the creditor for at least twelve months after the reporting date' (paragraph 4.7).

3.3.2 Adapting the balance sheet formats

SI 2015/980 allows companies to adapt the Companies Act formats for the balance sheet and profit and loss account. This has two key effects. First, it facilitates a style of presentation more in line with IFRS (particularly important for FRS 101 accounts, but not especially relevant for FRS 102 accounts). Second, it enables companies to use the newer, IFRS style terminology in FRS 102 as an option. So for example, whilst the Companies Act formats refer to Tangible Fixed Assets, FRS 102 calls them Property, Plant and Equipment. The effect of the option to adapt accounts essentially allows either new or old terminology to be used as long as it makes sense and is not misleading.

The option to adapt the formats is particularly significant for the balance sheet. This is because, like IFRS, adapted accounts distinguish between non-current assets (those expected to be realised after 12 months) and current assets (those expected to be realised within 12 months), whereas the Companies Act formats draw the slightly different distinction between fixed assets (those that are intended for use in the business on an ongoing basis) and current assets (assets that are not fixed assets).

Adapting the formats would, in general, have the effect that some assets previously presented under 'current assets' may well be moved to 'non-current assets'. This is because many companies present, say, long-term debtors within current assets, since they are not intended for continuing use in the business. However, under the adapted approach, these are amounts that are not expected to be settled within 12 months and would therefore be classified as non-current.

3 Financial statement presentation

If a company chooses to adapt its balance sheet then it must, as a minimum, present the following items, distinguishing between those that are current and non-current:

(a) property, plant and equipment;

(b) investment property carried at fair value through profit or loss;

(c) intangible assets;

(d) financial assets (excluding amounts shown under (e), (f), (j) and (k));

(e) investments in associates;

(f) investments in jointly controlled entities;

(g) biological assets carried at cost less accumulated depreciation and impairment;

(h) biological assets carried at fair value through profit or loss;

(i) inventories;

(j) trade and other receivables;

(k) cash and cash equivalents;

(l) trade and other payables;

(m) provisions;

(n) financial liabilities (excluding amounts shown under (l) and (m));

(o) liabilities and assets for current tax;

(p) deferred tax liabilities and deferred tax assets (classified as non-current);

(q) non-controlling interest, presented within equity separately from the equity attributable to the owners of the parent; and

(r) equity attributable to the owners of the parent.

Certain sub-classifications of the above items are also required, either on the face of the statement of financial position or in the notes:

(a) property, plant and equipment in classifications appropriate to the small entity;

(b) goodwill and other intangible assets;

(c) investments, showing separately shares and loans;

(d) trade and other receivables, showing separately amounts due from related parties, amounts due from other parties, prepayments and accrued income;

(e)   inventories, showing separately amounts of raw materials, work in progress and finished goods;

(f)   trade and other payables, showing separately amounts payable to trade suppliers, amounts payable to related parties, deferred income and accruals; and

(g)   classes of equity, such as called up share capital, share premium, retained earnings, revaluation reserve, fair value reserve and other reserves.

3.3.3   Other required information

There are few supplementary requirements in Section 4 of FRS 102 beyond the basic requirement to use one of the company law formats or adapted formats. In general, disclosures relating to individual line items are specified in the relevant sections of the standard rather than in this section.

Paragraphs 4.12 and 4.13 include additional disclosure requirements in respect of share capital or, where the entity has no share capital, equivalent disclosures for each category of equity. These include disclosing, for each class of share, numbers issued, par values, rights and restrictions but there is no requirement to disclose a reconciliation of the number of shares outstanding at the beginning and end of the period.

Finally, paragraph 4.14 sits as a slight afterthought to the rest of the section, setting out, very briefly, requirements to disclose details of disposal groups or individual assets where the entity has a binding commitment to sell the asset or group. It should be noted that this is the only part of the disposal requirements of IFRS 5 that has been brought in. The assets or groups to be disposed of are not remeasured, nor are they separately presented on the balance sheet: instead, brief disclosures are given, describing the assets, specifying their carrying amounts, and setting out the facts and circumstances of the sale.

3.3.4   Small entities

Small entities do not have to apply Section 4 but they do need to present a statement of financial position. Instead of prescribing formats, Section 1A simply points preparers to the requirements in Pt. 1 of Sch. 1 to the Small Companies Regulations or the Small LLP Regulations as appropriate.

Some additional guidance is given in Appendix A to Section 1A: in particular, it sets out what a small entity should do if it takes the company law permission to adapt the balance sheet formats, by specifying a list of line items that still must be included. These are similar to the line items for larger entities.

3.4   Statement of comprehensive income and income statement

Section 5 covers the items that appear in 'total comprehensive income', defined in the Glossary as 'the change in equity during a period resulting from transactions and other events, other than those changes resulting from transactions from equity participants (equal to the sum of profit or loss and other comprehensive income)', with the supporting definition of other comprehensive income (OCI) as 'items of income and expense (including reclassification adjustments) that are not recognised in profit or loss as required or permitted by this FRS'. The definitions of income and expense are included in **2.2.2**.

In general, the standard makes it quite clear whether any particular gain or loss should be included within profit or OCI: the default is inclusion within profit, but items such as revaluation gains, certain foreign currency gains in groups, and some hedging movements are reported in OCI, meaning they increase equity without having an effect on profit.

This split of results into two distinct types of gains and losses leads to two alternative presentations within the primary statements. The first option is to give a single statement of comprehensive income which shows first all the items in profit, then all the items in OCI, and sums to a figure for total comprehensive income for the period. Alternatively, entities may present an income statement and a second primary statement, with this second statement confusingly also called a statement of other comprehensive income, but only including the detail of items from OCI.

The choice of a single-statement or two-statement approach is a matter of accounting policy, so it is in the scope of Section 10 and cannot be changed unless this results in relevant and more reliable information.

Although both the single-statement and two-statement approaches take the formats from company law as their core, further requirements are layered on top of the basic formats, whichever approach is used.

- The components of other comprehensive income must be classified by nature, presented either net of related tax effects, or before tax followed by a single line for the aggregate of related income tax.

- The entity's share of other comprehensive income of associates and jointly controlled entities that are equity accounted must be shown separately.

- A total must be given for total comprehensive income.

- Turnover must appear as a line item on the face of the income statement or statement of comprehensive income.

- There must be a split of discontinued operations (see more below).

- Material items anywhere within total comprehensive income (i.e. in profit or OCI) must be shown separately either on the face or in the notes.

- Entities that disclose operating profit, or the results of operating activities, must not include non-operating items in that total.

- The single statement or two statements must show an allocation of both profit or loss and total comprehensive income between non-controlling interests and owners of the parent.

3.4.1   Single-statement approach

As is the case for the statement of financial position above, the formats prescribed in company law continue to apply to entities using FRS 102, unless the option is taken to adapt the profit and loss part of the statement of comprehensive income (see **3.4.3**).

Two possible formats are available for a company that is not a banking or insurance company. Unless adapted, the formats must be used even by entities that are not companies, and which are therefore not otherwise in the scope of company law.

Format 1

(1) Turnover

(2) Cost of sales

(3) Gross profit or loss

(4) Distribution costs

(5) Administrative expenses

(6) Other operating income

(7) Income from shares in group undertakings

(8) Income from participating interests

(9) Income from other fixed asset investments

(10) Other interest receivable and similar income

(11) Amounts written off investments

(12) Interest payable and similar charges

(13) Tax on profit or loss on ordinary activities

(14) Profit or loss on ordinary activities after taxation

(15) [Omitted]

(16) [Omitted]

(17) [Omitted]

(18) [Omitted]

(19) Other taxes not shown under the above items

(20) Profit or loss for the financial year

Format 2

(1) Turnover

(2) Change in stocks of finished goods and in work in progress

(3) Own work capitalised

(4) Other operating income

    (a) Raw materials and consumables

    (b) Other external charges

(5) Staff costs

    (a) Wages and salaries

    (b) Social security costs

    (c) Other pension costs

    (d) Depreciation and other amounts written off tangible and intangible fixed assets

    (e) Exceptional amounts written off current assets

(6) Other operating charges

(7) Income from shares in group undertakings

(8) Income from participating interests

(9) Income from other fixed asset investments

(10) Other interest receivable and similar income

(11) Amounts written off investments

(12) Interest payable and similar charges

(13) Tax on profit or loss on ordinary activities

(14) Profit or loss on ordinary activities after taxation

(15) [Omitted]

(16) [Omitted]

(17) [Omitted]

(18) [Omitted]

(19) Other taxes not shown under the above items

(20) Profit or loss for the financial year

The single-statement approach continues directly from the profit and loss component into other comprehensive income. Items of other comprehensive income (OCI) that are recognised outside of profit or loss as part of total comprehensive income include:

(a) foreign exchange component of a gain or loss on a non-monetary item when the gain or loss itself has been recognised in OCI (for example, any foreign exchange component of actuarial gains and losses or of the revaluation of property, plant and equipment); (FRS 102.30.11)

(b) foreign exchange differences on a net investment in a foreign operation in the financial statements that include the foreign operation and the reporting entity; (FRS 102.30.13)

(c) foreign exchange differences on translating assets, liabilities, income and expenses from a functional currency to the presentational currency; (FRS 102.30.18(c))

(d) remeasurement of a defined benefit pension liability, i.e. actuarial gains and losses, and the return on plan assets excluding the amount included in net interest; (FRS 102.28.23(d) and 25)

(e) the effective portion of the change in the fair value of hedging instruments in a cash flow hedge or (in consolidated financial statements) a net investment in a foreign operation; (FRS 102.12.23)

(f) changes in fair values of investments in subsidiaries, associates and joint ventures when the parent has made the accounting policy election to account for its investments in subsidiaries, associates and joint ventures at fair value through other comprehensive income; (FRS 102.17.15E–F; 9.26(b), 14.10 or 15.15)

(g) revaluation increases and decreases arising when the revaluation model is selected for the measurement of property, plant and equipment, heritage assets or intangible assets (unless reversing a loss charged to profit and loss); (FRS 102.17.15E–F, 34.49, and 18.18G–H)

(h) the movements in fair value of available-for-sale assets when an entity chooses under FRS 102.11.2 to apply IAS 39 for the recognition and measurement of its financial instruments; and

(i) deferred tax charges or credits arising on any items appearing in other comprehensive income (FRS 102.29.22).

The most commonly found items are those relating to revalued assets and actuarial gains and losses on defined benefit schemes, plus those relating to hedging and net overseas investments.

3.4.2   Two-statement approach

Under the two-statement approach, the income statement requirements are the same as for the first part of the single statement; that is in one of the permitted formats from company law, or an adapted presentation as set out in **3.4.3**.

The second statement, called the statement of other comprehensive income, starts with profit or loss, and then includes each component of OCI, so that it adds down to total comprehensive income. As described above, OCI items may be shown net of tax, or gross of tax followed by a single line for the aggregate tax charge or credit.

3.4.3   Adapting the profit and loss account format

A company choosing to adapt its profit and loss account formats must, as a minimum, include the following items:

(a)   revenue;

(b)   finance costs;

(c)   share of the profit or loss of investments in associates and jointly controlled entities accounted for using the equity method;

(d)   profit or loss before taxation;

(e)   tax expense excluding tax allocated to other comprehensive income or equity;

(f)   a single amount comprising the total of:

  (i)   the post-tax profit or loss of a discontinued operation; and

  (ii)   the post-tax gain or loss recognised on the remeasurement of the impairment or on the disposal of the assets or disposal group(s) constituting discontinued operations;

(g)   profit or loss;

(h)   each item of other comprehensive income classified by nature (excluding amounts in (i));

(i)   share of other comprehensive income of associates and jointly controlled entities accounted for by the equity method; and

(j)   total comprehensive income.

There is some flexibility to include additional line items or amend the descriptions and ordering where necessary to properly explain the financial position or performance, providing it is at least equivalent. [FRS 102.5.5C]

3.4.4 Fair value adjustments

FRS 102 requires the inclusion of fair value adjustments on listed investments and investment properties within the profit and loss account. There is no guidance as to which line item in the formats should be used, although Section 23 is clear that gains and losses of this nature do not constitute revenue.

Thus far it appears that companies are opting either to use the line 'other operating income' for this purpose or to include a line item from format 1 in Schedule 1 to SI 2008/409 and SI 2008/410, which has not previously been in frequent use, entitled 'Income from other fixed asset investments'. Indeed, this would appear a logical description. Alternatively, companies may take advantage of the option to adapt the formats (see **3.4.3**) and introduce an IFRS style of presentation, enabling them to include a line for something like 'other gains and losses'.

3.4.5 Operating profit

There is no requirement in FRS 102 to include the line 'operating profit', but if one is included, it should be struck at an appropriate level and not exclude items of an operating nature. FRS 102.5.9B states that 'it would be inappropriate to exclude items clearly related to operations (such as inventory write-downs and restructuring and relocation expenses) because they occur irregularly or infrequently or are unusual in amount. Similarly, it would be inappropriate to exclude items on the grounds that they do not involve cash flows, such as depreciation and amortisation expenses'.

Things are less clear when it comes to presenting fair value adjustments, however. Under IFRS, these adjustments often appear after operating profit and there is therefore an argument for the same approach to be taken under FRS 102, but there are exceptions to this. For example, in the case of a property investment company, it would seem more appropriate to present fair value movements in relation to investment property above operating profit as the properties are clearly linked to the ordinary operations of the company.

FRS 102 (2018) clarifies paragraph 5.9B to make it clear that while a profit or loss on a disposal of property, plant and equipment, investment property and intangible assets should typically appear above the operating profit line, a profit or loss on disposal of a discontinued operation must be presented after operating profit (see **3.4.6**).

3.4.6   *Discontinued operations*

A discontinued operation is defined in the Glossary as:

> 'A component of an entity that has been disposed of and:
>
> (a)   represented a separate major line of business or geographical area of operations;
>
> (b)   was part of a single co-ordinated plan to dispose of a separate major line of business or geographical area of operations; or
>
> (c)   was a subsidiary acquired exclusively with a view to resale.'

To support this, a component of an entity is defined as 'operations and cash flows that can be clearly distinguished, operationally and for financial reporting purposes, from the rest of the entity'.

Example 3.2

Company L makes ice creams and umbrellas. The two operations have distinct management teams and operate from separate premises. During 2018, L ceases its ice cream operations and sells off all the equipment. The ice cream business would be classified as a discontinued operation in the 2018 accounts.

Company M makes deck chairs and raincoats, but during 2018 it concludes that the summer business is not supportable, and begins the process of winding down its deckchair operations. No new stock is bought after November 2018, and the staff at the deckchair warehouse have been warned by December 2018 that they can expect redundancy in the new year. Sales of deckchairs continue, though, as the intention is to terminate the operations by selling out all of the stock. The deckchair operations are therefore not classified as discontinued in 2018, because the termination was not completed until 2019.

Company N had years of trading through significant operations in several European countries but during 2019 it withdrew completely from France, and also sold two of its small Spanish companies as part of a committed plan to withdraw entirely from Spain too. The French business will be classified as discontinued in 2019 because it represented a major geographical area of operations; it is likely that the Spanish subsidiaries that were disposed of will also be classified as discontinued because their disposal was part of a single co-ordinated plan to cease trading in Spain.

Once discontinued operations have been identified, the presentation is not complex: paragraph 5.7D requires the face of the income statement or statement of comprehensive income to include one figure representing the sum of the post-tax profit or loss of discontinued operations and the post-tax gain or loss attributable to the impairment, or on the disposal, of the relevant assets or disposal groups. This is then supplemented by a line-by-line analysis of discontinued operations in a separate column, with the result that the income statement or statement of comprehensive income will include three columns, for continuing operations, discontinued operations, and the total.

The requirements to give these splits apply to both the current and comparative periods for all operations that had been discontinued by the end of the reporting period.

Example 3.3

Company P, a retailer, discontinued its 'young and hip' shop brand in 2018.

In the 2018 accounts, the results of 'young and hip' are shown separately, as discontinued operations, in both the current year and comparative columns.

Then in 2019, P also discontinues its 'comfortable middle age' shop brand, closing 45 more stores. The discontinued operations column for 2019 will include only the results of 'comfortable middle age' but for 2018 will include the results of both 'comfortable middle age' and 'young and hip'.

While this point seems fairly obvious, it is important that the disclosures surrounding the discontinued operations are clear enough that users will not be misled into thinking, for instance, that they can look at the comparatives and understand the decline of 'comfortable middle age'. Such a conclusion would be flawed because the prior year figures include other discontinued operations too.

The Appendix to FRS 102 contains an example of the presentation of discontinued operations. This appendix shows 'profit or loss on disposal of operations' as falling below the operating profit line, but prior to the triennial review amendments in FRS 102, this item sat above the operating profit line. The current treatment is more consistent with that in IFRS 5 and old UK GAAP (FRS 3), as a profit or loss on sale of an operation is not part of the ongoing activities of the business.

3.4.7 Exceptional items

FRS 102 does not use the term exceptional items but that does not remove the requirement to consider whether additional items would be shown. Paragraph 5.9 requires 'additional line items, headings and subtotals … when such presentation is relevant to an understanding of the entity's financial performance'.

3.4.8 Small entities

As mentioned above, small entities are required to present an income statement but, if they have items of other comprehensive income, are only encouraged rather than required to present a statement of comprehensive income.

As with the statement of financial position, the formats are not reproduced in Section 1A but instead, preparers are pointed to Pt. 1 of Sch. 1 to the Small Companies Regulations or the Small LLP Regulations as relevant. More detail on using the formats is given in Appendix B to Section 1A, including the option to adapt the income statement format.

The disclosure of items which have an exceptional effect on profit or loss is one of the mandatory notes under Section 1A and therefore these requirements do apply to small entities (FRS 102.1AC.32). However, small entities are not required to present discontinued operations separately.

3.5   Statement of changes in equity and statement of income and retained earnings

Section 6 is very brief, simply outlining the required components of the statement of changes in equity, and the permissible alternative primary statement.

3.5.1   *Statement of changes in equity*

The statement of changes in equity summarises all the elements of the movement between the comparative and current year total equity. The three items required on the face of the statement are:

- total comprehensive income for the period (split between amounts attributable to owners of the parent and to non-controlling interests);

- the effects of retrospective application of the standard or retrospective restatement arising from changes in policy or errors, shown separately for each component of equity;

- a reconciliation of the opening carrying amount of each component of equity to its closing carrying amount, split between changes arising from:

  - profit or loss;

  - other comprehensive income; and

  - investments by, and dividends and other distributions to, owners.

The final component of the above reconciliation must split the movement between issues of shares, purchase of own shares, dividends and other distributions, and changes in ownership interests in subsidiaries that do not result in loss of control (see **4.2.5.6** of this guide).

In addition, an item by item analysis of other comprehensive income is required, either on the face of the statement of changes in equity or in the notes.

Example 3.4

This example sets out a statement of changes in equity that includes a range of items and complies with the requirements of Section 6. This is not the only way of meeting the requirements, and there may be more ways even for the same entity – it does not have all possible types of transaction, but at least indicates one mode of presentation.

As there is no exemption from providing comparatives, a similar table would, in each case, need to be provided for the previous period too, although this has not been shown here.

As the tables are not populated with numbers, rows or columns that are sums of others are clearly marked – this markup would not be needed in a normal set of financial statements.

	Share capital (1)	Share premium (2)	Retained earnings (3)	Revaluation reserve (4)	Total equity (1+2+3+4) (5+6)	Attributable to owners of parent (5)	Attributable to NCI (6)
Opening balance (A)	X	X	X	X	X	X	X
Profit for the period (B)			X		X	X	X
Other comprehensive income:							
Revaluation gains on PPE (C)				X	X	X	X
Change in value of hedging instruments (D)			X		X	X	X
Total comprehensive income (B + C + D) (E)			X	X	X	X	X
Shares issued (F)	X	X			X		
Dividends (G)			X		X		
Purchase of additional stake in subsidiary (H)			X		X		
Closing balance (A+E+F+G+H)	X	X	X	X	X		

As an alternative, the table can be shortened by having only one line item for other comprehensive income, and giving the disaggregation in a note to the accounts. Whether this option is useful will depend on how many components of OCI there are – in this example, where there are only two, it seems unnecessary to add another table.

3.5.2   Statement of income and retained earnings

In very simple situations where a company has minimal changes to equity outside of its profit or loss for the year, a statement of changes in equity adds very little to the financial statements.

Accordingly, paragraph 6.4 tightly defines a circumstance in which it is acceptable to replace the statement of comprehensive income and statement of changes in equity with a single statement of income and retained earnings. This is only permitted if the only changes in equity are:

- profit or loss for the period;
- payment of dividends;
- correction of prior period material errors;
- changes in accounting policy.

There is no requirement to replace the two statements with one where these conditions are met; it is purely an accounting policy option.

3.5.3   Changing which statement is presented

A question arises over what should be done in the situation where an entity is eligible in one year to prepare only a statement of income and retained earnings, but in the following year undertakes a transaction such as an issue of shares which means that a separate statement of comprehensive income and statement of changes in equity will be needed.

It seems that the requirement from paragraph 3.14, to provide comparative information except when the standard permits or requires otherwise, will be effective here, meaning that a full comparative statement of comprehensive income and statement of changes in equity will be needed even though these were not presented in the previous year. Perhaps the converse is more challenging: if an entity has a number of complex transactions in 2018, requiring the full set of primary statements, but in 2019 only has profits and payment of dividends, then it is not absolutely clear in the standard that it is acceptable to present the combined statement in 2019. Doing so would mean that important information from the comparatives would be omitted, and would prevent a successful reconciliation of 2018 opening to closing equity from the 2019 accounts.

In the absence of guidance from the standard, a judgment will be needed by preparers and may also need to be audited. On the one hand, the lack of comparatives if only a statement of income and retained earnings were to be presented for both periods might be seen as unimportant because users can get the information from the previous year's accounts. On the other hand, it might be argued that the primary statements which were required for 2018 were part of the 2018 financial statements (as they clearly were) and so they must be included to be a reasonable representation of 2018 as a comparative period for 2019.

Example 3.5

A statement of income and retained earnings for a simple company could be presented as follows, although as with the example statement of changes in equity above, there are other ways of presentation that would also comply with Section 6.

	2019	2018 as previously reported
Turnover	X	X
Cost of sales	X	X
Gross profit	X	X
Distribution costs	X	X
Administrative expenses	X	X
Interest payable	X	X
Tax	X	X
Profit after tax and retained profit for the year	X	X
Opening retained earnings	X	X
Dividends	X	X
Correction of prior period errors		X
Effects of changes in policy		X
Closing retained earnings	X	X

Note that the line items in respect of prior year adjustments (for correction of errors and changes in policy) are both shown as having entries only in the comparative column. For IFRS preparers making prior year adjustments and presenting a SOCIE, there would be no separate line item for these restatements – they would simply be taken into account in the reported figures.

3.5.4   Small entities

Small entities are encouraged but not required to present a statement of changes in equity or statement of income and retained earnings.

3.6   Statement of cash flows

The statement of cash flows reconciles movements in cash and cash equivalents over the reporting period. Most entities in the scope of FRS 102 will be required to prepare one, with the following exceptions from paragraphs 7.1A:

(a)   mutual and life assurance companies;

(b)   retirement benefit plans;

(c)   investment funds meeting all of the following conditions:

    (i)   substantially all of the entity's investments are highly liquid;

    (ii)   substantially all of the entity's investments are carried at market value; and

    (iii)   the entity provides a statement of changes in net assets.

Small entities are not required to comply with any of Section 7 of FRS 102.

In addition, paragraph 1.12 gives an exemption for any 'qualifying entity', that is 'a member of a group where the parent of that group prepares publicly available consolidated financial statements which are intended to give a true and fair view (of the assets, liabilities, financial position and profit or loss) and that member is included in the consolidation'.

3.6.1   Cash and cash equivalents

Cash equivalents are defined in paragraph 7.2 as 'short-term, highly liquid investments that are readily convertible to known amounts of cash and that are subject to an insignificant risk of changes in value' and it goes on to clarify that an investment with a maturity of three months or less from acquisition will normally be classified as a cash equivalent.

Some entities will find this leads to a discrepancy between the amounts included in cash equivalents and those included within cash on the balance sheet (if, for instance, the entity has funds in short term deposits which it classifies as current asset investments).

This possibility is acknowledged in paragraphs 7.20 and 7.20A, which state that balance sheet cash only includes 'cash and balances at central banks and loans and advances to banks repayable on demand'. They then require a reconciliation of the reported amounts in the two statements, presented in the notes, if the amounts differ.

3.6.2   *Basic format of the statement of cash flows*

The format prescribed by Section 7 has only a high level structure: cash flows are divided into those from operating, investing and financing activities. An example is given at the end of this part.

In general, gross cash receipts and payments are shown separately, but the standard includes some guidance setting out conditions where it is acceptable (but not required) to net them off. This applies to cash receipts and payments on behalf of customers when the cash flows reflect the customer's, rather than the entity's, activities, and to cash receipts and payments for items in which the turnover is quick, the amounts are large, and the maturities are short.

Examples of these are focused mainly on transactions which might be undertaken by financial institutions, such as where a bank accepts and repays demand deposits, or, as an example of the second type, where a credit card provider transacts with holders. There are some non-financial applications listed too, though, for instance the collection by a letting agency of rents on behalf of a landlord. This could apply to many agency-type arrangements where the reporting entity's role is strictly as an intermediary, although careful examination is needed to ensure this is truly the case. The issues surrounding the agent vs principal question are discussed further in **10.5.1** of this guide.

3.6.3   *Operating activities*

Operating activities are defined in paragraph 7.4 as 'the principal revenue-producing activities of the entity'. Most items above interest in the income statement will be included in this category, with an exception of profits or losses on disposal of fixed assets.

There is some flexibility in the mode of presentation of operating cash flows: in particular, there is a choice between the direct and indirect methods.

In the direct method, separate line items are shown for 'major classes of gross cash receipts and gross cash payments' such as receipts from customers and payments to suppliers and employees. Paragraph 7.9 gives some guidance on how to establish the appropriate figures, most of which is fairly intuitive (for instance, reaching a figure of cash receipts from customers by adjusting sales revenue for opening and closing trade receivables).

In the indirect method, in contrast, the statement of cash flows begins with profit or loss and is adjusted for the effects of non-cash transactions and those of cash transactions that are included elsewhere in the cash flow statement. Examples of non-cash items are depreciation, provisions, deferred tax, accrued income, unrealised foreign currency gains and losses, undistributed profits of associates, and non-controlling interests, although this list should not be seen as exhaustive, and nor does it dictate a required or permitted level of aggregation.

FRS 102 (2018) clarifies that the indirect method should commence with a measure of profit or loss disclosed in the income statement and the measure of profit/loss selected should be used consistently from year to year.

The standard also clarifies that the reconciliation to operating cash flow needs to be presented in the financial statements. This may be either on the face of the cash flow statement or in the notes.

3.6.4 *Investing activities*

Investing activities are defined in paragraph 7.5 as 'the acquisition and disposal of long-term assets and other investments not included in cash equivalents', with a long list of examples then given, including:

- payments to acquire (or construct) property, plant and equipment;
- payments to acquire intangible assets (including capitalised development costs, although expensed development costs would be included in operating activities);
- receipts from disposal of long-term assets;
- payments to acquire investments in other entities (equity or debt) and receipts from sales of these;
- cash advances and loans made to other parties and receipts from those (note that cash received as loans and advances would be included as a financing, not an investing, activity);
- cash payments and receipts relating to futures contracts, forward contracts, options, etc except when these are held for dealing or trading and classified as financing activities.

FRS 102 (2018) clarifies that cash flows from investing activities include net cash flows arising from obtaining or losing control of subsidiaries or other businesses.

Interest and dividends are covered separately in paragraphs 7.4–7.16: in short, there is a wide choice of location for such flows. The options can be summarised in a table:

	Operating	Investing	Financing
Interest paid	✓		✓
Interest received	✓	✓	
Dividends paid	✓		✓
Dividends received	✓	✓	

3.6.5   Financing activities

Financing activities are defined in paragraph 7.6 as 'activities that result in changes in the size and composition of the contributed equity and borrowings of an entity'. Again, the standard gives a number of examples:

- cash proceeds from issuing shares or other equity;

- cash proceeds from issuing debt;

- cash repayments of amounts borrowed, or outflows for redemption or repurchase of shares;

- cash payments for the reduction of the outstanding liability relating to a finance lease.

3.6.6   Special considerations

3.6.6.1   Foreign currency cash flows

When an entity has transactions in a foreign currency, the cash flows that are included relating to these transactions should be the exact functional currency equivalent, in other words the result of translating each transaction at the spot rate. This can be challenging to execute, though, so 7.11 permits 'a rate that approximates the actual rate' to be used. As in Section 30, with its similar allowance for income statement items, this relaxation is likely to be widely taken advantage of as few preparers have the resources or inclination to perform transaction-by-transaction translation.

The same applies to the translation of cash flows of a foreign subsidiary: ideally an actual rate would be used, but in practice it is permissible to use a weighted average.

In either case, and regardless of the method of translation used, opening and closing cash balances will not reconcile when foreign currency is involved, because of unrealised gains and losses included in year end balances. The requirement of the standard is that 'the entity shall remeasure cash and cash equivalents held during the reporting period at period-end exchange rates' with the resulting exchange gain or loss shown as a separate line item in the cash flow statement, outside the three categories of operating, investing and financing activities.

3.6.6.2 Income tax

Tax cash flows do not fall naturally into any of the categories so the standard approaches this by making it clear, in paragraph 7.7, that they are to be included as a separate line item within operating cash flows 'unless they can be specifically identified with financing and investing activities' which is unlikely to be the case in a jurisdiction such as the UK where a company's tax bill is based on its revenue and capital gains together.

It seems clear the income tax cash flows referred to here include only taxes on profits, not employment taxes or VAT, even though the latter is scoped into Section 29.

3.6.6.3 Non-cash transactions

Paragraphs 7.18–7.19 make what seems to be a reasonably obvious point: non-cash transactions are not reported in the statement of cash flows. Although it is clear when expressed this way, in practice application difficulties are sometimes seen. For example, an entity acquiring a piece of equipment under a finance lease has an increase in its assets and liabilities, so if the cash flow statement was prepared at speed, using the 'additions' line from the fixed asset note as the relevant cash outflow in its investing activities section, it would include the acquisition of this asset, even though no cash outflow has arisen from the transaction. Similarly, where a business combination is effected by issuing shares as part of the consideration, the amount shown as an outflow in investing activities is not the whole consideration, but only the cash component (similarly, deferred consideration would not be included).

If there are significant non-cash items such as the examples above, it will be helpful to provide an explanation, perhaps in the relevant notes, of why there are discrepancies between the amount shown as a cash flow and the year to year movement on the balance sheet.

3.6.6.4 Financial institutions

Section 7 contains a small number of special provisions for financial institutions.

First, cash advances and loans that they make to other parties must be included within operating rather than investing activities.

Second, as well as the situations described above when cash flows may be reported net, financial institutions may also net off each of the following (from paragraph 34.33):

(a) cash receipts and payments for the acceptance and repayment of deposits with a fixed maturity date;

(b) the placement of deposits with and withdrawal of deposits from other financial institutions; and

(c) cash advances and loans made to customers and the repayment of those advances and loans.

3.6.7 Example statement of cash flows

The example below is not populated with figures, but shows how a medium-sized company with a range of transactions might present a statement of cash flows that complies with all of the requirements of Section 7.

Example 3.6

Statement of cash flows for the year to 31 December 2019

	2019	2018
Operating activities		
Profit before tax	X	X
Adjustments for:		
Change in inventories	X	X
Change in debtors	X	X
Change in creditors	X	X
Depreciation	X	X
Loss on disposal of fixed assets	X	X
Amortisation	X	X
Interest paid	X̲	X̲
Income taxes paid	X̲	X̲
Total cash from operating activities	X	X
Investing activities		
Payments to acquire property, plant and equipment	X	X
Receipts from sale of property, plant and equipment	X	X
Purchase of shares in other entities	X̲	X̲
Total cash from investing activities	X	X
Financing activities		
Proceeds from issuing shares	X	X

	2019	2018
Dividends paid	X	X
Capital repayments on bank loans	X	X
Interest paid on bank loans	X	X
Total cash from financing activities	X	X
Net increase in cash and cash equivalents	**X**	**X**
Cash and cash equivalents at the beginning of the period	X	X
Exchange differences	X	X
Cash and cash equivalents at the end of the period	X	X

3.6.8   *Other cash flow disclosures*

FRS 102 requires disclosure of any material non-cash transactions not shown in the cash flow statement (paragraphs 7.18–19) as well as information about any cash not available for use by the entity (paragraph 7.21).

FRS 102 (2018) reintroduced the requirement to present a reconciliation of net debt by inserting paragraph 7.22:

> 'An entity shall disclose an analysis of changes in net debt from the beginning to the end of the reporting period showing changes resulting from:
>
> (a)   the cash flows of the entity;
>
> (b)   the acquisition and disposal of subsidiaries;
>
> (c)   new finance leases entered into;
>
> (d)   other non-cash changes; and
>
> (e)   the recognition of changes in market value and exchange rate movements.'

When several balances (or parts thereof) from the statement of financial position have been combined to form the components of opening and closing net debt, sufficient detail shall be shown to enable users to identify these balances. This analysis need not be presented for prior periods

3.7   Notes to the financial statements

Section 8, on notes to the financial statements, is unsurprisingly brief. It does not contain any account-balance specific requirements, as these are all included in the relevant sections of the standard; instead it sets out the aim of notes and a small number of general requirements.

3.7.1   Contents and structure

Paragraph 8.2 signposts the more specific requirements in the remainder of Section 8, and adds a general requirement to provide information that is necessary or relevant even where not specifically required by the standard.

There is a slightly odd paragraph setting out the order in which notes to the accounts are normally presented (with no suggestion that this is a recommended or mandated order): this begins with a statement of compliance (discussed at **3.2.1**), then a summary of significant accounting policies, supporting information for individual line items following their sequence in the primary statements, and finally 'any other disclosures'. An entity choosing to use a different order, perhaps by grouping notes thematically, or by describing certain accounting policies within the relevant note, would not be breaching anything within Section 8 of FRS 102.

3.7.2   Accounting policies

Although the detailed guidance on developing accounting policies appears in Section 10 of the standard (discussed in **2.3** of this guide), Section 8 of FRS 102 supplements this with a general requirement to include within the summary of accounting policies a disclosure of the measurement basis (that is, whether historical cost or fair value, or a mixture of the two) used in preparing the financial statements, and a disclosure of 'the other accounting policies used that are relevant to an understanding of the financial statements'.

No threshold is provided for determining relevance, and there is clearly some subjectivity here. The inclusion of a very detailed accounting policy for every account balance, even when only of trivial numerical value and unlikely to recur, does not improve the quality of financial reporting; it would be too broad-brush, though, to apply a principle of only making accounting policy disclosures for material line items.

3.7.3   Judgments and estimates

Two similar types of disclosure are required here: it can be hard to discern which is which.

First, it is necessary to disclose 'the judgements, apart from those involving estimations, that management has made in the process of applying the entity's accounting policies and that have the most significant effect on the amounts recognised in the financial statements' (paragraph 8.6). This contrasts with the requirement in the subsequent paragraph to disclose 'key assumptions concerning the future, and other key sources of estimation uncertainty at the reporting date, that have a significant risk of causing a material adjustment to the carrying amounts of assets and liabilities within the next financial year' (8.7), giving details of the nature of the relevant assets or liabilities, and their carrying amounts at the balance sheet date.

To clarify the distinction between these two areas, typical areas subject to estimation uncertainty might include:

- measurement of provisions, for instance relating to legal cases with uncertain outcomes;
- estimates of future pension liabilities, which use multiple assumptions about remaining service periods, mortality rates, etc.; and
- valuation of share based payments, which again use a number of assumptions.

Judgments, on the other hand, might include:

- the policy chosen for revenue recognition, including the determination of the point when risks and rewards are transferred;
- the decision process for classifying financial assets and liabilities at fair value; and
- the assessment of whether a lease is an operating lease or a finance lease.

Often, the judgments note will make reference to specific account balances and their values; it might, for instance, describe the assessment of a particular lease, and note that had it been classified differently, there would have been a (quantified) effect on profit and net assets.

3.7.4 Small entities

As mentioned above, small entities are not required to give the disclosures set out in Sections 8–35 of the standard. Unfortunately, this sits uneasily with the requirement to give a true and fair view, so paragraph 1A.17 states that 'because these disclosures are usually considered relevant to giving a true and fair view, a small entity is encouraged to consider and provide any of those disclosures that are relevant to material transactions, other events or conditions of the small entity in order to meet the requirement set out in paragraphs 1A.5 and 1A.16'.

Appendix C to Section 1A sets out the minimum disclosures for small entities, and these are discussed in the relevant sections, but they do not provide the reassurance of a checklist, because of this overarching requirement to consider the disclosures in the rest of the standard where it seems possible that they might be relevant.

4 Groups

4.1 Scope of this section

Although this section's title is 'Groups', its scope covers all aspects of preparing accounts where the reporting entity has an investment in another entity that gives it some rights to have influence and to receive a share of the investee's profits. This means it discusses the following sections of FRS 102:

- Section 9 *Consolidated and Separate Financial Statements*
- Section 14 *Investments in Associates*
- Section 15 *Investments in Joint Ventures*
- Section 19 *Business Combinations and Goodwill*

The corresponding standards in IFRS are:

- IFRS 10 *Consolidated Financial Statements*;
- IFRS 11 *Joint Arrangements Illustrative Examples*;
- IFRS 12 *Disclosure of Interests in Other Entities*;
- IAS 27 *Separate Financial Statements*; and
- IAS 28 *Investments in Associates and Joint Ventures*.

When the FRC consulted in 2016 on the approach to the triennial review, it asked for views on whether or not certain areas should be amended in line with IFRSs. In particular it suggested that the control model should be updated to bring in the IFRS 10 approach, which looks at the power to control and direct activities.

Respondents to the consultation disagreed with this suggestion. It was pointed out that most entities would end up with the same situation as they have under the current control model, but would need to go through a lengthy and potentially expensive exercise to establish this, so the cost of implementing it would far outweigh the benefits. The FRC has therefore decided not to amend these two areas for the time being, but the triennial review does add an additional disclosure requirement about unconsolidated structured entities to make sure users have enough information in this area.

Application to micro-entities: The micro-entity regime is not applicable to group accounts, and cannot be applied by a company that is required to prepare group accounts. A parent company can only qualify as a micro-entity if it heads a small group and is not required to prepare consolidated accounts (and is not included in consolidated accounts at a higher level). As such it is possible that a micro-entity could have subsidiaries.

In relation to individual financial statements, the definition of a subsidiary, an associate and a jointly controlled entity is the same in FRS 105 as in FRS 102. Section 9 of FRS 105 states that, in the individual accounts of the micro-entity such investments are held at cost less impairment. Jointly controlled operations and jointly controlled assets are accounted for in the same way as FRS 102.

FRS 105 does contain a section on trade and asset acquisitions (Section 14), which is based on Section 9 of FRS 102. The purchase method set out in Section 19 of FRS 102 is generally followed but with some exceptions:

(1)   intangible assets are not separated from goodwill;

(2)   deferred tax is not provided;

(3)   share-based payments are not accounted for until shares are issued; and

(4)   no disclosures are required.

Merger accounting is not referred to in FRS 105 and the definition of a group reconstruction does not appear in the Glossary. It is therefore not completely clear in the current standard whether the group reconstruction hybrid approach (as used in old UK GAAP) would be appropriate for use in the individual accounts of a micro-entity where a hive-up or hive-across of trade and assets takes place under common control. This is also unlikely to arise frequently in practice since most group entities are unable to qualify for the micro-entity regime (see **1.2.3**). In the absence of specific guidance, micro-entities should select an appropriate accounting policy in accordance with Section 8 of FRS 105.

The guidance on accounting for intermediate payment arrangements in FRS 105 is consistent with that in FRS 102.

4.2   Preparing consolidated accounts

4.2.1   Requirements, definitions and exemptions

Section 9 requires any entity that is a parent at its reporting date to prepare consolidated financial statements which include all of its investments in subsidiaries. (A parent is simply defined as an entity with one or more subsidiaries).

Since this is an area that is also addressed in the Companies Act, the FRS 102 exemptions from consolidation have been written to ensure that they are consistent with the Act. To save unnecessary clutter in the standard, most of the exemptions refer to additional conditions within s. 400 and 401 of the Act.

The exemption applies in any of the following circumstances, summarised here from paragraph 9.3:

(a) the parent is a wholly-owned subsidiary with an EEA immediate parent (s. 400(2));

(b) the parent is a majority-owned subsidiary and meets the conditions in the Act that apply to wholly-owned subsidiaries (s. 400(2) and 400(1)(b));

(c) the parent is a wholly-owned subsidiary of another entity which is established outside the EEA (s. 401(2));

(d) the parent is a majority-owned subsidiary meeting the same conditions as those in (c) and those in s. 401(1)(b);

(e) the parent and the group it heads both qualify as small (based on s. 383) and the group is not ineligible (s. 384);

(f) all of the subsidiaries are required to be excluded from consolidation by para. 9.9; or

(g) the parent entity's statutory framework does not require it to prepare statutory financial statements (where the parent is not reporting under the Act).

Put another way, a wholly-owned or majority-owned parent whose parent is within the EEA will not usually have to prepare group accounts, and nor will one whose parent is outside the EEA, provided certain conditions are met. Also, group accounts are not required if the relevant group would qualify as small, though they are required for medium-sized groups.

The Act sets out the detail of the conditions that apply when an exemption is taken based on being part of a larger EEA or non-EEA group.

- The company taking the exemption must be included in consolidated accounts for a larger group drawn up to the same date.

- Those accounts must be audited and prepared under the EU Accounting Directive (Directive 2013/34/EU) or IFRS (or, with a parent outside the EEA, principles equivalent to the EU Accounting Directive).

- The company taking the exemption must disclose this fact in its individual accounts.

- It must also state the name of the parent that draws up the relevant group accounts, and the country in which it is incorporated (or the address of its principal place of business, if it is unincorporated).

- When the exempt company's accounts are filed at Companies House, they must be accompanied by a copy of the relevant group accounts, annual report and auditor's report.

- If necessary, these must be accompanied by a certified translation into English.

Where the company taking the exemption is not wholly-owned, the exemption would be blocked if:

(a) the parent company holds 90% or more of the allotted shares in the company and the remaining shareholders do not approve the exemption; or

(b) shareholders holding more than 50% but less than 90% of the remaining shares, or 5% of the total shares in issue, were to serve notice requiring group accounts to be prepared, at least six months before the end of the relevant financial year.

4.2.1.1 Equivalence

The question of what it means for a parent company's accounts to be prepared in a manner equivalent to the provisions of the EU Accounting Directive (and prior to that, the Seventh Directive) has been problematic ever since company law introduced the possibility of an exemption for companies with a non-EEA parent. Previously this was addressed by UITF Abstract 43 *The interpretation of equivalence for the purposes of section 228A of the Companies Act 1985*. UITF 43 discussed a general approach to assessing equivalence and observed that EU-adopted IFRS would always meet the test of equivalence, and that many GAAPs based on IFRS (such as those of Australia, Hong Kong and South Africa) would meet the test too, providing that their divergences from IFRS represented restrictions rather than expansions of the available accounting options. Moving to GAAPs that are not linked to IFRS, the Abstract stated that accounts prepared in accordance with US GAAP, Japanese GAAP and Canadian GAAP would usually comply as well, although some key issues (for instance the scope of consolidation) would need to be carefully reviewed for each particular circumstance).

This assessment is still necessary under FRS 102, and some guidance is contained in the Application Guidance within FRS 100, which forms an integral part of that standard. The Application Guidance is consistent with the conclusions in UITF 43.

4.2.1.2 Small entities

Small entities applying Section 1A of the standard are not required to prepare consolidated financial statements (paragraph 1A.21). If, however, a small parent voluntarily prepares group accounts, it must follow the accounting in Section 9 and is also encouraged to give the disclosures in paragraph 9.23 (discussed at **4.2.9**).

4.2.2 Establishing which entities are included in the consolidation

As stated above, a parent must prepare consolidated accounts including all of its subsidiaries, being the entities that it controls.

4.2.2.1   Control

Control is defined in paragraph 9.4 as 'the power to govern the financial and operating policies of an entity so as to obtain benefits from its activities'. Control is presumed to exist when the parent has more than half of the voting power, but can also exist where the parent has less than half of the voting power but instead has at least one of:

(a)   power over more than half of the voting rights through an agreement with other investors;

(b)   power, under a statute or agreement, to govern the entity's financial and operating policies;

(c)   power to appoint or remove a majority of the board or governing body; or

(d)   power to cast the majority of votes at a meeting of the board or governing body.

Conversely, it is possible for an investor to have more than half of an investee's voting rights without controlling it, if the other party has a claim to control based on one of the circumstances above. Joint control, which is another possibility, is discussed further at **4.5.2**.

To complicate things further, control can also be achieved through the power to exercise or actual exercise of dominant influence, and through a situation where the parent and the investee 'are managed on a unified basis'.

When looking at shareholdings that give access to voting rights, currently exercisable options or convertible instruments are also taken into account.

These points are best illustrated through examples.

Example 4.1

Company A holds 40% of the equity share capital (and hence voting rights) of Company P. Although its holding is below the default 50% threshold for control, it has the right to appoint two-thirds of the board of the directors, and hence concludes that it controls P.

Company B holds 60% of the share capital and voting rights of company Q. It has an agreement, though, with the holder of the remaining 40% of the shares, whereby that other investor has the casting vote on all key decisions (this was set up on the understanding that B receives a greater share of profits by virtue of its majority shareholding). B does not control Q despite the level of its shareholding.

Company C holds 45% of the share capital of company S and has an investment in S's convertible debt which would, if converted, mean that C held 52% of S's total shares in issue. The debt includes a term that gives the holder an immediate conversion right should certain conditions be breached,

---

> and these have been breached in the period. From the point when the breach takes place and triggers the conversion option, C controls S even if it has not yet given notice to exercise, or does not intend to exercise, the option.
>
> Company D holds the remaining 55% of the share capital of company S, and has always accounted for it as a subsidiary. When the debt conditions are breached, though, so that C's options are convertible, D loses control of S, regardless of whether C intends to exercise its right to convert.

The conclusion for Company D in the above example is because, setting aside contractually agreed joint control, a company can only have one parent. It means that parents need to understand and monitor all of their subsidiaries' shares and options in issue, to ensure that it continues to be accurate to consolidate each subsidiary. It is reasonably unusual for situations like this to arise, as in general an entity's controlling party will cause the issue of dilutive shares and options to be restricted, in order to ensure that it cannot lose control.

4.2.2.2   Subsidiaries excluded from consolidation

There are only three circumstances in which a subsidiary must (or may), despite meeting the control conditions, be excluded from the parent's consolidated accounts.

Firstly, a subsidiary may be excluded from consolidation if its inclusion is not material (individually or collectively for more than one subsidiary) for the purposes of giving a true and fair view in the context of the group. FRS 102 (2018) contains this exclusion in a new paragraph 9.9A (with previous paragraphs 9.9A and 9.9B renumbered to 9.9B and 9.9C respectively). Previously, the exclusion was only in company law (CA 2006, s. 405(2)).

The second circumstance is where 'severe long-term restrictions substantially hinder the exercise of the rights of the parent over the assets or management of the subsidiary' (9.9(a)), in other words, where the parent has theoretical rights but there is a practical barrier in place which means it cannot use them. An example might be where a subsidiary is based outside the UK and the local government imposes new barriers on the conduct of foreign investments, perhaps by insisting on involving a government representative in decision-making, or by prohibiting cash movements in and out of the country. It should normally be relatively straightforward to determine whether such long-term restrictions exist.

The final circumstance may be harder to assess: it applies where 'the interest in the subsidiary is held exclusively with a view to subsequent resale' (9.9(b)) and the subsidiary has never been included in consolidated accounts prepared under FRS 102.

Assessing intention is always somewhat problematic but it is reasonable to expect that an investment bought for resale would have been flagged as such in board meetings, in any publicity surrounding the acquisition, and so on, with the important feature being that this discussion is contemporaneous to the acquisition. If a parent buys a subsidiary and disposes of it six months later, in the same financial year, because its results are disappointing, then both the acquisition and the disposal must be properly accounted for, and the six months of results while the subsidiary was owned must be included in the consolidation.

When a subsidiary is excluded from consolidation, clearly some alternative accounting is needed, the nature of which will depend on whether it is held as part of an investment portfolio (which is much more likely to be the case for exclusion on the second grounds than the first). Investments held as part of such a portfolio are measured at fair value, with changes reported in profit or loss; for the remainder the accounting policy options are the same as those for separate financial statements (discussed at **4.2.6**).

FRS 102 defines 'held as part of an investment portfolio' as follows:

'An interest is held as part of an investment portfolio if its value to the investor is through fair value as part of a directly or indirectly held basket of investments rather than as media through which the investor carries out business. A basket of investments is indirectly held if an investment fund holds a single investment in a second investment fund which, in turn, holds a basket of investments.'

FRS 102 (2018) includes the following sentence to add to the definition:

'In some circumstances, it may be appropriate for a single investment to be considered an investment portfolio, for example when an investment fund is first being established and is expected to acquire additional investments.'

The additional sentence removes the confusion expressed in the past by some.

Although it should be sufficient merely to set out positive requirements for exclusion from consolidation, by defining the only two circumstances in which it is permissible, the standard takes a 'belt and braces' approach by also describing two specific situations which do not justify exclusion:

(1) dissimilarity of the subsidiary's activities to those of the rest of the group (this should instead be dealt with through disclosures about the additional activities of the subsidiary); and

(2) a claim that the necessary information cannot be obtained without disproportionate expense or undue delay (presumably based on the idea that a parent has rights to the relevant information, and should be in a position to access it, if it truly does control the subsidiary).

It is helpful that these points are made specific in the standard, because the second differs from the requirements of company law (CA 2006, s. 404), which would permit (but not require) an exclusion based on disproportionate expense or undue delay.

4.2.2.3 Special purpose entities

Special purpose entities (SPEs) are not precisely defined in the standard: instead they are described as being created to accomplish a narrow objective, for instance to effect a lease, undertake research and development activities, securitise financial assets or facilitate the use of ESOPs. Post-employment benefit plans are covered separately in Section 28 of FRS 102 (see **14.7**) and intermediate payment arrangements have their own specific guidance later in Section 9 of FRS 102 (discussed at **4.2.7**).

The basic principle that applies is that any SPEs which an entity controls are included in its consolidated accounts, in the same way as if they were subsidiaries. The suggested circumstances which might indicate control (summarised from paragraph 9.11), aside from the general control principles applying to all subsidiaries, are as follows:

- the SPE's activities are being conducted on behalf of the entity;
- the entity has ultimate decision-making power even if it is not involved with day-to-day decisions; and
- the entity has the right to obtain the majority of related benefits, and may be exposed to incidental risks;
- the entity retains the majority of the residual or ownership risks related to the SPE or its assets.

This guidance is intended to capture the sort of structuring arrangements that were designed to keep liabilities off balance sheet, with the consequence of preventing investors from having a true understanding of an entity's full risk exposure. Clearly, significant judgment will be needed in determining whether there is control, particularly where some efforts have been made to structure a group so as to achieve an off balance sheet treatment, and it will usually be necessary to consider a balance of indicators.

In an attempt to improve transparency in this area, FRS 102 (2018) introduces an additional disclosure requirement targeted at SPEs – see **4.2.9.**

4.2.3   The mechanics of consolidation

Once an entity has determined which others it controls, it can go on to the preparation of consolidated accounts. The basic procedure is quoted here from paragraph 9.13:

'(a)   combine the financial statements of the parent and its subsidiaries line by line by adding together like items of assets, liabilities, equity, income and expenses;

(b)   eliminate the carrying amount of the parent's investment in each subsidiary and the parent's portion of equity of each subsidiary;

(c)   measure and present non-controlling interest in the profit or loss of consolidated subsidiaries for the reporting period separately from the interest of the owners of the parent; and

(d)   measure and present non-controlling interest in the net assets of consolidated subsidiaries separately from the parent shareholders' equity in them. Non-controlling interest in the net assets consists of:

(i)   the amount of the non-controlling interest's share in the net amount of the identifiable assets, liabilities and contingent liabilities recognised and measured in accordance with section 19 *Business Combinations and Goodwill* at the date of the original combination; and

(ii)   the non-controlling interest's share of changes in equity since the date of the combination.'

Step (a) is self-explanatory, describing the basic process of aggregation that is usually the first step of preparing a consolidation. It is not made clear, although we may assume it is the case, that the results of subsidiaries included in this consolidation are stated before any fair value adjustments that were recognised on their acquisition and have not yet been unwound (for instance, through additional depreciation on items of PPE brought in at a value above their previous carrying amount). Another consolidation journal is then needed each reporting date to reflect the cumulative fair value difference.

Step (b), eliminating the cost of investment with the parent's share of equity, is only a partial instruction, since it is also necessary at this stage to bring a goodwill balance in, so that a clean (and balancing!) consolidation journal can be executed representing the entries that initially arose:

• Dr share capital/share premium of subsidiary

• Dr pre-acquisition reserves

• Dr goodwill

   – Cr investment in subsidiary

   – Cr non-controlling interest

The calculation of goodwill is discussed in Section 19 of FRS 102 and at **4.3.2**.

Steps (c) and (d) then provide the final piece, adjusting the consolidated comprehensive income so that instead of including the whole amount from the subsidiary's accounts, only the parent's share is recognised. This is achieved by separating out the non-controlling interest's share of profit:

- Dr non-controlling interests (income statement)
  - Cr non-controlling interests (balance sheet)

Accounting for non-controlling interests is discussed more at **4.2.4**.

4.2.3.1 Synchronising policies and reporting dates

Although, as described above, the standard does not address how to deal with ongoing fair value adjustments to a subsidiary's results (for instance, additional depreciation when a property has been revalued upwards on acquisition for the purpose of the group accounts), it does give a more general requirement that the accounting policies used in preparing consolidated accounts must be consistent across the group. This could mean that a subsidiary's results need to be adjusted before they are aggregated in step (a) above, to bring the policies in line with the parent's.

It is also a general requirement that all the component financial statements included are made up to the same reporting date, for obvious reasons. There is an impracticability exemption, but if this is taken and the subsidiary's accounts are prepared to a different date, they must be to no more than three months before the parent's reporting date, and must be adjusted for 'significant items' occurring between the two dates. An alternative, if the subsidiary cannot change its year end, is for it to prepare interim accounts to the same reporting date as the parent, although this could be costly and time-consuming.

4.2.3.2 Intragroup balances and transactions

Aggregating the results and balances of all entities in the group, without adjustment, would lead to artificially grossed up assets and liabilities, income and expense, in any situation where there is intragroup trade or lending. This explains the requirement in paragraph 9.15 to eliminate all such balances and transactions in full, including eliminating unrealised profits in assets that are still held within the group.

Example 4.2

Subsidiary S sells inventories to Subsidiary R. They originally cost S £200,000; it sells them on to R at its normal margin, for proceeds of £250,000, and hence a profit of £50,000.

At the year end, R still has £125,000 of inventories in stock (i.e. half the original amount).

The carrying value of the inventories in R's books includes unrealised profits of £25,000; that is profits which only represent transfers within the group rather than actual crystallised increases in value. Accordingly, as well as the elimination of the intercompany sale/purchase, the value of inventory in the group balance sheet and used to calculate cost of sales is reduced by £25,000.

4.2.4   Non-controlling interests

In general, the explanation of accounting for non-controlling interests (familiar to UK preparers as 'minority interests' is not well explained in the standard: there are brief references in a number of places, but no comprehensive summary. Pulling together the various strands:

(1)   When a parent gains control of a subsidiary, a non-controlling interest is recognised, as a separate line item within equity. This is not actually stated anywhere in the standard, but comes as a consequence of the requirement in paragraph 19.14 to calculate goodwill based on the acquirer's interest in the fair values of assets and liabilities. The entry relating to the balance of the fair value of those assets and liabilities must be included as the opening balance for non-controlling interests.

(2)   Each reporting date, the carrying value of the non-controlling interest within equity is adjusted for the NCI's share of total comprehensive income (profit or loss and other comprehensive income), even where this leads to a debit balance on the NCI (9.22).

(3)   When a parent increases its stake in a subsidiary, no additional goodwill is recognised, and the carrying value of assets and liabilities on the balance sheet remains unchanged. The fair value of the proceeds is adjusted against the NCI (9.19D and 22.19).

(4)   Conversely, if a parent decreases its stake while retaining control the proceeds are recognised as an increase in the NCI, with no adjustment to goodwill (9.19A and 22.19).

(5)   When a parent disposes of a subsidiary entirely, or reduces its stake so that it no longer has control, the NCI balance is recycled as part of the valuation of profit or loss on disposal (indirectly from 9.18A, which requires that a profit on disposal is calculated with reference only to the parent's share of net assets, with the consequence that the NCI share must be removed).

Example 4.3

D Ltd pays £200,000 for a 90% share in L Ltd. At the time, L has net assets with a carrying value of £140,000 and fair value of £190,000. Goodwill is the difference between the consideration of £200,000 and D's 90% share of the fair value, i.e. £200,000 − £171,000 = £29,000.

The obvious way to value the NCI at the outset is to recognise it at 10% of the fair value of the net assets of L, i.e. £19,000. Although alternatives are available to IFRS preparers, these are ruled out in FRS 102 by the way that goodwill is defined.

4.2.5   Acquisitions and disposals

4.2.5.1   Inclusion in consolidation – general

The core principle for inclusion of subsidiaries' results in a consolidation is that a subsidiary is consolidated from its acquisition date to the date of its disposal. The acquisition date is the date that control passes (discussed in more detail at **4.3.2**) and the disposal date is the date that control is lost, whether this is through a sale, through a dilution which changes the percentage holding without the parent selling any shares, or through a forcible event such as the subsidiary coming under the control of a court or regulator.

4.2.5.2   Step acquisitions

Sometimes a parent will gain control over a subsidiary in a series of transactions, increasing its shareholding until it reaches the threshold for control.

An investment could move through three phases, with the accounting treatment being different for each phase.

Stage 1 – investments below 20%

Shareholdings of less than 20% will usually not give enough voting power for significant influence, so the investment will not be treated as an associate, but instead just as a trade investment (but see **4.4** below for more on this). This will be a financial asset in the scope of Section 11 of FRS 102 and will usually be classified as a basic financial instrument, and measured either at fair value (if the shares are publicly traded or the fair value can otherwise be reliably measured) or, otherwise, at cost less impairment.

Stage 2 – investments between around 20% and 50%

Investments in this category will usually be classified as associates, so in the group accounts they will be subject to equity accounting.

When the investor's shareholding is increased, the cost of the investment is determined by adding together the cost of each individual component.

Example 4.4

In 2017, Investor L acquires 15% of trading company T for consideration of £100,000. At the December 2017 year end this is measured at £100,000 (cost, with no impairment noted).

During 2018, L acquires a further 15%, this time for £130,000. The investment's cost is £230,000, being the sum of the amount paid for the two tranches, and this is used as the starting point for equity accounting.

Stage 3 – investments over 50%

Investments in this category will usually be classified as subsidiaries.

The business combination accounting in Section 19 of FRS 102, discussed at **4.3**, uses calculations and valuations at the date that control passes; that is, at the point when the shareholding changes from being insufficient for control to sufficient for control.

If an investor was applying IFRS to the transaction that gives rise to the change in control, it would have some careful accounting to do. Under IFRS, establishing the cost of the combination involves a notional surrender of the previously held investment for its fair value in exchange for the value of the investment. This means that a gain or loss would be recognised relating to the difference between the investment's carrying value and its fair value at completion date.

The FRS 102 model is much simpler, being the same as for the earlier stage of an investment becoming an associate: the cost of the investment in the subsidiary is simply the aggregate of the amounts paid for each tranche.

Example 4.5

Investor L from the above example is sufficiently impressed with the trade of T that it decides to buy sufficient shares to gain control. Accordingly, in 2019 it acquires yet another 15%, for £160,000 (each tranche is more costly than the last because T is so successful).

The cost of L's investment in the subsidiary is £390,000.

It would not be permissible to assign a notional higher value based on the latest price per share that L has paid (for instance to treat it as three tranches each now worth £160,000 and therefore initially record the investment at £480,000).

4.2.5.3   Increasing a controlling interest

When a parent already has a controlling interest in a subsidiary, and then increases this interest, there are no remeasurements. Instead, as set out in 9.19C–9.19D and 22.19, this is accounted for as a simple transaction with shareholders and the entries are all in equity. Goodwill is not revalued, and no other adjustments to net assets arise because the whole of the subsidiary's net assets are already included in the top half of the balance sheet.

4.2.5.4 Disposals where control is lost

A disposal of a subsidiary, which includes a partial disposal leading to loss of control, usually gives rise to a gain or a loss. This is calculated as the difference between:

- the proceeds from the disposal (or event resulting in loss of control) LESS

- the proportion of the carrying amount of the subsidiary's net assets, including any related goodwill, disposed of.

This amount is then adjusted for any amounts that were previously recognised in other comprehensive income and would generally be required to be recycled on a disposal, but not for cumulative foreign exchange differences recognised in equity.

Example 4.6

Parent P has a wholly-owned subsidiary S.

P originally paid £500,000 for its investment, at which point S had net assets with carrying value of £280,000 and fair value £400,000.

Goodwill was therefore initially calculated at £100,000.

Since the acquisition, S has made profits of £250,000 and not paid any dividends. It also has £50,000 of gains that were recognised in OCI, relating to hedging arrangements. Its net assets included in the consolidation are therefore £700,000.

P sells 60% of the shares in S for £500k, reducing it to being an associate (with a 40% holding).

At this date, the carrying amount of goodwill on the group balance sheet is £80,000 (after two years of amortisation based on a ten-year life).

The profit on disposal is calculated as:

Proceeds	£500,000
60% of assets	(£420,000)
60% of goodwill	(£48,000)
60% of OCI items to be recycled	£30,000
Profit on disposal	£62,000

Note that the example above makes a couple of assumptions about unspoken areas within the standard. First, it is assumed that the goodwill value to be included in the calculation is the amortised value and that previous amortisation is not written back (9.18A(b) refers only to 'any related goodwill'); this same assumption of proportion is made in respect of items previously included in equity via OCI being recycled at this point. While these are both reasonable assumptions and compatible with the standard, preparers should note the need to develop their own accounting policies in this area, and may consider whether other treatments could also be supported.

4.2.5.5   Accounting for the balances that remain

If any balance of an investment remains after a disposal, the treatment depends on the nature of the balance. Investments in associates or joint ventures are accounted for in accordance with Sections 14 and 15 of FRS 102 respectively; those that do not meet the threshold for significant influence are financial assets in the scope of Section 11 or Section 12. The initial carrying value in each of these cases is the value remaining after the disposal has been accounted for.

Example 4.7

In the example above, where P has reduced its holding in S to 40%, the opening carrying value of the investment in associate, to be subsequently equity accounted, is £312,000, being 40% of the previous goodwill value plus 40% of the previous asset value.

This can be checked by reference to the previous carrying value and amounts removed – in this case, £780,000 – £48,000 – £420,000 = £312,000.

Note that the requirement above to recycle into profit amounts previously included in equity via OCI has no bearing on the accounting by the entity being disposed of. Again looking at the example where P reduces its holding in S, if S still meets the conditions for recognising gains and losses relating to its hedging arrangement within OCI, it will continue doing so, and the balance on the relevant reserve is unaltered by the disposal. The accounting adjustment to recognise this as part of the gain or loss on disposal is something of a construct, representing as it does the crystallisation of a gain or loss at the point when the subsidiary leaves the group, even though the underlying hedge relationship (in this example) has not been terminated.

4.2.5.6   Disposals where control is retained

As above for the situation where shareholdings are increased without a change in control, the accounting for disposals while retaining control is all through equity, with no asset revaluations or adjustments to goodwill.

4.2.6   Individual and separate financial statements

4.2.6.1   Definitions

The distinction between individual and separate financial statements has always been elusive.

Individual financial statements are defined in FRS 102 as 'the accounts that are required to be prepared by an entity in accordance with the Act or relevant legislation', which for companies means individual accounts as set out in CA 2006, s. 394.

Within the category of individual financial statements, there is then the sub-group of separate financial statements, defined in the glossary as 'those prepared by a parent in which the investments in subsidiaries, associates or jointly controlled entities are accounted for either at cost or fair value rather than on the basis of the reported results and net assets of the investees.'

When a UK parent files consolidated accounts at Companies House, it is required to include its individual accounts with these too. These would be classified as separate financial statements.

If a company has no subsidiaries, it does not prepare consolidated accounts and its company-only accounts are 'individual' but not 'separate' (because the definition of 'separate' includes the condition of being a parent).

If a company has subsidiaries but has taken one of the exemptions from preparing consolidated accounts, the company-only accounts are treated as 'separate'.

4.2.6.2   Accounting options

The possibilities for accounting for investments in individual accounts are dependent on the type of investment and whether the accounts are included in the sub-category of 'separate'.

The guidance dispersed around the various sections is summarised as follows:

Reporting entity	Investment type	Accounting requirements
Parent – consolidated financial statements	Subsidiary	Consolidation – Section 9
Parent – consolidated financial statements	Associate	Equity method (unless part of an investment portfolio – FVTPL) – Section 14

Reporting entity	Investment type	Accounting requirements
Parent – consolidated financial statements	Jointly controlled entity	Equity method (unless part of an investment portfolio – FVTPL) – Section 15
Parent – consolidated financial statements	Jointly controlled asset	Recognise venturer's share of jointly controlled assets and liabilities, own liabilities, income from the sale or use of its share of output, share of expenses, own expenses – Section 15
Parent – consolidated financial statements	Jointly controlled operation	Recognise the assets that the venturer controls and the liabilities it incurs, with the expenses that it incurs and its share of income – Section 15
Parent – separate financial statements	Subsidiary, associate or any type of joint venture	Cost less impairment – Section 9 OR Fair value with changes in OCI – Section 9 OR Fair value with changes in profit (Sections 9/14/15)
Non-parent – individual financial statements	Associate or joint venture	Cost model OR Fair value with changes in OCI OR Fair value with changes in profit (Sections 14/15)

4.2.6.3   Transitional provisions

In Section 35, on transition to FRS 102, paragraph 35.10(f) allows an entity that is using the cost model in its individual or separate financial statements for its investments in subsidiaries, associates or jointly controlled entities to initially record these investments at a choice of cost or 'deemed cost', being the carrying amount at the date of transition as determined under the entity's previous GAAP. For instance, an investment in a foreign subsidiary which was financed by a foreign currency loan may, under old UK GAAP, have been retranslated at the end of each period, as permitted by SSAP 20. This is no longer permitted under FRS 102, but this exemption enables preparers to avoid unwinding pre-transition retranslations. However, as the vast majority of companies have transitioned from old UK GAAP (including the FRSSE), this exemption now offers limited relief.

4.2.7   Interests in investments acquired by exchange of businesses or other non-monetary assets

Guidance is given separately for accounting for investments in each of subsidiaries, associates and joint ventures. In general it assumes that payments for such investments will be through cash, shares or assumption of liabilities.

On occasion, though, an entity will acquire an interest in another by less conventional means such as providing a non-cash asset (for instance, a property) or by exchange for another investment it already holds.

The issue is how to value the assets and liabilities acquired, taking into account the fact that the investee has had its net assets adjusted by virtue of the transaction. The following guidance, summarised from 9.31, applies when an entity becomes a subsidiary, associate or jointly controlled entity (i.e. not to a transaction with an existing subsidiary, associate or jointly controlled entity, unless the transfer increases the parent's interest such that a previous associate or jointly controlled entity becomes a jointly controlled entity or subsidiary).

(1)   To the extent that the transferring entity retains an interest in the business or assets transferred, even if this is indirectly through another company, the asset's carrying value is not adjusted.

(2)   Goodwill is the difference between the fair value of the consideration given and the fair value of the entity's newly acquired share of the investee's net assets *measured before accounting for the new asset or business received.*

(3)   If the fair value of the consideration given is less than the fair value of the share of net assets (equivalent to negative goodwill) the investor recognises a gain immediately. If this gain is unrealised, it is recognised in OCI rather than profit.

(4)   If the value of the consideration received (i.e. the share of net assets) is less than the sum of the carrying amount of the business or asset (or part thereof) derecognised and goodwill, an impairment loss is recognised.

4.2.8   Intermediate payment arrangements

The most common example of an intermediate payment arrangement is a trust set up by a company to make payments to employees, although Section 9 of FRS 102 does allow for the possibility of other types of structure and other types of beneficiary. The crux of the requirements is that in general a payment that a company makes into this type of vehicle will not usually give rise to an expense for the company until the time when payments are made to the beneficiaries. This presumed treatment can only be rebutted if the company can demonstrate that either it will not at any point obtain future economic benefits from the amounts transferred or that it does not control the right or access to benefits it expects to receive.

Example 4.8

A company has an employee benefit trust. The payments it makes into the trust will be stored in assets and then used to make payments to employees. As is usual for this type of arrangement, the trust is set up so that its sponsoring company cannot control its actions (legally they are two distinct entities) although the company in this case has the right to appoint trustees.

Accordingly, although the company's directors may express their wishes about how the trust's assets are apportioned (and have set it up with some outlines in the trust deed, for instance payments only being to employees with certain characteristics, with caps on size of payments and so on) the actual payments are at the trustees' discretion.

The company may not record payments into the trust as an expense, but instead will show an expense whenever payments are disbursed to employees. To be able to charge the expense straight away, the company would need to demonstrate that it made the payment into the trust with no anticipation of any benefit, perhaps by showing that the trustees had such free choice about payments that they could, if they wished, pass all of the money out to animal charities, or choose never to make any payments at all, with no recourse for the company.

While it clearly would be possible to set up an arrangement with the features set out at the end of this example, such that it did mean payments into the trust were immediately expensed (and hence deductible for tax purposes), it seems hard to envisage how this would be commercial: one of a director's duties is to promote the success of the company (CA 2006, s. 172) and this seems hard to reconcile with actions involving making payments out of the company with no expectation of benefit. Of course, an exception could be where a company used a trust not for employee benefits but as a conduit for its charitable giving as part of its corporate social responsibility agenda, perhaps with trustees who were employees or representatives from the local community.

If a sponsoring entity places its own shares into an intermediary to use for employee payment arrangements, and if the sponsoring entity has control or de facto control of that intermediary, the effect is the same as if the sponsoring entity had directly purchased its own shares.

In this situation, the following accounting guidance is given (summarised from 9.37):

(1) the consideration paid for the entity's shares is deducted from equity (rather than shown as an investment), and the debit remains there until the shares vest unconditionally with the employees;

(2) consideration for the purchase or sale of the shares is shown as a separate line in the statement of changes in equity;

(3) the intermediary's other (non-share) assets and liabilities are included on the sponsoring entity's balance sheet as if they were its own assets and liabilities;

(4) purchases, sales or cancellations of the entity's own equity do not give rise to gains or losses;

(5) finance costs and administrative expenses are recognised on an accruals basis (rather than being aligned with when cash is paid to the intermediary);

(6) dividend income from the entity's own instruments is excluded from profit or loss and deducted from the aggregate of dividends paid in the statement of changes in equity (effectively, netted off against the accounting for dividends paid).

FRS 102 (2018) introduces a new paragraph, 9.33A, which acknowledges the possibility that a trust may not be controlled by the reporting entity and gives an example as follows:

'9.33A It is possible for an entity to be owned by a trust established for the benefit of employees without the entity controlling the trust. An example is when the entity is a co-operative, owned by its employees, and all of the shares are held in a trust for the benefit of the employees but the shares never vest in individual employees, with dividends from the company being distributed to employees solely in accordance with the provisions of the trust deed.'

In practice, this is likely to be relatively uncommon.

4.2.9 *Disclosures relating to consolidated and separate financial statements*

Paragraph 9.23 requires the following disclosures in consolidated financial statements:

(a) the fact that the statements are consolidated financial statements;

(b) the basis for concluding that control exists when the parent does not own, directly or indirectly through subsidiaries, more than half of the voting power;

(c) any difference in the reporting date of the financial statements of the parent and its subsidiaries used in the preparation of the consolidated financial statements;

(d) the nature and extent of any significant restrictions (e.g. resulting from borrowing arrangements or regulatory requirements) on the ability of subsidiaries to transfer funds to the parent in the form of cash dividends or to repay loans;

(e) the name of any subsidiary excluded from consolidation and the reason for exclusion; and

(f) the nature and extent of its interests in unconsolidated special purpose entities, and the risks associated with those interests.

The principle-based disclosure requirement (f) was added into FRS 102 (2018). It derives from IFRS 12 *Disclosure of Interests in Other Entities* and is intended to improve the information available to users about this specific type of entity.

For separate financial statements, it is necessary to disclose the fact that they are separate financial statements, and a description of the methods used to account for the investments in subsidiaries, jointly controlled entities and associates (9.27). If a parent claims an exemption from consolidation, it must disclose the grounds on which it is exempt (9.27A). If the policy choice is adopted to measure investments in subsidiaries, associates or jointly controlled entities at fair value through profit or loss, the disclosure requirements of Section 11 of FRS 102 apply to those investments (9.27B).

The disclosure requirements for intermediate payment arrangements, set out in 9.38, are generally described as being for sufficient information to enable users to understand the intermediary's significance in the context of the sponsoring entity's financial statements. This general requirement is then clarified as including:

(a) a description of the main features of the intermediary including the arrangements for making payments and for distributing equity instruments;

(b) any restrictions relating to the assets and liabilities of the intermediary;

(c) the amount and nature of the assets and liabilities held by the intermediary, which have not yet vested unconditionally with the beneficiaries of the arrangement;

(d) the amount that has been deducted from equity and the number of equity instruments held by the intermediary, which have not yet vested unconditionally with the beneficiaries of the arrangement;

(e) for entities that have their equity instruments listed or publicly traded on a stock exchange or market, the market value of the equity instruments held by the intermediary which have not yet vested unconditionally with employees;

(f) the extent to which the equity instruments are under option to employees, or have been conditionally gifted to them; and

(g) the amount that has been deducted from the aggregate dividends paid by the sponsoring entity.

4.3 Business combinations

4.3.1 Definition of a business combination

Accounting for business combinations is addressed by Section 19 of FRS 102.

A business combination is defined in paragraph 19.3 as 'the bringing together of separate entities or businesses into one reporting entity'. This can take a range of forms, including the acquisition of shares, purchase of net assets, assumption of liabilities, or purchase of a group of assets constituting a business.

As usual, although this definition seems straightforward, there can be some issues in applying it. In particular, there is a grey area around exactly how a 'business' is identified.

The Glossary to the standard defines a business as:

'An integrated set of activities and assets conducted and managed for the purpose of providing:

(a) a return to investors; or

(b) lower costs of other economic benefits directly and proportionately to policyholders or participants.

A business generally consists of inputs, processes applied to those inputs, and resulting outputs that are, or will be, used to generate revenues. If goodwill is present in a transferred set of activities and assets, the transferred set shall be presumed to be a business.'

So, at one end of the spectrum, the acquisition of a chain of retail stores with supplying warehouses, full inventory, employees, a management team, and a well-established revenue base, is clearly a business combination.

At the opposite extreme, the purchase of an empty untenanted building with no specialised features would not be a business combination. Although the building could be let out to generate revenues, and that might be the acquirer's intention, at the point of acquisition there are no inputs or processes applied to inputs (nor, for that matter, are there any outputs).

Careful judgment is needed for situations that are not so clear cut. An investment property being used by long term tenants and giving rise to an identifiable and secure revenue stream might be viewed as a business, although it could also be argued that it is simply an investment property asset, which is normally valued on the basis of its future revenue stream, so that it does not have anything 'extra' to force its classification as a business.

Another challenging situation is the acquisition of a group of all the assets and liabilities necessary to run a business where they are not currently being operated as such – perhaps when a factory has been mothballed but still contains all the plant and machinery, and raw materials, necessary to produce a saleable output. This would probably meet the 'will be used to generate revenues' condition, but each situation would need to be assessed on its own merits.

It should be noted that despite the name, it is not necessary for both combining parties to be a business, in order for the transaction as a whole to be classified as a business combination. So where, for instance, an individual investor chooses to invest in a trading company by setting up an empty shell company to buy the shares, this share purchase will be treated as a business combination despite the lack of previous activity in the legal acquirer. It might well be the case, here, that the legal acquiree is identified as the accounting acquirer, often known as a reverse acquisition (see **4.3.2.2** for more discussion of this point).

A transaction that is not a business combination, based on these definitions, will usually be accounted for simply as an asset acquisition (meaning, as one consequence, that goodwill will not be recognised, and nor will any fair value adjustments be made).

Most business combinations are accounted for using the purchase method, except for group reconstructions, where merger accounting is used, and public benefit entity combinations which are in substance a gift or are a merger, which are addressed by Section 34 of FRS 102 (see **17.2.2**).

4.3.2   Mechanics of the purchase method

4.3.2.1   Overview

The steps set out in Section 19 for purchase accounting are as follows:

(1)   identify the acquirer;

(2)   measure the cost of the combination;

(3)   allocate the cost of the combination to the assets acquired and liabilities (including provisions for contingent liabilities) assumed.

There are other implicit steps too, such as identifying the acquisition date, which are not covered in much detail within the standard and therefore need careful thought when an accounting policy is being developed and the exact accounting entries for a transaction are being determined.

4.3.2.2 Identifying the acquirer

When the purchase method is applied, the net assets of one of the entities, the accounting acquiree, will be remeasured to fair value for the purposes of calculation of goodwill and for inclusion in subsequent group accounts. This means it is crucial to get the identification of the acquirer and acquiree right, since the fair value review can make a significant change to the shape of the subject's balance sheet.

While for many business combinations it will be quite clear that the accounting acquirer is the same as the legal acquirer, it is important to check the definition in 19.8, which states that the acquirer is 'the combining entity that obtains control of the other combining entities or businesses'. If it is not obvious which of the parties this is, the following indications are suggested which might be helpful (summarised from 19.10):

(a) if there is a big difference between the fair values of the combining entities, the entity with the greater value is usually the acquirer;

(b) if the business combination is via the exchange of shares for cash or other assets, the entity giving up the cash or other assets is usually the acquirer (so the entity issuing the shares is the acquiree);

(c) if the management of one of the combining entities is expected to dominate the management of the combined entity, that dominant entity is likely to be the acquirer.

Example 4.9

(1) Companies A and B combine by B issuing shares to A for cash such that A gains 70% of the voting rights of B. In this situation, A is the acquirer.

(2) Companies C and D combine by having all of their shareholders transfer their holdings into a new shell company, E. E issues shares to the original holders in proportion to the value of their holdings in the respective entities. C has a fair value four times the size of D, and so, in the absence of any indications to the contrary, C is identified as the acquirer.

4.3.2.3 Determining the acquisition date

The acquisition date is defined in the Glossary as 'the date on which the acquirer gains control of the acquiree'.

The standard provides little guidance on determining this date, although 19.17 does point out that it is not always necessary for legal title to have passed before control is obtained, and requires 'all pertinent facts and circumstances' to be considered. It is vital to get this right because all fair values are established on this date, and it is the point from which consolidation begins.

Preparers looking for guidance on how to assess when control passes should look at the detail of their particular acquisition arrangements, which should specify when voting rights are effective, when board appointments will be made, and whether there are any special clauses in the agreement specifying an exposure to risks and benefits beginning earlier or later than the stated acquisition date. If, for instance, the sale and purchase agreement fixes a nominal completion date of 31 March but the acquirer has the right to change the board of directors in February, this gives good reason to look further at the details and consider whether control has actually passed over in February too.

4.3.2.4   Determining the cost of a business combination

Paragraph 19.11 requires that the cost of a combination is measured as the aggregate of:

(a) the fair values, at the acquisition date, of assets given, liabilities incurred or assumed, and equity instruments issued by the acquirer, in exchange for control of the acquiree; plus

(b) any costs directly attributable to the business combination.

As described at **4.2.5**, if control is achieved in stages (for instance by acquiring 40% of an investee's shares, then later another 15%), the cost of the combination for the purposes of applying the purchase method is the aggregate of the costs at each stage (although 19.11A, which sets out this requirement, does not explicitly mention directly attributable transaction costs, it would be reasonable to include them by analogy to the previous paragraph).

The reference to valuing consideration at the acquisition date is particularly relevant in transactions where part of the consideration is the acquirer's own equity. It is not acceptable to use a historic share price (or value), or the share price at the point when the transaction was agreed or announced.

Example 4.10

Company F agreed to acquire Company G for consideration of £1m plus 200,000 shares in company F. When the acquisition was announced, company F's shares each had an estimated value of £1.20, so the total consideration announced was £1.24m (£1m + £240,000).

> By the date, two weeks later, that the shares were issued and the transaction completed the value of F's shares had fallen to £1.10, so the consideration recognised in the accounts and used for the goodwill calculation is £1.22m.

The transaction date is also highly relevant if part of the consideration is in a foreign currency: this will be translated at the transaction date spot rate to give the investment cost, used in calculating goodwill.

Because most entities applying FRS 102 will be unlisted, establishing a fair value for shares will not be as simple as just looking at a share price. Although, again, the standard provides no comment on this, it would seem reasonable to use a valuation model of some type, which would need to comply with the principles for establishing fair value set out in Section 11 of the standard, including looking first at recent transactions, then to other similar assets, and finally to other valuation techniques to reach 'what the transaction price would have been on the measurement date in an arm's length exchange motivated by normal business considerations'.

The process of determining fair value in accordance with Section 11 is discussed in more detail at **7.5.2**.

Contingent consideration is relatively common in purchase arrangements, and is dealt with very simply in 19.12–19.13: an estimate of any further amounts payable is made at the outset, and the amount is recognised if the additional outflow is probable and can be measured reliably. Any adjustment to the measurement of contingent consideration adjusts the cost of the combination and, therefore, affects goodwill in the period in which the adjustment takes place.

If the contingent consideration is to be paid some time after the transaction date, it may be outstanding at one or more reporting dates. Although 19.13 requires that where an outflow that was not probable becomes probable, it is brought onto the balance sheet and adjusted through the cost of the combination, it does not set out what to do where an outflow ceases to be probable, or where the reliable estimate of the expected amount varies.

In the absence of guidance, a policy must be developed, and here it might seem reasonable to base the accounting on that for provisions, i.e. to keep adjusting the liability for the best estimate, but instead of reporting changes in profit, to continue adjusting through the cost of investment.

The cost of a business combination also includes any directly attributable costs incurred. Care is needed when assessing which costs to include. Only those which are incremental (i.e. would not have been incurred had the combination not taken place) should be included. Such costs could include professional fees (legal fees, accountancy fees, due diligence and so forth) but should not include, for instance, costs associated with issuing shares or raising finance to acquire another business. This is because these costs are required to be dealt with as transaction costs and are treated as a deduction from the relevant instrument, in accordance with Sections 11 and 22 of FRS 102.

4.3.2.5 *Identifying net assets acquired*

The general principle here is that the cost of the combination is allocated to the net assets acquired, based on their fair values, and then any balance that cannot be allocated to separate assets is defined as goodwill. As always, though, the devil is in the detail.

Paragraph 19.15 states that assets and liabilities on the acquiree's balance sheet are recognised at their acquisition date fair value, subject to the following conditions for separate recognition:

(a) For an asset, it is probable that future benefits will flow to the acquirer, and the fair value can be measured reliably.

(b) For a liability that is not a contingent liability, it is probable that an outflow of resources will be necessary, and the fair value of the outflow can be measured reliably.

(c) For contingent liabilities, the fair value can be measured reliably.

Previously, paragraph 19.15 contained a further exception for intangible assets. The removal of the exception means that an intangible asset will need to meet the probability test going forward if it is to be recognised separately in a business combination.

FRS 102 (2018) introduced a new accounting policy choice for intangible assets acquired as part of a business combination. By default, intangible assets are only recognised separately from goodwill when all the following three conditions are satisfied:

• the recognition criteria set out in paragraph 18.4 are met (i.e. it is probable that the expected future economic benefits that are attributable to the asset will flow to the entity and the cost or value of the asset can be measured reliably);

• the intangible asset arises from contractual or other legal rights; and

• the intangible asset is separable (i.e. capable of being separated or divided from the entity and sold, transferred, licensed, rented or exchanged either individually or together with a related contract, asset or liability).

However, as an alternative, they allow an entity to recognise intangible assets separately from goodwill for which condition (a) and only one of (b) or (c) above is met (i.e. what previous FRS 102 allowed). This is an accounting policy choice which must be applied consistently to all intangible assets in the same class and to all business combinations.

Where the latter option is taken, the standard requires disclosure of the nature of the intangible assets and the reason why they have been separated from goodwill.

It is important to note that the default option is not the same as the previous FRS 102 treatment. However, the amendments include a transitional provision (in Section 1 of FRS 102) which states that an entity 'shall only apply any change to an accounting policy arising from the Triennial review 2017 amendments to paragraph 18.8 prospectively (i.e. it shall not restate comparative information), and therefore shall not subsume intangible assets that previously have been separately recognised within goodwill'. Therefore, no retrospective adjustment is needed.

The difference in the two accounting policies can be illustrated by way of an example.

Example 4.11

On 1 January 2018, Company A acquired Company B for £10m. The fair value of Company B's net assets as shown in Company B's balance sheet at the date of acquisition was £8 million. Company B also holds the following internally generated intangible assets which were attributed fair values as part of the acquisition process:

Intangible asset	Fair value	Useful life
Patent	£500,000	3 years
Customer lists	£150,000	3 years
Unpatented technology	£500,000	3 years

Company A plans to amortise the goodwill arising on acquisition over ten years.

If the default option is taken, only the patent will be recorded as a separate intangible asset. Customer lists and unpatented technology do not arise from legal or contractual rights and will therefore be subsumed within goodwill.

The alternative accounting policy would allow all three of the above items to be capitalised separately. This affects not only the presentation in the financial statements but also the profit and loss profile, since the intangible assets will be amortised to profit or loss more quickly than the goodwill balance. The following table compares the two treatments.

Default treatment		Alternate treatment (as previous FRS 102)	
Date of acquisition:	£	Date of acquisition:	£
Dr Goodwill	1,500,000	Dr Goodwill	850,000
Dr Intangible asset	500,000	Dr Intangible assets	1,150,000
Dr Other net assets	8,000,000	Dr Other net assets	8,000,000
Cr Cash	10,000,000	Cr Cash	10,000,000
Subsequent annual amortisation charge		Subsequent annual amortisation charge	
Dr P&L	316,667	Dr P&L	468,333
Cr Goodwill	150,000	Cr Goodwill	85,000
Cr Intangible asset	166,667	Cr Intangible asset	383,333
For three years, then £150,000 for remaining seven years of the goodwill useful life.		For three years, then £85,000 for remaining seven years of the goodwill useful life.	

The requirement to bring contingent liabilities onto the acquisition balance sheet is also a slightly counter-intuitive one, since in Section 21 it is made clear that a contingent liability does not meet the definition of a liability as there is not a probable future cash outflow, and thus it is dealt with through disclosures rather than balance sheet recognition. Perhaps this requirement is an investor protection measure and an acknowledgement that a decision to purchase a business will be affected by both its probable and its possible future cash outflows – and since uncertainties like this will affect the negotiated price, they should also be reflected in the accounting.

Although the probability requirement does not apply to contingent liabilities, it is still necessary for their fair value to be able to be measured reliably, because it would otherwise, by definition, be impossible to attribute a fair value. The subsequent accounting (in 19.21) requires some careful work, because the initial recognition is in conflict with Section 21, so the requirement is that the 'liability' is subsequently measured at the higher of the amount it would be measured at under Section 21 and the initial amount less amounts already recognised as revenue.

Other special cases in initial allocation of fair value

The only other special cases when it comes to determining fair values are set out in paragraphs 19.15A–19.15C, inserted by the FRC to remove any possible ambiguity. All that these paragraphs do is refer preparers to relevant sections of the standard instead of requiring blanket fair value measurement, in relation to deferred tax (to be based on Section 29), employee benefit arrangements (to be based on Section 28) and share-based payments (to be based on Section 26). In each of these cases, establishing a fair value at a single point in time would not be consistent with the way that the assets or liabilities would otherwise be measured. Deferred tax is an accounting entry not directly linked to value; retirement benefit obligations are measured on a basis that mixes current value with carefully composed estimates of future cash flows; and share based payment obligations are not, if they are equity settled, recognised as a liability at all even though there is an associated obligation.

Costs that are expected to be incurred as a result of a business combination, such as restructuring, are not included as provisions on the acquisition balance sheet – the assessment of fair value is based only on the current situation at the acquisition date, not taking into account the acquirer's intentions. The only exception is where measures have already been put in place to implement these intentions, such as announcing to staff before the transaction that their jobs are in danger, in sufficient detail for this to meet the Section 21 criteria for a provision.

4.3.2.6   'Initial accounting' estimates of assets and liabilities

For some assets and liabilities, it can be hard at the outset to reach an accurate number for the fair value. Paragraph 19.19 recognises this by requiring, in this case, the recognition of 'provisional amounts' (the best possible estimate) in the first financial statements after the acquisition, with a twelve month period from the acquisition date during which these amounts can be adjusted (with a consequent effect on goodwill).

4.3.2.7   Goodwill

As set out above, goodwill arising on a business combination is measured as the difference between the cost of the combination and the acquirer's interest in the net amount of assets, liabilities and contingent liabilities on the acquisition balance sheet.

After this initial recording at cost, goodwill is then amortised over its useful life, if this can be reliably estimated, or over not more than ten years, if it cannot be reliably estimated. Note that in the originally issued version of FRS 102 (applicable for periods commencing on or after 1 January 2015), this was five years, but following amendments to company law made by SI 2015/980, FRS 102 was updated in line with the legal requirements to extend this to ten years (for periods commencing on or after 1 January 2016, but with early adoption available).

Determining the useful life is an exercise that will of necessity be highly entity-specific, and will involve looking at information such as the nature of the business acquired, management's expectations of it at the time, and so on. FRS 102 makes it clear that the ten year 'default' should only be applied in exceptional cases which implies the expectation is that a reliable estimate should be able to be reached.

4.3.2.8   *Negative goodwill*

When the acquirer's share of net assets acquired is higher than the consideration paid, 'negative goodwill' arises. The first requirement when this happens is to check very carefully the values attributed to the assets, liabilities and contingent liabilities, on the basis that such bargain purchases are highly unusual, so any apparent difference is likely to be due to mismeasurement. If, after this review, the negative goodwill still exists, then it is recognised as a separate line item on the balance sheet, directly under goodwill, with a subtotal then showing the total 'net' goodwill.

The credit balance is released to profit as follows:

- Amounts up to the fair value of the non-monetary assets (for instance property, plant and equipment, which are likely to give rise to most significant fair value adjustments) are released over the periods in which the assets' fair values are recovered.

- Any excess over those amounts is released 'in the periods expected to be benefited'.

Example 4.12

Company L pays £1m for 100% of the share capital of Subsidiary R. R has PPE with a fair value of £600,000 and other net assets with a fair value of £500,000. The resulting negative goodwill of £100,000 is lower than the value of the non-monetary assets so it is all released to match those non-monetary assets, probably over their weighted average depreciation period. The use of a weighted average period is a pragmatic way of matching the amortisation to the periods in which the assets' values are recovered. If one asset makes up almost all of the value, it may be sufficient simply to write back the negative goodwill over that single asset's life.

If, on the other hand, the fair value of other (non-monetary) assets were much higher, at £1.1m, then the negative goodwill value would be £700,000, so the first £600,000 would be allocated to the non-monetary assets and released based on their depreciation, and the remaining £100,000 would be looked at separately. If the fair value uplift on the monetary assets related, for instance, to a revised bad debt provision, then the £100,000 would be released when the debts in question were settled, as this would be the period expected to be benefitted.

4.3.3 Group reconstructions

4.3.3.1 Conditions

Certain transactions, despite involving one business acquiring another, are not in the scope of the purchase method. The relevant transactions are those defined as group reconstructions, set out in the Glossary as:

Any one of the following arrangements:

(a) the transfer of an equity holding in a subsidiary from one group entity to another;

(b) the addition of a new parent entity to a group;

(c) the transfer of equity holdings in one or more subsidiaries of a group to a new entity that is not a group entity but whose equity holders are the same as those of the group's parent; or

(d) the combination into a group of two or more entities that before the combination had the same equity holders.

So, it does not just apply to movements of shareholdings around groups, such as subsidiaries being moved under other subsidiaries, but also more widely to common control transactions, where the shareholder group and the proportions each shareholder holds are the same after the transaction as before it.

This is a multi-stage process, though, because once the basic definition is met, there are then a series of conditions which must be met if merger accounting is to be used, summarised here from paragraph 19.27:

(a) the use of merger accounting is permitted by company law or other relevant legislation;

(b) the ultimate equity holders remain the same, and the rights of the holders, relative to each other, are unchanged; and

(c) no non-controlling interest in the net assets of the group is altered by the transfer.

FRS 102 (2018) clarifies that merger accounting can also be applied where an unincorporated business is transferred from one entity under common control to another.

4.3.3.2 Merger accounting under company law

In this area, as with others, the FRC has attempted to avoid unnecessary length in the standard, and potential future clashes if the law changes, by referring to legislation rather than copying in relevant sections, but it does mean that preparers need to look to the law to understand how to apply condition (a). For UK companies, the requirements are in Sch. 6 to the Accounting Regulations, where para. 10 states that:

'The conditions for accounting for an acquisition as a merger are:

(a) that at least 90% of the nominal value of the relevant shares in the undertaking acquired (excluding any shares in the undertaking held as treasury shares) is held by or on behalf of the parent company and its subsidiary undertakings;

(b) that the proportion referred to in paragraph (a) was attained pursuant to an arrangement providing for the issue of equity share by the parent company or one or more of its subsidiary undertakings;

(c) that the fair value of any consideration other than the issue of equity shares given pursuant to the arrangement by the parent company and its subsidiary undertakings did not exceed 10% of the nominal value of the equity shares issued; and

(d) that adoption of the merger method of accounting accords with generally accepted accounting principles or practice.'

Running briefly through each of these conditions:

At least 90% held

Put another way, this requires that no more than 10% of the equity of the entity being moved around is held outside the group. So if parent A has a 75% subsidiary B and transfers its shareholding to its other, wholly-owned, subsidiary C, the transaction would fail the 90% condition and could not be dealt with using merger accounting.

Arrangement achieved mostly through issue of shares

Requirements (b) and (c) are best understood together. They clarify that for merger accounting to be possible, the acquiring company must have issued equity in exchange for the equity it receives. A certain amount of non-cash consideration is permitted – capped at 10% of the nominal value of shares issued – so this is not as restricting a requirement as it otherwise would be.

Example 4.13

Parent P has two wholly-owned subsidiaries, R and S. It decides to move R under S by having S pay £20,000 in cash and issue further shares to P in exchange for the whole share capital of R. S will issue 150,000 £1 shares, so the non-share component is within the permitted margin, being less than 10% of the nominal value of shares it issues.

If the consideration was adjusted slightly so that S instead paid £40,000 of cash and issued 100,000 shares, the non-share component would be too high and merger accounting would not be available.

Complies with generally accepted accounting principles or practice

This condition leads the circle back to the original requirements in FRS 102, looking back to continuity of ultimate shareholders and the value of the non-controlling interest.

Continuity of shareholders

The requirement from 19.27(b) effectively involves a strict numerical test. If, for instance, two companies with common shareholders are brought together, perhaps by the first issuing shares in exchange for the shares of the second, then the resulting enlarged group needs to have exactly the same distribution of equity rights as the individual companies had.

It is also necessary that non-controlling interests remain unchanged.

This is a highly limiting condition, effectively restricting the use of merger accounting to group reconstructions. It would be rare in practice for a merger that involves bringing together two separate entities to be able to meet this condition, since it would require that each had the same shareholders in the same proportion immediately before the transaction.

Transactions which are very like group reconstructions but do not meet the precise conditions (for example, a reconstruction where the non-share element is just over the permissible 10% threshold) must be accounted for using the purchase method, meaning a full fair value exercise and the recognition of goodwill. This leads to the awkward consequence that two very similar transactions can have two very different accounting treatments, but this is to be expected in any situation where accounting guidance exists and draws a distinction between two types of arrangement (the same could be said about the difference in accounting for finance leases and operating leases).

4.3.3.3   Issue of shares as consideration – interaction with company law

When shares are issued in consideration for a business combination, whether it is then subject to purchase accounting or merger accounting, careful consideration must be given to the overlap between accounting requirements from FRS 102, and the requirements or permissions of company law. In particular, s. 611–615 of the Act include details of the treatment of situations where the excess of investment value over nominal value of shares issued should be recorded (this would usually be in the share premium account).

Looking first purely at the Act's requirements:

(1) Under s. 611, if a wholly-owned subsidiary issues shares to its parent or to a fellow wholly-owned subsidiary, in exchange for non-cash

assets (which include shares), then there is a cap at the amount required to be recorded in the share premium account (see detail below). This is known as 'group reconstruction relief'.

(2) Under s. 612, if a company acquires shares in another company, such that after the transaction it owns more than 90% of that other company's equity, with the consideration being the acquirer's own shares, there is no requirement to record any amount in share premium. This is known as 'merger relief' and can only be used if section 611 does not apply.

(3) Under s. 615, if either of the reliefs above is taken, then it is also permissible to record the investment at a lower amount, reducing it by the value of the amount which is exempt from being recorded in the share premium account.

The 'minimum premium value' referred to in s. 611 is the difference between the 'base value of consideration' and the nominal amount of the shares, and the base value of consideration is:

• the lower of the cost of the assets to the transferring company and their carrying value in the transferor's books immediately pre-transfer; less

• the carrying value of the liabilities in the transferor's books.

These exemptions are best illustrated by examples.

Example 4.14 – group reconstruction relief

Parent P has two wholly-owned subsidiaries, R and S.

R acquires the whole share capital of S from P, by issuing 100,000 of its own shares, with nominal value £100,000 and fair value £250,000. P previously held its investment in S at its original cost of £120,000.

If none of the above reliefs applied or were taken, R would make a simple accounting entry recording the investment at cost and the other entry in share capital/share premium.

Dr investments	£250,000	
Cr share capital		£100,000
Cr share premium		£150,000

However, section 611 applies, so only the 'minimum premium amount' is recorded in share premium, being, in this case, the difference between nominal value of shares issued of £100,000 and the £120,000 at which P was carrying the investment, i.e. £20,000.

Applying no further reliefs, the entries would now be:

Dr investments	£250,000	
Cr share capital		£100,000
Cr share premium		£20,000
Cr other reserves		£130,000

If the relief from s.615 is then taken on top of this, the investment carrying value is reduced by the amount in other reserves, so the entries become:

Dr investments	£120,000	
Cr share capital		£100,000
Cr share premium		£20,000

Example 4.15 – merger relief

Entity X acquires the whole share capital of entity Y by issuing shares to Y's previous shareholders.

X issues 100,000 of shares, with nominal value £100,000 and fair value £250,000.

As in the group reconstruction relief example above, if no reliefs were taken the accounting entry would be

Dr investments	£250,000	
Cr share capital		£100,000
Cr share premium		£150,000

Applying the relief in s. 612, though, none of the excess needs to be recorded in share premium, so the entry can instead be

Dr investments	£250,000	
Cr share capital		£100,000
Cr other reserves		£150,000

Layering s. 615 on top of this example gives a much reduced initial value for the investment, and no entries in the share premium account:

| Dr investments | £100,000 | |
| Cr share capital | | £100,000 |

The main reason for choosing to take these reliefs where they are available is that the uses of the share premium account are highly limited. When the credit entry is instead made to other reserves (some companies choose to call this a merger reserve, though there is no requirement to do this), its application is more flexible: as an example, if the investment is later impaired, the impairment loss can be set off against this credit in reserves, rather than against distributable profits (although a merger reserve is not in itself distributable).

Now, considering the reliefs in the light of guidance in FRS 102, there is no prohibition on the use of merger relief and group reconstruction relief, as all that these do is allow a credit to be recognised in a different line item within equity, and in general FRS 102 includes no comment on the detail of the placing of items in equity. There may, however, be more care needed when it comes to taking the relief in s. 615. Paragraph 9.26 allows the three options of cost less impairment, fair value with changes in equity, and fair value with changes in profit, for measuring subsidiaries in the parent's company accounts.

No definition is given of 'cost' but if this is analogised to elsewhere in the standard, it might reasonably be defined as the fair value of consideration given, which when shares are issued for a purchase would be the fair value of those shares. However, although not clear from the words of the standard itself, Appendix IV to FRS 102 makes clear that 'cost' is intended to include 'cost' as determined using merger relief or group reconstruction relief:

> 'Paragraph 9.26 of FRS 102 requires that in an investor's separate financial statements its investments in subsidiaries are accounted for at cost less impairment, or at fair value. Where the cost model is applied, sections 611 to 615 of the Act set out the treatment where "merger relief" or "group reconstruction relief" are available. These reliefs reduce the amount required to be included in share premium; they also (in section 615) allow the initial carrying amount to be adjusted downwards so it is equal to either the previous carrying amount of the investment in the transferor's books or the nominal value of the shares issued, depending on which relief applies. If the fair value model in paragraph 9.26 is used, then the relief in section 615 is not available, so the investment's carrying value may not be reduced, although the provisions in sections 611 and 612 remain relevant in respect of amounts required to be recorded in share premium.'

4.3.3.4   Merger accounting method

After the difficulty of establishing that it is acceptable to use merger accounting, the mechanics of it are comparatively straightforward. The group accounts will be prepared in the name of the legal parent, showing its share capital and share premium, with the overarching principle that the resulting accounts should show the results of the new group as if it had always been in place. The key consequences are that no fair value exercise is performed, and no goodwill recognised, but further details included in paragraphs 19.29–19.31 include the following.

- The results of the combining parties are adjusted as necessary to ensure uniformity of accounting policies (a judgment will be needed on which of the entities' policies is chosen as the base line – there are no rules in this respect).

- The results and the cash flows of all combining entities are brought into the combined entity's financial statements from the beginning of the financial year in which the combination happened.

- The comparative information is prepared by including total comprehensive income for all entities and their statements of financial position.

- Any difference between the nominal value of shares issued plus fair value of other consideration and the nominal value of shares received in exchange is shown as a movement on other reserves in the consolidated accounts.

- Existing balances on the share premium account or the capital redemption reserve of the new legal subsidiary are brought in as a movement on other reserves.

- Merger expenses are charged to the statement of comprehensive income, as part of profit or loss, at the effective date of the reconstruction.

Example 4.16

Company M has one subsidiary, N. As part of its long term structural planning, M's shareholders wish to expand the group vertically, so that the top company is purely a holding company. This is to be achieved by setting up a new holding company, L, which will acquire all of M's share capital in exchange for its own shares.

This is a group reconstruction. If L issues shares on a strict one-for-one basis (for instance), the new shareholders of L will be exactly the same individuals, and in exactly the same proportions, as they previously were. This, combined with the lack of any non-equity consideration, means that the group reconstruction would be accounted for as a merger.

In the L group's first accounts, it will show a full 12 months for both the current and comparative periods, even though L has only been in existence from part way through the current period. These results will be virtually identical to those which were or would have been reported by a group headed by M, since no additional fair value adjustments are made. The key difference will be that the bottom half of the balance sheet will show L's share capital and share premium account, and will almost certainly have a merger reserve, to make it balance.

4.3.4   Disclosures on business combinations and group reconstructions

The disclosure requirements in Section 19 are reasonably lengthy.

Paragraph 19.26 requires, for all business combinations, a reconciliation of the opening and closing carrying amounts of goodwill, showing separately:

(a)   changes arising from new business combinations;

(b)   amortisation;

(c)   impairment losses;

(d)   disposals of previously acquired businesses; and

(e)   other changes.

A comparative movements table is not required, but 19.26A requires a similar table for 'negative goodwill'.

For business combinations effected during the period, the following disclosures are required by 19.25:

(a)   the names and descriptions of the combining entities or businesses;

(b)   the acquisition date;

(c)   the percentage of voting equity instruments acquired;

(d)   the cost of the combination and a description of the components of that cost (such as cash, equity instruments and debt instruments);

(e)   the amounts recognised at the acquisition date for each class of the acquiree's assets, liabilities and contingent liabilities, including goodwill;

(f)   [not used]

(fA) a qualitative description of the nature of intangible assets included in goodwill;

(g)   the useful life of goodwill, and if this exceeds five years, supporting reasons for this; and

(h)   the periods in which the excess recognised in accordance with paragraph 19.24 will be recognised in profit or loss.

Then, for each material business combination in the period, 19.25A requires disclosure of the revenue and profit or loss of the acquiree since the acquisition date included in the consolidated statement of comprehensive income for the period.

For group reconstructions (that do not qualify as business combinations), 19.33 requires disclosure of:

(a)   the names of the combining entities (other than the reporting entity);

(b)   whether the combination has been accounted for as an acquisition or a merger; and

(c)   the date of the combination.

Small entities applying Section 1A are exempt from these requirements; most small groups would not be expected to prepare group accounts in any case. However, if group accounts are prepared, small entities are encouraged to make the disclosures required by Section 9.

4.3.5   *Transition*

In Section 35, on transition to FRS 102, paragraph 35.10(a) allows an entity to choose not to apply Section 19 to business combinations that occurred before the transition date, though if it applies the section to any business combination before that date, it must then also apply it to all subsequent combinations.

When an entity has pre-transition business combinations that it chooses not to restate, then at the transition date it must measure assets and liabilities relating to those combinations in accordance with the remainder of Section 35, with two exceptions:

- intangible assets subsumed within goodwill are not separately recognised;
- no adjustments are made to the carrying value of goodwill.

4.4   Associates

4.4.1   *Definition*

Section 14 addresses the accounting for investments in associates.

An associate is defined in paragraph 14.2 as:

> ' ... an entity, including an unincorporated entity such as a partnership, over which the investor has significant influence and that is neither a subsidiary nor an interest in a joint venture ... '

To help with this, paragraph 14.3 then explains that 'significant influence is the power to participate in the financial and operating policy decisions of the associate but is not control or joint control over those policies'. Usually, a holding of 20% or more will give significant influence, and conversely significant influence will not exist at a holding less than this level, but both of these are rebuttable if it can be clearly demonstrated that other factors outweigh the equity proportion.

Example 4.17

Investor I has several subsidiaries and two smaller investments.

The first small investment, in Company A, is a holding of 18% of the issued equity. This would normally not be classified as an associate because the holding is below the 20% threshold, but as part of the shareholder agreement, I has the right to appoint one quarter of the Board. I is also A's most significant customer, making up around 60% of A's sales each year.

These factors, in combination, mean that I would probably be judged to have significant influence over A, and therefore would account for it as an associate.

The second smaller investment is in company B, where I holds 21%. One other entity holds the remaining 79% and also has all four of the board seats, since B's Articles state that a 25% holding is needed to give entitlement to board representation. Despite the shareholding over 20%, it does not seem likely in this fact pattern that I would be judged to have significant influence over B, so it would not be classified as an associate.

4.4.2 Accounting policy choices

The required accounting, or accounting policy options, for investments in associates depends on whether the investor is or is not a parent, and if so whether it is preparing individual or group accounts.

The options are summarised in the table at **4.2.5**; as a reminder:

- A parent company, in its consolidated accounts, accounts for all investments in associates using the equity method (14.4A).

- As an exception, in the special case of an investor that is a parent but holds its investment in an associate as part of an investment portfolio, the investment is measured in the consolidated accounts at fair value with changes in profit or loss.

- A parent company, in its separate financial statements (that is, its company-only financial statements) makes an accounting policy choice between cost less impairment, fair value with changes in other comprehensive income, and fair value with changes in profit (9.26).

- An investor that is not a parent has a choice between the cost model, fair value with changes in other comprehensive income, and fair value with changes in profit (14.4).

4.4.2.1 Cost model

The cost model is available in the investor's individual/separate financial statements and is the most straightforward to apply: investments are initially recorded at cost, and adjusted for impairment in accordance with Section 27 (discussed in **5.6** of this guide).

Dividends and other distributions from the investee are recognised in income (that is, rather than by adjusting the carrying amount of the investment).

4.4.2.2   Measurement at fair value

There are two fair value accounting policy choices for measurement of an associate in the investor's individual/separate financial statements. Either way, the investment is measured initially at its transaction price, and then remeasured to fair value each reporting date. In one option, changes in fair value are recognised in other comprehensive income; in the other, they are recognised through profit or loss.

In the consolidated financial statements of the investor, measurement at fair value through profit or loss is required instead of the equity method where the associate is held as part of an investment portfolio.

No guidance is given in Section 14 about how to determine fair value: instead, preparers are referred to Section 11 (discussed in **7.3.4**).

4.4.2.3   Equity method

The equity method is only available in the consolidated financial statements. The basic principle of the equity method is that initial recognition is at the transaction price, including transaction costs. This should represent the investor's share of the fair value of the associate's net assets at acquisition, plus any goodwill arising on the acquisition (this goodwill is not shown as a separate item: it is just part of the cost, having influenced the price that was set).

Subsequently the investor continues to recognise its share of the associate's results by increasing the investment carrying value each period for the amount of profit and other comprehensive income to which it is entitled (measured using the investor's accounting policies), and reducing it for any distributions received. Taking this to an extreme, if an associate paid out all of its profits in dividends each year then the carrying value in the investor's books would never change, as it would be increased and then decreased by the same amount each year.

A number of additional details on the application of this method are set out in paragraph 14.8, and discussed point by point below.

(1)   Measuring the investor's share of profit (14.8(b))

This clarifies that when an investor includes its share of profit and other comprehensive income in the carrying value of the investment, this is based on its current voting rights, even though if it has potential voting rights too these may also have been taken into account in its assessment of whether it has significant influence.

(2)   Implicit goodwill and fair value adjustments (14.8(c))

As described above, the original amount recorded for the investment reflects the fair values of assets and liabilities acquired, plus goodwill. In subsequent years, the share of profits will therefore also need to be adjusted for the notional effects of these fair value adjustments, for instance if at acquisition the property had a fair value higher than its carrying value, then the depreciation charge of which the group recognises a share should be based on the fair value not on the carrying value in the holder's books.

(3)   Impairment (14.8(d))

If there is an indication of impairment, a full impairment review is performed based on Section 27, treating the investment as a single asset (rather than as a group of shares of smaller assets, plus goodwill). It can be assumed that this also means that if an impairment charge is necessary, it will simply be taken off the investment carrying amount, rather than being viewed as an impairment of the inherent goodwill.

(4)   Transactions between an investor and its associates (14.8(e))

Where there are transactions between the two parties in an investor/ associate relationship, they cannot be cancelled out in the group accounts because only the investor's percentage of the associate's results is included. The requirement instead is to eliminate unrealised profits and losses resulting from upstream or downstream transactions 'to the extent of the investor's interest in the associate'.

(5)   Date of financial statements

Ideally, the associate's financial statements should be prepared to the same date as those of the investor, but where this is not possible (perhaps the associate has a parent with a different year end, so is aligned to that instead) the most recent financial statements are used instead, adjusted for 'the effects of any significant transactions or events occurring between the accounting period ends'. No limit is set on the permissible gap between period ends, so in theory an investor with a December 2015 year end could find itself incorporating its share of the results of an associate with a March 2015 year end (for instance) as these would be the most recent available.

If this was the case, then common sense and good judgment would be needed in assessing which items between those two dates required adjustment. Probably the most important need is to have 12 months of the associate's results included: if the associate is in a period of growth or decline then the investor's reported share will lag behind this reported change, but since there is no provision in the accounts for including a composite set of 12 months, this is an unavoidable consequence. In circumstances where there are no significant transactions but just a period of change, the directors may consider it helpful to provide additional disclosures, perhaps even with a pro forma statement of comprehensive income and balance sheet showing the effect of including results on a different basis – though this would need to be very clearly explained and not given undue prominence.

Significant events that would need to be adjusted for might include the associate's acquisitions or disposals of subsidiaries or large pieces of PPE, or the taking on of debt which has a material effect on the balance sheet. It will be vital to keep excellent records to ensure that transactions adjusted out of one accounting period are then adjusted back into the next, so that none of the consequences for the investor are omitted from the accounts.

(6)   Losses in excess of investment

If an associate makes losses after the investor purchases its stake, these will reduce the carrying amount of the investment each period, and if this continues then it may happen that the associate continues to make losses even after the carrying amount in the investor's books reaches zero.

The default treatment of this situation is that at this point the investor stops recognising its share of losses. Instead, they are recorded in a memo account, and if the associate returns to profitability then the investor does not recognise any share of profits until its notional share of the losses in that time has been 'absorbed'.

Example 4.18

Investor J paid £300,000 for its 25% share of associate B, but after two years this investment was written down to zero due to B's continuing losses.

In the subsequent year B makes further losses of £200,000. J's share of the losses is not included in J's accounts, but it keeps note of the unrecognised 25% share, being £50,000.

The year after this, B makes a profit of £100,000, so J would be entitled to £25,000, but it does not recognise this, instead reducing its noted value of unused losses to £25,000.

Another year further on, B makes a profit of £400,000. J is entitled to £100,000 of this, and recognises £75,000, being the difference between its entitlement and the remaining, previously unrecognised, losses. The carrying amount of its investment at the end of this period will therefore, assuming no dividends, also be £75,000.

The only exception to this requirement not to recognise losses that would take the investment balance below zero is where the investor 'has incurred legal or constructive obligations or has made payments on behalf of the associate'. Effectively, this is bringing the accounting back to the core definitions from the early sections of the standard: usually, an investor in an associate has no obligations to make good the associate's losses (a standard equity shareholder in a limited liability company can lose no more than their capital), so if a provision is to be recognised, it is in the rare situation where the investor has a more than typical commitment in respect of its investee.

(7) Discontinuing the equity method

The equity method may only be used for as long as the investor has significant influence, and its use stops from the date that significant influence is lost. This could change through disposal of a shareholding, or through a deemed disposal where the investee issues additional shares to another party such that the other investors' stakes are diluted. It could also happen through a change in the shareholder agreement or in the composition of the Board, since these can affect whether there is significant influence despite the level of the investor's holding.

The accounting when the equity method is discontinued depends on what caused the loss of significant influence.

If there was a full or partial disposal, then firstly a profit or loss is recognised based on the difference between the proceeds of the disposal and the previous (equity accounted) carrying amount of the investment. For a partial disposal, the relevant proportion would be applied to this investment, e.g. if a 20% holding was reduced to a 10% holding, then half of the carrying value would be included in the profit or loss calculation. The carrying value of the remaining balance becomes the opening cost for the resulting financial asset, which is then accounted for in accordance with Section 11 or 12, as appropriate.

If the loss of significant influence is not through a disposal, then there is clearly no profit or loss to account for, so the investment balance is instead simply redesignated as a financial asset and its carrying value at that point becomes the opening cost for its accounting in accordance with Section 11 or 12.

The standard makes no mention of which of these treatments applies to a deemed disposal, that is whether a dilution of the investor's shareholding should give rise to a profit or loss or simply a reclassification of amounts on the balance sheet. It may therefore be possible to argue this either way and effectively to have a choice of two accounting treatments, although the best way of following the principles behind the guidance would seem to be to include it as a special type of disposal, since the shareholding is being reduced even where no proceeds change hands.

As a further refinement, paragraph 14.8 briefly addresses the treatment of amounts that had, under equity accounting, been included in other comprehensive income in relation to the associate. Wherever the standard would normally require such gains or losses to be recycled, this is applied on the disposal too, and the recycled amounts adjust the profit or loss recognised. There is no explicit comment stating that it is the whole amount from OCI that is recycled, rather than just a proportion based on the proportion of the asset disposed of, but it seems reasonable to assume that it is the whole amount that is recycled, since when equity accounting ceases the investor will no longer be recording its share of movements relating to assets and liabilities on the balance sheet. In other words, this is comparable to a disposal of the underlying asset.

Example 4.19

Investor K has a 20% interest in associate A, which it purchased for £500,000.

During the period of K's significant influence, A has reported profits of £1m and other comprehensive income of £150,000, relating to gains on a hedging instrument. Accordingly, K's share included in its group accounts has been made up of profit share of £200,000 and other comprehensive income share of £30,000. The carrying value of the investment in A at the end of this time is therefore £730,000.

K then disposes of half of its investment in A, for proceeds of £400,000. The profit on disposal is calculated as follows:

Cash proceeds	£ 400,000	
Less carrying value of investment disposed of	(£ 365,000)	(half of total carrying value)
Add gains previously recognised in OCI	£ 30,000	(full value)
Net profit on disposal	£ 65,000	

The remaining carrying value of £365,000 will then become the beginning point, the deemed cost, for the investment's subsequent treatment as a financial asset.

4.4.3 Disclosures

The financial statements should disclose (paragraph 14.12):

(a) the accounting policy for investments in associates;

(b) the carrying amount of investments in associates;

(c) the fair value of investments in associates accounted for using the equity method for which there are published price quotations.

Where the cost model is used, paragraph 14.13 requires disclosure of the amount of dividends and other distributions recognised in income.

Where the equity method is used, paragraph 14.14 requires disclosure of the investor's share of the profit or loss of such associates and its share of any discontinued operations.

Where the fair value model is used, the disclosure requirements are in Section 11.

Finally, under paragraph 14.15A, the individual financial statements of an investor that is not a parent must provide summarised financial information about the investments in the associates, along with the effect of including those investments as if they had been accounted for using the equity method. Investing entities that are exempt from preparing consolidated financial statements, or would be exempt if they had subsidiaries, are exempt from this requirement.

Small entities are exempt from the disclosure requirements of Section 14 unless necessary for a true and fair view.

4.5   Joint ventures

Section 15 addresses the accounting for joint ventures in a parent company's consolidated and separate financial statements, and in the financial statements of an investor that is not a parent.

4.5.1   Definitions

Section 15 defines a joint venture, then sets out three sub-categories into which joint ventures can be assigned.

The definition of a joint venture relies first on that of joint control:

> 'Joint control is the contractually agreed sharing of control over an economic activity, and exists only when the strategic financial and operating decisions relating to the activity require the unanimous consent of the parties sharing control (the venturers). (15.2)'

A joint venture, then, is:

> 'a contractual arrangement whereby two or more parties undertake an economic activity that is subject to joint control. Joint ventures can take the form of jointly controlled operations, jointly controlled assets, or jointly controlled entities. (15.3)'

This is a tightly drawn definition of joint control. In particular, the requirement to have a contractually agreed sharing of control means that an arrangement where two entities have no connection except for that they happen each to own 50% of a third entity would not meet this definition: they would need an agreement in place to enforce the position where decisions could not be taken without mutual consent.

In fact, although many think of joint ventures as being ventures with a 50/50 split, this is not a requirement at all. A joint venture can, for instance, involve more than two investors – perhaps three, each with a third of the shares, and with an arrangement that requires unanimous consent from these three investors for each decision. It may also be the case that an entity has several investors, not all of whom share control, for instance where two parties hold 40%, another holds 10%, and there is a formal agreement specifying sharing of control between the two larger-stake investors. Equally, though this may be less common, that arrangement including three shareholders with unequal proportions of the voting rights may give rise to joint control between all three investors if there is a separate agreement setting this out and overriding the default position based on equity rights.

After the stage is set with this definition of a joint venture, Section 15 then goes on to discuss the three kinds of joint ventures: jointly controlled operations, jointly controlled assets, and jointly controlled entities. Each has its own accounting requirements, so establishing the right classification at the outset is crucial.

4.5.1.1   Jointly controlled operations

A jointly controlled operation is one that:

> 'involves the use of the assets and other resources of the venturers rather than the establishment of a corporation, partnership or other entity, or a financial structure that is separate from the venturers themselves. (15.4)'

The key feature is the lack of a distinct legal or financial structure, so although there is a definable business, it is not ring fenced or self contained.

4.5.1.2   Jointly controlled assets

A jointly controlled asset is jointly controlled, and often also jointly owned, by the investors, and is dedicated to the purposes of the joint venture.

4.5.1.3   Jointly controlled entities

A jointly controlled entity is any joint venture where the operations are run through a distinct corporation, partnership or other entity in which each venturer has an interest.

4.5.2   Accounting requirements

The accounting requirements for the first two categories of joint venture, jointly controlled operations and jointly controlled assets, apply regardless of the status of the investor, i.e. whether or not it is a parent, and if a parent, whether it is preparing consolidated accounts. For jointly controlled entities, there are more nuanced requirements, discussed below and also summarised in the table at **4.2.5**.

4.5.2.1   Jointly controlled operations

An investor in a jointly controlled operation recognises:

(a) the assets that it controls and the liabilities that it incurs; and

(b) the expenses that it incurs and its share of the income that it earns from the sale of goods or services by the joint venture.

4.5.2.2   Jointly controlled assets

An investor in a jointly controlled asset recognises:

(a) its share of the jointly controlled assets, classified according to the nature of the assets;

(b) any liabilities that it has incurred;

(c) its share of any liabilities incurred jointly with the other venturers in relation to the joint venture;

(d) any income from the sale or use of its share of the output of the joint venture, together with its share of any expenses incurred by the joint venture; and

(e) any expenses that it has incurred in respect of its interest in the joint venture.

4.5.2.3   Jointly controlled entities

For jointly controlled entities, the accounting treatment depends on whether the investor is a parent and, if so, whether it is preparing consolidated accounts.

A venturer that is not a parent has three accounting policy options:

(a) the cost model;

(b) fair value with changes in other comprehensive income; or

(c) fair value with changes in profit.

A venturer that is a parent has the same three choices in its company-only accounts, although these are via paragraph 9.26 rather than section 15.

A venturer that is a parent must, in its consolidated accounts, use equity accounting for all of its investments in joint ventures, unless the investment is held as part of an investment portfolio, in which case it is measured at fair value, with changes each period recognised in profit or loss.

The cost model, equity method, and fair value model (plus the additional option of using fair value with changes in profit) are all the same as set out for associates in Section 14, and discussed at **4.4**.

4.5.3   Other joint venture accounting issues

4.5.3.1   Transactions between venture and venturer

The complexity of the relationship between a venturer and a venture is illustrated by the tensions surrounding treatment of transactions between them. Because venturers share control, their transactions with the venture may be neither totally commercial nor totally disinterested, so the accounting must be carefully judged to reflect the substance of the individual arrangement.

When a venturer sells or contributes assets to a joint venture, the accounting profit that arises is only partially crystallised, since the venturer retains shared control of the operation as a whole. This means that so long as the assets are still held in the venture, the venturer only recognises 'that portion of the gain or loss that is attributable to the interests of the other venturers' (paragraph 15.16). The only exception is when the contribution or sale gives evidence of an impairment loss, in which case the full loss is recognised immediately – it would be inappropriate to defer recognition of a known loss.

Looking at the opposite situation where a venturer purchases assets from a joint venture, the joint venture may show a profit in its own books, but the venturer's share of this profit is not included in the venturer's accounts until the asset is sold on to a third party. It can be seen that this may mean the profit is never recognised, if for instance the asset is used by the receiving venturer until the end of its useful life, and is then scrapped.

Example 4.20

Joint venturer J has a 50% interest in joint venture V, and a contractual agreement to share control with the other joint venturer K.

J sells a property with carrying value of £700,000 to V for £1m, giving rise to a notional gain of £300,000.

Assuming that all significant risks and rewards of ownership are transferred, J will recognise only half of its book gain, being £150,000 (the proportion attributable to K).

The double entry for the disposal will depend on the type of joint venture, but effectively involves recognising on the venturer's balance sheet a lower value for the transferred asset than the value that is attributed on the books of the joint venture itself. This would be achieved through an adjustment either to the share of the asset value (in a jointly controlled operation or jointly controlled asset) or to the carrying value of the equity accounted investment (in a jointly controlled entity).

In the same period, V sells a piece of machinery to K. The machinery had been on V's books at £200,000 but K pays £300,000 for it.

Although in its company accounts, V will recognise a gain of £100,000, K may not recognise a share of this gain until it sells the machinery on. J, on the other hand, will recognise its £50,000 share immediately as it is not involved in the transaction.

4.5.3.2   Other investors in a joint venture

The accounting requirements discussed so far here have all related to the accounting by the venturers that share control in a joint venture. However, as described above, a joint venture may have investors who have an interest but do not share control.

In this situation, paragraph 15.18 directs the investor, as might be expected, to Sections 11 and 12, which set out the accounting for financial assets. In other words, there is no special treatment needed by a minority investor in a joint venture, any more than one would be needed by a minority investor in a subsidiary.

4.5.4   Disclosures

Unsurprisingly, the disclosure requirements are very similar to those for investments in associates:

The financial statements shall disclose (paragraph 15.19):

(a) the accounting policy for recognising investments in jointly controlled entities;

(b) the carrying amount of investments in jointly controlled entities;

(c) the fair value of investments in jointly controlled entities accounted for using the equity method for which there are published price quotations; and

(d) the aggregate amount of [the investor's] commitments relating to joint ventures, including its share in the capital commitments that have been incurred jointly with other venturers, as well as its share of the capital commitments of the joint ventures themselves.

Where the equity method is used, paragraph 15.20 requires disclosure of the investor's share of the profit or loss of such jointly controlled entities and its share of any discontinued operations.

Where the fair value model is used, the disclosure requirements are in Section 11.

Finally, under 15.21A, the individual financial statements of an investor that is not a parent must provide summarised financial information about the investments in the jointly controlled entities, along with the effect of including those investments as if they had been accounted for using the equity method. Investing entities that are exempt from preparing consolidated financial statements, or would be exempt if they had subsidiaries, are exempt from this requirement.

Small entities are exempt from the disclosure requirements of Section 14 unless necessary for a true and fair view.

5 Tangible and intangible assets and impairment

5.1 Scope of this section

This section is very broad in scope, pulling in several sections of the standard. These are grouped together because of their commonalities: while intangible assets clearly differ from property, plant and equipment (PPE), they share a long-term nature, a requirement to be written off against profit over their lives, and a need to be reviewed for impairment. Investment properties, a special category of PPE, are dealt with here too because although they have a unique accounting treatment, there is a fallback to the standard PPE accounting where measures of fair value are not available. The section addresses the following areas of the standard:

- Section 17 *Property, plant and equipment*

- Section 16 *Investment properties*

- Section 18 *Intangible assets*

- Section 34 *Other long-term assets (heritage assets and assets relating to extractive industries)*

- Section 27 *Impairment of assets*

5.2 Property, plant and equipment

Property, plant and equipment is covered by Section 17. The equivalent standard in IFRS is IAS 16 *Property, Plant and Equipment*.

> **Application to micro-entities:** Micro-entities can only apply the cost model to measure property, plant and equipment; the revaluation model is not available. There is no exemption from full retrospective restatement of property, plant and equipment. Therefore, any such assets previously held at valuation will need to be restated to depreciated historic cost on first-time adoption of FRS 105.
>
> The other requirements are generally consistent with FRS 102, except that borrowing costs may not be capitalised as part of the cost of an item of property, plant or equipment; they must be expensed as incurred.

5.2.1   Scope and definitions

The Glossary defines property, plant and equipment as tangible assets that:

(a) are held for use in the production or supply of goods or services, for rental to others or for administrative purposes; and

(b) are expected to be used during more than one period.

None of the following are within the scope of Section 17 but are all within the scope of *Specialised Activities*, Section 34:

(a) biological assets related to agricultural activity (discussed in **6.2.9**);

(b) heritage assets (discussed at **5.5**); and

(c) mineral rights and mineral reserves, such as oil, natural gas and similar non-regenerative resources (discussed at **5.5**).

Section 17 also applies to investment properties (Section 16, discussed at **5.3**) where the property is let out to another group member and the accounting policy choice is made to apply the cost model rather than fair value.

5.2.2   Initial recognition

5.2.2.1   Items to be recognised

An entity only recognises the cost of an item of property, plant and equipment as an asset if (17.4):

(a) it is probable that future economic benefits associated with the item will flow to the entity; and

(b) the cost of the item can be measured reliably.

Separable assets, such as land and buildings, must be accounted for separately even when they are acquired together.

In general, there is little difficulty in applying this condition. Virtually all fixed asset purchases will be clear-cut, with a well-defined invoice price. Exceptions might be where the price an entity pays for an asset is determinable based, for instance, on output levels. This might apply to custom machinery, where efficiency is hard to predict until a running in period is over. In this case, it would seem appropriate to recognise the floor price when the asset is received, and to adjust the cost when it is finalised (which, if it is at the end of the running-in period, will coincide with the point when depreciation starts).

5.2.2.2 Spare parts and stand-by equipment

Paragraph 17.5 of FRS 102 (2018) says items such as spare parts, stand-by equipment and servicing equipment are recognised in accordance with Section 17 when they meet the definition of property, plant and equipment. Otherwise, such items are classified as inventory. This clarified what was previously stated.

5.2.2.3 Replacements

Parts of some items of property, plant and equipment may require regular replacement (e.g. the roof of a building). In such a case, the cost of replacing part of such an item is added to the carrying amount of the related item of property, plant and equipment when that additional cost is incurred, providing that the replacement is expected to provide incremental future benefits to the entity. At the same time, the entity must derecognise any carrying amounts of the parts that are replaced. Where there are major components of an item of property, plant and equipment that have significantly different patterns of consumption of economic benefits, the initial cost of the asset is allocated to its major components and each such component is depreciated separately over its useful life.

FRS 102 (2018) notes derecognition of replaced parts is required regardless of whether the replaced parts had been depreciated separately. It does, however, allow that if it is impracticable for an entity to identify the carrying amount of the replaced part, it can be estimated using the current cost of the replacement part to represent the original cost of the replaced part and adjusting it for depreciation and impairment. This is a useful practical expedient which is likely to represent an approach companies have taken previously in practice.

5.2.2.4 Regular inspections

In some industries, e.g. the travel industry, an item of property, plant and equipment such as a plane or a bus can only be operated if the entity carries out regular major inspections for faults regardless of whether parts of the item are replaced. The cost of performing each major inspection is recognised in the carrying amount of the item of property, plant and equipment as a replacement where the recognition criteria (see above) are satisfied. At the same time, any remaining carrying amount relating to the cost of previous major inspections (as distinct from physical parts) is derecognised. This is done regardless of whether the cost of the previous major inspection was identified in the transaction in which the item was acquired or constructed. If necessary, the estimated cost of a future similar inspection may be used as an indication of what the cost of the existing inspection component would have been when the item was acquired or constructed.

5.2.3   Measurement at initial recognition

5.2.3.1   The basic rule

On initial recognition, items of property, plant and equipment are measured at cost.

5.2.3.2   Elements of cost

Paragraph 17.10 states that the cost of an item of property, plant and equipment comprises all of the following:

(a) its purchase price, including legal and brokerage fees, import duties and non-refundable purchase taxes, after deducting trade discounts and rebates;

(b) any costs directly attributable to bringing the asset to the location and condition necessary for it to be capable of operating in the manner intended by management. These can include the costs of site preparation, initial delivery and handling, installation and assembly, and testing of functionality;

(c) the initial estimate of the costs, recognised and measured in accordance with Section 21 *Provisions and Contingencies*, of dismantling and removing the item and restoring the site on which it is located, the obligation for which an entity incurs either when the item is acquired or as a consequence of having used the item during a particular period for purposes other than to produce inventories during that period;

(d) any borrowing costs capitalised in accordance with paragraph 25.2.

Note that stamp duty on an asset purchase would normally be viewed as part of the asset's cost, since it is a 'non-refundable purchase tax'.

Paragraph 17.11 then goes on to clarify that costs that are connected to an item of property, plant and equipment but that are not directly attributable to the asset cannot be capitalised and must be recognised as an expense when incurred. These include:

(a) costs of opening a new facility;

(b) costs of introducing a new product or service (including costs of advertising and promotional activities);

(c) costs of conducting business in a new location or with a new class of customer (including costs of staff training); and

(d) administration and other general overhead costs.

The income and related expenses of incidental operations during construction or development of an item of property, plant and equipment are recognised in profit or loss if those operations are not necessary to bring the item to its intended location and operating condition. This would include any subletting income that could be earned on a property constructed in stages.

5.2.3.3   Spares, replacements and maintenance

While many assets are clear individual objects, some are more complex. The standard sets a base position that spare parts are treated as inventory (i.e. not included in the cost of property, plant and equipment), unless they are major and expected to be used in more than one period.

Where certain components of an asset are expected to be replaced over its life, these components are capitalised and depreciated separately. One well-known example is a furnace with a replaceable lining.

For assets that need regular major inspections, the cost of the inspection itself must be capitalised. No guidance is given on depreciating this incremental cost, but it would seem reasonable to argue either for using the whole asset's remaining life or, if known, the period until the next inspection. When that next inspection happens, any cost remaining in the balance sheet from the last inspection is treated as having been disposed of (i.e. it is charged to profit).

5.2.3.4   Initial measurement of cost

Paragraph 17.13 states that the cost of an item of property, plant and equipment is the cash price equivalent at the recognition date. If payment is deferred beyond normal credit terms, the cost is the present value of all future payments.

If, instead of using cash, an asset is purchased using non-monetary assets, paragraph 17.14 applies:

An entity shall measure the cost of the acquired asset at fair value unless:

(a)   the exchange transaction lacks commercial substance; or

(b)   the fair value of neither the asset received nor the asset given up is reliably measurable. In that case, the asset's cost is measured at the carrying amount of the asset given up.

The standard does not give any guidance on what should be recorded when the exchange of assets lacks commercial substance. Each situation would need to be considered on its own merits including whether title has been genuinely transferred.

Example 5.1

Entity P acquires a new forklift truck but, instead of using cash, negotiates to pay the supplier with its own products.

The forklift has a list price of £12,000 and the goods supplied have a list price of £13,000 but a cost to P of £10,000.

The new vehicle is initially recorded at £12,000, with the assumption that its list price is a good proxy for its fair value (being what would normally be asked for and paid in the open market).

Interestingly, the accounting here would generate a £2,000 profit for P (since the stock was only being held at £10,000) but this would appear not to meet the definition of a realized profit (because the forklift is non-monetary) and hence would not be distributable.

5.2.3.5   Self-constructed assets

The standard has no guidance on accounting for self-constructed assets. In general, the principles for what can be capitalised can be expected to be the same as those for purchased assets; care is needed, though, in determining when capitalisation should stop, and depreciation begin.

Entities will need to develop their own policies, though given the absence of directly relevant guidance within the standard they may choose to use the option to look to full IFRS. IAS 16.22 points to the principles for capitalising costs on an acquired asset, and also observes that if an entity constructs an asset for its own use that is the same as an asset it sells to others, the cost should be the same in both cases. Also, it states that abnormal amounts of wasted material, labour or other resources used in self-construction should not be capitalised within the asset's cost – though it leaves the meaning of 'abnormal' open to interpretation.

5.2.4   *Measurement after initial recognition*

5.2.4.1   *Policy choices*

After initial recognition, there is a class-by-class choice between the cost model and the revaluation model. A class of assets is a group which all have a similar nature, function or use in the business.

5.2.4.2   *Cost model*

Under the cost model, each asset is measured at cost less accumulated depreciation (**5.2.5**) and accumulated impairment losses (**5.6**).

5.2.4.3   Revaluation model

Under the revaluation model, an item of property, plant and equipment whose fair value can be measured reliably is carried at a revalued amount. This amount is the asset's fair value at the date of revaluation less any subsequent accumulated depreciation and subsequent accumulated impairment losses.

The standard does not give any guidance on frequency of revaluations, beyond the statement in paragraph 17.15B that 'revaluations shall be made with sufficient regularity to ensure that the carrying amount does not differ materially from that which would be determined using fair value at the end of the reporting period'. This has the practical consequence that the frequency of valuation will depend on the item involved, the volatility of the market and geographical location. We might look to IAS 16, which points out that the values of some assets change quickly, meaning they would need annual revaluation, whereas with others, it might be acceptable to revisit the value only every three or five years.

Paragraph 17.15C states that professionally qualified valuers are normally needed to determine the fair value of land and buildings, with the implication that a market appraisal (which can be performed by the asset's owner) would usually be enough for other types of asset. Further guidance on determining fair value is given in Section 11 of FRS 102, discussed in **7.3.4** of this guide.

In some cases, there will be no market-based evidence of fair value because a piece of PPE is specialised in nature and is rarely sold, except as part of a continuing business. In these cases, paragraph 17.15D suggests an income or depreciated replacement cost approach.

5.2.4.4   Reporting gains and losses on revaluations

If there is an upward revaluation, so that an asset's carrying amount is increased, the increase is recognised in other comprehensive income and accumulated in equity. (This is different to valuation movements on investment property, discussed at **5.3**, which are always taken to profit or loss.) The exception is where, or to the extent that, the revaluation gain reverses a revaluation decrease of the same asset previously recognised in profit or loss, in which case this part is also recognised in profit or loss.

The standard does not say where in equity revaluation gains have to be reported, nor even that they need to be in a separate component of equity – in other words, there is no requirement for a separate revaluation reserve. However, entities subject to UK law on distribution of profits will probably find it easiest to continue having a revaluation reserve in place, since revaluation gains are not legally distributable.

A downward revaluation might be recognised in two places: first in other comprehensive income, to reverse any gain already recorded on that asset, then any excess in profit. In other words, a fall in value on a revalued asset may not give an impairment charge to profit, if the value is still higher than depreciated historic cost.

Example 5.2

On 1 January 20X1, an entity acquired a property for £100,000 which has a residual value of £20,000.

The property is expected to have a useful life of 20 years and is depreciated on a straight line basis.

Neither the residual value nor useful life of the asset need to be revised for the purposes of this example. Taxation has been ignored.

On 31 December 20X1, the property was revalued upwards to £120,000.

On 31 December 20X2, the property was not revalued.

On 31 December 20X3, the property was revalued downwards to £80,000.

On 31 December 20X4, the property was revalued upwards to £110,000.

This will be reflected as follows:

Date	Opening NBV at 1 January	Depreciation	Valuation movement in year	Closing NBV at 31 December
20X1	100,000	-4,000	24,000	120,000
20X2	120,000	-5,263	0	114,737
20X3	114,737	-5,263	-29,474	80,000
20X4	80,000	-3,529	33,529	110,000

	Year ended 31 December 20X1	Year ended 31 December 20X2	Year ended 31 December 20X3	Year ended 31 December 20X4
Income statement				
Depreciation	4,000	5,263	5,263	3,529
Impairment/ (reversal)			5,474	-(5,474)

Date	Opening NBV at 1 January	Depreciation	Valuation movement in year	Closing NBV at 31 December
OCI				
Revaluation (gain)/loss		(24,000)		24,000 (28,056)
	At 31 December 20X1	At 31 December 20X2	At 31 December 20X3	At 31 December 20X4
Balance sheet				
PPE – cost or valuation	120,000	120,000	80,000	110,000
PPE – accumulated depreciation	0	5,263	0	0
PPE – NBV	120,000	114,737	80,000	110,000
Revaluation reserve	24,000	24,000	0	28,056

5.2.5   Depreciation

5.2.5.1   Asset components

Sometimes, the major components of an item of property, plant and equipment have significantly different patterns of consumption of economic benefits. In this case, paragraph 17.16 requires that the initial cost of the asset is allocated to its major components with each component then depreciated separately over its useful life.

In all other cases, assets are depreciated over their useful lives as a single asset. However, there are some exceptions such as land which generally has an unlimited useful life and is therefore not usually depreciated. As noted above, land and buildings should be accounted for separately even when they are acquired together.

5.2.5.2   Recognition of the depreciation charge

The depreciation charge for each period is recognised in profit or loss unless another section of FRS 102 requires the cost to be recognised as part of the cost of an asset (for instance where the depreciation of manufacturing property, plant and equipment is included in the cost of inventories). There is no prescribed location within the income statement, so there is freedom to include the charge in the line item the preparer considers to be the most appropriate. It is common to split the charge between more than one line (perhaps including depreciation of shop fittings in cost of sales, while depreciation of office furniture is within cost of sales).

5.2.5.3   Depreciable amount

To calculate the depreciation charge for each period, the depreciable amount is allocated on a systematic basis over the asset's useful life. The depreciable amount is the cost of the asset, or other amount substituted for cost in the financial statements (e.g. revalued amount), less the residual value of the asset.

The residual value of an asset is defined in the glossary as 'the estimated amount that an entity would currently obtain from the disposal of an asset, after deducting the estimated costs of disposal, if the asset were already of the age and in the condition expected at the end of its useful life'.

Residual value could be affected by factors such as:

- a change in how an asset is used;
- significant unexpected wear and tear;
- technological advancement; and
- changes in market prices.

As well as indicating a possible change in the residual value of an asset, the above factors may also indicate that the useful life of an asset has changed since the most recent annual reporting date. If such indicators are present, it will be important to review all previous estimates and, if necessary, to amend the residual value, depreciation method or useful life. These changes will then be accounted for as a change in an accounting estimate on a prospective basis, as discussed in **2.4.1** of this guide (Section 10 of FRS 102).

5.2.5.4   Depreciation period – useful life

Depreciation of an asset starts from the point that it is available for use, i.e. when it is in the location and condition necessary for it to be capable of operating in the manner intended by management. Depreciation of an asset ceases when the asset is derecognised and not when it becomes idle or is retired from active use unless it is fully depreciated. However, the depreciation charge could be zero when there is no production under usage methods of depreciation.

ECONOMIC LIFE OF ASSET			
	USEFUL LIFE		
Asset's commissioning period	Asset becomes available for use and is used in the manner intended	Asset becomes idle or retired from active use but is not fully depreciated	Asset becomes fully depreciated or is derecognised
	DEPRECIATION PERIOD		

Paragraph 17.21 states that all of the following factors should be considered in determining the useful life of an asset:

- the expected usage of the asset. Usage is assessed by reference to the asset's expected capacity or physical output;

- expected physical wear and tear, which depends on operational factors such as the number of shifts for which the asset is to be used and the repair and maintenance programme, and the care and maintenance of the asset while idle;

- technical or commercial obsolescence arising from changes or improvements in production, or from a change in the market demand for the product or service output of the asset; and

- legal or similar limits on the use of the asset, such as the expiry dates of related leases.

5.2.5.5   Depreciation method

The depreciation method should reflect the pattern in which the entity expects to consume the asset's future economic benefits. Possible depreciation methods according to paragraph 17.22 include:

- the straight-line method;

- the diminishing balance method; and

- a method based on usage such as the units of production method.

The depreciation method, as with all other key decisions, should be reviewed if there are indications of significant change in the factors that influenced the original choice of method. If this leads to a change in method, it is dealt with prospectively as a change in accounting estimate according to Section 10 (discussed in **2.4.1**).

In 2014, the IASB clarified that under IFRS, a revenue-based depreciation method would not be appropriate. This does not absolutely prohibit an FRS 102 preparer from arguing that an asset's pattern of revenue generation is the best proxy for its pattern of consumption, but anyone proposing this treatment would need to address the question of why they were interpreting the concepts in a way that is different from IFRS, with

141

reference to the hierarchy in Section 10 – in other words, they would need to argue that this treatment could be derived from elsewhere within FRS 102.

5.2.5.6   Recognition and measurement of impairment

Paragraph 17.24 requires an entity to apply Section 27 *Impairment of Assets* at each reporting date to determine whether an item or group of items of property, plant and equipment is impaired and, if so, how to recognise and measure the impairment loss by determining the recoverable amount of an asset. This is discussed in detail at **5.6**. Any plan to dispose of an asset earlier than expected would be an indicator of impairment that would trigger the calculation of the asset's recoverable amount for the purpose of determining whether the asset is impaired. Even if the asset is not impaired, an indication of impairment may indicate a need to review the remaining useful life, depreciation method or residual value of an item of property, plant and equipment.

5.2.5.7   Compensation for impairment

Compensation from third parties for items of property, plant and equipment that were impaired, lost or given up is included in profit or loss only when the compensation is virtually certain.

5.2.6   Derecognition

Paragraph 17.27 states that:

An entity shall derecognise an item of property, plant and equipment:

(a) on disposal; or

(b) when no future economic benefits are expected from its use or disposal.

The gain or loss arising from the derecognition of an item of property, plant and equipment is the difference between the net disposal proceeds, if any, and the item's previous carrying amount. The gain or loss is recognised in profit or loss when the item is derecognised (unless Section 20 *Leases* requires otherwise on a sale and leaseback). The gains are not classified as revenue but would typically be included in other income or expense.

To determine the date of disposal of an item, it will usually be necessary to look to the criteria for recognising revenue from the sale of goods in Section 23, but Section 20 applies to disposal by a sale and leaseback.

5.2.7   *Presentation and disclosure*

Under Section 4, *Statement of Financial Position*, an entity which is not a bank or insurance company must present its property, plant and equipment in accordance with the formats in company law (unless adapting the formats as set out in **section 3** of this guide). The formats require 'Tangible assets' to be presented on the face of the statement of financial position with the notes giving an analysis of the following categories:

- land and buildings;
- plant and machinery;
- fixtures, fittings, tools and equipment;
- payments on account and assets in course of construction.

Under FRS 102, paragraph 17.31 requires several disclosures for each class of property, plant and equipment. These are listed below together with a reference to the equivalent Companies Act disclosure requirement:

(a)   the measurement bases used for determining the gross carrying amount;

(b)   the depreciation methods used;

(c)   the useful lives or the depreciation rates used;

(d)   the gross carrying amount [see also SI 2008/410, Sch. 1, para. 51(1)(a) and 51(2)] and the accumulated depreciation (aggregated with accumulated impairment losses) at the beginning and end of the reporting period [see also SI 2008/410, Sch. 1, para. 51(2) and 51(3)];

(e)   a reconciliation of the carrying amount at the beginning and end of the reporting period showing separately:

(i)   additions [see also SI 2008/410, Sch. 1, para. 51(1)(b)(ii)];

(ii)   disposals [see also SI 2008/410, Sch. 1, para. 51(1)(b)(iii)];

(iii)   acquisitions through business combinations;

(iv)   revaluations [see also SI 2008/410, Sch. 1, para. 51(1)(b)(i)];

(v)   transfers to or from investment property if a reliable measure of fair value becomes available or unavailable;

(vi)   impairment losses recognised or reversed in profit or loss in accordance with section 27 *Impairment of Assets* [see also SI 2008/410, Sch. 1, para. 51(2) and 51(3)];

(vii)   depreciation [see also SI 2008/410, Sch. 1, para. 51(2) and 51(3)]; and

(viii) other changes [see also SI 2008/410, Sch. 1, para. 51(1)(b)(iv) which refers to any transfers to this category].

This reconciliation need not be presented for prior periods.

In addition, an entity shall also disclose the following (17.32):

(a) the existence and carrying amounts of property, plant and equipment to which the entity has restricted title or that is pledged as security for liabilities; and

(b) the amount of contractual commitments for the acquisition of property, plant and equipment.

For items of property, plant and equipment stated at revalued amounts, the following shall be disclosed (17.32A):

(a) the effective date of the revaluation [see also SI 2008/410, Sch. 1, para. 52(a) which requires disclosure of the years (so far as they are known to the directors) in which the assets were severally valued and those several values];

(b) whether an independent valuer was involved;

(c) the methods and significant assumptions applied in estimating the items' fair values; and

(d) for each revalued class of property, plant and equipment, the carrying amount that would have been recognised had the assets been carried under the cost model.

In addition, in the case of assets that have been valued during the financial year, SI 2008/410, Sch. 1, para. 52(b) requires disclosure of the names of the persons who valued them or particulars of their qualifications for doing so and (whichever is stated) the bases of valuation used by them.

There is also an additional disclosure required by the Companies Act which is not referred to, which requires disclosures in respect of land and buildings to include an analysis of freehold, long leasehold (i.e. those leases with 50 years or more to run at the end of the reporting year) and short leasehold property. (SI 2008/410, Sch. 1, para. 53)

5.2.7.1   Example reconciliation note

		Freehold property	Long leasehold property	Fixtures and fittings	Plant and equipment	Total
Cost/revaluation						
As at 1 January 20X1		X	X	X	X	X
Additions		X	X	X	X	X
Disposals		(X)	(X)	(X)	(X)	(X)
Acquisitions		X	X	X	X	X
Revaluations		X	X	X	X	X
Transfers:						
	From/(to) investment property to/ (from) owner-occupied property	X	X	-	-	X
Other changes		X	X	X	X	X
As at 31 December 20X1		X	X	X	X	X
Accumulated depreciation						
As at 1 January 20X1		X	X	X	X	X
Charge in year		X	X	X	X	X
Eliminated on disposal		(X)	(X)	(X)	(X)	(X)
Impairment charge / (reversal)		X	X	X	X	X
Transfers:						
	To investment property from owner-occupied property	(X)	(X)	-	-	(X)
Other changes		X	X	X	X	X
As at 31 December 20X1		X	X	X	X	X
Net book value						
As at 31 December 20X1		X	X	X	X	X
As at 1 January 20X1		X	X	X	X	X

There are no exemptions for qualifying entities in respect of property, plant and equipment under paragraphs 1.12–1.13 of FRS 102.

5.2.7.2   *Disclosures for small entities applying FRS 102 Section 1A*

The disclosure requirements for small companies in respect of property, plant and equipment are included in paragraphs 1AC.12–1AC.18. The detail is not reproduced here, but it can be noted that the basic fixed asset movement tables needed are essentially the same, though there is some reduction in narrative information needed, for instance, there is no explicit requirement to disclose depreciation methods, useful lives or rates. Small entities also need to disclose any assets pledged as security to liabilities. The overall volume of disclosures for small entities in respect of tangible assets is unlikely to be appreciably smaller than the volume for larger entities.

5.2.8   Transition

Under paragraph 35.10(c) of FRS 102, an entity may elect to measure the deemed cost of an item of property, plant and equipment at the date of transition to FRS 102 at either:

- its fair value at the date of transition; or

- a previous GAAP revaluation at, or before, the date of transition to FRS 102.

It should be noted that this transition exemption applies to an individual item and does not need to be applied to a whole class of assets.

It has the advantage of enabling an entity to strengthen its reported balance sheet without creating onerous obligations for the future. It would be costly, though, to undertake a full revaluation exercise as a one-off, so the more common use of the exemption will probably be by entities that already had a revaluation policy but plan to revert to cost on adopting FRS 102; this gives a final opportunity to update valuations.

This transition exemption should be easy to implement when calculating transition adjustments. The first option to fair value at the date of transition could be taken whether or not the entity expected to reliably fair value all assets in the relevant class in the future as it would not compel the entity to subsequently adopt the revaluation model.

There is also a transition option, in 35.10(l) in respect of decommissioning liabilities. An entity that incurs a decommissioning obligation, (either when an item of property, plant and equipment is acquired or as a consequence of using it during a particular period for purposes other than to produce inventories during that period), must include an initial estimate of the decommissioning costs of dismantling and removing the item and restoring the site on which it is located in the cost of that item. However, a first-time adopter may elect to measure this component of cost at the date of transition to FRS 102, rather than on the date(s) when the obligation initially arose.

5.3   Investment properties

5.3.1   Scope and definitions

This section covers the accounting requirements from Section 16 for investment property. The equivalent standard in IFRS is IAS 40.

The only properties in the scope of Section 16 are investments in land or buildings that meet the definition of investment property (see below) and some property interests held by a lessee under an operating lease that are treated like investment property where fair value can be measured reliably on an ongoing basis.

All other investment property, where fair value cannot be measured reliably on an ongoing basis, is accounted for as property, plant and equipment using the cost model in Section 17. This cost model will apply from initial recognition if a reliable fair value is not available at that time or from the date when a reliable fair value is no longer available even though the property has initially been accounted for under Section 16. The property remains within the scope of Section 17 unless a reliable measure of fair value becomes available and it is expected that fair value will be reliably measurable on an ongoing basis. In the latter case, the property will be transferred to investment properties and accounted for under this section.

Property held primarily for the provision of social benefits, e.g. social housing held by a public benefit entity, is not classified as investment property. It shall be accounted for as property, plant and equipment in accordance with Section 17.

FRS 102 (2018) excludes from the scope of Section 16 investment property that is rented to another group entity and transferred to PPE – see **5.3.3.**

> **Application to micro-entities:** FRS 105 does not allow the use of fair value measurement, so investment property is measured in the same way as other property, i.e. at cost less depreciation and impairment. As for property, plant and equipment, FRS 105 requires full retrospective restatement of any previously revalued assets.
>
> There is no exemption from full retrospective restatement, but there is some relief in how it is applied to investment property, in the form of a transitional exemption. If the exemption is taken, a micro-entity can apply depreciation

to an investment property based on the useful life of the most significant component of the investment property, rather than having to identify useful lives for separate major components (which would normally be required). To apply this exemption, a micro-entity would follow this somewhat lengthy procedure to allocate depreciation.

(1)   Determine the total cost of the investment property including all of its components. This can be calculated by reversing any revaluation gains or losses previously recorded in equity reserves.

(2)   Separate the cost of land from buildings.

(3)   Estimate the total depreciated cost of the investment property (excluding land) at the date of transition to FRS 105 by recognising accumulated depreciation since the date of initial acquisition calculated on the basis of the useful life of the most significant component of the item of investment property (e.g. the main structural elements of the building).

(4)   Allocate a portion of the estimated total depreciated cost calculated in step (3) to each of the other major components (i.e. excluding the most significant component identified above) to determine their depreciated cost. The allocation should be made on a reasonable and consistent basis. For example, a possible basis of allocation is to multiply the current cost to replace the component by the ratio of its remaining useful life to the expected useful life of a replacement component.

(5)   Allocate any amount of the total depreciated cost not allocated under step (4) to the most significant component of the investment property.

FRS 105 also does not permit the same treatment as FRS 102 for properties held on operating leases by lessees. This is linked to the fact that FRS 105 does not allow fair value measurement; FRS 102 only allows operating leases to be treated as investment property if they can be fair valued.

There is no guidance on transfers into or out of investment property in FRS 105; this is because micro-entities do not need to distinguish between investment property and other fixed assets in their balance sheets or for measurement purposes, so reclassification is irrelevant.

5.3.1.1   Definition of investment property

In the context of investment property, 'property' could be in the form of land, an entire building, a part of a building or a mixture of land and buildings. The Glossary defines it as follows:

'Investment property is property ... held either by the owner or by the lessee under a finance lease to earn rentals or for capital appreciation or both, rather than for:

(a)   use in the production or supply of goods or services or for administrative purposes; or

(b)   sale in the ordinary course of business.'

This means that for the purposes of individual accounts of the lessor (but not in the consolidated accounts), the definition of investment property includes properties leased to other members in the same group.

In addition, a property interest that is held by a lessee under an operating lease may in some cases be classified and accounted for as investment property. This only applies if (paragraph 16.3):

*   the property would otherwise meet the definition of an investment property; and

*   the lessee can measure the fair value of the property interest on an ongoing basis.

This classification alternative for properties held under an operating lease is available on a property-by-property basis so does not have to be applied to all properties held under an operating lease that otherwise meet the definition of investment property.

Note FRS 102 (2018) removed the reference to undue cost or effort from paragraph 16.3.

Where property has mixed use then it will need to be separated for accounting purposes between investment property and property, plant and equipment if the resulting portions could be sold separately or leased out separately under a finance lease. This would most likely be done on a square footage basis with the assistance of a professional valuer.

5.3.1.2 Changes in classification

Sometimes, an entity will change its plans for the use of a property, for instance by consolidating its activities into a smaller part of an office building and letting out the remainder, or by moving into a property of which it had previously been the landlord.

When a change in circumstance occurs which causes the property to fail to meet the definition of investment property, it will fall to be treated under either Section 17 or Section 13 *Inventories*. A change in circumstance is a matter of fact, not a change of accounting policy, and the accounting will therefore need to change once the change in circumstance takes place.

If an entity decides to sell an investment property, this would not usually trigger a reclassification out of the category of investment properties, since this would merely be evidencing a choice to crystallise the capital appreciation for which the property was held. The only slightly grey area would be if the entity's main business was buying and selling properties, so that the property in question effectively became inventory, but it is likely that in such a business, sale would be relatively rapid so that effects of a reclassification might not be significant.

FRS 102 (2018) introduces requirements for where the classification of a property changes from or to investment property, inserting three new paragraphs (paragraphs 16.9A-C) into Section 16 as follows:

When a property ceases to meet the definition of an investment property (for example it becomes owner-occupied or inventory), the deemed cost for subsequent accounting as property, plant and equipment (in accordance with Section 17) or inventory (in accordance with Section 13 *Inventories*) shall be its fair value at the date of change in use.

If an owner-occupied property becomes an investment property, an entity shall apply Section 17 up to the date of change in use. The entity shall treat any difference at that date between the carrying amount of the property in accordance with Section 17 and its fair value in the same way as a revaluation in accordance with Section 17.

For a transfer from inventories to investment property that will be carried at fair value, any difference between the fair value of the property at that date and its previous carrying amount shall be recognised in profit or loss.

5.3.2   *Measurement on initial recognition of investment property*

On initial recognition an investment property is measured at cost. The basis of calculation will depend on the nature of the property as follows:

(a)   purchased investment property

The cost of a purchased investment property comprises its purchase price and any directly attributable expenditure such as legal and brokerage fees, property transfer taxes and other transaction costs. The key point is that the costs that are capitalised would not have occurred had the property not been purchased. If payment is deferred beyond normal credit terms, the cost is the present value of all future payments. This will be calculated by scheduling out the payments and then discounting them at a rate based on the entity's cost of borrowing. Unsurprisingly, this is not different from the initial measurement of any purchased property, regardless of its purpose.

(b)   self-constructed investment property

The cost of a self-constructed investment property will be determined on the same basis as an item of self-constructed property, plant and equipment.

(c)   property interest held under a lease

The initial cost of a property interest held under a lease and classified as an investment property is calculated as if the lease were a finance lease, regardless of what its classification would be under Section 20. Accordingly, the asset is recognised at the lower of the fair value of the property and the present value of the minimum lease payments with an equivalent amount recognised as a liability. Any premium paid for a lease is treated as part of the minimum lease payments for the purpose of calculating the original cost and is therefore included in the cost of the asset but it is excluded from the liability.

Example 5.3

On 1 January 20X1, Entity X enters into an agreement to lease a property from Entity Y with the purpose of earning rentals and capital appreciation. It is expected that the fair value of the property interest held by Entity X (the lessee) can be measured on an ongoing basis. If the lease had been within the scope of Section 20, *Leases*, it would have been classified as an operating lease.

The terms of the lease are as follows:

Initial premium payable on inception	£1,000,000
Lease term	5 years
Annual payments (payable 31 December each year)	£600,000
Discount rate, r	7%
Fair value of property interest on inception of lease	£3,500,000
Fair value of property on inception of lease	£25,000,000

Minimum lease payments

	Time (n)	Cash flow	$1/(1+r)^n$	Discounted cash flow
		£		£
Lease premium	On inception	1,000,000	1.0000	1,000,000
	Year X1	600,000	0.9346	560,748
	Year X2	600,000	0.8734	524,063
	Year X3	600,000	0.8163	489,779
	Year X4	600,000	0.7629	457,737
	Year X5		0.7130	427,792
Initial cost of asset				3,460,118
Initial liability (excludes premium)				2,460,118

Asset		
Record at the lower of the:	a) fair value of the property interest; and	3,500,000
	b) present value of the minimum lease payments	3,460,118

5.3.3 Measurement after initial recognition

Investment property whose fair value can be measured reliably must be measured at that fair value at each reporting date, with changes in fair value recognised in profit or loss (except for property rented out to another group company where there is a choice as discussed below). The Appendix to Section 2 provides guidance on determining fair value.

If a property interest held under a lease is classified as investment property, the item accounted for at fair value is that interest and not the underlying property. Guidance on determining fair value is given in Section 11 of FRS 102, discussed in **7.3.4** of this guide.

All other investment property (i.e. that which is not held at fair value) is accounted for as property, plant and equipment using the cost model in Section 17.

Example 5.4

The property in example A will initially be recorded at £3,460,118. Over time it is believed that a fair value can be obtained. As the end of the lease term approaches the fair value decreases are taken to the profit and loss account.

Time	Opening balance	Fair value movement	Closing balance
	£	£	£
On inception			3,460,118
Year X1	3,460,118	-580,118	2,880,000
Year X2	2,880,000	-645,000	2,235,000
Year X3	2,235,000	-685,000	1,550,000
Year X4	1,550,000	-750,000	800,000
Year X5	800,000	-800,000	0

The lease liability is calculated as follows based on an effective interest rate of 7%:

Time	Opening balance	Finance cost	Cash flow	Closing balance
	£	£	£	£
On inception				-2,460,118
Year X1	-2,460,118	-172,208	600,000	-2,032,327
Year X2	-2,032,327	-142,263	600,000	-1,574,590
Year X3	-1,574,590	-110,221	600,000	-1,084,811
Year X4	-1,084,811	-75,937	600,000	-560,748
Year X5	-560,748	-39,252	600,000	0

Subsequent measurement of investment property in FRS 102 will need to be at fair value, since the 'undue cost or effort' exception has been removed. However, there is an exemption for property let out to another group member, where FRS 102 (2018) introduces an accounting policy choice between cost (under Section 17) and fair value, as set out in new paragraphs 16.4A and B:

An entity that rents investment property to another group entity shall account for those properties either:

(a) at fair value with changes in fair value recognised in profit or loss in accordance with this section (the Appendix to Section 2 provides guidance on determining fair value); or

(b) by transferring them to property, plant and equipment and applying the cost model in accordance with Section 17.

An entity choosing to apply (b) above shall provide all the disclosures required by Section 17, other than those related to fair value measurement.

When only part of a property is rented to another group entity and the remainder is used for other purposes (such as being rented to an external third party or owner-occupied), paragraph 16.4A only applies to the component of that property that is rented to another group entity.

5.3.4   Transfers to or from investment property

Transfers may be made to, or from, investment property only when a property first meets, or ceases to meet, the definition of investment property – see **5.3.1.2**.

5.3.5 **Presentation and disclosure**

5.3.5.1   *Presentation and disclosure for investment property accounted for at fair value through profit or loss*

Presentation and disclosures required for all investment property accounted for as property, plant and equipment are given in Section 17.

For investment property accounted for at fair value through profit or loss, para. 16.10 has the following requirements:

(a) the methods and significant assumptions applied in determining the fair value of investment property;

(b) the extent to which the fair value of investment property (as measured or disclosed in the financial statements) is based on a valuation by an independent valuer who holds a recognised and relevant professional qualification and has recent experience in the location and class of the investment property being valued. If there has been no such valuation, that fact shall be disclosed;

(c) the existence and amounts of restrictions on the realisability of investment property or the remittance of income and proceeds of disposal;

(d) contractual obligations to purchase, construct or develop investment property or for repairs, maintenance or enhancements; and

(e) a reconciliation between the carrying amounts of investment property at the beginning and end of the period, showing separately:

  (i)   additions, disclosing separately those additions resulting from acquisitions through business combinations;

  (ii) net gains or losses from fair value adjustments;

  (iii) transfers to and from property, plant and equipment (see paragraphs 16.9 to 16.9B);

  (iv) transfers to and from inventories (see paragraphs 16.9, 16.9A and 16.9C); and

  (v)   other changes.

This reconciliation need only be presented for the current period, i.e. it is not required for prior periods.

Paragraph 16.11 also requires an entity to give all relevant disclosures about leases it has entered into as required by section 20 both as a lessor and lessee.

The treatment required by SSAP 19 was consistent with paragraph 32(2) of Sch. 1 to the Regulations which allows tangible fixed assets to be measured under the alternative accounting rules at '*a market value determined as at the date of their last valuation or at their current cost'.* All gains and losses resulting from movements in an asset's value (other than those relating to permanent diminutions in value) were recognised in the revaluation reserve under para. 35(1) of Sch. 1 to SI 2008/410. However, para. 33 still required the depreciation rules to be applied in such circumstances – hence the need, under SSAP 19, for a true and fair override to be given because of the non-provision of depreciation.

Paragraph 39(2) of Sch. 1 to the regulations allows investment properties to be measured at fair value with movements in fair value recognised in the profit and loss account. There is no requirement to provide depreciation. This treatment is consistent with FRS 102. As a result, there is now no need for a true and fair override to be given in UK GAAP accounts prepared under FRS 102 because of the non-provision of depreciation.

5.3.5.2   Example reconciliation note

		Investment property
		£
As at 1 January X1		X
Additions		X
Acquisitions		X
Fair value adjustments		X
Transfers:		X
	From/(to) inventories and owner-occupied property	X
Disposals		(X)
Other movements		X
As at 31 December X1		X

5.3.5.3   Disclosures for small entities applying FRS 102 Section 1A

Small entities are required to provide a basic movements table but are spared the detailed requirements for instance to disclose the extent to which the fair value is based on a valuation by an independent valuer. Any assets pledged as security to liabilities should also be disclosed.

5.3.6   *Transition*

Under paragraph 35.10(c) of FRS 102, an entity may elect to measure the deemed cost of an investment property at the date of transition to FRS 102 at either:

- its fair value at the date of transition; or
- a previous GAAP revaluation at, or before, the date of transition to FRS 102.

This transition exemption should be easy to implement when calculating transition adjustments.

5.4   Intangible assets

5.4.1   Scope and definitions

The objective of Section 18 *Intangible Assets other than Goodwill* is to prescribe the accounting treatment for any intangible assets that are not dealt with elsewhere in the standard. In so doing, it sets out the general principle for recognising intangible assets as well as the initial and subsequent measurement of intangible assets within the scope of the standard.

The equivalent standard in IFRS is IAS 38.

Interestingly, the classification of software costs is not addressed so preparers will need to make their own assessments of whether to treat them as tangible or intangible.

The Glossary defines an intangible asset:

'An intangible asset is an identifiable non-monetary asset without physical substance. Such an asset is only identifiable when:

(a) It is separable, i.e. capable of being separated or divided from the entity and sold, transferred, licensed, rented or exchanged, either individually or together with a related contract, asset or liability; or

(b) It arises from contractual or other legal rights, regardless of whether those rights are transferable or separable from the entity or from other rights and obligations.'

Accordingly, an entity would not be permitted to recognise a team of skilled staff as an intangible asset even if it could identify direct future economic benefits from those skills and the staff were not expected to leave in the near future. The staff are not an accounting asset of any sort as the entity would not have control over the expected future economic benefits arising from the team of skilled staff: the employees can always choose to leave.

Section 18 applies to all intangible assets meeting the above definition other than:

- goodwill (which is covered in Section 19 *Business Combinations and Goodwill*); and

- intangible assets held by an entity for sale in the ordinary course of business (which is covered in Section 13 *Inventories* and Section 23 *Revenue*).

Paragraph 18.3 also explicitly scopes out financial assets, heritage assets and mineral rights and mineral reserves, an exclusion which is necessary because of the breadth of the definition of an intangible asset, which could otherwise be read as scoping some of these items in.

Example 5.5

An entity trades in transferable licences which entitle the holder to fish in specified waters and to catch a certain tonnage. The entity does not own a boat nor does it intend to catch fish. It therefore advertises these licences to the general public at a price 50% more than it paid for them.

The licences would be considered inventories even though they otherwise meet the definition of intangible assets, as they are assets held for sale in the ordinary course of business and so would be accounted for under Section 13.

Example 5.6

An entity owning a purchased brand which has a trademark attached would recognise the brand as an intangible asset because the asset is non-monetary in nature (it is neither a currency held nor an asset receivable in a fixed or determinable amount of currency), it is without physical substance as it is a legal right, it is identifiable as the brand is protected legally through the trademark and it can be sold in its own right, i.e. it is separable.

Example 5.7

An entity owning software licences used by staff in their work would recognise these licences as intangible assets. In this situation the licences would actually meet both of the criteria in the Glossary for the asset to be 'identifiable' although only one of the criteria need be met for an intangible to be recognised (so long as it is also a non-monetary asset without physical substance). This is because the licences (which are non-monetary in nature and have no physical substance) can both be sold in their own right, i.e. they are separable, and arise from purchased legal rights.

> **Application to micro-entities:** The definition of an intangible asset in FRS 105 is the same, but FRS 105 only allows the recognition of separately acquired intangible assets. Intangible assets acquired in a business combination are not separated from goodwill and internally generated assets cannot be capitalised.
>
> Separately acquired intangible assets can only be measured at cost less amortisation and impairment. The revaluation model is not available.

5.4.2   Recognition

Paragraph 18.4 requires that:

> 'An entity shall apply the recognition criteria in para. 2.27 in determining whether to recognise an intangible asset. Therefore, the entity shall recognise an intangible asset if, and only if:
>
> (a)   it is probable that the expected future economic benefits that are attributable to the asset will flow to the entity; and
>
> (b)   the cost or value of the asset can be measured reliably.'

In assessing the expected future economic benefits, it is necessary to use 'reasonable and supportable assumptions that represent management's best estimates of the economic conditions that will exist over the useful life of the asset' (18.5). This requires judgment on the likelihood of associated cashflows based on evidence currently available giving greater weight to external evidence. However, where an intangible asset is separately acquired, it is assumed that the probability criterion is satisfied.

5.4.2.1   Acquisition as part of a business combination

Paragraph 18.8 tells us that intangible assets acquired in a business combination shall be recognised separately from goodwill when all the following three conditions are satisfied:

(a)   the recognition criteria set out in Paragraph 18.4 are met;

(b)   the intangible asset arises from contractual or other legal rights; and

(c)   the intangible asset is separable (i.e. capable of being separated or divided from the entity and sold, transferred, licensed, rented or exchanged either individually or together with a related contract, asset or liability).

As discussed further in **4.3.2.5** of this guide, there is an accounting policy choice for recognising intangible assets as part of a business combination where an entity may choose to recognise intangible assets separately from goodwill for which condition (a) and only one of (b) or (c) above is met.

5.4.2.2 *Internally generated intangible assets*

In assessing whether an internally generated intangible asset meets the criteria for recognition, the generation of the asset is classified into a research phase and a development phase. If the classification between these phases cannot be made, the entity shall treat the expenditure on the project as if it was incurred in the research phase only (that is, expensed immediately).

Paragraph 18.8C lists out a number of types of expenditure which will always be recognised as an expense rather than as an intangible asset:

(a) internally generated brands, logos, publishing titles, customer lists and items similar in substance;

(b) start-up costs which include establishment costs such as legal and secretarial costs incurred in setting up a legal entity, expenditure to open a new facility/business in either an existing or new location (pre-opening costs) and expenditure for starting new operations or launching new products or processes including costs of advertising and promotional activities (pre-operating costs);

(c) training activities;

(d) advertising and promotional activities (unless they meet the definition of inventories held for distribution at no or nominal consideration in Section 13, discussed in **6.2.1** of this guide);

(e) relocating or reorganising part or all of an entity;

(f) internally generated goodwill.

Payments made in advance of delivery of the goods or rendering of the services of the above items would still be recognised as a prepayment.

5.4.2.3 *Research phase*

Research expenditure is always recognised as an expense when incurred. This is because on an internal project, for example, an entity cannot demonstrate that probable future economic benefits will be generated.

Some examples of research activities given in 18.8G are as follows:

(a) activities aimed at obtaining new knowledge;

(b) the search for, evaluation and final selection of applications of research findings;

(c) the search for alternatives for materials, devices, products, processes, systems or services;

(d)   the formulation, design, evaluation and final selection of possible alternatives for new or improved material, devices, projects, processes, systems or services.

5.4.2.4   Development phase

In 18.8H, a number of conditions are set out for the recognition of an intangible asset arising from development:

(a)   the technical feasibility of completing the intangible asset so that it would be available for use or sale;

(b)   [the entity's] intention to complete the intangible asset and use or sell it;

(c)   [the entity's] ability to use or sell the intangible asset;

(d)   how the intangible asset will generate probable future economic benefits. Among other things, the entity can demonstrate that there is a market for the output of the intangible asset itself or, if it is to be used internally, the usefulness of the intangible asset;

(e)   the availability of adequate technical, financial and other resources to complete the development of the intangible asset and to use or sell the intangible asset;

(f)   [the entity's] ability to measure reliably the expenditure that is attributable to the intangible asset during its development.

It will be easier for an entity to identify an intangible asset and demonstrate probable future economic benefits during the development phase of a project as it is further advanced than the research phase.

Paragraph 18.8J gives the following examples of development activities:

* the design, construction and testing of pre-production or pre-use prototypes and models;

* the design of tools, jigs, moulds and dies involving new technology;

* the design, construction and operation of a pilot plant that is not of a scale economically feasible for commercial production;

* devices, products, processes, systems or services.

Example 5.8

An entity has developed a formula for baby milk for babies who are intolerant to cows' milk protein. The formula milk is the leading product in the market because of its distinct ingredients which are only known to the owner of the entity; no competitor has been able to replicate the formula which is not protected by a patent.

The formula would meet the definition of an intangible asset: it is identifiable and capable of being separated from the entity and sold. The formula is also non-monetary because it is neither currency held nor an asset receivable in a fixed or determinable amount of cash.

As explained above, expenditure on internally generated intangible assets in a development phase may only be recognised as an asset if certain criteria are met. In this example, a judgment would have to be made over the probability of future economic benefits and the certainty of the market, i.e. how likely is it that the current barrier to entry will be removed and competitors will enter the market with possibly an even better product. Any expenditure incurred before that critical point where the development phase is judged to have started will need to be expensed.

Example 5.9

Entity A develops a successful brand that allows it to charge a premium for its products. Entity A continues to spend money on maintaining this brand and also in developing it further.

The costs incurred in developing the brand such as on sponsorship deals, sponsoring local sports events and advertising do not satisfy the recognition criteria as they cannot be distinguished from costs incurred in respect of developing the business as a whole. The costs therefore would not be recognised as an intangible asset but would be recognised as an expense as incurred

---

Where a policy is adopted of capitalisation of qualifying expenditure in the development phase then this policy needs to be applied consistently to all such expenditures. Expenditure not meeting the criteria must be expensed as incurred.

5.4.3   Initial measurement

On initial recognition, an intangible asset is measured at cost.

5.4.3.1   Separate acquisition

The cost of a separately acquired intangible asset includes:

(a) its purchase price, including import duties and non-refundable purchase taxes, after deducting trade discounts and rebates; and

(b) any directly attributable cost of preparing the asset for its intended use.

5.4.3.2   Internally generated intangible assets

The cost of an internally generated intangible asset is that expenditure incurred from the date that the recognition criteria were first met. It therefore includes directly attributable costs that have been incurred to create, produce and prepare the asset so that it is capable of operating in the manner intended by management. Examples of directly attributable costs include:

- costs of materials and services used or consumed in generating the intangible asset;

- costs of employee benefits arising directly from the generation of the intangible asset;

- professional fees arising directly as part of the asset's development, e.g. registering a legal right;

- amortisation of patents and licences used to generate the intangible asset;

- costs of testing whether the asset is functioning properly, e.g. does the software work as intended and not interfere with other applications.

Capitalisation ends, then, when the asset is ready for operation in the manner intended by management.

Section 25 *Borrowing Costs* (discussed in **13.2** of this publication) specifies the criteria required for the recognition of interest as an element of the cost of an internally generated intangible asset.

5.4.3.3   Acquisition as part of a business combination

Where an intangible asset is acquired as part of a business combination and meets the recognition criteria (see **5.4.2**) then its initial cost is its fair value at the acquisition date.

The fair value guidance comes from Section 11, with references to shares being read as they would apply to intangibles. A quoted price for an identical asset in an active market provides the most reliable estimate of the fair value of an intangible asset. The appropriate market price would be the current bid price but if this was not available then the price of the most recent similar transaction would provide a basis from which to measure fair value. However, any significant changes in the economic circumstances between the recent transaction and the acquisition date would need to be considered in determining the appropriate fair value.

Active markets are not common for intangible assets but may exist in some jurisdictions for items such as freely transferable taxi licences, fishing licences or production quotas. However, an active market cannot exist for unique assets such as brands, newspaper mastheads, music and film publishing rights, patents or trademarks.

The standard includes no explicit guidance on valuation techniques for assets acquired in a business combination. Directors will need to choose an appropriate technique that reflects current transactions and practices in the relevant industry. Techniques that might be used (based on current practice outside UK GAAP) include:

(a) discounting estimated future net cash flows from the asset; or

(b) estimating the costs that the entity avoids by owning intangible assets, e.g. by not having to:

    (i) license it from another party in an arm's length transaction; or

    (ii) recreate or replace it (as in the cost approach).

5.4.3.4 Acquisition by way of a grant

Paragraph 18.12 requires that an intangible asset acquired by way of a grant is recognised at cost, where cost is the fair value of the asset at the date the grant is received/receivable in accordance with Section 24 *Government Grants* (discussed in **10.7**).

Example 5.10

On 1 January 20X3 the government allocated a 10 year broadcasting licence for free to a local entity in a specific jurisdiction to help develop local ownership. The fair value of the broadcasting licence was £10,000 and no specified future performance conditions were imposed on the entity.

In accordance with Section 24 of FRS 102, the entity receiving the licence recognises the licence as an intangible asset at £10,000 (its fair value) on initial recognition and, as the other side of the entry, also recognises £10,000 of income.

5.4.3.5 Exchange of assets

Intangible assets are not always paid for in cash: they can be acquired in exchange for either monetary or non-monetary assets or even a combination of both. An intangible asset acquired in this manner is recognised at its fair value unless (paragraph 18.13):

(a) the exchange transaction lacks commercial substance; or

(b)   the fair value of neither the asset received nor the asset given up is reliably measurable. In this case, the asset's cost is measured at the carrying amount of the asset given up.

Example 5.11

An entity receives landing rights to an airport in an arm's length transaction. In return, the entity gives to the airport 1,500 litres of aviation fuel, which had a cost of £1 per litre.

The landing rights received are recognised as an intangible asset and are initially measured at their fair value, i.e. the cost of the asset given up which can be reliably measured at £1,500.

Example 5.12

An entity receives landing rights to an airport in an arm's length transaction. In return the entity gives to the airport 1,200 litres of aviation fuel, which had a cost of £1 per litre, and £300 of cash.

The landing rights received are again initially measured at £1,500 (their fair value). The fair value of the landing rights is determined by reference to the fair value of the aviation fuel of £1,200 plus the £300 cash given up in the arm's length exchange transaction.

5.4.3.6   Past expenses not to be recognised as an asset

Expenditure incurred on an intangible asset that was initially recognised as an expense may not then be included as part of the cost of an asset at a later date. An appropriate judgment should have been made at the time that the costs were written off in that they did not meet the intangible asset recognition criteria, and so a retrospective adjustment would not be justified.

5.4.4   Subsequent measurement

5.4.4.1   Models

After initial recognition an intangible asset is measured using either the cost model or the revaluation model. The revaluation model may be applied if the fair value is determined through an active market for the asset.

If the revaluation model is selected, then it must be applied to all intangible assets in the same class. However, if an intangible asset is within a revalued class but a particular asset cannot be revalued because it has no active market then this asset is carried at cost less any accumulated amortisation and impairment losses.

5.4.4.2   Measurement under the cost model

Under the revaluation model, the intangible asset is initially recognised at cost and then carried at a revalued amount, i.e. the asset's fair value at the date of revaluation less any subsequent accumulated amortisation and impairment losses. This model can be applied provided the fair value is determined based on an active market for the asset.

The revaluation applies to the whole intangible asset even if the initial costs incurred on the item were written off because, at the time, the capitalisation criteria were not met.

The revaluation model does not permit:

(a)   the revaluation of intangible assets that have not been previously been recognised as assets; or

(b)   the initial recognition of intangible assets at amounts other than cost.

Revaluations should be made sufficiently regularly to ensure that the carrying amount does not differ materially from that which would be determined using fair value at the end of the reporting period, though the standard gives no hint as to how frequently this might be. Management judgment will be needed.

Should the fair value of a revalued intangible asset no longer be determined by reference to an active market, then the asset moves to being measured at the carrying amount of the asset at its last revaluation less any subsequent accumulated amortisation and impairment losses. *Assets and Goodwill* which required

5.4.4.3   Reporting gains and losses on revaluations

Revaluation gain

If an asset's carrying amount is increased as a result of a revaluation, the increase is generally recognised in other comprehensive income and accumulated in equity. The exception that is that to the extent a revaluation gain reverses a revaluation decrease previously recognised in profit, the gain is also recognised in profit. As explained in **5.6.3**, though, the reversal of an impairment loss will never increase the carrying amount of the asset above the amount that would have been determined (net of amortisation) had no impairment loss been recognised for the asset in prior years.

Drawing an analogy to the requirements for property, plant and equipment, it would seem that once a reversal of an impairment loss is recognised, the amortisation charge for the asset in future periods is adjusted to allocate the asset's revised carrying amount, less its residual value (if any), on a systematic basis over its remaining useful life.

Revaluation loss

The decrease of an asset's carrying amount as a result of a revaluation is recognised in other comprehensive income to the extent of any previously recognised revaluation increase accumulated in equity in respect of that particular asset.

If a revaluation decrease exceeds the accumulated revaluation gains accumulated in equity in respect of that asset, then the excess is recognised in profit or loss. This differs from FRS 11 *Impairment of Fixed Assets and Goodwill* which required all revaluation losses caused by a clear consumption of economic benefits to be recognised in the profit and loss account irrespective of whether previous valuation gains had been recognised on an asset (and also required revaluation losses not classified as impairments, i.e. those not caused by a clear consumption of benefits, to be recognised in the STRGL rather than affecting profit).

Example 5.13

On 1 January 20X1, an entity acquired a licence for £100,000. It has a useful life of 20 years and a nil residual value. It is amortised on a straight line basis on the opening book amount.

Neither the residual value nor useful life of the asset needs to be revised at any time for the purposes of this example. Taxation has been ignored.

On 31 December 20X1, the licence was revalued upwards to £120,000.

On 31 December 20X2, the licence was not revalued.

On 31 December 20X3, the licence was revalued downwards to £80,000.

On 31 December 20X4, the licence was revalued upwards to £110,000.

This will be reflected as follows:

Date	NBV at 1 January...	Additions	Amortisation	Overall valuation movement in year	NBV at 31 December...	Restriction on valuation uplift	Revaluation movement in income statement	Revaluation movement in OCI
20X1	0	100,000	-5,000	25,000	120,000	0	0	25,000
20X2	120,000		-6,316	0	113,684	0	0	0
20X3	113,684		-6,316	-27,368	80,000	0	-2,368	-25,000
20X4	80,000		-4,706	34,706	110,000	-139	2,229	32,477

If the £27,368 impairment had not been recognised in the year ended 31 December 20X3, the opening NBV at 1 January 20X4 would have been £82,368 (instead of £80,000) so amortisation in the year ended 31 December 20X4 would have been £4,845 (i.e. (£82,368 over 17 years) and not £4,706. The £139 difference must therefore reduce the credit taken to the profit and loss on the valuation uplift in the year ended 31 December 20X4. The result is that the credit to OCI (and revaluation reserve) of £32,477 is the same as if the impairment had not incurred (i.e. £110,000 − (£82,368-£4,845)).

	Year ended 31 December 20X1	Year ended 31 December 20X2	Year ended 31 December 20X3	Year ended 31 December 20X4
Income statement				
Amortisation	5,000	6,316	6,316	4,706
Impairment/(reversal)			2,368	-2,229
OCI				
Revaluation	25,000	0	-25,000	32,477
Balance sheet				

Intangible assets

	Year ended 31 December 20X1	Year ended 31 December 20X2	Year ended 31 December 20X3	Year ended 31 December 20X4
Cost/valuation b/f	0	120,000	120,000	95,000
Additions	100,000			
Revaluation uplift/decrease	20,000	0	-25,00	15,000
Cost/valuation c/f	120,000	120,000	95,000	110,000
Accumulated depreciation b/f	0	0	-6,316	-15,000
Amortisation in year	-5,000	-6,316	-6,316	-4,706
Impairment charge/(reversal)			-2,368	2,229
Reversed on revaluation	5,000			17,477
Accumulated depreciation c/f	0	-6,316	-15,000	0
Net book value	120,000	113,684	80,000	110,000
Revaluation reserve				
At start of year	0	-25,000	-25,000	0
Valuation gain/loss in year	-25,000	0	25,000	-32,477
At end of year	-25,000	-25,000	0	-32,477

5.4.5   Amortisation over useful life

All intangible assets are considered to have a finite useful life under FRS 102. The useful life of an intangible asset that arises from contractual or other legal rights should not exceed the period of the contractual or other legal rights but may be shorter depending on the period over which the entity expects to use the asset.

However, where the contractual or legal rights are for a specified period of time and this can be renewed, then the useful life of the intangible asset will include the renewal period only if there is evidence to support the renewal by the entity without incurring significant costs. 'Evidence to support the renewal' is a somewhat opaque phrase, but might be read as meaning 'evidence to support the entity's intention and ability to renew'.

The useful life of an asset is:

- the period over which an asset is expected to be available for use by an entity; or

- the number of production or similar units expected to be obtained from the asset by an entity.

The useful life of an intangible asset is not the same as its economic life: the economic life is the period during which the asset can produce economic benefits regardless of who enjoys those benefits.

Therefore, if an entity has an asset with an economic life of eight years but it intends to sell the asset after year three then from the reporting entity's point of view, the useful life is three years and a residual value would need to be calculated (which might coincidentally be five-eighths of the opening value, giving the same depreciation charge each year as would have arisen if the entity had planned to use the asset for its whole economic life).

Factors that would be considered in determining an asset's useful life include:

- the expected usage of the asset by the entity;

- typical product life cycles for the asset;

- expected actions by competitors and potential competitors;

- the level of maintenance expenditure required to obtain the expected future economic benefits from the asset and the entity's ability and intention to achieve such a level.

If the entity is unable to make a reliable estimate of the useful life of the intangible asset then the life shall not exceed ten years (18.20).

Example 5.14

An entity acquires a computer program with a three year licence. The entity expects to use this software for only two years until it has developed its own software.

The best estimate of the useful life of the software is two years. The fact that the entity can use the software for three years does not extend its useful life beyond that period over which the entity expects to use the asset. This illustrates the requirement in 18.19 stating that an asset's useful life cannot be longer than any relevant contractual rights, but may be shorter.

5.4.5.1   Amortisation period and method

Amortisation of intangibles works in the same way as depreciation: the depreciable amount of an intangible asset is allocated on a systematic basis over its useful life. The amortisation for each period is then recognised in profit or loss unless a different section of FRS 102 requires capitalisation, e.g. amortisation may in some cases be included in the cost of inventories or property, plant and equipment.

Amortisation only begins when the intangible asset is available for use, i.e. the asset is in its location and condition necessary for intended usage. It ceases when the asset is derecognised.

The selected amortisation method should reflect the pattern in which the entity expects to consume the assets future economic benefits. If the entity is unable to determine this reliably then the straight line method is used.

When assessing 'the pattern in which it expects to consume the asset's future economic benefits' an entity must be mindful that every asset on its statement of financial position represents a bundle of future economic benefits. Those benefits may be direct or indirect. With an intangible asset, the objective is to select an amortisation method which approximates the pattern in which the bundle of economic benefits diminishes over time. There are several methods that can be used to allocate amortisation over the asset's useful life. The three most common are as follows:

- the straight-line method: the asset's depreciable amount is allocated evenly over its useful life. Hence, straight-line amortisation results in a constant amortisation charge over the useful life of the asset and, as stated above, it is the default method;

- the reducing balance method: the annual amortisation charge is a fixed percentage of the opening carrying amount. This results in higher amortisation in earlier years than under the straight-line basis; and

- the unit of production method: the asset's depreciable amount is allocated over its useful life based on the asset's usage, activity or units produced instead of the passage of time.

5.4.5.2 Residual value

It is always assumed that the residual value of an intangible asset is zero unless:

(a) there is a commitment by a third party to purchase the asset at the end of its useful life; or

(b) there is an active market for the asset and:

 (i) residual value can be determined by reference to that market; and

 (ii) it is probable that such a market will exist at the end of the asset's useful life. (18.23)

Residual value is the estimated amount that an entity would currently obtain from disposing of the asset after deducting the estimated costs of disposal, if the asset were already of the age and in the condition expected at the end of its useful life.

Example 5.15

An entity acquires a patent for five years for a product that is expected to be a source of net cash inflows for at least five years.

The patent is amortised over its five year useful life to a nil residual value.

5.4.5.3 Review of amortisation period and amortisation method

Factors such as a change in how an intangible asset is used, technological advancement and changes in market prices may indicate that the residual value or useful life of an intangible asset has changed since the most recent reporting date.

If such indicators are present, an entity shall review its previous estimates and if current expectations differ, amend the residual value, amortisation method or useful life. The entity shall account for the change in residual value, amortisation method or useful life as a change in accounting estimate, in accordance with Section 10 (discussed in **2.4.1**).

5.4.5.4 Recoverability of the carrying amount – impairment losses

Guidance on when an impairment loss should be recognised or reversed is given in Section 27, discussed at **5.6**.

5.4.6   Retirement and disposals

Paragraph 18.26 states that:

An entity shall derecognise an intangible asset, and shall recognise a gain or loss in profit or loss:

(a)   on disposal; or

(b)   when no future economic benefits are expected from its use or disposal.

5.4.7   Presentation and disclosure

Under Section 4 *Statement of Financial Position*, an entity which is not a bank or insurance company (and which does not adapt the formats as set out in **section 3** of this guide) must present its intangible assets in accordance with the *Large and Medium-sized Companies and Groups (Accounts and Reports) Regulations* 2008 (SI 2008/410), Sch. 1. This requires 'Intangible assets' to be presented on the face of the statement of financial position with the notes giving an analysis of the following sub-headings:

- concessions, patents, licences, trademarks, and similar rights and assets;
- development costs;
- goodwill;
- payments on account.

The disclosure requirements for intangible fixed assets are governed by para. 51 of Sch. 1 to the *Large and Medium-sized Companies and Groups (Accounts and Reports) Regulations* 2008 (SI 2008/410). These requirements are identical to those for tangible fixed assets.

The requirements in FRS 102 refer to disclosures for each 'class' of intangible assets. A class is a grouping of assets of a similar nature and use in an entity's operations such as:

(a)   brand names;

(b)   mastheads and publishing titles;

(c)   computer software;

(d)   licences and franchises;

(e)   copyrights, patents and other industrial property rights, services and operating rights;

(f)   recipes, formulas, models, designs and prototypes; and

(g) intangible assets under development.

Under paragraph 18.27, an entity must give several disclosures for each class of intangible assets. These are listed below together with a reference to the equivalent Companies Act disclosure requirement, where appropriate:

(a) the useful lives or the amortisation rates used and the reasons for choosing those periods;

(b) the amortisation methods used;

(c) the gross carrying amount [see also SI 2008/410, Sch. 1, para. 51(1)(a) and 51(2)] and any accumulated amortisation (aggregated with accumulated impairment losses) at the beginning and end of the reporting period [see also SI 2008/410, Sch. 1, para. 51(2) and 51(3)];

(d) the line item(s) in the statement of comprehensive income (or in the income statement, if presented) in which any amortisation of intangible assets is included; and

(e) a reconciliation of the carrying amount at the beginning and end of the reporting period showing separately:

   (i)   additions, indicating separately those from internal development and those acquired separately [see also SI 2008/410, Sch. 1, para. 51(1)(b)(ii)];

   (ii)   disposals [see also SI 2008/410, Sch. 1, para. 51(1)(b)(iii)];

   (iii) acquisitions through business combinations;

   (iv) amortisation [see also SI 2008/410, Sch. 1, para. 51(2) and 51(3)];

   (v)   revaluations [see also SI 2008/410, Sch. 1, para. 51(1)(b)(i)];

   (vi) impairment losses recognised or reversed in profit or loss in accordance with Section 27 *Impairment of Assets* [see also SI 2008/410, Sch. 1, para. 51(2) and 51(3)];

   (vii) other changes [see also SI 2008/410, Sch. 1, para. 51(1)(b)(iv) which refers to any transfers to this category].

This reconciliation does not need to be presented for prior periods.

An entity should also disclose (18.28):

(a) a description, the carrying amount and remaining amortisation period of any individual intangible asset that is material to the entity's financial statements;

(b) for intangible assets acquired by way of a grant and initially recognised at fair value:

   (i)   the fair value initially recognised for these assets; and

173

(ii)   their carrying amounts.

(c)   the existence and carrying amounts of intangible assets to which the entity has restricted title or that are pledged as security for liabilities; and

(d)   the amount of contractual commitments for the acquisition of intangible assets.

Then, paragraph 18.29 requires that:

'An entity shall disclose the aggregate amount of research and development expenditure recognised as an expense during the period (i.e. the amount of expenditure incurred internally on research and development that has not been capitalised as an intangible asset or as part of the cost of another asset that meets the recognition criteria in this FRS).'

For any intangible assets accounted for at a revalued amount, an entity should disclose the items below (the equivalent Companies Act disclosure requirement is also referred to where appropriate):

(a)   the effective date of the revaluation [see also SI 2008/410, Sch. 1, para. 52(a) which requires disclosure of the years (so far as they are known to the directors) in which the assets were severally valued and those several values];

(b)   whether an independent valuer was involved;

(c)   the methods and significant assumptions applied in estimating the assets' fair values; and

(d)   for each revalued class of intangible assets, the carrying amount that would have been recognised had the assets been carried under the cost model.

In addition to the above requirements from Section 18, in the case of assets that have been valued during the financial year, SI 2008/410, Sch. 1, para. 53(b) requires disclosure of the names of the persons who valued them or particulars of their qualifications for doing so and (whichever is stated) the bases of valuation used by them.

Where a company has applied one of the alternative accounting rules to any intangible fixed asset, the notes must disclose the years in which the assets were separately valued (so far as the directors know these) and also the separate values. If any assets are valued during the financial year in question, the notes must also disclose the valuers' names or particulars of their qualifications and the basis of valuation used by them. [SI 2008/410, Sch. 1, para. 52].

Under Section 4, *Statement of Financial Position*, an entity which is a bank must present its intangible assets in accordance with Sch. 2 to the *Large and Medium-sized Companies and Groups (Accounts and Reports) Regulations* 2008 (SI 2008/410), and an insurance company must present its intangible assets in accordance with Sch. 3 to that SI. The disclosure and presentation requirements under these Schedules are very similar to those stipulated in Sch. 1 and described above.

5.4.7.1 Disclosures for small entities applying FRS 102 Section 1A

Small entities applying section 1A have disclosure requirements in parallel with those for property, plant and equipment: in other words, a movements table is required, and information about valuations, though less than is required for non-small entities. There is no requirement for small entities to disclose the amount of research and development costs recognised as an expense in the period.

5.4.8 Transition

Under paragraph 35.10(c) and (d), an entity may elect to measure the deemed cost of an intangible asset which meets the recognition criteria and the criteria for revaluation at the date of transition to FRS 102 at either:

- its fair value at the date of transition; or

- a previous GAAP revaluation at, or before, the date of transition to FRS 102.

In addition, paragraph 35.10(n) allows a first-time adopter to elect to measure the carrying amount of development costs deferred in accordance with SSAP 13 *Accounting for research and development* at the date of transition to FRS 102 as its deemed cost at that date.

Both of these transition exemptions should be easy to implement when calculating transition adjustments.

5.5 Other non-current assets

There are two other areas in the standard where guidance is given on assets that are long-term in nature but outside the scope of Section 17 or Section 18. Here we briefly describe the prescribed accounting for heritage assets and for extractive activities.

> **Application to micro-entities:** FRS 105 contains a section on specialised activities (Section 27), but this only deals with agriculture. Heritage assets and extractive activities are highly unlikely to be relevant to micro-entities. In rare cases where they are relevant the micro-entity should design an appropriate accounting policy in line with Section 8 of FRS 105 and the pervasive principles in Section 2.

5.5.1   Heritage assets

Heritage assets are defined in the Glossary as:

> 'Tangible and intangible assets with historic, artistic, scientific, technological, geophysical, or environmental qualities that are held and maintained principally for their contribution to knowledge and culture.'

Examples might include oil paintings hung on board room walls, historical properties, and so on.

As seen at **5.2** and **5.4**, the standard accounting for a tangible or intangible asset is initial capitalisation at cost, followed by systematic depreciation and, if chosen, periodic revaluations. Such assets are then regularly reviewed for impairment (**5.6**).

The guidance in paragraphs 34.51–34.54 does not require anything radically different, continuing to point entities to using the cost model or the revaluation model, but adding an important additional exemption: if information is not available on the cost of the asset (usually because it was purchased a long time ago) then the asset is not brought on to the balance sheet at all, and instead is simply disclosed in the notes to the accounts. This prevents entities from having to undergo an arduous and costly valuation exercise on transition.

Section 34 also includes specific disclosure requirements for heritage assets (note that these do not apply to heritage assets that are used in an entity's day to day business, such as 'historic buildings used for teaching by education establishments', although paragraph 34.50 points out that the additional disclosures may nonetheless be informative for users.

The requirements are surprisingly detailed, which may be an acknowledgement of an expectation that many entities holding this type of assets will claim the 'cannot determine cost' exemption, meaning that without a formal set of disclosure requirements, users of their accounts could be unaware of, or at least ill-informed about, the assets' existence and value. Paragraph 34.55, in full, states:

An entity should disclose the following for all heritage assets it holds:

(a) an indication of the nature and scale of heritage assets held by the entity;

(b) the policy for the acquisition, preservation, management and disposal of heritage assets (including a description of the records maintained by the entity of its collection of heritage assets and information on the extent to which access to the assets is permitted);

(c) the accounting policies adopted for heritage assets, including details of the measurement bases used;

(d) for heritage assets that have not been recognised in the statement of financial position, the notes to the financial statements shall:

(i)   explain the reasons why;

(ii) describe the significance and nature of those assets; and

(iii) disclose information that is helpful in assessing the value of those heritage assets;

(e) where heritage assets are recognised in the statement of financial position the following disclosure is required:

(i)   the carrying amount of heritage assets at the beginning of the reporting period and the reporting date, including an analysis between classes or groups of heritage assets recognised at cost and those recognised at valuation; and

(ii) where assets are recognised at valuation, sufficient information to assist in understanding the valuation being recognised (date of valuation, method used, whether carried out by external valuer and if so their qualification and any significant limitations on the valuation);

(f) A summary of transactions relating to heritage assets for the reporting period and each of the previous four reporting periods disclosing:

(i)   the cost of acquisitions of heritage assets;

(ii) the value of heritage assets acquired by donations;

(iii) the carrying amount of heritage assets disposed of in the period and proceeds received; and

(iv) any impairment recognised in the period.

The summary shall show separately those transactions included in the statement of financial position and those that are not;

(g) in exceptional circumstances where it is impracticable to obtain a valuation of heritage assets acquired by donation, the reason shall be stated.

Disclosures can be aggregated for groups or classes of heritage assets, provided this does not obscure significant information.

Paragraph 34.56 then adds an exemption relating to 34.55(f), allowing comparatives on the transaction summary to be presented for just one previous period where it is impracticable to establish the relevant information for all four previous periods.

Small entities are subject to no specific disclosures about heritage assets, but would need to consider whether disclosure is necessary to give a true and fair view if such assets were held.

5.5.2   Extractive activities

While in IFRS, extractive activities ('the exploration for and/or evaluation of mineral resources') merit a dedicated standard, IFRS 6, they are a highly specialist activity so the decision was taken to afford them only a small part of Section 34. Those expecting to find guidance here, though, will be disappointed, as its main gist (in paragraph 34.11) is to refer entities engaging in extractive activities to IFRS 6, with the proviso that references within that standard to other IFRS standards should be read as referring to the relevant section in FRS 102. The only exception is the reference to IFRS 8 (requiring that a cash generating unit or group of cash generating units is no larger than an operating segment) which should be read as referring to an operating segment as defined in the glossary (since there is no section in FRS 102 on operating segments).

Summarising IFRS 6 is out of the scope of this publication, but it permits a very broad range of options for the capitalisation of costs relating to extractive activities, and allows considerable flexibility on areas such as the assessment of impairment.

This part of Section 34 also includes a transition exemption, separate from all others in Section 35, allowing that:

On first-time adoption of this FRS if it is not practical to apply a particular requirement of paragraph 18 of IFRS 6 to previous comparative amounts an entity shall disclose that fact.

Paragraph 18 of IFRS 6, for completeness, refers to the requirement to perform an impairment review of exploration and evaluation assets when facts and circumstances suggest that their carrying amount may not be recoverable. So the transition exemption appears to be saying that there is no need to review the transition date balances or those on the comparative balance sheet if this is not practical. This is more generous than the treatment for 'normal' tangible and intangible assets.

It should be noted that this is only relevant for exploration-stage companies. Those that have moved into production will need to look to Sections 17 and 18 as appropriate.

Again, small entities are not subject to any specific disclosure requirements here.

5.6   Impairment

5.6.1   Scope and definitions

Section 27 *Impairment of Assets* prescribes the accounting treatment for the impairment of non-financial assets other than those dealt with in another section of FRS 102 or that are within the scope of FRS 103, *Insurance Contracts*.

The equivalent standard in IFRS is IAS 36.

Essentially an impairment loss occurs when the carrying amount of an asset exceeds its recoverable amount. Various disclosures are required in respect of any impairment recognised in the income statement.

Section 27 applies to all assets that have been impaired except the following:

(a)   assets arising from construction contracts (dealt with in Section 23 *Revenue*);

(b)   deferred tax assets (dealt with in Section 29 *Income Tax*);

(c)   assets arising from employee benefits (dealt with in Section 28 *Employee Benefits*);

(d)   financial assets within the scope of Section 11 *Basic Financial Instruments* or Section 12 *Other Financial Instruments Issues*;

(e)   investment property measured at fair value (dealt with in Section 16 *Investment Property*); and

(f)   biological assets related to agricultural activity measured at fair value less estimated costs to sell (dealt with in Section 34 *Specialised Activities*).

Section 27 does not apply to the impairment of deferred acquisition costs and intangible assets that arise from contracts covered by FRS 103 *Insurance Contracts*.

Typical assets that Section 27 will apply to are therefore items of plant, property and equipment, intangible assets, inventory and investments in subsidiaries, joint ventures and associates not held at fair value.

Application to micro-entities: The requirements for impairment are largely consistent with those in FRS 102. If it is necessary to allocate goodwill arising on a trade and asset acquisition to CGUs, FRS 105 refers preparers to Section 27 of FRS 102 for further guidance.

5.6.2 Impairment of inventories

Inventories merit special treatment because they are usually short-term assets, and have one (relatively predictable) expected cash flow, since the only purpose of holding them is to sell them.

At each reporting date, an entity determines whether its inventories have been impaired, by comparing the carrying amount of each item of inventory with its selling price less costs to complete and sell. If inventory is impaired, the carrying amount of the inventory is written down to its selling price less costs to complete and sell, with an impairment recognised in profit or loss.

It is important to note that the comparison of the carrying value is made to the selling price less costs to complete and sell *as at the balance sheet date*. If selling prices have moved after the year end this is not necessarily indicative of the sales price at the year end, as an external factor could have arisen after the year end and influenced later selling prices. For example, a competitor may have announced a new product after the year end which made the entity's own product obsolete. However, the impairment had not occurred at the year end as it only arose after that date.

If the entity is unable to determine the selling price less costs to complete and sell for inventories on an item by item basis, it is acceptable to group items of inventory relating to the same product line that have similar purposes or end uses and are produced and marketed in the same geographical area for the purpose of assessing impairment.

Should there be an increase in selling price less costs to complete and sell (for instance where the circumstances that caused the impairment no longer exist), the impairment loss previously recognised is reversed (the reversal is limited to the amount of the original loss) so that the new carrying amount is the lower of the cost and the revised selling price less costs to complete and sell.

5.6.3   *Impairment of assets other than inventories*

For assets other than inventories, if the asset's recoverable amount is less than its carrying amount then the carrying amount of the asset is written down to that recoverable amount.

The impairment loss is recognised immediately in profit or loss, unless the asset is carried at a revalued amount. An impairment loss of a revalued asset is treated as a revaluation decrease in accordance with the relevant section (e.g. Section 17, *Property, Plant and Equipment* or Section 18, *Intangible Assets Other than Goodwill*.)

Example 5.16

At 31 December 2019 an entity has catering equipment that was acquired for a cost of £25,000 on which accumulated depreciation of £15,000 has been recognised (including depreciation of £5,000 for year ended 31 December 2019). The catering equipment has an estimated useful life of five years and a residual value of £nil. The asset is depreciated using the straight-line method, and is tested for impairment at 31 December 2019.

The recoverable amount for the asset at 31 December 2019 is determined to be £9,000. The assessment of the equipment's useful life, depreciation method and residual value are unaffected by the impairment.

The impairment of the catering equipment is recorded as follows:

Dr Profit or loss (loss on impairment)	£1,000
Cr Accumulated impairment loss (equipment)	£1,000

The £1,000 charge is calculated as the difference between the £10,000 NBV at the reporting date, and the £9,000 recoverable amount.

5.6.3.1   *Indicators of impairment*

Entities must, at each reporting date, review their assets for indicators of impairment. Note that this is a preliminary step, and is not the same as performing an impairment review.

If there are no indicators of impairment, then no further work is needed. If, however, there are any such indicators, a formal impairment review is necessary.

The following internal and external indications should be considered when an entity assesses if an asset has been impaired (summarised from 27.9):

External sources of information:

(a) During the period the asset's market value declines significantly more than would be expected.

(b) There are significant changes that could affect the asset's value such as new technology being introduced which could make the asset redundant or there are changes in legal requirements that would make using the asset in the future either impossible or uneconomic.

(c) Market interest rates or other market rates of return on investments have increased during the period with a potentially material effect on the discount rate to be applied when calculating an asset's fair value less costs to sell or value in use.

(d) The carrying amount of the entity's net assets is more than the estimated fair value of the entity as a whole.

Internal sources of information:

(a) Evidence is available that would suggest the asset has become obsolete or damaged.

(b) There have been, or are expected to be, significant changes within the entity that would suggest the asset would not be used in the future or may be sold or used for another purpose which could affect the asset's value.

(c) Internal reporting information suggests economic performance, e.g. in terms of operating results and cash flows, is or will be inferior to what was expected.

The list of impairment indicators above must not be seen as an exhaustive list. Even where there is an indicator of impairment, meaning a review is performed, but the result is that there is no impairment charge, the very existence of the indicator is telling. It might, for instance, suggest that the entity should review the remaining useful life of an asset or, alternatively, its depreciation or amortisation rates or methods or the asset's residual value in accordance with Section 17 or Section 18.

Example 5.17

Entity Q owns a specialised machine for shrink-wrapping cucumbers. The machine is held at depreciated cost.

In 2017, when the machine has four years of useful life remaining, legislation is announced with effect from 2019 requiring that cucumbers will be sold unpackaged.

Q performs an impairment review and concludes that the carrying value is still supported (based on a high value in use) but also takes the decision to revise the machine's remaining useful life to two years (the time before the new legislation will render it obsolete) and its residual value to zero. This means that the depreciation charge will be higher in 2018 and 2019 than it would otherwise have been.

5.6.3.2   Measuring recoverable amount

If the recoverable amount of an individual asset cannot be estimated, then instead an estimate is made of the recoverable amount of the cash-generating unit to which the asset belongs. This technique will need to be used where individual assets do not generate cash flows by themselves. A cash-generating unit is 'the smallest identifiable group of assets that generates cash inflows that are largely independent of the cash flows from other assets or groups of assets'.

Example 5.18

Entity B makes biscuits and has a factory full of plant. Its wrapping machinery generates no distinct cash flows, because it simply performs the end function in the many steps of producing biscuits ready to sell. So when testing for impairment, the asset has to be considered within its whole production line as a CGU.

Entity C, on the other hand, has a similar set-up but also has a distinct revenue stream from packing goods for others. One of its wrapping machines is used solely for contract packing, and this asset can be assessed for impairment individually, unlike C's other wrapping machines which only give rise to cash inflows as part of a larger CGU.

The standard does not give detailed guidance on determining cash-generating units or what constitutes largely independent cash inflows. However, it would be expected that factors such as the presence of vertical or horizontal integration of the business, the actual businesses concerned, the nature of product lines and individual geographical locations or regional areas would all be relevant. In addition, the process that management follows in deciding whether to continue using or to dispose of a particular asset or an operation would be a useful indicator. In the absence of requirements and guidance in the standard, entities could also make use of the permission in paragraph 10.5 to look to full IFRS, and refer to IAS 36 *Impairment of Assets*.

The recoverable amount of an asset or a cash-generating unit is the higher of its fair value less costs to sell and its value in use. However, it is not always necessary to ascertain both of these amounts, because if either of these amounts are higher than the asset's carrying amount, the asset is not impaired, so no further work is needed.

If the entity expects that the value in use will be lower or not materially higher than fair value less costs to sell, then it need not calculate value in use: instead the fair value less costs to sell can be used as the asset or cash-generating unit's recoverable amount. This situation could arise when an asset or cash-generating unit is expected to be disposed of (so has little value in use because the period of further use will be short).

5.6.3.3   Fair value less costs to sell

Fair value less costs to sell is 'the amount that would be received from the sale of an asset or a cash-generating unit at an arm's length transaction between knowledgeable, willing parties less the costs of disposal' (27.14). Prices would be likely to be different where the transacting parties are related (i.e. not an arm's length transaction) as either a discount or a premium might well be given on the sale price (depending on the nature of the relationship).

The best evidence of fair value less costs to sell is therefore a price in a binding sale agreement in an arm's length transaction or a market price in an active market, i.e. one in which willing buyers and sellers can normally be found at any time, the items traded are homogeneous and prices are available to the public.

Where neither of these amounts is available, fair value less costs to sell is based on the best information available to reflect the amount that the entity could obtain from the disposal in an arm's length transaction after deducting disposal costs. Such a figure would need to be estimated with reference to the outcomes of recent transactions for similar assets within the same industry and possibly within similar geographic locations.

Consideration should also be given to the effect on the fair value less costs to sell of any restrictions imposed on the asset as this could either increase the costs of disposal (by way of additional costs to remove the restriction to allow its sale) or reduce the fair value of that asset, if the restrictions will be transferred with the asset. An example might be a commercial property that has usage restrictions imposed by the local planning department. Anything that reduces a buyer's options is also likely to reduce the size of the pool of potential buyers, which may depress the sale price as there is less competition.

5.6.3.4   Value in use

The value in use of an asset is the present value of the future cash flows that are expected to arise from that asset.

To undertake a present value calculation, these steps are followed:

Step 1 – identify whether the asset can be tested individually for impairment or whether it needs to be tested as part of a cash generating-unit. (This would also apply when assessing the asset's fair value less costs to sell.)

Step 2 – estimate the future cash inflows and outflows that will arise from the asset's or cash-generating unit's continued use of the asset and from its ultimate disposal.

Step 3 – determine an appropriate discount rate.

Step 4 – apply the discount rate to the cash flows to derive value in use.

Paragraph 27.16 requires that the calculation of value in use reflect:

'(a) an estimate of the future cash flows the entity expects to derive from the asset;

(b) expectations about possible variations in the amount or timing those future cash flows;

(c) the time value of money, represented by the current market risk-free rate of interest;

(d) the price for bearing uncertainty inherent in the asset; and

(e) other factors, such as illiquidity, that market participants would reflect in pricing future cash flows the entity expects to derive from the asset.'

When estimating future cash flows, it is not permissible to include any cash flows relating to financing activities or income tax receipts and payments, but paragraph 27.17 dictates that the estimate must include:

'(a) projections of cash inflows from the continuing use of the asset;

(b) projections of cash outflows that are necessarily incurred to generate the cash inflows from continuing use of the asset (including outflows to prepare the asset for use) and can be directly attributed or allocated on a reasonable and consistent basis, to the asset;

(c) net cash flows, if any, expected to be received (or paid) for the disposal of the asset at the end of its useful life in an arm's length transaction between knowledgeable, willing parties.'

An obvious starting point for making the necessary estimates is recent financial budgets or forecasts. These can be used to estimate cash flows over the period presented and also beyond that by extrapolating the projections using a steady or declining growth rate (unless an increasing rate can be justified). It is hard to envisage a good justification for using an increasing growth rate, and a preparer choosing to do so should expect challenge from its auditor, and may be encouraged to give explanatory information in its accounts.

It should be noted that future cash flows are estimated for the asset in its current condition. This means that expected cash flows arising from a future restructuring to which the entity is not yet committed (and for which no provision has therefore been made) or from improving or enhancing the asset's performance are not included. This ensures that the cash flows used in the present value calculation are the ones associated with the asset in its condition as at the balance sheet date.

Example 5.19

Entity V is assessing a major piece of plant for impairment after a key product that the plant was used for was threatened by a low-priced competitor. V has been researching modifications to the plant which will, when implemented, significantly reduce the unit production cost, restoring the product to profitability even at the sales price now needed to be competitive.

In performing the value in use calculation, the planned improvement expenditure must be ignored, along with the expected resulting cost savings. This may mean an impairment charge is recognised even where there is a well-progressed plan for improving the assets' ability to generate value.

5.6.3.5   Discount rate

The discount rate used in the present value calculation is a pre-tax rate which reflects the current market assessments of the time value of money and the risks specific to the asset for which the future cash flow estimates have not been adjusted. In order to avoid double counting, the discount rate does not reflect risks for which the future cash flow estimates have been adjusted.

In practice, it can be hard to establish a perfect discount rate, and many preparers argue that their cost of debt is a reasonable starting point. This may well be the case where borrowings are either specific to the asset in question (e.g. a loan actually secured on an asset) or general (but are not specific to a different asset). It can be worth performing a sensitivity analysis on the rate chosen – e.g. if an entity uses 6% because this is its cost of borrowing or WACC, and this gives a value in use materially higher than the carrying value, then a second calculation can be performed to establish what the discount rate would need to be in order for a problem to arise. If this calculation showed that even a 20% rate would not show an impairment, it gives a level of additional comfort; conversely, if it transpires that a rate of 6.2% would lead to an impairment charge, it behoves management to revisit their chosen rate and to be prepared to explain and defend it.

5.6.3.6   Assets held for service potential

For assets held for their service potential, i.e. those held primarily for use by the entity, a cash flow driven valuation such as value in use may not be appropriate. Instead the standard introduces a specific concept of 'value in use (in respect of assets held for their service potential)'. This is based on the asset's remaining service potential plus the net amount the entity will receive from its disposal and may, in some cases, be taken to be costs avoided by possession of the asset (for instance saved operating lease rentals, through using rather than hiring a fleet of photocopiers). A more suitable measurement model may therefore be depreciated replacement cost although other approaches may be appropriate depending on facts and circumstances.

5.6.3.7   Recognising and measuring an impairment loss for a cash-generating unit

An impairment loss is recognised for a cash-generating unit if, and only if, the recoverable amount of the unit is less than the carrying amount of the unit.

Paragraph 27.21 requires that:

> 'The impairment loss is allocated to reduce the carrying amount of the non-monetary assets of the unit in the following order:
>
> (a)   first, to reduce the carrying amount of any goodwill allocated to the cash-generating unit; and
>
> (b)   then to the other assets of the unit pro rata on the basis of the carrying amount of each asset in the cash-generating unit.'

The application is restricted by the requirement that the carrying amount of an asset in the cash-generating unit is never reduced below the highest of:

(a)   its fair value less costs to sell (if determinable);

(b)   its value in use (if determinable); and

(c)   zero.

Any excess amount of the impairment loss that cannot be allocated to an asset because of the above restriction is allocated to the other assets of the unit pro rata on the basis of the carrying amount of those other assets.

Example 5.20

An entity has a cash-generating unit comprising goodwill, other intangible assets, PPE and inventory with a total carrying amount of £7,000. Management has noted an indicator of impairment so undertook a value in use calculation which showed that the cash-generating unit had a recoverable amount of £3,600. An impairment of £3,400 therefore needs to be recognised. This is firstly taken against the carrying amount of the goodwill in the unit (of £3,000) and then the excess £400 needs to be recorded pro rata against the other assets of the cash-generating unit based on the carrying amount of each asset.

The initial allocation of the impairment charge (in column 4 below) gives a revised carrying value for stock of £450 (impaired from £500) but this is less than the highest of its fair value less costs to sell (of £480), its value in use (of £480) and zero. There is therefore an impairment loss of £30 that cannot be allocated to stock because of this restriction so this needs to be allocated to the other assets of the unit, i.e. other intangibles and PPE, pro rata on the basis of the carrying amount of those other assets.

	Carrying Amount £	Impairment of goodwill £	% of amounts of remaining assets in CGU %	Impairment of other assets £	Initial revised carrying amount £	FV less costs to sell £	Value in use £	Excess impairment £	Re-allocation of excess impairment loss £	% of carrying amounts in initially revised CGU %	Final revised carrying amount £
Goodwill	3,000	-3,000				0					0
Other intangible assets	1,000		25.0	-100	900	800	700	-	-9	28.6	891
PPE	2,500		62.5	-250	2,250	2,100	2,200	-	-21	71.4	2,229
Stock	500		12.5	-50	450	480	480	30	30		480
	7,000	-3,000	100.0	-400	3,600					100.0	3,600
Recoverable amount	3,600			-400							
Impairment to recognise	3,400	-3,000									

5.6.3.8 Additional requirements for impairment of goodwill

Goodwill is not a separable asset so it cannot be sold in its own right nor can it generate cash flows independently from other assets. Its value is therefore only supported in conjunction with an entity's other assets. Consequently, the fair value of goodwill cannot be measured directly and it has to be derived from measuring the fair value of the cash-generating unit(s) of which the goodwill is a part.

When goodwill is acquired in a business combination it is allocated to each of the acquirer's cash-generating units that are expected to benefit from the synergies of the combination, irrespective of whether other assets or liabilities of the acquiree are assigned to those units. The allocation of goodwill therefore requires judgment and, in a large group, goodwill could be allocated to several cash-generating units. The allocation of goodwill to units that do not contain any assets or liabilities of the acquired business may be perplexing to some readers, and will merit careful explanation in the accounts (perhaps the acquired entity had recently sold off some assets but retained the related staff who will add value to other areas of the acquiree, as one example).

If it is impracticable to allocate goodwill to individual cash-generating units or groups of cash-generating units on a non-arbitrary basis, then, paragraph 27.27 requires that:

'For the purposes of goodwill impairment testing, the entity shall determine the recoverable amount of either:

(a) the acquired entity in its entirety, where the goodwill relates to an acquired entity that has not been integrated. In this context, "integrated" means the acquired business has been restructured or dissolved into the reporting entity or other subsidiaries; or

(b) the entire group of entities, excluding any entities that have not been integrated, where the goodwill relates to an entity that has been integrated.'

So on acquisition, goodwill will be separated into tranches: that which relates to entities which have been integrated, and that which does not. To calculate the recoverable amount of the acquired entity or group of entities, the principles above for CGUs need to be applied.

Example 5.20

Entity B acquires 100% of Entity X on 1 January 20X1. B and its new subsidiary X each have only one cash-generating unit; goodwill of £20,000 arises on the acquisition relating to costs that will be saved in entity X's cash-generating unit only.

For the purposes of impairment testing, the £20,000 of goodwill shall be allocated to entity X's cash-generating unit and no goodwill will be allocated to entity B's cash-generating unit.

Where an entity owns less than 100% of a subsidiary, part of the recoverable amount of a cash-generating unit is attributable to the non-controlling interest in goodwill. For the purpose of testing for impairment of a non-wholly-owned cash-generating unit with goodwill, paragraph 27.26 specifies that the following steps should be carried out:

(a)   notionally adjust the carrying amount (say C) of that cash-generating unit by grossing up the carrying amount of goodwill allocated to it so that it includes the goodwill attributable to the non-controlling interest (say G). There is no guidance in FRS 102 as to how this should be done but, unless another systematic basis is more appropriate, it would seem that the recognised goodwill would be increased by a factor of NCI/(100–NCI) (where NCI is the percentage of the entity held outside the group) and then adjusted if, for example, factors indicate that a discount should be applied to the goodwill relating to the non-controlling interest;

(b)   compare this notionally adjusted carrying amount, say N, (which is C + G) with the recoverable amount of the unit (say R) to determine whether the cash-generating unit is impaired. If the recoverable amount is less than the uplifted carrying amount an impairment loss is calculated (of N – R). However, some of this 'loss' relates to the notional goodwill so, in order to calculate the impairment loss to be recognised, the total impairment 'loss' initially calculated is reduced by the amount of goodwill attributable to the non-controlling party. Any impairment loss in excess of G is then recognised firstly against goodwill recognised by parent and then, secondly, the non-monetary assets held on a pro rata basis.

5.6.3.9   Reversal of an impairment loss

An impairment loss recognised for all assets except goodwill, is reversed in a subsequent period if and only if the reasons for the impairment loss (or part of it) have ceased to apply. The July 2015 amendments to FRS 102 changed the requirements so that impairment losses on goodwill are now not reversed – before this, the same rules applied to goodwill as to all other assets.

At each reporting date an entity shall assess whether there is any indication that an impairment loss recognised in prior periods may no longer exist or may have decreased. Indications of this would generally be the opposite of the indicators of impairment set out above. If any such indication exists, the entity needs to assess whether all or part of the prior impairment loss should be reversed. The procedure for making that determination will depend on whether the prior impairment loss on the asset was based on:

(a)   the recoverable amount of that individual asset; or

(b)   the recoverable amount of the cash-generating unit to which the asset belongs.

5.6.3.10   *Reversal where recoverable amount was estimated for an individual impaired asset*

Paragraph 27.30 states that:

'When the original impairment loss was based on the recoverable amount of the individual impaired asset, the following requirements apply:

(a)   The entity shall estimate the recoverable amount of the asset at the current reporting date.

(b)   If the estimated recoverable amount of the asset exceeds its carrying amount, the entity shall increase the carrying amount to recoverable amount, subject to the limitation described in (c) below. That increase is a reversal of an impairment loss, and is recognised immediately in profit or loss unless the asset is carried at revalued amount in accordance with another section of this FRS (e.g. the revaluation model in Section 17). Any reversal of an impairment loss of a revalued asset is treated as a revaluation increase in accordance with the relevant section of this FRS.

(c)   The reversal of an impairment loss shall not increase the carrying amount of the asset above the carrying amount that would have been determined (net of amortisation or depreciation) had no impairment loss been recognised for the asset in prior years.

(d)   After a reversal of an impairment loss is recognised, the entity shall adjust the depreciation (amortisation) charge for the asset in future periods to allocate the asset's revised carrying amount, less its residual value (if any), on a systematic basis over its remaining useful life.'

5.6.3.11   *Reversal where recoverable amount was estimated for a cash-generating unit*

Paragraph 27.31 states that in this case the entity is required to begin by estimating the recoverable amount of the relevant CGU at the current reporting date. If the recoverable amount is higher than the carrying amount, the excess is treated as the reversal of an impairment loss. This is allocated pro-rata to the assets of the unit (excluding goodwill), though a cap applies similar to that for allocating losses in the first place. A reversal allocated to an asset must not take its carrying amount above the lower of:

(a)   its recoverable amount; and

(b)   the carrying amount it would have had, if no impairment had previously been recognised (this calculation includes the effects of the depreciation or amortisation that would have been charged in the time since the impairment).

Where the cap is reached, impairment loss reversals that cannot be allocated to one asset are reallocated among the others.

Reversals of impairment losses are recognised immediately in profit unless they relate to revalued assets, in which case they are dealt with as revaluation increases, e.g. in Section 17.

As would be expected, the final step after allocating the reversal of an impairment loss is to revisit the depreciation or amortisation charges for relevant assets so that their revised carrying amounts (less residual values) will be written off over their remaining lives.

5.6.4   *Presentation and disclosure*

For each of the following classes of assets indicated below, paragraph 27.32 requires disclosure of both the amount of impairment losses and the reversals of those impairment losses that are recognised in profit or loss during the period as well as the line item(s) in the statement of comprehensive income (or in the income statement, if presented) in which those impairment losses are included or reversed:

(a)   inventories;

(b)   property, plant and equipment (including investment property accounted for by the cost method);

(c)   goodwill;

(d)   intangible assets other than goodwill;

(e)   investments in associates; and

(f)   investments in joint ventures.

An entity shall also disclose a description of the events and circumstances that led to the recognition or reversal of the impairment loss.

There are no specific references to disclosures for investments in subsidiaries as these are covered in Section 9.

Statutory Instrument 2008/410, the *Large and Medium-sized Companies and Groups (Accounts and Reports) Regulations* 2008 requires that provisions for diminution in value are made in respect of any fixed asset that has diminished in value if the reduction in its value is expected to be permanent. Where such provisions are not shown in the profit and loss account, para. 19 and 20 of Sch. 1 to SI 2008/410 require that they are disclosed (either separately or in aggregate) in a note to the financial statements. Specific disclosure requirements are also given in para. 51(3) of Sch. 1 to SI 2008/410. These disclosures are:

• the cumulative amount of provisions for depreciation or diminution in value of assets included under that item at the beginning of the financial year and at the balance sheet date;

- the amount of any such provisions made in respect of the financial year;

- the amount of any adjustments made in respect of any such provisions during that year in consequence of the disposal of any assets; and

- the amount of any other adjustments made in respect of any such provisions during that year.

5.6.4.1   *Disclosures for small entities applying FRS 102 Section 1A*

Small entity disclosure requirements in respect of impairments are minimal: they need only disclose provisions for impairments and any reversals of these, if they are not already shown separately in the income statement.

6 Inventories

6.1 Scope of this section

This chapter covers Section 13 of FRS 102 *Inventories*.

It deals with the recognition, measurement, presentation and disclosure of most items treated as inventories under FRS 102. FRS 102 excludes from the scope of Section 13 some specialised inventories.

The comparable standard in IFRS is IAS 2 *Inventories*.

> **Application to micro-entities**: FRS 105 is consistent with the requirements of FRS 102 in this area.

6.1.1 Scope

As noted above, Section 13 of FRS 102 deals with most inventories but there are some types of inventory which are outside its scope.

Section 13 does not apply to:

- work in progress which arises under construction contracts, including any directly related service contracts;
- financial instruments; and
- biological assets related to agricultural activity and agricultural produce at the point of harvest.

Construction contracts give rise to slightly different considerations from those that apply with normal inventories. In particular, the normal requirement applying to inventories that no profit element be included within their carrying value would come up with inappropriate results, and lead to financial statements that arguably would not reflect the activities of the business over the reporting period. As a result, they are dealt with separately and using different principles. The accounting requirements applicable to construction contracts are covered in **10.4.4**.

The second exclusion is unsurprising. Financial instruments (see **7**) are dealt with in Sections 11 and 12 of FRS 102, depending on whether they fall within the definition of basic financial instruments or not.

Biological assets and agricultural produce (see **6.2.9**) are dealt with in Section 34 of FRS 102, together with various other specialised activities. They give rise to issues of cost determination which are very different to those that generally arise with other types of inventory.

There is also a more specific exemption in Paragraph 13.3:

'This section does not apply to the measurement of inventories measured at fair value less costs to sell through profit or loss at each reporting date. Inventories shall not be measured at fair value less costs to sell unless it is a more relevant measure of the entity's performance because the entity operates in an active market where sale can be achieved at published prices, and inventory is a store of readily realisable value.'

This differs from the equivalent paragraph in the IFRS for SMEs, which specifically refers to:

(a)   producers of agricultural and forest products, agricultural produce after harvest, and minerals and mineral products, to the extent that they are measured at fair value less costs to sell through profit or loss; or

(b)   commodity brokers and dealers that measure their inventories at fair value less costs to sell through profit or loss.

However, it is likely that only these types of inventory would meet the revised exception in FRS 102. It should be noted that it would be necessary to apply a true and fair override of company law to account for such items at fair value through profit or loss. This is because inventories are not permitted to be accounted for under the fair value accounting rules. Company law does permit use of the alternative accounting rules, enabling inventories to be carried at current cost, but this is not an accepted treatment under FRS 102.

6.1.2   Definition

FRS 102 provides something that is close to a definition of inventories, which is helpful in determining to which types of asset the requirements of Section 13 apply. The Glossary states:

'... Inventories are **assets**:
(a)   held for sale in the ordinary course of business;
(b)   in the process of production for such sale; or
(c)   in the form of materials or supplies to be consumed in the production process or in the rendering of services.'

This stresses the point that inventories are assets. While this may sound an obvious point, it does present somewhat of a problem for FRS 102. An asset is defined as:

'A resource controlled by the entity as a result of past events and from which future economic benefits are expected to flow to the entity.'

This definition is fairly familiar to most accountants, and in line with that they will have seen in FRS 5. The problem is that FRS 102 has specific rules for inventories which are held for distribution at no or nominal consideration. Yet such items would not fall within a normal reading of the definition of an asset, if the definition of an asset implies that future economic benefits will flow to the entity. This point is made clear in Paragraph 2.16 which goes further in noting that future economic benefits must be sufficiently certain to warrant the recognition of an asset in a statement of financial position, and in Paragraph 2.17 which specifically mentions that future economic benefits must contribute, directly or indirectly, to the flow of cash and cash equivalents to the entity.

It is hard to see how an item which will be given away for nothing, and therefore will not generate any cash inflows, could fall within the definition of an asset. This problem could be resolved by taking a much broader reading of what is meant by future economic benefit, particularly insofar as it relates to public benefit entities, which are the most likely to have items they will provide free of charge or at nominal charge. This is clearly tempting, and seems consistent with the intention behind FRS 102, but would involve specifically ignoring Paragraph 2.17. The danger with this approach is that it allows considerable override of the specific requirements included in FRS 102. In effect, what is the limit to the extent to which apparently clear requirements in FRS 102 can be ignored. Does this mean that entities which are not public benefit entities could also ignore the requirement for cash or cash equivalent inflows? This cannot have been the FRC's intention, but the standard is drafted in a way that gives rise to precisely problems of this type.

It should be noted that inventories are assets, but that no mention is made of whether they are tangible. This means that some inventories may be intangible. This may apply to service providers, although see below, as this is not as important as it might appear. It does mean that where an entity trades in assets that are themselves intangible, such as quotas or licences, then those items may be inventories.

Most situations are fairly clear, and there are normally few questions about whether items are inventory or not. One area where problems might arise is in relation to property where the dividing line between inventory (properties acquired or developed for short-term sale) and investment property might not always be clear, particularly where a site might be developed for a dual purpose. The definition of an investment property also allows for sale, albeit usually over a longer period.

6.2   Accounting requirements

6.2.1   *Basic measurement principles*

'An entity shall measure inventories at the lower of cost and estimated selling price less costs to complete and sell.'

This applies only where an entity has not measured inventories at fair value less costs to sell.

There is an exception to this rule. The exception is primarily likely to affect public benefit entities, although this is not a specified requirement of the standard.

Under Paragraph 13.4A:

'Inventories held for distribution at no or nominal consideration shall be measured at cost adjusted, when applicable, for any loss of service potential.'

Such inventories are defined in the Glossary to the standard as:

'**Assets** that are:
(a)   held for distribution at no or nominal consideration in the ordinary course of operations;
(b)   in the process of production for distribution at no or nominal consideration in the ordinary course of operations; or
(c)   in the form of material or supplies to be consumed in the production process or in the rendering of services at no or nominal consideration.'

(This definition makes use of the defined term **'Assets'**. The problems arising from this are noted above.)

Such a special rule for items held for distribution is not unusual, and is for example included in International Public Sector Accounting Standards (IPSAS).

However, it is clear that the definition, while probably aimed primarily at public benefit entities, can apply to commercial entities as well. When dealing with intangible assets, Section 18 of FRS 102 provides a list of items that must be treated as giving rise to an expense and not treated as intangible assets. Included in the list in paragraph 18.8C are:

'[Expenditure on] advertising and promotional activities (unless it meets the definition of inventories held for distribution at no or nominal consideration (see paragraph 13.4A)).'

This clearly implies that some items which might otherwise be treated as advertising and promotion costs could qualify as inventories, and be recorded in accordance with the special measurement rules.

6.2.2 Measuring cost

The basic rule for determination of the costs of inventories, included in paragraph 13.5, is consistent with the requirements set out in SI 2008/410:

An entity shall include in the cost of inventories all costs of purchase, costs of conversion and other costs incurred in bringing the inventories to their present location and condition.

FRS 102 then goes on to deal with the various elements that may be included in the determination of such cost.

There is a slightly different rule, set out in paragraph 13.6, where the inventory has been acquired as a result of a non-exchange transaction:

'Where inventories are acquired through a **non-exchange transaction**, their cost shall be measured at their **fair value** as at the date of acquisition. For **public benefit entities** and entities within a **public benefit entity group**, this requirement only applies to inventories that are recognised as a result of the requirements for incoming resources from non-exchange transactions as prescribed in Section 34 *Specialised Activities*.'

A non-exchange transaction is itself defined as:

'A transaction whereby an entity receives value from another entity without directly giving approximately equal value in exchange, or gives value to another entity without directly receiving approximately equal value in exchange.'

While only part of the rule makes specific reference to public benefit entities, it is unlikely that such transactions will be common for entities that are aiming to make a profit. In the unusual case where a commercial enterprise were to receive inventories as a result of a non-exchange transaction, and if this were not a form of funding provided by equity holders, then this would appear to give rise to an immediate profit.

The requirements that apply to public benefit entities that are party to non-exchange transactions are covered in **17.2.1** of this guide.

6.2.3 Purchase cost

Where inventories are purchased, rather than made, there are usually few accounting problems that arise in the determination of their cost. The simplest case is where goods are bought and then sold on in the same condition, that is, without any work having been done on them. This might be a typical situation for a wholesaler or retailer. The cost of stock will then simply be the cost of the goods that were purchased for resale, plus the costs (if any) of bringing the goods to the site at which they are to be sold. The other costs that are incurred may be the costs of selling, marketing and distributing the goods, which would not be included in the cost of stock.

The basic rule is set out in paragraph 13.6:

> 'The costs of purchase of inventories comprise the purchase price, import duties and other taxes (other than those subsequently recoverable by the entity from the taxing authorities), and transport, handling and other costs directly attributable to the acquisition of finished goods, materials and services. Trade discounts, rebates and other similar items are deducted in determining the costs of purchase.'

FRS 102 also includes a specific prohibition on the inclusion of 'abnormal amounts of wasted materials, labour or other production costs' in the cost of inventories. This should cover nearly all situations where costs are incurred that might not be considered to be in the normal course of business.

6.2.4   Deferred settlement

FRS 102 also deals specifically with the treatment of deferred settlement terms. In some cases inventories might fall within the definition of a qualifying asset. However, the definition of a qualifying asset is one that ' ... necessarily takes a substantial period of time to get ready for its intended use or sale'. While this may apply to some inventories, it will not apply to inventories that are purchases in the same, or virtually the same, state as that in which they are to be sold or used. The definition of a qualifying asset makes the exclusion entirely clear by an explicit statement that assets 'that are ready for their intended use or sale when acquired are not qualifying assets'. The treatment of qualifying assets and associated borrowing costs is covered in **13.2** of this guide.

In all other cases where inventories are acquired on substantially deferred payment terms, the cost of inventory should reflect the cost that would be incurred were the inventory to be acquired for cash, or on normal credit terms. The difference between this and the nominal amount that is payable is then treated as an interest expense over the period of the financing. The principle behind this is quite logical, and consistent with other areas of accounting such as the requirements that are applied to financial instruments. For example, an alternative method of acquiring inventory might be to pay immediately (or on normal credit terms) but then obtain a loan to cover the payment required. In substance, there is really no difference between this and paying a higher amount to the provider with a significant deferral of payment. Judgment will be needed in applying this requirement. For example, companies will need to determine what is considered a normal credit period and will apply this requirement only where the period is in excess of this. Where there is no obtainable cash price, (or price on normal credit terms) companies will need to determine the interest rate that should be applied to the actual price to be paid to arrive at the present value of that price.

Example 6.1

A company acquires inventory for a contracted price of £100,000. This amount is payable in 18 months. The price on normal credit terms of one month would be £91,500.

The inventory will be stated at its cost of £91,500, and the liability will be initially recorded at the same amount. The liability will then be increased, using the effective interest method, to grow to the required balance of £100,000, eighteen months after the initial recording.

A company acquires inventory for a contracted price of £100,000. The amount is payable in two years. The inventory was made to order, so no equivalent price on normal credit terms is available. The company estimates its borrowing rate for trade finance to be 6% per annum.

The cost of the inventory will be £100,000 discounted for two years at 6%, so:

$$100,000 \times \frac{1}{(1+0.06)^2} = 89,000$$

The inventory will be stated at its cost of £89,000, and the liability will be initially recorded at the same amount. The liability will then be increased, using the effective interest method (which in this case we know involves a discount rate of 6%) to grow to the required balance of £100,000, two years after the initial recording.

6.2.5   Costs of conversion

As noted above, determining costs where inventories are acquired in the same state in which they will be sold or used normally gives rise to few accounting problems.

More complex issues normally arise where inventory is produced or modified. In these situations we need to take account of the costs of production.

The basic rules are set out in paragraph 13.8:

> 'The costs of conversion of inventories include costs directly related to the units of production, such as direct labour. They also include a systematic allocation of fixed and variable production overheads that are incurred in converting materials into finished goods. Fixed production overheads are those indirect costs of production that remain relatively constant regardless of the volume of production, such as depreciation and maintenance of factory buildings and equipment, and the cost of factory management and administration. Variable production overheads are those indirect costs of production that vary directly, or nearly directly, with the volume of production, such as indirect materials and indirect labour.'

In practice this means that the determination of the cost of inventories for a company that produces or modifies items usually involves two parts:

- the calculation of the direct costs attributable to each unit; and
- the calculation of the proportion of the total overhead costs that can be attributed to each unit.

The identification of the direct costs is normally the simpler part of the exercise. Direct costs would include items such as:

- costs of the basic raw materials;
- costs of additional raw materials and components;
- costs of direct labour; and
- production overheads that vary directly (or as the standard mentions 'nearly directly') with the level of production (described as variable production overheads).

The more complex part of the exercise is the determination of the fixed overheads and their allocation to units of production.

This stage can itself be broken down into two:

- the determination of the total overheads that are to be allocated; and
- the method of allocation to be used.

FRS 102 provides little guidance on the specific costs that can be included as production overheads. However, exactly the same can be said of IAS 2 and most other accounting standards that deal with inventories or stocks. The key test is whether the cost is related to production, rather than any other activity of the entity, and this requires the application of a reasonable approach in determining whether a cost is related to production or otherwise.

There is one specific area where FRS 102 makes it clear that production overheads may be included in the cost of inventory. Paragraph 13.8A states:

'Production overheads include the costs for obligations (recognised and measured in accordance with Section 21 Provisions and Contingencies) for dismantling, removing and restoring a site on which an item of **property, plant and equipment** is located that are incurred during the **reporting period** as a consequence of having used that item of property, plant and equipment to produce inventory during that period.'

FRS 102 also provides, at paragraph 13.13, a list of specific items that should not be included within the costs of inventory, although this is provided in the form of a list of examples rather than a list which is intended to be comprehensive.

Examples of costs excluded from the cost of inventories and recognised as expenses in the period in which they are incurred are:

(a) abnormal amounts of wasted materials, labour or other production costs;

(b) storage costs, unless those costs are necessary during the production process before a further production stage;

(c) administrative overheads that do not contribute to bringing inventories to their present location and condition; and

(d) selling costs.

Items (b) to (d) on this list should be interpreted as a clarification of the basic requirement that costs of conversion should include only production overheads, rather than as separate requirements.

These requirements are consistent with the requirement in SI 2008/410 that the costs of stock should not include distribution costs, a phrase which should be interpreted widely in this context.

Apart from determining the total costs that can be allocated to inventories there is also the second issue of the basis on which the cost should be allocated. The basic rule in FRS 102, set out at paragraph 13.9, is that this should be based on the normal level of production:

'An entity shall allocate fixed production overheads to the costs of conversion on the basis of the normal capacity of the production facilities. Normal capacity is the production expected to be achieved on average over a number of periods or seasons under normal circumstances, taking into account the loss of capacity resulting from planned maintenance. The actual level of production may be used if it approximates normal capacity. The amount of fixed overhead allocated to each unit of production is not increased as a consequence of low production or idle plant. Unallocated overheads are recognised as an expense in the period in which they are incurred. In periods of abnormally high production, the amount of fixed overhead allocated to each unit of production is decreased so that inventories are not measured above cost. Variable production overheads are allocated to each unit of production on the basis of the actual use of the production facilities.'

This can be supplemented by the requirement in paragraph 13.13(a) quoted above in relation to any abnormal costs that may have been incurred.

While this guidance is useful, it lacks some of the detail that was previously included in an Appendix to SSAP 9. There is no reason to believe that the FRC intended any substantive change in this area; SSAP 9 noted that in determining a normal level of activity this would reflect:

(a)   the volume of production which the production facilities are intended by their designers and by management to produce under the working conditions (e.g. single or double shift) prevailing during the year;

(b)   the budgeted level of activity for the year under review and for the ensuing year;

(c)   the level of activity achieved both in the year under review and in previous years.

The normal level of activity is not intended to be a theoretical maximum which could not realistically be achieved. So, for example, in determining the costs to be allocated to unit of production accounts can be taken of normal levels of wastage at reasonable efficiency.

FRS 102 is specific when dealing with abnormally high production, with the guidance requiring that costs allocated are reduced in these circumstances. This avoids the possible issue where the production overheads allocated in aggregate to inventories exceed the actual level of production overheads.

6.2.6   Other costs

In order to avoid the omission of any costs that are genuinely relevant, FRS 102 at paragraph 13.11 also includes a catch-all requirement to deal with any other costs that may be incurred:

An entity shall include other costs in the cost of inventories only to the extent that they are incurred in bringing the inventories to their present location and condition.

While this is drafted in a way that looks permissive, it is intended to avoid entities including other costs in the cost of inventories, unless they are clearly able to demonstrate that such costs meet the basic requirements that apply to all costs that should be included in the cost of inventories. This paragraph is effectively a restatement of the description of the measurement rule generally applicable to inventories as a requirement.

There is a specific example in paragraph 13.12 of an additional cost that can be included in the inventories of an entity holding commodities and which also make use of complex financial instruments for the purposes of hedging:

'Paragraph 12.19(b) provides that, in some circumstances, the change in the fair value of the **hedging instrument** in a hedge of fixed interest rate risk or commodity price risk of a commodity held adjusts the carrying amount of the commodity.'

This is a specific application of the general rule in Section 12 that allows entities which have met the hedge accounting criteria applicable to the commodity price risk of a commodity that they hold, or on which they have firm commitment, to include changes in the fair value of the hedging instrument in the carrying amount of the commodity. Hedge accounting is covered in **7.4.7** of this guide.

6.2.7   Joint products and by-products

A further problem that can arise is where a single production process does not give rise to a single product, but to two or more. Whilst the normal methods of allocating costs to the production process, as set out above, can be applied to the production process as a whole this still leaves the issue of the allocation of costs between the individual products.

FRS 102 distinguishes between joint products and by-products. Unfortunately, neither term is defined. Normally, the distinction between the two is based on materiality. Two or more outputs of a process are considered to be joint products if they are all considered to be material. Where at least one of the outputs has a value that is immaterial to the total value then it is considered a by-product, and the other product is considered the main product. FRS 102 reflects this, although the description used in paragraph 13.10 is not entirely helpful:

> '... Most by-products, by their nature, are immaterial ... '

It is the 'most' that causes the problem. This raises the possibility that there might be cases where a by-product is material. In the absence of a definition it is unclear what such cases might be. (As noted below, when stating the accounting policy that must be applied for by-products FRS 102 also notes that this method means that the carrying amount and cost of the main product are not materially different; this can be correct only if by-products are not material.)

In all cases, there will need to be a judgment as to whether products which result from the same production process are joint products or by-products. Despite the lack of clarity in the standard, this will continue to be based on a judgment concerning materiality.

If products are considered to be joint products then FRS 102 does not prescribe a single mandatory method for cost allocation, but paragraph13.10 does require that:

> ' ... When the costs of raw materials or conversion of each product are not separately identifiable, an entity shall allocate them between the products on a rational and consistent basis ... '

It then provides, as an example of such a method, allocation by reference to the relative sales value of each product, whether this is based on the value at the date at which the products become separable or at the stage they are completed.

With by-products, paragraph 13.10 is more prescriptive:

> '... the entity shall measure them at selling price less costs to complete and sell and deduct this amount from the cost of the main product. As a result, the carrying amount of the main product is not materially different from its cost.'

Example 6.2

Joint Products

A company's production process has two outputs, A and B. For a particular production run the costs incurred are £500,000. There are no further costs prior to sale for either product.

The outputs are 10,000 kg of A and 4,000 kg of B.

The sales value of a kilo of A and B are £40 and £55 respectively. Costs are allocated on the basis of sales value.

The total sales value is £620,000, being £400,000 for A and £220,000 for B.

The costs will be allocated pro-rata so the cost of A will be 400,000/620,000 × 500,000, being £322,581, or £32.26 per kilo. The cost of B will be 220,000/620,000 × 500,000, being £177,419 or £44.35 per kilo.

One of the obvious implications of this approach is that the margin on both of the products will necessarily be the same.

By-products

The facts are the same as above, except that the sales value of A is £60 per kg and the sales value of B is £3 per kg. B is considered a by-product.

In this case the amounts are not pro-rated. Instead, first the sales value of B is determined. This is 4,000 × 3 or £12,000.

This is then deducted from the total costs incurred, being £500,000 – £12,000 or £488,000.

The cost is then allocated to each unit of A, being £488,000/10,000 or £48.80.

In this case, no profit or loss arises on the sale of the by-product, and all profits are recorded in respect of sales of the main product.

In some cases a process might give rise to a combination of joint products and by-products.

In such situations, the by-products would be dealt with first, to give rise to the total costs that need to be allocated to the joint products. Then the total costs remaining would be allocated to the joint products on the same basis as in the example above (or some other rational and consistent basis).

6.2.8   Service providers

FRS 102 also deals with inventories that are held by service providers, in addition to any physical inventories that service providers may have such as consumables. Paragraph 13.14 stresses that the basic principles are exactly the same as for any other type of inventory, other than that there may be differences in the balance of the types of cost that may have been incurred.

To the extent that service providers have inventories, they measure them at the costs of their production. These costs consist primarily of the labour and other costs of personnel directly engaged in providing the service, including supervisory personnel, and attributable overheads. Labour and other costs relating to sales and general administrative personnel are not included but are recognised as expenses in the period in which they are incurred. The cost of inventories of a service provider does not include profit margins or non-attributable overheads that are often factored into prices charged by service providers.

In practice, the occurrence of inventory held by service providers is likely to be fairly infrequent. While this might be thought to refer to much of the normal work in progress that service providers may have, it is worth pointing out that most such work in progress will fall within the areas covered by Section 23, on revenue recognition, when dealing with the rendering of services. In some cases this may arrive at the same result, particularly if, for example, it is not possible to come up with a reasonable estimate of the profit that may be made on a contract (although a loss is not expected) so the contract is in fact carried at its cost. However, this determination can only be made after the principles of Section 23 have been applied. Revenue recognition for service contracts is dealt with in **10.4.2** of this guide.

6.2.9   Agriculture

FRS 102 also has special rules for the determination of the cost of agricultural produce that has been harvested from biological assets. Paragraph 13.15 states:

> 'Section 34 requires that inventories comprising agricultural produce that an entity has harvested from its biological assets should be measured on initial recognition, at the point of harvest, at either their fair value less estimated costs to sell or the lower of cost and estimated selling price less costs to complete and sell. This becomes the cost of the inventories at that date for application of this section.'

This rule is secondary, and simply seeks to clarify the cost that should be used for any further activities which the entity may undertake in relation to harvested biological products.

The additional guidance in Section 34 covers both recognition and measurement. First, in paragraph 34.3:

> 'An entity shall recognise a biological asset or an item of agricultural produce when, and only when:
>
> (a)   The entity controls the asset as a result of past events;
>
> (b)   It is probable that future economic benefits associated with the asset will flow to the entity; and
>
> (c)   The fair value or cost of the asset can be measured reliably.'

This is uncontroversial, and summarises standard requirements for any asset.

For a biological asset ('a living animal or plant', such as a sheep for slaughter, a dairy cow, or a potato plant), or agricultural produce ('the harvested product of the entity's biological assets', such as meat from a slaughtered animal, milk from a cow, or potatoes), there are two options for measurement the fair value model, or the cost model.

Under the fair value model, a biological asset is measured at fair value on initial recognition, and remeasured at each reporting date, with changes in the fair value less costs to sell reported within profit. When agricultural produce is then harvested from these assets, this produce is measured at fair value less costs to sell at the point of harvest, and this measurement becomes its cost at the point when the produce moves into the scope of Section 13. As an exception to this model, and distinct from the application of the cost model, is a special provision in paragraph 34.6A stating that if the fair value of a biological asset cannot be measured reliably, the cost model is applied to that asset until such time as the fair value can once more be reliably measured. Since this is an exception within the fair value model, the relevant disclosures are included with those relating to this model (see **3** for a list of required disclosures).

Under the cost model, biological assets are measured at cost less accumulated depreciation and any accumulated impairment losses. Agricultural produce from these assets is then, at the point of harvest, measured at either fair value less costs to sell, or at the lower of cost and estimated selling price less costs to complete and sell. Again, this becomes the cost for the purposes of accounting for this produce under Section 13.

6.2.10   Cost assumptions

Apart from determining the costs to be allocated to inventories as a whole, entities also need to determine the costs relevant to those items which are in fact held at any particular point in time, and most relevantly at the end of a reporting period. This is a slightly different issue, since it reflects how costs may change over a period.

FRS 102 reflects the fact that, in those cases where it can be used, the actual cost of the specific unit is the best method of costing. As paragraph 13.17 states:

> 'An entity shall measure the cost of inventories of items that are not ordinarily interchangeable and goods or services produced and segregated for specific projects by using specific identification of their individual costs.'

Since the cost of each inventory item is the actual cost that has been incurred in its production, it does not involve the inevitable assumptions and averaging procedures that affect all of the alternative methods. The unit cost is a practical method of determining cost for wholesalers and retailers who deal in low-volume high-value goods, where there are virtually no problems with the allocation of overheads. In such cases, the only costs to be included will normally be those of purchase and transportation inwards. There may be cases where other costs need to be included, for example, costs of necessary storage, but this would be unusual.

In manufacturing or producing companies, as well as many wholesaler and retailers dealing with bulk items, this method often cannot be used, since the costs of maintaining the necessary information would be out of all proportion to the benefit, and the items are likely to be interchangeable. Where there is a high volume of production it may be impossible, or at least impractical, to determine the individual costs to be attributed to each unit of production.

In other cases, a cost flow assumption needs to be applied. The allowed methods are set out in paragraph 13.18:

> 'An entity shall measure the cost of inventories, other than those dealt with in paragraph 13.17, by using the first-in, first-out (FIFO) or weighted average cost formula. An entity shall use the same cost formula for all inventories having a similar nature and use to the entity. For inventories with a different nature or use, different cost formulas may be justified. The last-in, first-out method (LIFO) is not permitted by this FRS.'

Under FIFO the underlying assumption is that the goods which are produced or purchased first are sold first. The items that remain as inventory at the end of the period are those which have been produced or purchased at the most recent levels of cost. For most businesses this is a realistic assumption and should reflect the physical flow of goods from production or purchase to sale. The performance statements should provide a very close approximation to the actual costs incurred in the production or purchase of each unit of sales.

Under the weighted average cost method, the total costs of production (or total costs of purchase) over a period are divided equally between all of the goods produced (or purchased) in that period. A period for the purposes of the use of this method need not be the same as the company's accounting period. For example, while a company may produce financial statements on an annual basis it may use a monthly basis for the calculation of the cost of its stock; however, the company will then have to make an additional assumption about the flow of units between the months. In theory, the weighted average cost method may mean that the performance statements do not quite reflect the actual costs incurred in the production or purchase of each actual unit of sales. Nonetheless, in practice the differences that will result are unlikely to be large unless there is a very high rate of inflation, or if the period used for averaging purposes is excessively long. It is for this reason that weighted average cost has often been used in the UK and that FRS 102 allows its use.

FRS 102 also includes the requirements for consistency for similar types of inventory, whilst allowing different methods where different types of inventory are held.

Having stated which methods can be used for determining the costs of stock it is perhaps a little odd that FRS 102 then goes on to state a single method which is specially prohibited, LIFO.

6.2.11   Other methods of determining cost

While the basic methods of determining cost of units are all reasonable in principle, they can be immensely complex to apply in practice for entities which, for example, produce a very wide range of separate products or which stock a very large number of goods.

In practice, various methods have been developed over the years to enable the cost of items to be determined in such cases. FRS 102 allows the use of alternative methods, subject to the crucial criterion that the methods must approximate to actual cost. There is clearly a slight logical problem with this. In order to determine the extent to which such methods come up with similar results to actual cost we would need to know what actual cost is. If we know what actual cost is then there is no need to use a method of approximation. However, in practice what this means is that the bases used must be regularly monitored, and updated whenever necessary, so that it is reasonable to assume that there is no material difference between the results that have been obtained and the amounts that would be obtained if the normal methods were to be applied. Paragraph 13.16 mentions three particular methods that may be used, although it also opens the possibility of others so long as they are likely to arrive at similar results:

> 'An entity may use techniques such as the standard cost method, the retail method or most recent purchase price for measuring the cost of inventories if the result approximates cost. Standard costs take into account normal levels of materials and supplies, labour, efficiency and capacity utilisation. They are regularly reviewed and, if necessary, revised in the light of current conditions. The retail method measures cost by reducing the sales value of the inventory by the appropriate percentage gross margin.'

The standard cost method involves the creation of cost standards for the quantity and price of inputs of labour, materials and overheads to be used in the manufacture of products. Cost standards could be loosely described as detailed budgets. The standards are normally set prior to production, by reference to product specifications, expected levels of cost, operating volumes and efficiency. The standards are then altered as the experience of actual production grows. The alteration of a standard does not necessarily imply that the original standard was incorrectly calculated. Standards are often altered, particularly with a relatively new product, to reflect the increased experience and expertise of the staff involved in production. As experience grows, the rate of production will often increase, and methods of using materials and other resources more efficiently may be found.

At the end of a period the profit actually earned can be analysed by reference to the 'standard' profit on the volume of sales achieved and variances from this standard amount. For example, if staff are paid at a higher wage rate than was originally expected, then there will be an adverse variance arising from the labour cost attributable to production. Similarly, if fewer materials are used for the actual volume of production than would have been expected from the standard, then this will give rise to a favourable variance.

The use of standard costs for valuing stock is acceptable under FRS 102, but as noted above when standard costs are used they must be reviewed frequently to ensure that they continue to bear a reasonable relationship to actual cost. If variances are large and frequent then this indicates that it is the standards themselves that do not accurately reflect the costs involved in production, and so need to be revised. Standard costing, where properly operated, has the advantage that it applies the requirement that costs carried forward be based on the normal level and manner of operating, and not on unusual circumstances.

The retail method allows the cost of stock to be determined by applying the estimated profit margin to the selling price. This is on the condition that it is possible to demonstrate that this provides a reasonable approximation of the actual cost and that margins are reviewed very regularly to ensure that they continue to accord with the actual levels that are being achieved. This method is used by some organisations with fixed margins, usually because it is the only practical method they can adopt. It is described as the 'retail method', as its most common use is by retailers.

The most recent purchase price is, in effect, a very simple basis which avoids the need to track the records that are required in order to use a cost flow assumption, such as weighted average or FIFO. It works best where prices are not very volatile so that any inaccuracy introduced is likely to be very small. It also works well where the value of the inventory affected is unlikely to be material whatever method is used.

FRS 102 makes no mention of the base stock method. It is, however, mentioned specifically in the Statutory Instruments made under the *Companies Act* 2006. This involves stating a fixed quantity of inventory at a fixed price. This level is deemed to be the minimum amount of inventory needed by an entity to continue to operate and is, in effect, treated as though it were a long term asset. All amounts over and above this base level must be valued using a separate cost flow assumption. The method is acceptable under the *Companies Act* 2006 if:

- the amount involved comprises 'raw materials and consumables' rather than any other category;

- the overall value is not material in assessing the state of affairs of the company; and

- the quantity, value and composition are not subject to material variation.

This method is likely to be acceptable under FRS 102 since company law only allows the use of the base stock method where the amount involved is 'not material to assessing the company's state of affairs' so it cannot conflict with FRS 102, since the standard does not apply to immaterial items.

6.2.12 Impairment

Paragraph 13.19 states:

'Paragraphs 27.2 to 27.4 require an entity to assess at the end of each reporting period whether any inventories are impaired, ie the carrying amount is not fully recoverable (eg because of damage, obsolescence or declining selling prices). If an item (or group of items) of inventory is impaired, those paragraphs require the entity to measure the inventory at its selling price less costs to complete and sell, and to recognise an **impairment loss**. Those paragraphs also require a reversal of a prior impairment in some circumstances.'

This ties the impairment of inventories into the general requirement for impairment, hence the references to Section 27. It also avoids the term 'net realisable value' that is familiar to UK accountants. But 'selling price less costs to complete and sell' is basically a definition of net realisable value, as this term used to be applied.

It should be noted that no reference is made to the value at which goods could be sold in their current state. Selling price less costs to complete and sell is not the same as the current market price of the goods involved, in their current state. It is fairly common for companies to hold stocks of goods that they could not sell for the price they paid. Some of these goods may actually have no commercial value in their present state. However, this is not relevant if those goods are to be included in other finished items which will realise at least the total costs that have been incurred in their production.

A simple example of this situation is work in progress. Where an asset is partially completed it may have no or negligible value in its present state. It will no longer have any value as raw materials, since they may no longer be in a usable form. At the same time the good is incomplete and cannot be sold. The only value the item may have is its scrap value, if any. This does not mean that the total costs incurred in producing all work in progress should be written off, as long as the items currently under production will be completed.

It is acceptable for a company to start by using a pre-determined formula to perform the initial calculation of the value of its inventory. For example, the formula might take account of the age of the inventory held, the scrap value of the goods involved, the current level of trading and previous experience. Nonetheless, the simple application of any formula will never be sufficient to provide the final result. In all cases, consideration must be given to any special factors that may affect the value of the items. Each item, or group of items, must be considered individually.

While the impairment section makes no mention of it, the normal rule cannot be applied to inventories held for distribution at no or nominal consideration, since this would always result in a full or partial write down. The basic measurement rule refers to a loss of service potential, which should be used as an alternative basis. Loss of service potential is likely to involve consideration of qualitative factors as well as quantitative. This seems appropriate when dealing with the sorts of situation where this issue arises, but of course ultimately a quantified measure of impairment is required. Disclosure of how this has been determined will be crucial.

6.2.13 Expense recognition

FRS 102 contains specific rules on when expenses in relation to inventories must be recognised. Apart from impairment, which is dealt with separately, the basic rules can be summarised as:

- for inventories that are sold, the carrying amount is recognised as an expense when the revenue is recognised; and

- for inventories that are distributed at no or nominal consideration, the carrying amount is recognised as an expenses when those inventories are distributed.

FRS 102 also deals with the issue of inventories that are used in connection with other assets, for example where materials are used to construct an item that qualifies as property, plant and equipment. In this case, the treatment above is modified. The cost of the inventory is added to the cost of the other asset. After this point the accounting treatment will be governed by the rules that normally apply to assets in that category, and the rules on inventory are no longer of any relevance.

So, for example, if a company were to use inventories in the construction of an item of equipment then there would be no expense recorded initially, and the inventory cost would be added to the costs of the plant. An expense would then be recorded in the future as the asset is depreciated, or impaired if relevant, or in the calculation of any subsequent profit or loss on disposal.

6.3 Disclosure

FRS 102 contains, in paragraph 13.22, a short list of disclosures:

'An entity shall disclose the following:

(a) the accounting policies adopted in measuring inventories, including the cost formula used;

(b) the total carrying amount of inventories and the carrying amount in classifications appropriate to the entity;

(c) [not used]

(d) impairment losses recognised or reversed in profit or loss in accordance with section 27; and

(e) the total carrying amount of inventories pledged as security for liabilities.'

Examples might include:

(1) Inventories are valued at the lower of cost and selling price less costs to complete and sell. Cost is defined as the actual cost of raw materials and an appropriate proportion of labour and overheads in the case of work in progress and finished goods. Provision is made for obsolete and slow-moving items and for unrealised profits on items of inter-company manufacture.

(2) Stocks have been valued at the lower of cost and selling price less costs to complete and sell. The cost of the stock is calculated by deducting the appropriate departmental gross profit margin from the normal selling price.

(3) Finished products are valued at the lower of purchase price, manufacturing cost and selling price less costs to complete and sell. Distribution and administration expenses are not included in the valuation. Work in progress is valued at the cost of materials plus manufacturing labour and overheads. Raw materials are valued at purchase price but are reduced to net replacement cost if this is lower. Account is always taken of any slow-moving or obsolete items.

The total carrying amount of inventories, in appropriate categories, is also not a new requirement. For companies, it will also be necessary to consider the formats included in the appropriate Schedule to SI 2008/410. Under Sch. 1, the formats include the following sub-categories for stock:

(1) raw materials and consumables;

(2) work in progress;

(3) finished goods and goods for resale;

(4) payments on account.

Whether or not entities have previously disclosed the amount of inventories recognised as an expense in the period will depend on what they do and exactly how they have produced financial statements in the past. Some companies will have done so, if their cost of sales has related solely to the cost of goods sold. For other companies, and entities which are not companies, this may be a new disclosure, although it is one that any accounting system should be able to provide easily.

The requirement to disclose impairment losses (or their reversal) is strictly new, although again this information should be easily available.

The total carrying amount of inventories pledged as security for liabilities is not new, although previously this disclosure has been required as a subset of the requirement to disclose all assets which are pledged as security for liabilities.

Companies will also be required to disclose where there is a material difference between the value of inventories as included in the statement of financial position and their replacement cost (or the most recent actual purchase price or production cost prior to the end of the period). This information should be provided in a note to the financial statements. The directors should determine whether it is the replacement cost, latest purchase price or latest production cost that is the most appropriate standard of comparison. Disclosure is not required if the items are stated at their actual cost, that is, a cost flow assumption (such as FIFO or weighted average) has not been used.

Entities choosing the fair value model for biological assets must disclose the following (from paragraph 34.7):

(a) a description of each class of biological asset;

(b) the methods and significant assumptions applied in determining the fair value of each class of biological asset;

(c) a reconciliation of changes in the carrying amount of each class of biological asset between the beginning and the end of the current period. The reconciliation shall include:

    (i)   the gain or loss arising from changes in fair value less cost to sell;

    (ii) increases resulting from purchases;

    (iii) decreases attributable to sales;

    (iv) decreases resulting from harvest;

    (v)   increases resulting from business combinations; and

    (vi) other changes.

This reconciliation need not be presented for prior periods.

In addition, paragraph 34.7A requires that if any individual biological assets are measured at cost by virtue of their fair value not being reliably measurable, this must be explained.

Finally, the method and significant assumptions used in determining the fair value of agricultural produce at the point of harvest must be disclosed, class by class.

For entities using the cost model, the disclosure requirements are set out in paragraph 34.10 for each class of biological asset:

(a) a description of each class of biological asset;

(b) [not used]

(c) the depreciation method used;

(d) the useful lives or the depreciation rates used; and

(e) a reconciliation of changes in the carrying amount of each class of biological asset between the beginning and the end of the current period. The reconciliation shall include:

(i) increases resulting from purchases;

(ii) decreases attributable to sales;

(iii) decreases resulting from harvest;

(iv) increases resulting from business combinations;

(v) impairment losses recognised or reversed in profit or loss in accordance with Section 27 *Impairment of Assets*; and

(vi) other changes.

This reconciliation need not be presented for prior periods.

Similarly to the requirements above for the fair value model, entities using the cost model must also disclose, for agricultural produce measured at fair value less costs to sell, the methods and significant assumptions applied in determining the fair value at the point of harvest, for each class.

6.3.1 Disclosure requirements for small entities

Section 1A does not give any explicit disclosure requirements for small entities in respect of inventories, besides the requirement to disclose any assets pledged as security to liabilities, which applies to all assets. They should continue to bear in mind, though, the overarching requirement to ensure the accounts give a true and fair view, so entities where inventory is significant in value or risk may conclude that notes expanding on the single balance sheet line item may still be helpful.

7 Financial instruments

7.1 Scope of this section

The sections of FRS 102 covered here are:

- Section 22 *Liabilities and Equity* (discussed at **7.2**)
- Section 11 *Basic Financial Instruments* (discussed at **7.3**)
- Section 12 *Other Financial Instruments Issues* (discussed at **7.4**)

FRS 102 (2018) provides further clarification and guidance to Section 11 and 12 than FRS 102 (2015), specifically around classifying debt instruments as basic and small entities recognising directors' loans.

Application to micro-entities: There are no differences with regards to the requirements in Section 17 of FRS 105 around liabilities and equity; these must still be identified and, where necessary, separated.

There are, however, significant differences with regard to the accounting for financial instruments. First, there is no alternative option to revert to IFRS; micro-entities must apply the requirements in Section 9 of FRS 105. There is also no distinction between 'basic' or 'other' financial instruments; this is because fair value accounting is not permitted under FRS 105. Financial instruments are therefore measured at cost or amortised cost. In particular, fixed asset investments are measured at cost less impairment; derivatives are measured at cost, with the transaction price (if any) allocated to profit or loss over the term of the contract; and other financial instruments are accounted for using a simplified version of amortised cost.

For debt instruments, the amortised cost method is similar to that in FRS 102, although transaction costs are dealt with in a simpler manner. If they are immaterial they are expensed to profit or loss immediately; if they are material, they are added to (if an asset) or deducted from (if a liability) the proceeds of the loan and spread over the life of the loan on a straight-line basis (i.e. there is no need to calculate an effective interest rate). The interest rate used is the contractual rate; there is no need to obtain a market rate of interest where loans are not made at a market rate.

Finally, micro-entities do not have the option to apply hedge accounting. However, there is an exception where a transaction is to be settled at a contracted foreign exchange rate, or a related or matching forward contract is taken out against a transaction. In these cases, the contracted rate must be used to translate the transaction rather than the spot rate.

7.1.1   *Option to revert to IFRS*

Sections 11 and 12 are unique within FRS 102 in that preparers have the choice of setting aside these Sections and instead applying either the recognition and measurement requirements of IAS 39 or of IFRS 9. If either of these alternative options is taken, preparers are still required only to apply the less demanding disclosure requirements of Sections 11 and 12. In practice, it seems most companies are opting for the requirements of Sections 11 and 12, but the flexibility is useful for those that previously applied FRS 26 because they will be able to continue with the same accounting but now under the name of IAS 39. It is also helpful for entities with complex or exotic financial instruments and hedging arrangements (particularly those using macro-hedging) who may find IAS 39 or IFRS 9 a better fit for their needs. The detail of the contents of IAS 39 and IFRS 9 is beyond the scope of this guide.

FRS 102 (2018) clarifies that entities adopting IAS 39 recognition and measurement provisions within FRS 102 may continue to apply IAS 39 even after it is withdrawn by the IASB. This option is likely to remain available until either (a) the FRS 102 requirements for the impairment of financial assets are amended to reflect IFRS 9, or (b) the FRC decides not to amend FRS 102 further in relation to IFRS 9. A copy of IAS 39 is retained for reference on the FRC website and is available on Croner-I Tax and Accounting.

7.1.2   *Key definitions*

All of the requirements in Sections 11, 12 and 22 depend upon the definitions of key terms that appear throughout the Sections. These key definitions, taken from the Glossary, are as follows:

A *financial instrument* is a contract that gives rise to a financial asset of one entity and a financial liability or equity instrument of another.

A *financial asset* is any asset that is:

(a) cash;

(b) an equity instrument of another entity;

(c) a contractual right:
  (i)   to receive cash or another financial asset from another entity; or
  (ii) to exchange financial assets or financial liabilities with another entity under conditions that are potentially favourable to the entity; or

(d) a contract that will or may be settled in the entity's own equity instruments and:

(i) under which the entity is or may be obliged to receive a variable number of the entity's own equity instruments; or

(ii) that will or may be settled other than by the exchange of a fixed amount of cash or another financial asset for a fixed number of the entity's own equity instruments.

For this purpose, the entity's own equity instruments do not include instruments that are themselves contracts for the future receipt or delivery of the entity's own equity instruments.

A *financial liability* is any liability that is:

(a) a contractual obligation:

    (i) to deliver cash or another financial asset to another entity; or

    (ii) to exchange financial assets or financial liabilities with another entity under conditions that are potentially unfavourable to the entity; or

(b) a contract that will or may be settled in the entity's own equity instruments and:

    (i) under which the entity is or may be obliged to deliver a variable number of the entity's own equity instruments; or

    (ii) will or may be settled other than by the exchange of a fixed amount of cash or another financial asset for a fixed number of the entity's own equity instruments. For this purpose the entity's own equity instruments do not include instruments that are themselves contracts for the future receipt or delivery of the entity's own equity instruments.

Equity is the residual interest in the assets of the entity after deducting all its liabilities.

These definitions are, it can be seen, worded in a way that is clearly very technically careful but can be a little overwhelming. A one sentence summary is that an entity has a financial liability if it has a contractual obligation to pay out cash or something like cash; it has a financial asset if it has a contractual right to receive cash or something like it.

Typical examples of financial assets and liabilities in a relatively uncomplicated set of accounts might include:

- cash (part (a) in the asset definition);

- trade debtors (receivables) (part (c)(i) in the asset definition);

- trade creditors (payables) (part (a)(i) in the liability definition);

- bank loans payable (part (a)(i) in the liability definition);

- investments in shares or debt of other companies (part (b) in the asset definition);

- forward currency contracts (part (c)(ii) in the asset definition, or (a)(ii) in the liability definition).

The main function of this brief list is to illustrate how broad the definitions are, and therefore how relevant these Sections are to all preparers, not just to those with complex financial affairs.

Common assets and liabilities that are **not** financial instruments include prepayments (which give a right to receive a future service, not to receive cash), tax balances (which are statutory, rather than contractual, obligations) and deferred income (which usually represents an obligation to provide goods or services, rather than to repay cash).

7.1.3 Scope of Sections 11 and 12

Having set out the definitions, though, not all items meeting the definition of a financial asset or financial liability are in the scope of Sections 11 and 12. There are eight categories of exclusion from Section 11 set out in paragraph 11.7, all of which are covered in more detail in a different section of the standard:

(1) investments in subsidiaries, associates and joint ventures (Sections 9, 14 and 15);

(2) instruments meeting the definition of own equity (Sections 22 and 26);

(3) leases (Section 20) – though there are some aspects of lease contracts that may still give rise to an asset or liability in the scope of Sections 11 or 12, discussed where relevant below;

(4) rights and obligations under employee benefit plans (Section 28);

(5) share based payment arrangements (Section 26) except those explicitly scoped into Section 12;

(6) insurance contracts issued and reinsurance contracts held (paragraph 1.6 requires the application of FRS 103 to insurance contracts (including reinsurance contracts) that the entity issues and reinsurance contracts that it holds);

(7) instruments issued by the entity with a discretionary participation feature (also scoped into FRS 103 by paragraph 1.6); and

(8) reimbursement assets and financial guarantee contracts (Section 21).

The scope of Section 12 is slightly different. It repeats the above, excludes any instruments in the scope of Section 11 and adds two further exclusions:

- contracts for contingent consideration in a business combination (the exemption is for the acquirer, not the vendor);

- any forward contract between an acquirer and a selling shareholder to buy or sell an acquiree that will result in a business combination at a future acquisition date.

These final exclusions appear primarily to be aimed at ensuring that business combinations are always cleanly accounted for by the acquirer using only the guidance in Section 19. Otherwise, in a situation where a buyer and seller had reached contractual agreement on a business combination but had not yet completed the deal, then as at the acquirer's year end the acquirer would have to recognise a financial liability and there would then be complications in washing the transaction out post year end when the purchase was completed.

Neither of these two additional exclusions is necessary in Section 11, because such arrangements would never be classified as basic instruments based on the definitions, so would be out of scope already.

Finally Section 12 adds into its scope 'contracts to buy or sell non-financial items if the contract can be settled net in cash or another financial instrument, or by exchanging financial instruments as if the contracts were financial instruments'. If a company effectively speculates on a commodity price by contracting to buy a commodity at a fixed price, but with an agreement that it is not obliged to take delivery of the commodity but instead can net settle (i.e. pay or receive only the differential between the spot price and the contracted price at the date of completion) then this derivative is scoped into Section 12, and will be accounted for at fair value.

The only time this would not be the case is when what is commonly known as the 'own use exemption' applies: this covers 'contracts that were entered into and continue to be held for the purpose of the receipt or delivery of a non-financial item in accordance with the entity's expected purchase, sale or usage requirements'. As an example, this would apply where a company used oil as one of its raw materials, and had entered into a forward purchase contract based on its expected needs for the period but with a net settlement option there just as a backstop, the contract would not be accounted for under Section 12, but instead as a normal purchase contract.

7.1.4   Scope of Section 22

Section 22 *Liabilities and Equity* covers instruments that the preparer issues, and sets out how to establish whether these are classified as equity or as a financial liability. For those classified as equity, it goes on to specify how they should be accounted for; those classified as financial liabilities are in the scope of Section 11 or Section 12, depending on their exact nature. The scope exclusions in paragraph 22.2 are exactly the same as those in Section 11, except that Section 11 scopes out an entity's own equity instruments issued, and these clearly need to be covered by Section 22.

7.2   Liabilities and equity

7.2.1   The distinction between liabilities and equity

Interestingly, Section 22 talks about distinguishing equity from liabilities, rather than from financial liabilities. Accordingly, it calls not upon the Glossary's definition of a financial liability but instead on the more general definition of a liability:

> 'A liability is a present obligation of the entity arising from past events, the settlement of which is expected to result in an outflow from the entity of resources embodying economic benefits.'

Section 22 also expands upon the definition of equity, to be clearer on the breadth of the scope of the term:

> 'Equity includes investments by the owners of the entity, plus additions to those investments earned through profitable operations and retained for use in the entity's operations, minus reductions to owners' investments as a result of unprofitable operations and distributions to owners.'

So, the section has a wider reach than might be expected: it does not simply aim to tell companies what to do when they issue instruments which are legally shares but have some equity-style characteristics, but instead looks more broadly at the accounting for amounts received by an entity which are not income but where there may be associated obligations or expectations. Having said this, the bulk of the guidance in the section is, as might be expected, focused on the question, familiar already to those who have wrestled with FRS 25, of whether funding and financing instruments will end up on the top or bottom half of the balance sheet.

7.2.1.1   Principles of classification

The basic principle from Section 11 is that an instrument is a financial liability if it gives the issuer an unconditional obligation to pay out cash or another financial asset.

Example 7.1

A simple example is a share that is redeemable in the future at the holder's option. Even if the exercise of this option is considered unlikely, it is still an obligation that the issuer cannot do anything to avoid, and as such the share would be classified as a liability (assuming it does not also have equity features – compound instruments are discussed further below).

Preference shares that have a fixed coupon will also be classified as financial liabilities (again assuming there is not also an equity component) because, again, from the issuer's point of view there is no way to avoid paying out the cash. This also applies to shares which give the holder a right to a predetermined share of profits, because there is a contractual obligation here even if it is possible that in practice there may be years when the company will have nothing to pay out because it has made a loss.

As with all financial instruments guidance, though, there are layers of refinement and exception, and paragraph 22.3A sets out a very specific treatment where the issuer has an unconditional obligation to settle on the occurrence of events that are beyond the issuer's and the holder's control. Usually such a contingent settlement provision will mean the issuer must classify the instrument as a financial liability, on the grounds that it cannot do anything to prevent the contingent event from happening. There are three situations, though, in which the instrument would be classified as equity despite the contingent settlement provision.

- The element of the contract relating to the cash outflow is 'not genuine', perhaps through its being based on such far-fetched conditions that no one would have any realistic expectation that they would take place.

- The only event triggering settlement of the obligation is the liquidation of the issuer.

- The instrument meets the 'residual interest' conditions discussed further below.

Example 7.2

A company issues 'A' shares which have the same terms for dividends and return of capital as its ordinary shares. The only difference is that in the event of a Martian invasion of London, the company must redeem the shares in full.

Prima facie the shares have a liability component because the company cannot through any actions of its own avoid redeeming them. However, there is no genuine possibility of a cash outflow, so the shares would be classified purely as equity.

225

7.2.1.2   Residual interest in net assets

There is a very lengthy expansion of the concept of an equity instrument, which represents the residual interest in an entity's net assets. As well as the special treatment described above for some instruments with contingent settlement provisions, there are broadly two categories of instrument described in paragraph 22.4 which would appear to meet the definition of a financial liability but will nonetheless be classified as equity because of this 'residual interest' feature:

(a)   Instruments that are subordinate to all other classes and give a right to a share of net assets only on liquidation. An example might be where all the classes of an entity's shares have a right to receive a fixed coupon and a share of assets on liquidation, and all classes but one give holders the right to demand redemption. The one class which is not redeemable is subordinate to all of the others so although it has the financial liability feature of a contractual obligation to pay cash, in the shape of the fixed coupon, it will nonetheless be classified as equity. This condition means that it will be relatively unusual to see a company with all of its shares classified as liabilities, because the 'bottom rung' instruments will often meet this condition to be classified as equity.

(b)   Certain puttable instruments.

A puttable instrument is one that includes a condition allowing the holder to sell it back to the issuer for cash or is automatically redeemed 'on the occurrence of an uncertain future event or the death or retirement of the instrument holder'. These would normally be classified as liabilities because of the issuer's unavoidable obligation to pay cash, such as in the example above of a redeemable share. Such an instrument is, however, classified as equity if five strict conditions are met.

(i)   It entitles the holder to a pro rata share of the entity's net assets in the event of the entity's liquidation. The entity's net assets are those assets that remain after deducting all other claims on its assets.

(ii)   The instrument is in the class of instruments that is subordinate to all other classes of instrument.

(iii) All financial instruments in the class of instruments that is subordinate to all other classes of instruments have identical features.

(iv)   Apart from the contractual obligation for the issuer to repurchase or redeem the instrument for cash or another financial asset, the instrument does not include any contractual obligation to deliver cash or another financial asset to another entity, or to exchange financial assets or financial liabilities with another entity under conditions that are potentially unfavourable to the entity, and it is not a contract that will or may be settled in the entity's own equity instruments.

(v)   The total expected cash flows attributable to the instrument over the life of the instrument are based substantially on the profit or loss, the change in the recognised net assets or the change in the fair value of the recognised and unrecognised net assets of the entity over the life of the instrument (excluding any effects of the instrument). (Paragraph 22.4)

Again, effectively these conditions are there to ensure that an instrument at the very bottom of the pile will be classified as equity even if it has typical liability features. Condition (iii) helps to ensure that there are no misinterpretations of a 'class' of instrument, since it is made clear that in order to qualify as a 'class' all the instruments in a group must have exactly the same features. Condition (iv) rules out instruments that come with obligations in addition to redemption, such as a redeemable share that also carries a fixed coupon, and also excludes shares that give the holder the option to have them redeemed or converted into ordinary shares (since then they would be a contract that 'may be settled in the entity's own equity instruments').

Condition (v) is more complex, although it is designed to ensure that only a certain relatively simple type of instrument is captured. Examples of features that would cause this test to be failed are:

*   a redemption value linked to a share index or interest rate, meaning an inflation-proofing guarantee of sorts is given to the holder, but the link directly to entity performance is lost;

*   the existence of a premium on redemption that is only triggered if certain external events take place, such as a share index reaching a predetermined threshold, or even a more company-specific condition such as a public listing.

So, a rule of thumb is that the 'unavoidable obligation' test will usually show whether an instrument is a financial liability, and if it is not one, then it is equity – but a follow up check is always necessary to ensure it is not one of the special cases discussed here.

Example 7.3

Company M and company N each have several classes of share in issue, all of which include some kind of redemption rights. For each company, there is one class of shares meeting conditions (i) to (iv) of paragraph 22.4.

For company M, the redemption value of the shares is to be calculated using a formula based on the change in fair value of M's net assets between issue and redemption.

For company N, which hoped at the date of issue that it would list on AIM in the medium term, the redemption value is based on the change in the FTSE AIM All-share index between issue and redemption.

M's lowest class of shares will be classified as equity, because condition (v) is met; N's will be classified as a compound instrument (see **7.2.4**) because condition (v) is not met – the factor determining the redemption amount is not sufficiently linked to the company's performance. This does not prevent classification of part of the instrument as equity, but merely forces recognition of a liability component, too.

7.2.2   Accounting for the issue of shares

Paragraphs 22.7–22.10 cover the basic accounting for the issue of shares classified as equity instruments. They are included in equity on the balance sheet and initially measured at the fair value of the consideration received, which would usually be cash, but may be calculated as a discounted amount if there is a deferred payment element and the time value of money is material.

Guidance is given in two consecutive paragraphs on the treatment of costs associated with issuing shares: Paragraph 22.8 refers to measuring them at the fair value of proceeds 'net of transaction costs' and then paragraph 22.9 explicitly requires that 'transaction costs of an equity transaction [are accounted for] as a deduction from equity,'. In a typically simple situation, the transaction costs will be administrative and legal, and it will be straightforward to determine which are incremental to the transaction, if this is all that has taken place. More complexity arises, though, if, for instance, equity instruments such as warrants are issued at the same time as debt, or if costs are incurred which seem to be incidental to the issue of the shares.

Fortunately the guidance is structured to point preparers to their own relevant legislation in addition to the accounting rules. Paragraph 22.10 states that:

'How the increase in equity arising on the issue of shares or other equity instruments is presented in the statement of financial position is determined by applicable laws. For example, the par value (or other nominal value) of shares and the amount paid in excess of par value may be presented separately.'

For UK preparers, this can be seen to have two effects:

(1)   it lets them apply, without contradiction, the *Companies Act* 2006, s. 610(1), which provides that any amount received over the nominal value of a share must be recognised in the share premium account;

(2)   it also brings in s. 610(2) of the Act, which allows the share premium to be used to write off the expenses of the share issue, including any commission paid relating to it.

Following on from this second point, FRS 102 defines transaction costs, in the Glossary, as:

> '...incremental costs that are directly attributable to the acquisition, issue or disposal of a financial asset or financial liability...An incremental cost is one that would not have been incurred if the entity had not acquired, issued or disposed of the financial instrument...'

Preparers could also look to paragraph AG13 of IAS 39, which states that:

> 'Transaction costs include fees and commissions paid to agents (including employees acting as selling agents), advisers, brokers and dealers, levies by regulatory agencies and securities exchanges, and transfer taxes and duties. Transaction costs do not include debt premiums or discounts, financing costs or internal administrative or holding costs.'

Since the Companies Act does not expand upon 'the expenses of share issue' it seems reasonable to apply the definition here. So, the costs that could be deducted from equity would include legal fees for the share issue but not, for instance, an allocation of the company secretary's salary.

FRS 102 (2018) paragraph 22.8 reads: 'An entity shall measure equity instruments, other than when merger relief or group reconstruction relief under sections 611 to 615 of the Act are applied or those accounted for in accordance with paragraph 22.8A, at the fair value of the cash or other resources received or receivable, net of transaction costs. If payment is deferred and the time value of money is material, the initial measurement shall be on a present value basis'. In other words, this explicitly allows for the provisions in the Act.

Paragraph 22.7 includes a blank sub-paragraph (a) because the original draft of the standard prescribed the accounting when shares had been issued but not yet paid for – but this clashed with the *Large and Medium-sized Companies and Groups (Accounts and Reports) Regulations* 2008, which prescribe a line item either alone or within debtors on the balance sheet for 'called up share capital not paid'. Because there is no guidance in the FRS, UK companies do not face any clash by using the accounts formats from company law. The remainder of paragraph 22.7 should also not give rise to any potential legal problems, requiring only that if proceeds are received before shares are issued, these are included in equity provided that:

- the entity cannot be required to repay them (which would lead to a liability classification); and

- where instruments have been subscribed for but not issued, and no cash has been received, no accounting entries are made.

FRS 102 (2018) introduced a new paragraph 22.8A to clarify that no gain or loss need be recognised when a financial liability is extinguished by issuing equity instruments if this option was in the contractual terms of the original liability, or if it is a transaction between owners in their capacity as owners:

> 'An entity shall not apply paragraph 22.8 to transactions in which a financial liability is extinguished (partially or in full) by the issue of equity instruments if:
>
> (a)   the creditor is also a direct or indirect shareholder and is acting in its capacity as a direct or indirect existing shareholder;
>
> (b)   the creditor and the entity are controlled by the same party or parties before and after the transaction and the substance of the transaction includes an equity distribution by, or contribution to, the entity; or
>
> (c)   the extinguishment is in accordance with the original terms of the financial liability.
>
> In these circumstances there is no gain or loss recognised in profit or loss as the result of such a transaction.'

7.2.3   *Options, rights and warrants*

Paragraph 22.11 briefly directs preparers to apply the principles for accounting for the issue of equity to the sale also of 'options, rights, warrants and similar equity instruments'. The elimination of doubt is always useful, although without this paragraph most readers may well have assumed this to be the case anyway, but care is needed to ensure that this paragraph is not viewed as overriding the scope Section, which is clear that share-based payment arrangements covered by Section 26 are excluded from Section 22. This means that paragraph 22.11 has a narrower reach than it would seem to were it read without context:

- share options issued to employees in return for services are excluded;

- warrants issued in lieu of arrangement fees for debt are likely to be excluded;

- share options issued as payment for goods or services are excluded.

Put another way, the only types of options, rights and warrants which are covered by Section 22 are those where the definition of a share-based payment in Section 26 is not met, in other words where the entity has not received goods or services in exchange for them. This is likely to be a reasonably rare situation, since this type of instrument is usually used as part of a commercial transaction rather than being issued for cash.

7.2.4   Capitalisation or bonus issues of shares and share splits

Paragraph 22.12 gives examples of ways in which the number of shares in issue can change without affecting total equity. There is no accounting guidance, but just a simple requirement that 'an entity shall reclassify amounts within equity as required by applicable laws'.

In a bonus issue, current shareholders all receive new shares in proportion to their existing holdings, so that each retains the same proportion of the company but has more shares, for instance if the company issues one share per ten already held. The company's number of shares in issue has increased, but no proceeds have been received and no accounting entries are needed, aside from accounting for any costs of the bonus issue.

In a share split, a company's existing share capital is divided into multiple shares, either by cancelling all of the old shares and reissuing new ones at some multiple, or by just issuing the appropriate additional number. Again, the holders' relative rights are unchanged, and there is no accounting to do.

The section does not cover the converse situation, of a share consolidation, where the number of shares in issue is reduced (usually by a complete cancellation and reissue) so a holder might now only own one share for each five he previously owned. It is understandable that this is not addressed in a Section devoted to the issue of equity, but it can nonetheless be noted that the common sense approach, of once more making no accounting entries, appears the most reasonable and is consistent with paragraph 22.12.

7.2.5   Compound instruments including convertible debt

7.2.5.1   Identifying a compound instrument

Compound financial instruments are defined in the glossary to the standard as being financial instruments that 'from the issuer's perspective, contain both a liability and an equity element'. The most common example is convertible debt, where the holder pays cash to the issuer and in exchange receives a promise to return the capital, usually a commitment to pay interest either periodically or at the end of the instrument's life, and an option to have the capital settled in shares instead of cash (which might be at the holder's or the issuer's option). The obligation to pay interest and redeem the capital gives the liability element, and the possibility of conversion into shares will often be classified as an equity element, though this depends on the precise conditions.

Example 7.4

(1)   A company issues £100,000 of debt to four investors. The debt has a three year term, and pays interest annually at 6% on the nominal value. At the end of the term, it will be redeemed at its nominal value, or, if the holders wish, at 1 share in the company per £2 of nominal value (so, if it were all converted, 50,000 shares would be issued). This conversion ratio was determined at the point of issue based on an expectation that the shares would have a market value of around £2 at the end of the debt's life, so the expected return to holders who choose to convert is anticipated to be very similar to the value of their capital, though if the market value is much higher, the holders will benefit as the number of shares they will receive is fixed. They are also protected from a drop in value, because they can choose not to convert, but instead to have their capital returned to them in full.

This debt has an equity element because of the right of the holders to receive a pre-determined number of shares in exchange for their capital.

(2)   The same company issues a further £100,000 of debt to another investor. The interest rate is lower, at 5%, and the conversion option is also slightly different. Instead of the holder being exposed to the risks of changes in market price of the shares, they are protected by having an option to convert the debt into the number of shares which have an aggregate market value of £100,000 at the conversion date.

This second instrument does not have an equity component because it meets part (b)(i) of the definition in the glossary of a financial liability, being 'a contract that will or may be settled in the entity's own equity instruments and under which the entity is or may be obliged to deliver a variable number of the entity's own equity instruments'. This is commonly known as failing the 'fixed for fixed' criterion; a derivative contract or equity conversion feature that does not deliver a fixed number of shares for a fixed consideration cannot qualify as equity. Because there is no equity component, the whole instrument is a liability and would be dealt with under Section 11 or 12, not Section 22.

The way in which these instruments are treated very differently for accounting purposes despite having terms which are likely to have similar commercial consequences illustrates the care needed in applying these parts of the standard.

7.2.5.2   *Accounting for a compound instrument*

The guidance on this issue in the body of Section 22 is surprisingly brief given that compound instruments have already proved to be an area of some difficulty for UK preparers. In recognition of this difficulty, though, there is an appendix to Section 22 which provides a comprehensive worked example.

Three pieces of instruction are given:

(1) On initial recognition of a compound instrument, allocate the proceeds between liabilities and equity by first determining the fair value of the liability component (based on the value of a similar liability without the conversion feature or similar equity component) and then allocating the residual amount to equity. Allocate transaction costs between the two components on the basis of their relative fair values.

(2) Do not revisit the allocation in subsequent periods.

(3) Use the effective interest method to allocate systematically to profits the difference between the amount initially recognised for the liability and the ultimate amount repayable at maturity.

Example 7.5

A company issues debt with a conversion option that meets the definition of a compound instrument. The initial proceeds, which are equal to the fair value, are £1.1m, and the fair value of a comparable liability with no equity component is £1m.

Assuming, for the sake of simplicity, there are no transaction costs, the initial accounting entry is:

Dr Cash	£1.1m
Cr Liability	(£1m)
Cr Equity	(£100k) (the balancing entry)

The liability component is then accreted up to its redemption amount using the process (and figures) in the example at **7.2.3**. No adjustments are made to the equity component during the instrument's life.

7.2.5.3 Presentation of the equity component of a compound instrument

No mention is made of where the equity component of a compound instrument should be shown on the statement of financial position. The most straightforward and literal treatment would be to have a single line item titled 'equity components of compound instruments', which has the advantage of clarity for an informed reader, though those not familiar with split accounting may find it confusing. But although this works for an item such as convertible debt, it will be more challenging when applied to an instrument that is legally a share but in accounting terms has both equity and liability elements. Company law requires that the nominal value of a share is shown in share capital, and any excess of proceeds over this nominal value in share premium, which forces an entry to the equity part of the balance sheet which is, in aggregate, equal to the whole proceeds of the instrument. But this would result in a double entry that did not reflect the liability/equity split in the accounting – what is needed is some way of showing that the amount shown in share capital and share premium for legal purposes is higher than the amount accounted for as equity.

The two most common approaches each have flaws, and neither has any particular force as there is no guidance in FRS 102, UK company law, or elsewhere, about this issue which only arises because of the curious interaction between accounting requirements and local law. These are demonstrated using an example of a company which issues redeemable shares of total nominal value £10 for proceeds of £100. The values attributed to the equity and liability components are £30 and £70 respectively.

Dr Cash	£100 (proceeds of issue)
Dr Equity	£70 (balancing figure)
Cr Liability	(£70)
Cr Share capital	(£10)
Cr Share premium	(£90)

Approach 1 – introduce a separate debit line within shareholders' funds

This would involve showing a line item that subtracted from other positive values. The main problem is naming, since 'equity component of compound instruments' is not quite accurate, 'adjustment to equity to reflect accounting for compound instruments' is unwieldy, and 'balancing entry' would probably attract unwelcome attention. Nonetheless it has the virtue of clarity for recording purposes, and is very visible for the later occasion when the instrument is extinguished and closing entries are needed (in itself something of an issue, as discussed further below).

Alternatively, the line could be named 'other reserves' and then explained further in a note.

Approach 2 – use the P&L reserve

Since FRS 102, like IFRS, rarely offers any guidance on the detail of the bottom half of the balance sheet, there is always the option of using the P&L reserve, or retained earnings, as a repository for items with no other clear location.

The main advantage to this approach is ease; the main disadvantage is the resulting lack of clarity for readers on what the retained earnings balance represents. In particular, for UK companies, there may historically have been an expectation that the P&L reserve is a good indicator of the level of a company's distributable profits so entries such as this one, that appear to show a reduction in that balance even though that is not their true effect, may be unwelcome (and similarly for those which increase retained earnings without being available for distribution). This may well be such a pervasive issue by now, though, that the waters are already muddy, and investors will learn to accept that they cannot determine distributable profits merely from examining a balance sheet.

A middle line between these approaches is to adopt a general-purpose 'other reserve' line in the balance sheet, which includes this and any other balancing entries, and is accompanied by a detailed explanatory note. There is nothing in either FRS 102 or company law prohibiting this approach, but adopting it does require a certain discipline on the part of the preparer, to maintain accurate records that will keep track of the entries within this reserve, so that they can be unwound as appropriate, and so distributable profits can always be accurately determined.

The effective interest rate calculation is discussed in more detail at **7.3.3**, but it is worth noting first that the guidance here is very similar, but not identical, to that in IAS 32. The main difference is that while Section 22 requires the 'proceeds' of issue to be allocated between the two components, IAS 32 requires the fair value of the whole instrument to be allocated between the two, meaning that for an instrument that is issued at an off-market value, the initial carrying value under FRS 102 would not be the same as that under IAS 32. When IAS 32 requires transaction costs in respect of a compound instrument to be allocated 'in proportion to the allocation of proceeds' rather than 'on the basis of their relative fair values' which is the requirement in 22.13, these two methods will have the same effect on the split of transaction costs, since both are based on the relative fair values of the components rather than a treatment of equity as a balancing figure.

Example 7.6

To understand this theoretical difference in initial accounting between IAS 32 and FRS 102, consider a compound instrument which is issued at a discount, perhaps because it is to a related party. The proceeds are £100,000, but the fair value of the whole instrument is £120,000. The fair value of the liability element alone, based on a comparable liability with no equity component, is determined to be £95,000, and transaction costs are £10,000.

Under IAS 32, the fair value of the equity component is determined as the difference between the fair value of the whole instrument and that of the liability, i.e. £120,000 – £95,000 = £25,000. Transaction costs were allocated 95/120 to the liability and 25/120 to the equity, i.e. £7,900 to liability, £2,100 to equity. Because the instrument was issued at under value, there would be a balancing debit entry, which could be to equity if the instrument was issued to existing shareholders or to expenses if it was part of another transaction. (This balancing entry is unrelated to the transaction costs: it will always arise where the initial fair value of a compound differs from the proceeds.) In summary, the entries would have been:

Dr Cash	£90,000 (£100,000 less £10,000 transaction costs)
Dr [appropriate account]	£20,000
Cr Liability	£87,100 (£95,000 – £7,900)
Cr Equity	£22,900 (£25,000 – £2,100)

The difference between the liability's initial carrying amount of £87,100 and its eventual redemption amount of £100,000 is £12,900 and this will be recognised in profit over the instrument's life.

This contrasts with the approach under Section 22, where the values initially allocated to equity and liabilities would be based only on splitting the proceeds; that is £95,000 to liabilities and only £5,000 to equity. The allocation of costs, though, will still be based on the relative fair values, so will be as in the IAS 32 example. This will result in the following entries:

Dr Cash £90,000 (£100,000 less £10,000 transaction costs)

Cr Liability £87,100

Cr Equity £3,900 (£5,000 – £2,100)

The amount charged to profit in respect of the liability component will be the same as in the example above, but the value attributed to equity is significantly lower, and in truth carries little meaning.

It is not clear why the drafting of the standard allows the simplification of allocating only the instrument's proceeds rather than its fair value: if it was to reduce the burden to preparers, then we might have expected it to carry this through into the method required for allocation of transaction costs. As it is, preparers will need to establish the fair value not just of the liability component but also of the whole instrument (or of the equity component, since the value of the two components should add to the value of the whole).

7.2.5.4　Redemption or conversion of a compound instrument

FRS 102 gives no guidance on the accounting for the end of a compound instrument's life, but this is a common area of confusion in practice. Drawing on guidance from IAS 32 (as permitted by Section 10 for developing an accounting policy on an area not covered by FRS 102), the process set out here may be appropriate.

If an instrument is redeemed at the end of its life, the cash paid should equal the liability's carrying amount, because the effective interest rate was calculated to achieve this. So the first accounting entry matches cash and liability. The equity component then remains, despite the instrument's having been settled, so it should be reclassified within equity. The most straightforward way to achieve this is through a reserves transfer, which will be shown in the statement of changes in equity or the statement of income and retained earnings. No gain is recognised.

If the instrument is, instead, converted at the end of its life, then the proceeds for the shares issued are equal to the liability that has been surrendered, giving an accounting entry of:

Dr Liability (carrying value)

Cr Share capital (nominal value of shares issued)

Cr Share premium (balancing figure)

Again there is a stray line item remaining, being the initial entry made to equity – as in the example above, this should be reclassified to reserves.

If the instrument is redeemed or converted part way through its life then great care is needed to get the accounting right. The guidance on this in IFRS might be considered slightly surprising. IAS 32 paragraph AG33 requires that when a convertible instrument is redeemed (not converted), the proceeds are allocated to liabilities and equity based on the original split when it was issued. This makes the amount that is recognised in profit smaller than it would have been if the whole proceeds were allocated to the liability.

Example 7.7

Looking at the compound instrument from the example above, at the end of year 1 the balance in liabilities is £1,119,000 and the unaltered original equity component is £100,000.

If the instrument is redeemed at this point for £1.2m, then 1/1.1 × £1.2m = £1,091,000 will be allocated to liabilities, and the remaining £109,000 to equity. Therefore a gain of £28,000 will be recorded relating to the liability, and none relating to the equity.

Dr Liabilities	£1,119,000
Dr Equity component	£100,000
Dr Reserves	£9,000
Cr Cash	(£1,200,000)
Cr Profit on liability settlement	(£28,000)

(The final line is to clear out the remaining balance on the line for the instrument's equity component.)

In contrast, if the instrument is converted early then the accounting is more straightforward, with the carrying amount of the liability at the conversion date being deemed to be the proceeds of the shares. So no gain or loss would be recognised, and the original equity entry would be reclassified to reserves as before. This is the conventionally accepted accounting, even though some might question the implicit assumption that amortised cost is a proxy for value throughout an instrument's life.

Example 7.8

In the example above, if the instrument is converted at the end of year 1 rather than redeemed, the shares are treated as being issued for £1,119,000.

Dr Liability	£1,119,000
Cr Share capital/share premium	(£1,119,000)
Dr Equity component	£100,000
Cr Reserves	(£100,000)

To reiterate, none of this accounting for the extinguishment of an instrument is specified in FRS 102. Where a policy is needed, though, this method, using the guidance in IAS 32, is the most obvious approach to turn to.

7.2.6   Treasury shares

Only minimal guidance is given on accounting for treasury shares, which appear when a company reacquires its own equity. The fair value of consideration paid for the shares is deducted from equity, and no gain or loss is recognised on the purchase, sale, issue or cancellation of treasury shares (paragraph 22.16).

Again this treatment should hold no particular challenges for preparers familiar with old UK GAAP, as treasury shares have been required to be shown as a deduction from equity rather than as an investment for some years now.

The treatment of equity instruments held by employee benefit trusts (EBTs) and employee share ownership plan trusts (ESOP trusts) is addressed by the intermediate payment arrangements guidance in Section 9 of FRS 102 (see **4.2.8**).

7.2.7   Distributions

The accounting for distributions to owners is also addressed only briefly, in paragraphs 22.17–22.18. Distributions – usually in the form of dividends on shares – are shown as a deduction from equity, net of any related income tax benefits (although UK companies would not generally receive any tax benefits from paying dividends). If, however, distributions are made in the form of non-cash assets (for instance by giving property from the company to an owner) then there is the slightly cryptic requirement in paragraph 22.18:

'An entity shall disclose the fair value of any non-cash assets that have been distributed to its owners during the reporting period, except when the non-cash assets are ultimately controlled by the same parties both before and after the distribution.'

This disclosure requirement is not accompanied by an accounting requirement, so it seems reasonable to assume that the expectation is that such distributions are accounted for at the book value of the assets transferred (the disclosure requirement is a significant watering down of what would be necessary in full IFRS under IFRIC 17, where the distribution would actually need to be measured at fair value, rather than the value just being disclosed). If assets are simply moved around a group, for example between subsidiaries, the disclosure is not needed, meaning that a 49% shareholder of a subsidiary would not be able to see, from the accounts, the full ramifications if that subsidiary sold an asset at under value to another subsidiary (removing the minority shareholder's ability to share in as yet uncrystallised gains, e.g. capital appreciation). Minority shareholders and creditors do benefit from some protection under UK law, since distributions may only legally be made if a company has a surplus on its reserves, but this does not prevent value from being transferred to the majority shareholder in such a way that the accounts do not show the full picture, reporting only book values because of the control-based exemption.

7.2.8 Non-controlling interests

Non-controlling interests (previously known as minority interests) are included on the consolidated balance sheet as a part of equity. The guidance covering their accounting treatment is spread across Sections 9, 19 and 22 of the standard and is discussed more fully in **4.2.4**, but briefly, the one issue tackled in Section 22 is the accounting where a parent changes its percentage holding in a subsidiary without losing control, for instance by increasing its stake from 75% to 80%, or reducing it from 75% to 60%. Such an event is treated as a transaction with equity holders and therefore does not give rise to a gain or a loss, and nor does it trigger any revaluation of the assets involved. In particular, paragraph 22.19 is clear that 'an entity shall not recognise any change in the carrying amounts of assets (including goodwill) or liabilities as a result of such transactions'.

Example 7.9

Parent P has a 75% investment in subsidiary S. When this stake was purchased, S had net assets with a carrying value of £1m and fair value of £1.2m, so the non-controlling interest was initially recorded at £300,000, being 25% of the fair value of the net assets. Up to the end of 2015, S has made profits of £500,000 and paid no dividends so the carrying value of the non-controlling interest on the group balance sheet has increased to £425,000 (£300,000 + [25% × £500k]).

239

On the first day of 2016, the parent's stake changes, when the book value of S's assets is £1.5m and the fair value is £1.8m.

The parent buys 5% of S's share capital from existing shareholders for £90,000, to increase its holding to 80%;

The parent sells some of its shares, for £270,000, to reduce its holding to 60%.

In situation (i), the fair value of the non-controlling interest has changed through both a reduction in its percentage holding and an increase in the fair value of the underlying assets. However only the former change is accounted for, by adjusting for 5% of the carrying value of assets, with no further adjustments to reflect the changes in the fair values. A balancing entry is recorded in equity:

Dr Non controlling interests	£75,000	
Dr Equity	£15,000	
Cr Cash (consideration)		£90,000

Similarly, in situation (ii), although the NCI is now entitled to 40% of S's profits in future, its carrying value is adjusted only incrementally for the further 15% of the book value of the assets.

Dr Cash	£270,000	
Cr Non-controlling interest		£225,000
Cr Equity		£45,000

In each case, the value now attributed to the non-controlling interest is effectively a hybrid of the initial accounting as a share of fair value, the subsequent share of profits, and then the change-of-stake adjustment based on carrying values.

7.3   Basic financial instruments

7.3.1   *Definition of a basic financial instrument*

As described above, the FRS 102 accounting for financial instruments is dependent on the initial assessment of whether each instrument is basic or not (sometimes referred to for convenience in this section as 'non-basic', although this is not a term used in the standard).

The assessment of whether or not an instrument is basic may, for many, be the hardest part of the accounting. Instead of there being a straightforward definition, paragraph 11.8 gives the following list of categories of instrument which would be classified as basic:

(a) cash;

(b) a debt instrument (such as an account, note, or loan receivable or payable) that meets the conditions in paragraph 11.9 and is not a derivative financial;

(bA) a debt instrument that, whilst not meeting the conditions in paragraph 11.9, nevertheless is consistent with the description in paragraph 11.9A, and is not a derivative financial instrument;

(c) a commitment to receive a loan that:

  (i) cannot be settled net in cash; and

  (ii) when the commitment is executed, is expected to meet the conditions in paragraph 11.9 or be consistent with the description in paragraph 11.9A;

(d) an investment in a non-derivative financial instrument that is equity of the issuer (e.g. most ordinary shares and certain preference shares).

Categories (a), (c) and (d) are each quite self-contained, and between them cover all eligible financial assets and financial liabilities which are not debt receivable or payable. For debt instruments, the conditions from paragraph 11.9 referred to above required to qualify as basic are:

(a) the contractual return to the holder (the lender), assessed in the currency in which the debt instrument is denominated, is:

  (i) a fixed amount;

  (ii) a positive fixed rate or a positive variable rate over the life of the instrument[1];

  (iii) [not used]

  (iv) a combination of a positive or a negative fixed rate and a positive variable rate (e.g. LIBOR plus 200 basis points or LIBOR less 50 basis points, but not 500 basis points less LIBOR).

(aA) The contract may provide for repayments of the principal or the return to the holder (but not both) to be linked to a single relevant observable index of general price inflation of the currency in which the debt instrument is denominated, provided such links are not leveraged.

(aB) The contract may provide for a determinable variation of the return to the holder during the life of the instrument, provided that:

---

[1] *Footnote 10, to para 11.9(a)(ii)*

10 A variable rate for this purpose is a rate which varies over time and is linked to a single observable interest rate or to a single relevant observable index of general price inflation of the currency in which the instrument is denominated, provided such links are not leveraged.

    (i)   the new rate satisfies condition (a) and the variation is not contingent on future events other than:

        (1)   a change of a contractual variable rate;

        (2)   to protect the holder against credit deterioration of the issuer;

        (3)   changes in levies applied by a central bank or arising from changes in relevant taxation or law; or

    (ii)   the new rate is a market rate of interest and satisfies condition (a).

Contractual terms that give the lender the unilateral option to change the terms of the contract are not determinable for this purpose.

(b)   There is no contractual provision that could, by its terms, result in the holder losing the principal amount or any interest attributable to the current period or prior periods. The fact that a debt instrument is subordinated to other debt instruments is not an example of such a contractual provision.

(c)   Contractual provisions that permit the issuer (the borrower) to prepay a debt instrument or permit the holder (the lender) to put it back to the issuer before maturity are not contingent on future events other than to protect:

    (i)   the holder against the credit deterioration of the issuer (e.g. defaults, credit downgrades or loan covenant violations), or a change in control of the issuer; or

    (ii)   the holder or issuer against changes in levies applied by a central bank or arising from changes in relevant taxation or law.

The inclusion of contractual terms that, as a result of the early termination, require reasonable compensation for the early termination to be paid by either the holder or the issuer does not, in itself, constitute a breach of the conditions in paragraph 11.9.

(d)   [not used]

(e)   Contractual provisions may permit the extension of the term of the debt instrument, provided that the return to the holder and any other contractual provisions applicable during the extended term satisfy the conditions of paragraphs (a) to (c).

Although this set of conditions seems horribly complex, it is trying to achieve a relatively simple goal: to ensure that straightforward instruments used in trade or for simple financing, without introducing new risk exposures, are accounted for in a correspondingly straightforward manner.

For instance, debt instruments with characteristics like any of the following would prima facie be classified as basic:

- trade receivables and payables;

- a bank loan with a fixed rate of interest and a fixed term;

- a bank loan on a standard variable rate;

- a loan issued that provides for early repayment if covenants are breached or the borrower's credit rating changes.

Conditions in debt instruments to look out for, because they would breach the conditions for being classified as basic, include:

- a loan with an interest rate pegged to a share index or commodity price;

- a loan that has a specified maturity date but where either party has the option to end the arrangement early (except on the very specific grounds set out in (c));

- most investments in convertible debt (the value of the return the holder receives will usually depend on share prices and potentially on interest rates, so the conditions in paragraph 11.9(a) will not be met);

- a loan that is only repayable if certain external conditions are made such as the FTSE reaching a predetermined level, the company achieving an agreed profit figure, or similar. This would breach condition paragraph 11.9(c);

- an unconventionally structured interest rate that consists of a fixed rate less a variable element, such as 7% less the base rate. This would breach condition paragraph 11.9(a) even though an instrument bearing interest at 6.5% plus the base rate (giving, as at the time of writing, the same starting interest rate) would be as described in paragraph 11.9(a)(iv) and therefore be classified as basic.

Clearly these are not all terms that are very commonly seen in loans to or from private companies, but nor are they so esoteric that their possible existence can be ignored. A bank that habitually lends to riskier borrowers may have complex terms included in its standard loan agreements.

FRS 102 (2018) introduces a more general, principles-based definition of a basic debt instrument in addition to the detailed rules set out previously:

'A debt instrument not meeting the conditions in paragraph 11.9 shall, nevertheless, be considered a basic financial instrument if it gives rise to cash flows on specified dates that constitute repayment of the principal advanced, together with reasonable compensation for the time value of money, credit risk and other basic lending risks and costs (eg liquidity risk, administrative costs associated with holding the instrument and lender's profit margin). Contractual terms that introduce exposure to unrelated risks or volatility (eg changes in equity prices or commodity prices) are inconsistent with this.'

The rules set out in paragraph 11.9 have not changed under FRS 102 (2018), but the introduction of this principles-based definition means that even if an instrument breaches one or more of the rules, it could still be basic if it falls within that definition. To help in this assessment, further examples of basic and non-basic debt instruments have been included in Section 11.

The introduction of this principles-based definition means that even if an instrument breaches one or more of the rules, it could still be basic if it falls within this definition. The intention is that more instruments should meet the 'basic' definition going forward, and non-basic instruments will end up being typically those where there is some exposure to something unusual or unrelated. It also means, though, that more judgment will be needed when assessing financial instruments classification. To help in this assessment, further examples of basic and non-basic debt instruments have been included in the amendments. These are reproduced as follows:

Example 3A A loan with interest payable at the bank's standard variable rate plus 1 per cent throughout the life of the loan – the bank's standard variable rate is negative

The combination of a positive bank's standard variable rate plus a fixed interest rate of 1 per cent meets the condition in paragraph 11.9(a)(iv). However, the conditions in paragraph 11.9(a) do not explicitly address the case when the bank's standard variable rate is negative and such a rate may not meet the conditions.

The interest rate is consistent with the description in paragraph 11.9A provided the bank's standard variable rate reflects prevailing economic conditions and monetary policies. In this case the negative interest rate represents reasonable compensation for basic lending risks.

Example 4A A loan with a condition that the interest rate is reset to a higher rate if a set number of payments are missed

In this case the change in interest rate is contingent on a set number of payments being missed. The missed payments are an indicator of credit deterioration of the issuer. The interest rate reset condition therefore meets the condition in paragraph 11.9(aB)(i)(2) (provided the new rate meets the conditions in paragraph 11.9(a)), and the interest rate reset condition would not result in the loan being measured at fair value in accordance with Section 12.

Example 8 Early repayment of a loan is not permitted during an initial two-year period, but is thereafter

The terms of a ten-year loan include that it may not be repaid within the initial two-year period, but thereafter it may be repaid at the issuer's option, subject only to the payment of reasonable compensation for early termination.

The early repayment condition is not contingent on future events, but automatically comes into effect with the passage of time, and therefore it meets the condition in paragraph 11.9(c) and would not result in the loan being measured at fair value in accordance with Section 12.

Example 9 Early repayment on subordinated debt contingent on repayment of senior debt

Bank A lends CU10 million to Entity S. Entity S has an option to repay this loan at any time. Entity S's parent, Entity P, also lends it CU10 million. The loans have the same maturity date but the loan from Bank A is senior to the loan from Entity P. Entity S has the right to repay the loan to Entity P at par plus accrued interest at any time after the loan from Bank A has been repaid.

Early repayment terms that are within the control of the issuer are not contingent on future events. Therefore if early repayment of both loans is within Entity S's control then the prepayment option in the loan from Entity P is not considered to be contingent, does not breach the condition in paragraph 11.9(c) and does not therefore cause the loan from Entity P to be measured at fair value in accordance with Section 12.

If the terms were such that early repayment of the loan from Bank A was not within the control of Entity S, then the prepayment option in the loan from Entity P would be contingent on a future event other than those listed in paragraph 11.9(c). The nature of the contingent event may be an indicator when assessing whether a debt instrument is consistent with the description in paragraph 11.9A, but is not in itself a determinative factor. The restriction on the prepayment feature in the loan from Entity P would be consistent with the description in paragraph 11.9A because it exists simply to enforce its subordination relative to another debt instrument. The restriction on Entity S's ability to exercise the prepayment option in the loan from Entity P would not therefore cause the loan from Entity P to be measured at fair value in accordance with Section 12 by Entity S.

Example 10 A loan with interest equal to a percentage of the profits of the issuer

The contractual return is neither a fixed rate or amount, nor a variable rate linked to a single observable interest rate or index of general price inflation. Therefore, the return breaches the conditions in paragraph 11.9(a).

In addition, the loan is inconsistent with the description in paragraph 11.9A because the linkage to the profits of the issuer introduces exposure to a risk that is not consistent with a basic lending arrangement.

The instrument is within the scope of Section 12 and will be measured at fair value by the holder. However, the issuer will need to consider whether measurement at fair value is permitted by the Small Companies Regulations, the Regulations, the Small LLP Regulations or the LLP Regulations (see paragraph A4.12A). These regulations prohibit the measurement of financial liabilities at fair value, except for those held as part of a trading portfolio, those that are derivatives and when permitted by IFRS as adopted in the EU. An example of the latter category is financial liabilities with embedded derivatives that meet certain conditions. However, this would exclude instruments with "a non-financial variable specific to a party to a contract".

Therefore, if the issuer concludes that the issuer's profits are "a non-financial variable specific to a party to a contract" and that the instrument could not otherwise be measured at fair value under IFRS as adopted in the EU, then it must measure the instrument at amortised cost, rather than at fair value, in accordance with paragraph 12.8(c).

7.3.2   *Initial measurement of basic financial instruments*

Almost all basic financial assets and liabilities are initially measured at their transaction price.

For those which are subsequently measured at amortised cost (see below), this transaction price is reported net of transaction costs (discussed at **7.2.2** with respect to the issue of equity instruments – the same principles apply here). For instruments subsequently measured at fair value, there would be no point in including transaction costs in the initial carrying amount, as these would immediately reach profit or loss as soon as the item was first remeasured to fair value.

Section 11 gives some examples of the initial measurement of basic financial instruments. These include simple trading balances, recorded initially at transaction price, and simple long-term loans, which are clearly financing transactions and are therefore recorded at the present value of future amounts payable or receivable. The most interesting example, though, is of an item sold to a customer on two-year interest-free credit.

This is clearly considered to be in the nature of a financing transaction but the example states that the value of the receivable is recognised as 'the current cash sale price for that item', with the present value of the receivable being used as a proxy only if the current cash sale price is not available. This seems to be an expansion of the measurement requirements in paragraph 11.13: where the agreed price is not a suitable measure because it is a financing transaction, a current cash equivalent of the transaction price should be used in preference to using a discounted cash flow. Theoretically, these two values might be expected to be the same, assuming rational consumers, but the standard treats them as distinct.

7.3.2.1   Financing transactions and off-market loans

The exception to initial measurement at transaction price is when the arrangement constitutes a financing transaction, in which case the initial amount recorded is 'the present value of the future payments discounted at a market rate of interest for a similar debt instrument' (Paragraph 11.13). Little explanation is given of what it means for an arrangement to constitute a financing transaction, beyond a note that this situation can arise not just with explicit loans, but also with trading balances where unusually generous credit terms are given. The most common application of this requirement, though, is in relation to intragroup and related party loans, which are commonly made at a below-market rate or are interest free.

Where a loan is made or received at a non-market rate of interest, FRS 102 requires the loan to be recognised initially at the present value of the future cashflows under that loan, discounted at a market rate of interest, rather than the contractual interest rate. This means that there will be a difference between the amount of cash advanced under the loan and the amount actually recorded as a loan in the accounts.

If the off-market loan is made between group companies or between a company and its owner, the generally accepted view is that there are two components to the transaction: a loan and a gift to the company – the gift, essentially, being the fact that they have loaned the money at no interest. This 'gift' – the difference between the cash advanced and the amount recorded as a liability - will typically be treated as a capital contribution or distribution (depending on the direction of the loan and the relationship of the lender to the borrower). This is because in most cases, it will have been made because an ownership relationship exists (e.g. parent/subsidiary).

The exception to this approach is where the loan is repayable on demand. In this case, the loan could, theoretically, be called for repayment at any time without notice. Therefore, there is no time period over which to discount and the loan is therefore recorded at the value of the net proceeds received.

In practice, establishing a market rate may prove challenging, especially if the loan was first made many years ago, since the effective interest rate should be established at inception of the loan. Often the company will have borrowed from a related party because it would have struggled to borrow on market terms. In these situations, arriving at a market rate will need some work and investigation. This could involve looking back at historic interest rates and seeking input from one or more lenders to establish an interest rate which is, in all material respects, a market rate. In the most complex scenarios, specialist advice may be needed to calculate an appropriate rate.

Example 7.10

Iridium Ltd has lent £100,000 interest free for five years to its subsidiary. The market rate of interest is 10%. FRS 102 requires that the loan amount is discounted to its present value using a market rate of interest:

£100,000 / 1.10^5 = £62,092.

On receipt of the loan, the subsidiary makes the following entries:

Dr Cash	£100,000
Cr Loan payable (liability)	£62,092
Cr Capital contribution (equity)	£37,908

The parent makes the following entries:

Dr Cash	£100,000
Dr Loan receivable (asset)	£62,092
Dr Cost of investment	£37,908

The treatment of the loan over the five years then follows the amortised cost method set out at **7.3.3**, using the market rate of interest to calculate the interest payable/receivable in profit or loss each year.

The amount recorded in equity by the subsidiary is not subsequently remeasured and nor is the increase to the cost of investment in the parent (unless there are indicators of impairment).

In contrast, if the loan had been repayable on demand, the loan would have simply been recorded at £100,000 in the accounts of both the parent and the subsidiary, with no discounting required.

7.3.2.2   Loans from directors to small entities

In FRS 102 (2018), small entities do not need to find a market rate of interest where they have borrowings with director-shareholders or close family of the director-shareholders. Instead, they can simply use the transaction price.

This exemption only extends to directors who are 'natural persons', so loans with corporate directors would not qualify for the exemption (for LLPs, 'directors' should be read as 'members'). Likewise, any other related party loans – intragroup loans and so on – still need to be accounted for at present value using a market rate of interest.

Small entities will still need to disclose these transactions, as off-market transactions with directors and their family are covered by the related party disclosure requirements in Section 1A.

If an entity ceases to be eligible for the exemption (because it is no longer small), the financial liability is remeasured to present value prospectively from the first reporting date after it ceases to be a small entity. The present value is determined on the basis of the facts and circumstances existing either at that time or at the date the financing arrangement was entered into.

If an entity becomes eligible for the exemption, it is applied fully retrospectively so the comparatives would need to be restated to reflect the transaction price rather than the amortised cost of the loan.

Relief has also been extended, on a similar basis, to small LLPs.

Loans from directors, or shareholders with a participating interest, to a small entity that are non-interest bearing, or bear interest at a non-market rate, fall within the disclosure requirements of paragraphs 1AC.35 or 1AD.51. Small entities are encouraged to consider whether disclosure about such loans from other parties is necessary for the purposes of giving a true and fair view.

7.3.2.3   Treatment of transaction costs

The initial measurement of a financial asset or financial liability is described as including transaction costs, defined in the glossary as:

> 'Incremental costs that are directly attributable to the acquisition, issue or disposal of a financial asset or financial liability, or the issue or reacquisition of an entity's own equity instrument. An incremental cost is one that would not have been incurred if the entity had not acquired, issued or disposed of the financial asset or financial liability, or had not issued or reacquired its own equity instrument.'

No further information is given on how to establish which costs would qualify, but the definition above should usually be straightforward to apply: it would include items such as arrangement fees for loans, legal costs of share issues, and so on, and would exclude allocations of employee costs to loan negotiations, marketing costs associated with a share issue (since these would be incurred regardless of whether or not shares were eventually issued), and similar.

A more interesting question arises when we consider the situation where an entity pays an arrangement fee for a loan facility but does not immediately make any drawdowns on the loan. While such fees, when included as part of the initial loan measurement, would normally be netted off against the loan liability, it is not clear how they should be accounted for when no loan liability has yet been recognised. While the costs are in the nature of a prepayment, it is something of a stretch to fit them into the definition of an asset, since the right to borrow money at a market rate is not usually considered an economic benefit, as such. On the other hand, it appears unreasonable to expense the costs if it is known that they were an inescapable part of the loan arrangement and that they fully meet the definition of transaction costs so would, had the timing been different, have been netted off the loan liability. Preparers will need to use judgment, including of materiality levels, when choosing their accounting here.

7.3.3   Subsequent measurement

The measurement after initial recognition depends on the nature of the instrument, which will be classified in one of three categories:

(1)   Debt instruments;

(2)   Commitments to make or receive a loan;

(3)   Investments in shares.

7.3.3.1   Debt instruments

Debt instruments within the scope of Section 11 are, after initial recognition, measured at amortised cost using the effective interest method. As ever, there is an exception, this time being items payable or receivable within one year: here, no discounting is required, and they are just recorded at the amount payable or receivable. It seems likely that this would, in most circumstances, give materially the same outcome as performing a discounting calculation over such a short period. The exception to the exception is short term arrangements that are financing transactions, where the subsequent measurement is the same as the initial measurement, i.e. at the present value of future payments discounted at a market rate of interest for a similar debt instrument. In practice, again this seems unlikely to give a materially different outcome from any of the other methods, given the short term nature of the arrangements.

The use of amortised cost has the effect of giving a constant rate of return on the asset's or liability's carrying amount over its life. At any given point, the carrying amount will be the initial carrying amount adjusted in the following ways (summarised from paragraph 11.15):

- add the interest charge or credit calculated using the effective interest method (see below);

- subtract amounts repaid;

- subtract (from assets) any necessary allowances for impairment.

The effective interest rate is defined in paragraph 11.16 as 'the rate that exactly discounts estimated future cash payments or receipts through the expected life of the financial instrument or, when appropriate, a shorter period, to the carrying amount of the financial asset or financial liability'. In practical terms, given a schedule of expected cash flows, the simplest way to determine the effective interest rate is to set up a spreadsheet showing the columns below and use the 'goalseek' function to establish the rate that gives a final carrying amount of zero.

Example 7.11

On 1 January 2018, a company draws down a bank loan of £1m. No cash interest is charged and there are no transaction costs, but a total amount of £1.4m is repayable on 31 December 2020.

On a spreadsheet, the calculation will appear as follows:

	B	C	D	E
	Opening carrying amount	Interest charged at 11.87%	Cash flows	Closing carrying amount
2018	1,000,000	118,689		1,118,689
2019	1,118,689	132,776		1,251,465
2020	1,251,465	148,535	(1,400,000)	0

In each row, the initial carrying amount is multiplied by the interest rate shown shaded in column C then reduced by any cash flows in column D to give the closing value in column E, which is then carried on to the beginning of the next row. The key is that this spread sheet can be set up with an arbitrary figure for the interest rate, and then the goalseek function will calculate the exact value necessary to end up at zero.

There are two refinements of detail on calculating the effective interest rate. First, 11.17 makes it clear that the estimated cash flows used should be based on the instrument's contractual terms (including the effects of conditions such as prepayment options if these are considered likely to be exercised) and should take account of known credit losses, but not possible future credit losses. Then, in 11.18, it is set out that usually fees, finance charges paid or received, transaction costs and other premia or discounts are dealt with over the instrument's life by including them in the effective interest rate calculation (in the example above, this would be achieved by deducting these costs from the liability's opening carrying value, thus increasing the total amount charged to profit over the whole life). A shorter period would only be used if the relevant costs were linked explicitly to something less than the

---

instrument's life, for instance if there was a fee linked to a discounted interest rate for the first two years before a loan reverted to a market rate: in this case the relevant fee would be amortised over the two years rather than the whole life. One outcome of performing calculations in this way is that the interest charge recognised for accounting purposes will very often be different from the actual cash outflows, and will also not be the same as amounts shown on any loan statements.

The treatment of changes in expected cash flows depends on whether the instrument bears interest at a fixed or a variable rate. For variable rate assets or liabilities, where initial measurement was at the amount of the principal repayable, a change in interest rates would usually only change future payments rather than affecting the carrying amount.

For other assets or liabilities, though, paragraph 11.20 requires that:

'If an entity revises its estimates of payments or receipts, the entity shall adjust the carrying amount of the financial asset or financial liability (or group of financial instruments) to reflect actual and revised estimated cash flows. The entity shall recalculate the carrying amount by computing the present value of estimated future cash flows at the financial instrument's original effective interest rate. The entity shall recognise the adjustment as income or expense in profit or loss at the date of the revision.'

Example 7.12

A company takes out a bank loan of £2m which charges interest, paid annually, at 9% on the nominal amount, and has an initial term of five years after which, if not repaid, it reverts to the bank's standard variable rate. The initial expectation is that it will repay the loan after seven years (that is, five at the fixed rate and two at the variable rate). It is predicted that the bank's variable rate after five years will be 6.25%.

After three years, the company assesses its cash flow forecasts and establishes that it will be able to repay the loan earlier than it had predicted, at the end of the original fixed term of five years.

Based on initial expectations, the effective interest rate on the loan is calculated to be 8.36%, and so its carrying value after three years is £1.959m (this is below the £2m face value because the interest charge to the income statement in the early years is a little lower than the cash interest paid each year).

When the reforecast takes place, at the end of year 3, only two more years of cash flows are predicted: £180,000 in one year's time, and £2.18m in two years' time (being the fixed interest and capital repayment). When these flows are discounted using the original effective interest rate of 8.36%, they give a present value of £2.023m, and so the loan carrying value is adjusted to this balance, through profit:

> Dr Income statement (finance charge)   £64,000
>
> Cr Liability   (£64,000)
>
> The same effective interest rate then continues to be used for the remainder of the instrument's life, so that after the remaining two payments the balance is nil.

This way of treating a change in expected cash flows arguably involves more work than just performing a recalculation of the effective interest rate based on the existing carrying value and new flows. It would be hard to ignore on the grounds of materiality though, without first doing the calculation. Accounts including such a charge relating to re-estimates of cash flows are likely to need an explanatory note so that readers can understand why there is a one-off charge (or credit).

7.3.3.2   Commitments to make or receive a loan

This category includes any commitment to receive a loan that cannot be settled net in cash and that will, when the commitment is executed, give rise to a loan that meets the conditions to be classified as a basic instrument. Although this sounds a little obscure, it would apply where, for instance, a borrower has a loan arrangement in place with a bank with a fixed schedule of drawdowns, not all of which have yet taken place.

These commitments are, after initial recording at transaction price, subsequently measured at cost less impairment. The standard notes in passing that cost may be zero, which seems the most likely option as it would be unusual for a fee to change hands simply in respect of a drawdown structure, as distinct from an arrangement fee for the loan itself, which would be dealt with as part of the accounting for the loan rather than as a separate instrument.

7.3.3.3   Investments in shares

The default for subsequent measurement of investments in another entity's equity instruments other than a non-derivative instrument that is equity of the issuer (e.g. most ordinary shares and certain preference shares) is measurement at fair value, with changes reported in profit or loss.

In other words, investments will only be accounted for at fair value in the accounts of the holder if they meet the definition of equity for the issuer, or if they are non-basic. If they are basic and meet the definition of liabilities for the issuer, they will be accounted for as any other basic debt instrument, i.e. at amortised cost.

If fair value is not available (because the shares in question are not publicly traded and there is no other reliable means of determining their value) then they are measured at cost less impairment.

7.3.4   *Guidance on determining fair value*

FRS 102 (2018) contains guidance on fair value in an Appendix to Section 2 (previously it was contained in Section 11).

The central point is the hierarchy set out in paragraph 2A.1, summarised here:

(a)   a quoted price for an identical asset in an active market, usually the current bid price, will always be the best evidence of fair value;

(b)   in the absence of quoted prices, a recent transaction price for an identical asset should be used, assuming there have been so significant changes or lapses of time. The only reason not to use this information, if available, is if for some reason it is not a good approximation of fair value, in which case it would be adjusted; and

(c)   if neither of the above types of information is available, a valuation technique is used 'to estimate what the transaction price would have been on the measurement date in an arm's length exchange motivated by normal business transactions'.

Five possible valuation techniques are mentioned:

(1)   using recent arm's length market transactions for an identical asset;

(2)   reference to the current fair value of another asset that is substantially the same;

(3)   discounted cash flow analysis;

(4)   option pricing models;

(5)   any valuation technique commonly used by market participants that has been demonstrated to give reliable estimates.

If a source of fair value is used other than quoted market prices in an active market, then paragraph 2A.4 sets out two conditions for the value to be classified as 'reliably measurable':

(a)   the variability in the range of reasonable fair value estimates is not significant for that asset; or

(b)   the probabilities of the various estimates within the range can be reasonably assessed and used in estimating fair value.

In practice, the 'not reliably measurable' condition should not be used as a justification for not attempting to measure fair value. For investments in unlisted shares, which might be one of the more common assets a private company would be attempting to value, current or historic quoted prices will not be available, but an estimate might be made based on peer companies which are quoted, or by taking advantage of investor access to financial information about the company to perform a discounted cash flow calculation based on forecasts. If this is not available, then the value of the expected dividend stream, or of the net assets, might be used as proxies. In short, the fallback to cost should only be used if these valuation methods have been explored and their results fail the test. Directors should think carefully before making an assertion that they cannot value their assets, as stakeholders might reasonably question, in the face of this type of statement, why the assets are being held and how they are being managed if it is impossible to know what they are worth.

Where an asset has been measured at fair value but this has ceased to be reliably measurable, its carrying amount at the last valuation is used as cost, and the asset is held at cost less impairment until a reliable measure of fair value becomes available again.

7.3.5   Impairment

The guidance on impairment is one of the parts of the standard which may well be subject to change. After the standard was issued, the relevant part of IFRS 9 was finalised by the IASB. Under the new version of IFRS 9, there is a significant shift from the previous 'incurred loss' model to a new 'expected loss' model which looks at the probability of default. It is probable that this model will be incorporated, in some form, into FRS 102 at some stage, but as discussed in **1.5** of this guide, it is unclear when or how this may take place.

In outline:

- for all financial assets held at cost or amortised cost, an assessment must be made at each reporting date of whether there is 'objective evidence of impairment';

- where there is objective evidence of impairment, a charge is recognised immediately;

- assets may be assessed individually or grouped by their credit risk characteristics, but each asset that is individually significant must be assessed separately, as must all 'equity instruments' (that is, presumably, investments in another entity's equity instruments);

- the value to be assessed in the impairment calculation depends on whether the asset is held at cost or at amortised cost.

7.3.5.1   Assessing when there has been an impairment

The concept of objective evidence of impairment is a critical one, and the standard gives five examples of evidence that will usually be sufficient to trigger a review, as well as some more indications of areas to consider.

Paragraph 11.22 sets out the following 'loss events' that would usually give objective evidence of impairment:

(a)   significant financial difficulty of the issuer or obligor;

(b)   a breach of contract, such as a default or delinquency in interest or principal payments;

(c)   the creditor, for economic or legal reasons relating to the debtor's financial difficulty, granting to the debtor a concession that the creditor would not otherwise consider;

(d)   it has become **probable** that the debtor will enter bankruptcy or other financial reorganisation;

(e)   observable data indicating that there has been a measurable decrease in the estimated future cash flows from a group of financial assets since the initial recognition of those assets, even though the decrease cannot yet be identified with the individual financial assets in the group, such as adverse national or local economic conditions or adverse changes in industry conditions.

Other indicators suggested in paragraph 11.23 include significant changes in the technological, market, economic or legal environment in which the issuer operates.

Most of these indicators are reasonably self-explanatory, although the final point from paragraph 11.22 is quite densely worded. An example of a situation meeting this description would be where an entity has customers operating in an industry relating to which new regulation has recently been introduced that is expected to have significant adverse effects on the cash flows of companies in the industry (an example would be the cigarette industry, if smoking were suddenly outlawed).

Note that looking at the list of 'loss events' through the lens of assessing trade receivables shows the important point that a customer does not need to have been declared bankrupt as at the year end for an impairment review to be triggered. Instead, it may just be that the customer is known to be in financial difficulties, or has asked for (and been granted) an extension of its credit terms (this would fit into condition (c) above).

7.3.5.2 Performing an impairment review

An impairment review involves comparing an asset's balance sheet carrying amount to some proxy for its value, and recognising a charge if the value is lower than its cost or amortised cost, as applicable.

For an asset held at amortised cost, for instance a typical loan receivable, the value used in the comparison is the present value of estimated cash flows discounted at the asset's original effective interest rate (if the interest rate is variable, the current rate is used).

For an asset held at cost, the value used is the best estimate of the amount the owner would receive for the asset if it were to be sold at the reporting date.

Example 7.13

(1) A company has a trade receivables balance of £435,000 owed by one customer. This was initially recorded at the cash sales price, with an expectation that it would be settled within the company's normal 90 day credit terms. This balance is technically held at amortised cost even though there is no additional finance income to recognise.

At the company's year end, a review of the trade press indicates that the customer has entered into liquidation proceedings, and that the liquidator has announced that creditors should expect to receive only 20 pence in the pound.

The value of the receivable is estimated, therefore, at £87,000 (assuming here that the effect of discounting would be trivial, based on predicted timescales). An impairment charge of £348,000 is therefore recognised.

(2) The same company holds a 12% investment in an unquoted company of which the remaining 88% is held within a larger group. It is held at cost because the fair value is not reliably measurable (the unquoted company is not material to the larger group's accounts so these do not yield any useful information). The investment was bought some years previously for £100,000, and the investee company has been profitable and cash-generative such that there have been no indications of impairment of the investment. In the current year, though, its main product has been rendered effectively obsolete by technological developments meaning that a rival product with many more features can be sold at a much lower cost to consumers. It seems likely that the company will be allowed to become dormant (rather than being closed or sold); accordingly the best estimate of the amount that the shares could be sold for is nil. The whole investment value is accordingly written off at the year end, through a charge to profit.

The procedure for calculating the impairment charge for an asset held at amortised cost illustrates the difficulty that preparers might find themselves in if they are accustomed to booking general bad debt provisions, for instance at 5% of the total debtor book. If all of a company's customer base operates in one industry, and there are difficulties within that industry, as discussed above, then this may be classified as objective evidence of impairment (the standard explicitly permits entities to review a group of financial assets together, providing that any which are individually significant have first been extracted), but could still be very challenging to measure. Estimated future cash flows may be impossible to predict unless customers are in such a bad state that the creditor expects to receive nothing, and an estimate based on prior experience of recovery rates is unlikely to be relevant in this particular situation where there has been a blow to an industry. Conversely, a general provision of a set percentage based on a history of defaults across a customer base, while quite possibly being an accurate estimate that can be justified in a common-sense way with reference to past events, will not generally be supportable for the purposes of recognising an impairment loss unless there is objective evidence of impairment-causing events relating to the particular assets held as at the year end.

7.3.6   Summary of measurement requirements

Type of basic instrument	Initial measurement	Subsequent measurement
Trade debt (receivable or payable) due within one year	Transaction price including transaction costs	Expected settlement amount (undiscounted) less impairment/ allowance for uncollectibility
Trade debt (receivable or payable) due after more than one year	Transaction price including transaction costs	Amortised cost less impairment/allowance for uncollectibility
Financing debt (receivable or payable) due within one year	Present value of future payments	Present value of future payments less impairment/allowance for uncollectibility
Financing debt (receivable or payable) due after more than one year	Present value of future payments (discounted at a market rate of interest if a financing transaction)	Amortised cost less impairment/ allowance for uncollectibility
Commitment to receive a loan	Transaction price including transaction costs	Cost less impairment/ allowance for uncollectibility
Investment in shares that are publicly traded or where the fair value can be measured reliably	Transaction price excluding transaction costs	Fair value with changes in profit or loss

Type of basic instrument	Initial measurement	Subsequent measurement
Investment in shares where fair value cannot be measured reliably	Transaction price including transaction costs	Cost less impairment

7.3.7 Derecognition

Derecognition refers to the process of removing financial assets or financial liabilities from the balance sheet. Although it might be the case that all that is necessary is to take the item off the balance sheet when it is disposed of or settled, there are in practice several common complications that mean more detailed guidance is necessary.

7.3.7.1 Derecognition of financial liabilities

Paragraph 11.36 sets out that 'an entity shall derecognise a financial liability (or part of a financial liability) only when it is extinguished – i.e. when the obligation specified in the contract is discharged, is cancelled or expires'.

Some of the more common ways that this might come about are:

- settlement of a trade payable;

- the waiving, by the lender, of a loan payable (most common with intercompany or related party loans);

- the 'timing out' of a promise to pay out cash, perhaps in competition prizes or similar.

Where a liability is derecognised, if there is a difference between its carrying amount and the consideration transferred, this is recognised in profit or loss (so, for instance, a gain is recorded if part of a liability is waived).

7.3.7.2 Capital contributions made through loan waivers

The standard is silent on the required accounting in the situation where an entity has a liability to one of its owners which is subsequently waived. While it seems that this would be covered by the requirement above to recognise the gain within profit, this does not sit comfortably with the definition of income in paragraph 2.23(a) which states that this excludes '[amounts] relating to contributions from equity investors'.

Since there is an apparent contradiction here, it will be important to develop and stick to a clear accounting policy for matters such as this. It would appear very reasonable to argue that Section 2 overrides Section 11 in this regard, and that a waiver of a loan from an owner should be treated as a capital contribution (that is, shown directly in equity) rather than as an income statement item.

7.3.7.3   Exchange of financial instruments

Section 11 summarises, in one paragraph (11.37) quite a difficult piece of accounting, for when one financial instrument is exchanged for another. It states that when these two instruments have 'substantially different terms', the original financial liability is derecognised, and a new financial liability with the new terms recognised (with a consequential effect on the income statement). This also applies when there is a 'substantial modification' of the terms of all or part of an existing liability.

This paragraph is actually a densely packed shorthand, seemingly designed to have the same effect as a more detailed section in IAS 39. The intention is to identify when a renegotiation should be treated as simply a change to an existing loan arrangement, which is dealt with over a long period, usually the remaining life of the instrument, and when it should, instead, be treated as if it were the cancellation of the old instrument and the recognition of a new one. This second option would lead to an immediate income statement impact relating to the first instrument's derecognition.

Example 7.14

A loan liability has an amortised cost carrying amount of £250,000. Its terms are changed to extend its life, with all other terms remaining unchanged.

If the change in terms is established as not being substantial, the modification will be dealt with by reperforming the effective interest rate calculation so that the remaining charge is recognised over the new, longer, remaining life (so the charge each period is lower than it would have been before the modification).

If, however, it is determined that the change is substantial, then the whole £250,000 carrying amount will be derecognised. In its place a new liability will be recognised based on the full terms of the renegotiated instrument including the shorter life. This new liability will be recognised at fair value at the outset. The difference between the fair value of the new liability and the carrying amount that was derecognised will be taken to the income statement immediately.

Unfortunately, no guidance is given on what it means for terms to be substantially different. This means that preparers need to look to the guidance in Section 10 on developing accounting policies. A definition of a term is needed, though, and there is nothing comparable in the remainder of the standard. The next step might be to resolve simply that such changes are assessed on a case by case basis, looking at the substance of each renegotiation, and taking into account management intentions at the time, the tone of discussion with lenders, and so on. This would appear to be compatible with the standard, although it gives little stability for application in practice, and it could be time consuming to perform a subjective assessment each time a balance is renegotiated (if this is common practice for an entity).

The alternative is to use the permission in paragraph 10.6 to look to EU-adopted IFRS for additional guidance. IAS 39.AG62 states that:

> '...the terms are substantially different if the discounted present value of the cash flows under the new terms, including any fees paid net of any fees received and discounted using the original effective interest rate, is at least 10% different from the discounted present value of the remaining cash flows of the original financial liability...'

This gives a precise calculation to be performed, which to some minds will produce a simple binary answer, although others read the passage from the Application Guidance as merely giving an example of terms which are substantially different. It should be reiterated, though, that there is no requirement to use the guidance in full EU-adopted IFRS, so while this may be seen as helpful, it is not the only permissible method.

Exchange of a financial liability for equity

A particular issue arises in the special situation where an entity has a loan in issue which is repayable in cash but, for some reason, negotiates with the lender and settles it in shares instead. (This is only problematic where the equity option is not already included in the loan terms: if it is built in to the loan then the relevant accounting is that set out for compound instruments, discussed at **7.2.4**.)

Section 11 does not address this question, so entities undertaking this type of transaction will need to work to develop a policy setting out how the relative values will be established – options might include:

- take the debt's carrying value as the amount settled, and use this as the value of the shares issued (seems unlikely to give a company law-appropriate value for the shares);
- fair value the debt, and attribute this value to the shares issued;
- fair value the shares issued, and recognise a gain or loss when comparing this value to the previous carrying value of the debt.

Those choosing to use the option to look to full IFRS will find that IFRIC 19 addresses this issue, prescribing (in summary) that the equity instruments issued in such a transaction are fair valued (giving the final of the options above), but if this cannot be reliably measured then the equity instruments are measured based on the fair value of the liability extinguished (not its carrying value). There is good logic behind this approach, and it may be helpful to those devising policies, although as in all such situations there is no requirement to comply with or even acknowledge the guidance in IFRS.

Additional guidance regarding the exchange of a liability for equity between entities under common control as included in Section 22 of FRS 102 (2018) is explained at **7.2.2**.

7.3.7.4   *Derecognition of financial assets*

The guidance on derecognition of financial assets is even less straightforward than that for liabilities. This complexity is because of the range of ways in which it is possible for a financial asset to change hands while still leaving traces with the previous owner, meaning that there are often real difficulties in establishing when exactly it should be removed from the transferor's balance sheet.

In practice, though, for entities outside financial services most derecognition of financial assets will be very simple: the asset will be taken off the balance sheet when it is settled in cash.

This is achieved by compliance with the first part of the following set of conditions in paragraph 11.33:

'An entity shall derecognise a financial asset only when:

(a)   The contractual rights to the cash flows from the financial asset expire or are settled, or

(b)   The entity transfers to another party substantially all of the risks and rewards of ownership of the financial asset, or

(c)   The entity, despite having retained some, but not substantially all, risks and rewards of ownership, has transferred control of the asset to another party and the other party has the practical ability to sell the asset in its entirety to an unrelated third party and is able to exercise that ability unilaterally and without needing to impose additional restrictions on the transfer. In this case, the entity shall:

　　(i)   Derecognise the asset; and

　　(ii)   Recognise separately any rights and obligations retained or created in the transfer.'

Looking through these possibilities in turn, case (a) will normally be represented by simple cash transfer, such as when a trade debtor settles an invoice.

For case (b), a classic example is when an entity enters into an arrangement to raise finance on its trade receivables. It may sell its whole loan book to a third party for an upfront payment, with the third party having all administrative responsibility for the debt collection, retaining all cash collected, and bearing all bad debt risk. In this case, it seems that substantially all risks and rewards have been transferred, so the selling entity would derecognise the loan book and account for the proceeds received from the finance provider.

Case (c) then covers the most challenging ground, dealing with the situation where an entity has transferred control of an asset but has retained some of the risks and rewards of ownership. Remaining with the example of factoring arrangements, this might apply to a situation similar to the above but where the transferring entity continues to be responsible for cash collections, passing on remittances to the third party as they are received. In this situation, some of the 'risk' (in this case, administrative burden) of ownership is retained, but most has been transferred, as the factor has no recourse to the original owner if the debts go bad.

In this situation, Section 11 requires that the original asset is derecognised, but a new asset or liability (or both) is recognised at fair value, representing any new rights or obligations arising from the transfer.

In a situation where some rights and obligations from the original asset are retained and some are transferred (instead of a distinct new asset or liability being created), the relative fair values are established at the transfer date to determine the value to be taken off the balance sheet and the value to be retained.

Example 7.15

Company G sells its £1m loan book to a third party, handing over the collection obligations. In consideration, the third party contracts to pass 80% of the cash collected back to G (this is instead of an upfront payment, and means that G effectively pays a 20% fee, and both parties share bad debt risk).

G has transferred control but retained the rights to 80%, so it retains an asset of £800,000 and derecognises the remainder. This leads to an immediate £200,000 charge to the income statement.

When a transfer of control does not result in derecognition, because substantially all risks and rewards have been retained, paragraph 11.34 requires that the whole asset remains on the balance sheet but a separate liability is also recognised to the value of consideration received. Presumably the liability is then subject to the derecognition requirements set out earlier in Section 11.

7.3.7.5   Collateral

Finally in this part, paragraph 11.35 gives guidance on the treatment where a transferor provides non-cash collateral (for instance debt or equity) to the transferee. The required accounting depends on what rights the transferee has in respect of being able to sell or repledge the collateral. If it has free rein over this, then the transferor reclassifies the relevant asset in its balance sheet to make it clear that the asset is in a special position with regard to future movements. The transferee would not recognise the collateral as an asset (until and unless the transferor defaults and thus surrenders its right to have it returned) but if it sells or repledges it, would account for a liability recognising its obligation to surrender value back to the transferor if the terms are met.

If, on the other hand, the transferee does not have the right to sell or repledge the collateral, no accounting entries are needed and the matter is dealt with by disclosure.

7.4   Other financial instruments

7.4.1   Definition of an 'other' financial instrument

Section 12 addresses 'other financial instruments'; that is those not classified as 'basic' and therefore not in the scope of Section 11. For convenience, in this section such instruments are sometimes referred to as 'non-basic', although this is not a term used in the standard.

The precise scope of each section is set out at **7.1**.

7.4.2   Initial measurement

Instruments in the scope of Section 12 are measured initially at fair value, which is normally the transaction price.

7.4.3   Subsequent measurement

Subsequent measurement is at fair value with changes in profit or loss, with two exceptions:

- investments in equity instruments that are not publicly traded and where there is no other way of reliably measuring fair value (and contracts to deliver such instruments) are measured at cost less impairment; and

- hedging instruments in designated hedging relationships are accounted for in accordance with the special hedging guidance (see **7.4.7**).

Since there is scope for instruments to move in and out of this first category, paragraph 12.9 provides that where a measure of fair value ceases to be available, its last reliable measure is taken as the instrument's cost, and the accounting from then onwards is based on this deemed cost less impairment. If fair value becomes reliably measurable again after a time, the instrument reverts to being measured at fair value.

7.4.4 Determining fair value

Most of the guidance on determining fair value appears in Section 11 and is discussed in **7.3.4** above.

Two additional points are made in Section 12, though: first that the fair value of a financial liability repayable on demand cannot be less than the amount payable on demand, discounted from the earliest date it could be expected to be paid (which is applicable particularly in the case of intercompany loans that are repayable on demand; see **7.3.2.1**), and second, that transaction costs are not included in the initial measurement of items held at fair value through profit or loss.

7.4.5 Impairment

For instruments measured at fair value with changes in profit or loss, being most of those in the scope of Section 12, there are no requirements around impairment because any fall in value is already reflected in the fair value measurement (and thus already charged to profit).

For those measured at cost less impairment, preparers are referred back to the relevant parts of Section 11, discussed here in **7.3.5**.

7.4.6 Recognition and derecognition

The principles for recognition and derecognition of non-basic financial instruments are, again, the same as those for basic instruments, so preparers are directed back to Section 11 (discussed here in **7.3.7**).

7.4.7 Hedge accounting

7.4.7.1 Background to hedge accounting

The requirements in Sections 11 and 12 are, in general, very prescriptive with respect to how any particular financial instrument is measured and accounted for, with little account being taken of the purpose of the instruments.

If there was no provision for hedge accounting, then this prescriptiveness would mean that it would often be impossible for directors to choose a method of financial reporting which reflected their commercial intentions. A simple example is where the risk associated with foreign currency debt is mitigated by the taking out of a forward contract to buy the appropriate amount of currency at the repayment date. The business plan is perfectly clear here, but the accounting would be likely to put the loan into the scope of Section 11, where it would be held at amortised cost with a systematic interest charge over the period, and with a foreign exchange gain or loss each period based on the movement in the spot rate each reporting date.

The forward contract, on the other hand, would not be classified as basic, so it would be in the scope of Section 12 and would be fair valued each year end, with all movements in profit. This would lead to an accounting mismatch which clearly does not reflect the underlying intention.

The idea of hedge accounting is to have rules in place allowing for special accounting in such situations so that the business intention is better reflected. While hedge accounting under IFRS has a reputation of being difficult to apply and highly technical, the requirements in FRS 102 are arguably simpler.

FRS 102 (2018) makes it possible to hedge a portfolio of financial assets or liabilities (often known as 'macro-hedging'). Paragraph 12.15A allows that, for a fair value hedge of interest rate exposure of a portfolio of financial assets or financial liabilities (and only for such a hedge), an entity may apply the hedge accounting requirements in IAS 39 instead of those in FRS 102. Where this is the case, the entity must also apply the specific requirements for the fair value hedge accounting for a portfolio hedge of interest rate risk and designate as the hedged item a portion that is a currency amount rather than the individual assets or liabilities.

7.4.7.2   General conditions for hedge accounting

Paragraphs 12.18, 12.18A, and 12.16 set out five conditions that must all be met for an arrangement to qualify for hedge accounting.

> 'An entity may apply hedge accounting to a hedging relationship from the date all of the following conditions are met:
>
> (a)   the hedging relationship consists only of a hedging instrument and a hedged item as described in paragraphs 12.16 to 12.17C;
>
> (b)   the hedging relationship is consistent with the entity's risk management objectives for undertaking hedges;
>
> (c)   there is an economic relationship between the hedged item and the hedging instrument;
>
> (d)   the entity has documented the hedging relationship so that the risk being hedged, the hedged item and the hedging instrument are clearly identified; and
>
> (e)   the entity has determined and documented causes of hedge ineffectiveness.
>
> An economic relationship between a hedged item and hedging instrument exists when the entity expects that the values of the hedged item and hedging instrument will typically move in opposite directions in response to movements in the same risk, which is the hedged risk. (12.18A)'

The first few conditions are basically expanded upon by the fuller details on what is a permitted hedged item or hedging instrument, but the later parts are more interesting.

Unlike in IFRS 9 (or IAS 39 before it), there is no requirement that an entity expects a hedge to be effective when it is designated. Instead, it is simply necessary that the entity has understood what will cause hedge ineffectiveness. In practice, it is also important to be able to measure this ineffectiveness, since this is what will affect profit, but the consequence of wording the requirements in this way is that it is perfectly permissible to enter into a massive over-hedge (for instance, taking out a currency contract covering five times the value of currency expected to be needed), with the simple plan of designating the whole contract as a hedging instrument and then recognising a large ineffective portion. This would not have been acceptable under IAS 39, where a hedge outside the range of 80%–125% effectiveness would be automatically excluded from hedge accounting.

7.4.7.3 Risks that can be hedged

The standard is relatively permissive on the type of item that can be hedged, in paragraph 12.16 and the clarifying paragraphs that follow:

A hedged item can be a recognised asset or liability, an unrecognised firm commitment, a highly probable forecast transaction or a net investment in a foreign operation, or a component of any such item, provided the item is reliably measurable.

For hedge accounting purposes, only assets, liabilities, firm commitments or a highly probable forecast transaction with a party external to the reporting entity can be a hedged item. Hedge accounting can be applied to transactions between entities in the same group only in the individual financial statements of those entities, except for:

(a) transactions with subsidiaries, where the subsidiaries are not consolidated in the consolidated financial statements;

(b) the foreign currency risk of intragroup monetary items that result in an exposure to foreign exchange gains or losses that are not fully eliminated on consolidation in accordance with Section 30 *Foreign Currency Translation*; and

(c) the foreign currency risk of highly probable forecast intragroup transactions, provided the transactions are denominated in a currency other than the functional currency of the entity entering into the transactions and the foreign currency risk affects consolidated profit or loss.

A group of items, including components of items, can be an eligible hedged item provided that all of the following conditions are met:

(a) it consists of items that are individually eligible hedged items;

(b) the items in the group share the same risk;

(c)   the items in the group are managed together on a group basis for risk management purposes; and

(d)   it does not include items with offsetting risk positions.

A component of an item comprises less than the entire fair value change or cash flow variability of an item. The following components of an item (including combinations thereof) may be a hedged item:

(a)   changes in the cash flows or fair value attributable to a separately identifiable and reliably measureable specific risk or risks, including cash flow and fair value changes above or below a specified price or other variable;

(b)   one or more selected contractual cash flows; or

(c)   a specified part of the nominal amount of an item.

It is easiest to see how these conditions are applied when we look at the three permitted types of hedging arrangement.

7.4.7.4   Permissible hedging instruments

Most instruments measured at fair value through profit or loss can be designated as hedging instruments, whether these are derivatives or other instruments at FVTPL. The only conditions that must be met by an instrument are set out in paragraph 12.17 and clarified by paragraphs 12.17A–12.17C:

'12.17

(a)   it is a financial instrument measured at fair value through profit or loss;

(b)   it is a contract with a party external to the reporting entity (i.e. external to the group or individual entity that is being reported on); and

(c)   it is not a written option, except as described in paragraph 12.17C.

12.17A An instrument (or a combination of such instruments) meeting the conditions of paragraph 12.17, may only be a hedging instrument:

(a)   in its entirety;

(b)   by designating a proportion of such an instrument or a proportion of a combination of such instruments, e.g. 50% of the nominal amount of the instrument; or

(c)   by separating the spot risk element of a foreign currency contract and excluding the forward element, or by separating the intrinsic value of an option and excluding the change in time value.

12.17B For a hedge of foreign currency risk, the foreign currency risk component of a financial instrument, provided that it is not a derivative financial instrument, may be a hedging instrument.

12.17C A written option is not a hedging instrument unless the written option is an offset to or is combined with a purchased option and the effect of the offset or combination is not a net written option. An example of a combination of a written and a purchased option that is not a net written option is a zero cost interest rate collar.'

Some of the details in this definition are designed to close very specific (and reasonably rare) loopholes; the main point of interest is that it is clearly acceptable to designate either a whole instrument or part of an instrument (for example, if an entity holds a forward contract to purchase $2m at an agreed rate, it can designate part of this contract in a hedging relationship with a known need for dollar outflows in the future, providing the other conditions are met).

7.4.7.5 Permitted types of hedge

After setting out the basic conditions for a hedging instrument, hedged item and hedge relationship, Section 12 defines three types of hedge relationship and briefly outlines the accounting for each. Here, we briefly discuss the three types: cash flow hedges, fair value hedges and hedges of a net investment in a foreign operation; however, the detail of the application of the requirements is beyond the scope of this guide. Although hedge accounting is much more achievable under FRS 102 than under IFRS, it is still not likely to be particularly popular in practice with most small and medium-sized entities with simple operations.

The first type of hedge set out in the standard is the **fair value hedge**. This is defined as:

'a hedge of the exposure to changes in fair value of a recognised asset or liability or an unrecognised firm commitment, or a component of any such item, that are attributable to a particular risk and could affect profit or loss.'

To give an example of when this might be used, where an entity has fixed rate borrowings, it has certainty over its cash flows, but will miss out on any benefit when interest rates fall, as well as being protected from adverse consequences if they rise. Another fairly common example is a commitment to purchase a commodity at a fixed price, or a foreign currency forward: in each case the cash flows are fixed but the entity does not benefit or lose from changes in the commodity price and exchange rate respectively.

In these cases, the hedged item is usually measured at amortised cost, and therefore its changes in fair value are not reflected in the accounts. Where a derivative is used to hedge the risk, though, for instance a fixed to floating interest rate swap in the case of the fixed rate loan above, this derivative is a non-basic instrument and is therefore measured at fair value, with changes in each period reported directly in profit.

If the conditions for hedge accounting are met, and a hedged item and hedging instrument are designated as part of a fair value hedge, paragraph 12.20 specifies two consequences:

(a) the gain or loss on the hedging instrument shall be recognised in profit or loss; and

(b) the hedging gain or loss on the hedged item shall adjust the carrying amount of the hedged item (if applicable) and be recognised in profit or loss. When a hedged item is an unrecognised firm commitment, the cumulative hedging gain or loss on the hedged item is recognised as an asset or liability with a corresponding gain or loss recognised in profit or loss.

In simple terms, the hedging instrument (e.g. the interest rate swap) will be accounted for exactly as it would have been were no hedge in place, but the hedged item changes to being measured on a hybrid basis, adjusted for changes in fair value relating to the hedged risk. This is sometimes described in shorthand terms as measurement of the hedged item at fair value, but this is not accurate, because only fair value changes relating to the hedged risk are relevant.

The second type of hedge, a **cash flow hedge**, is defined as:

'a hedge of the exposure to variability in cash flows that is attributable to a particular risk associated with all, or a component of, a recognised asset or liability (such as all or some future interest payments on variable rate debt) or a highly probable forecast transaction, and could affect profit or loss.'

An example of when a cash flow hedge might be used is when an entity has made a commitment to purchase a significant asset in a later accounting period, with the payment due in a foreign currency. It hedges its exposure to variability in cash flows arising from moving exchange rates, by purchasing a forward currency contract to buy the same amount of currency as it will need, at the same time as the asset purchase, for a fixed rate.

The main outcome of a cash flow hedge is, as suggested by the name, predictability of cash flows. Entities use this type of arrangement to give themselves certainty over their actual exposure, even if this means they do not get the 'best value' (in the example above, for instance, if foreign exchange rates move the opposite way from those expected, then the purchasing entity would have been better off waiting to buy the necessary currency in the market on the day it paid for the asset).

Without hedge accounting for this type of arrangement, the accounts can show considerable income statement volatility even though the arrangement was set up to avoid exposure and uncertainty. In the example above, if hedge accounting was not applied, nothing would be recognised on the balance sheet in respect of the asset purchase commitment until the purchase itself took place. The foreign currency forward, on the other hand, would be recognised immediately, and at any reporting date between inception and close it would be revalued with a consequent charge or credit to the income statement, even though it related to an item that would be on the balance sheet once recognised.

It seems clear that this outcome does not quite represent what an entity might be trying to achieve commercially, so if the conditions are met for a hedging relationship in general, and then for a cash flow hedge in particular, paragraph 12.23 gives the following lengthy instructions.

'(a) The separate component of equity associated with the hedged item (cash flow hedge reserve) is adjusted to the lower of the following (in absolute amounts):

  (i) The cumulative gain or loss on the hedging instrument from the date the conditions of paragraph 12.18 are met; and

  (ii) The cumulative change in fair value on the hedged item (i.e. the present value of the cumulative change of expected future cash flows) from the date the conditions of paragraph 12.18 are met.

(b) The portion of the gain or loss on the hedging instrument that is determined to be an effective hedge (i.e. the portion that is offset by the change in the cash flow hedge reserve calculated in accordance with (a)) shall be recognised in other comprehensive income.

(c) Any remaining gain or loss on the hedging instrument (or any gain or loss required to balance the change in the cash flow hedge reserve calculated in accordance with (a)), is hedge ineffectiveness that shall be recognised in profit or loss.

(d) The amount that has been accumulated in the cash flow hedge reserve in accordance with (a) shall be accounted for as follows:

  (i) If a hedged forecast transaction subsequently results in the recognition of a non-financial asset or non-financial liability, or a hedged forecast transaction for a non-financial asset or non-financial liability becomes a firm commitment for which fair value hedge accounting is applied, the entity shall remove that amount from the cash flow hedge reserve and include it directly in the initial cost or other carrying amount of the asset or liability;

  (ii) For cash flow hedges other than those covered by (i), that amount shall be reclassified from the cash flow hedge reserve to profit or loss in the same period or periods during which the hedged expected future cash flows affect profit or loss (for example, in the periods that interest income or interest expense is recognised or when a forecast sale occurs); and

  (iii) If the amount is a loss, and all or part of that loss is not expected to be recovered, the amount of the loss not expected to be recovered shall be reclassified to profit or loss immediately.'

Again, a detailed example is beyond the scope of this guide, but in short the hedged item is usually accounted for as it would have been with no hedge accounting, but gains and losses on the hedging instrument are recognised in equity rather than in profit. This applies in the early part of the relationship, but then as the hedged item begins to affect profit (for instance, when there are interest flows on debt, or when a hedged asset purchase takes place and the asset starts to be depreciated), the amounts previously deferred in equity, relating to the hedging instrument, are recognised in profit, in a way that mitigates the profit effect of the hedged item, and very broadly matches the timing.

The final type of hedge is a **hedge of a net investment in a foreign operation** which refers to the situation where an entity has a foreign currency investment (for instance through having bought shares in an overseas subsidiary whose net assets are denominated in a foreign currency) and is therefore exposed to exchange risk even if the subsidiary breaks even each year, just due to the fluctuation in net asset values from exchange rates.

Under Section 30 of FRS 102, on consolidation a foreign operation's net assets are retranslated at the closing rate. A difference will, therefore, arise when the closing net assets (at closing rate) are compared to the sum of the opening net assets (at opening rate, as included in the previous year's balance sheet) and the profit for the year (at an actual or average rate). This difference is usually accounted for within other comprehensive income, that is outside of profit.

If an entity chooses to manage its exposure, though, for instance by taking out a foreign currency loan of broadly equivalent value to the investee's net assets, then the loan would ordinarily be retranslated each year as a 'normal' foreign currency liability, meaning that gains or losses are recognised in profit. This does not mirror the treatment of the net asset exposure, even though the loan is taken out purely for risk mitigation purposes.

Paragraph 12.24 sets out the following accounting procedure for the hedge of a net investment, emphasising that this includes the hedge of a monetary item that is accounted for as part of a net investment:

'(a)   the portion of the gain or loss on the hedging instrument that is determined to be an effective hedge shall be recognised in other comprehensive income (see paragraphs 12.23(a) and (b)); and

(b)   the ineffective portion shall be recognised in profit or loss.

However, the cumulative gain or loss on the hedging instrument relating to the effective portion of the hedge that has been accumulated in equity shall not be reclassified from equity to profit or loss on the disposal or partial disposal of the foreign operation.'

7.4.7.6   *Other points of note on hedge accounting*

There are three other particular items of interest relating to hedge accounting. First, the standard makes it clear that any hedge can be voluntarily discontinued at any point. The accounting that follows such an election depends on the type of hedge; it is the same as that which would be followed if the discontinuation was not voluntary, for instance if the hedged item or hedging instrument ceased to meet the conditions to qualify.

Second, for some entities that want to reflect their commercial decisions in their accounting but do not have the resource to concentrate on formal hedge accounting, there is a 'short cut' option that will sometimes be available, namely designating the hedged item at fair value through profit or loss. Where the item qualifies, and is hedged by a derivative, there is a natural matching of profit effects, since the derivative will change in value with a roughly opposite effect from the other item's change in value (assuming they were set up with this aim in mind).

Most basic debt instruments are permitted to be designated at fair value through profit or loss and so where doing this 'eliminates or significantly reduces an accounting mismatch' by showing a profit effect in the same period as the hedging instrument's profit effect, it will be permissible, and a rough and ready sort of hedge accounting will be achieved. Entities wishing to pursue this path will need, of course, to check the detail of the definitions, since the standard includes a key caveat that designation at fair value through profit or loss is permissible only where this is not prohibited by EU law.

Finally, fair value hedging for a portfolio of financial instruments, often called macro-hedging, is possible in FRS 102 (2018). As noted at **7.4.7**, Section 12 of FRS 102 cross refers to the requirements in IAS 39 in relation to macro-hedging. This enables entities to apply the macro-hedging provisions of IAS 39 but otherwise apply the recognition and measurement requirements of FRS 102.

7.5 Transition

There are a number of transition exemptions relating to financial instruments, some mandatory and some optional. The mandatory exclusion, relating to derecognition, is discussed in **section 19** of this guide, the optional exemptions (one of which also relates to hedge accounting) are discussed here.

7.5.1 Compound financial instruments

Paragraph 35.10(g) states that:

> 'Paragraph 22.13 requires an entity to split a compound financial instrument into its liability and equity components at the date of issue. A first-time adopter need not separate those two components if the liability component is not outstanding at the date of transition to this FRS.'

This exemption does not, in truth, save very much work for most preparers. It says that if a compound instrument was issued some time ago, but the liability was settled pre-transition date, then there is no need to revisit the calculations to allocate a separate component of equity to the equity component. Since, for many preparers, the settlement of a compound instrument via payment of cash or issue of shares will trigger a 'cleaning up' exercise in equity, the exemption will probably only rarely be relevant.

7.5.2   *Designation of previously recognised financial instruments*

Paragraph 35.10(s) states that:

> 'This FRS permits a financial instrument (provided it meets certain criteria) to be designated on initial recognition as a financial asset or financial liability at fair value through profit or loss. Despite this an entity is permitted to designate, as at the date of transition to this FRS, any financial asset or financial liability at fair value through profit or loss provided the asset or liability meets the criteria in paragraph 11.14(b) at that date.'

This exemption saves a lot of work in establishing historical fair values. If designation at FVTPL were only permitted as at the date of initial recognition, then entities wishing to use this option for instruments already held or in issue at the transition date would need to look back to the acquisition or issue, determine the fair value at that point, and then recognise the movement in value between initial recognition and transition date as an adjustment to opening equity. This simplification allows a straightforward test against the designation conditions at the transition date, and then a single accounting entry to bring the asset or liability on to the balance sheet at fair value.

7.5.3   *Hedge accounting*

The July 2014 amendments to FRS 102 included an attempt by the FRC to clarify the options available for beginning hedge accounting on transition to the standard. As with other aspects of the new requirements, the intention was to stop it from being too onerous for entities to use hedge accounting for arrangements that were already in place; drafting an exemption that achieved this resulted in a densely written paragraph, the new 35.10(t):

(i) A hedging relationship existing on the date of transition

A first-time adopter may choose to apply hedge accounting to a hedging relationship of a type described in paragraph 12.19 which exists on the date of transition between a hedging instrument and a hedged item, provided the conditions of paragraphs 12.18(a) to (c) are met on the date of transition to this FRS and the conditions of paragraphs 12.18(d) and (e) are met no later than the date the first financial statements that comply with this FRS are authorised for issue. This choice applies to each hedging relationship existing on the date of transition.

Hedge accounting as set out in Section 12, *Other Financial Instruments Issues* of this FRS may commence from a date no earlier than the conditions of paragraphs 12.18(a) to (c) are met. In a fair value hedge the cumulative hedging gain or loss on the hedged item from the date hedge accounting commenced to the date of transition, shall be recorded in retained earnings (or if appropriate, another category of equity). In a cash flow hedge and net investment hedge, the lower of the following (in absolute amounts) shall be recorded in equity (in respect of cash flow hedges in the cash flow hedge reserve):

(a)   the cumulative gain or loss on the hedging instrument from the date hedge accounting commenced to the date of transition; and

(b)   the cumulative change in fair value (i.e. the present value of the cumulative change of expected future cash flows) on the hedged item from the date hedge accounting commenced to the date of transition.

(ii) A hedging relationship that ceased to exist before the date of transition because the hedging instrument has expired, was sold, terminated or exercised prior to the date of transition.

A first-time adopter may elect not to adjust the carrying amount of an asset or liability for previous GAAP accounting effects of a hedging relationship that has ceased to exist.

A first-time adopter may elect to account for amounts deferred in equity in a cash flow hedge under a previous GAAP, as described in paragraph 12.23(d) from the date of transition. Any amounts deferred in equity in relation to a hedge of a net investment in a foreign operation under a previous GAAP shall not be reclassified to profit or loss on disposal or partial disposal of the foreign operation.

(iii) A hedging relationship that commenced after the date of transition

A first-time adopter may elect to apply hedge accounting to a hedging relationship of a type described in paragraph 12.19 that commenced after the date of transition between a hedging instrument and a hedged item, starting from the date the conditions of paragraphs 12.18(a) to (c) are met, provided that the conditions of paragraphs 12.18(d) and (e) are met no later than the date the first financial statements that comply with this FRS are authorised for issue.

The choice applies to each hedging relationship that commenced after the date of transition.

(iv) Entities taking the accounting policy choice under paragraphs 11.2(b) or (c) or paragraphs 12.2(b) or (c) to apply IAS 39 Financial Instruments: Recognition and Measurement or IFRS 9 Financial Instruments

A first-time adopter adopting an accounting policy set out in paragraphs 11.2(b) or (c) or paragraphs 12.2(b) or (c) shall not apply the transitional provisions of paragraphs (i) to (iii) above. Such a first-time adopter shall apply the transitional requirements applicable to hedge accounting in IFRS 1 *First-time adoption of International Financial Reporting Standards*, paragraphs B4–B6, except that the designation and documentation of a hedging relationship may be completed after the date of transition, and no later than the date the first financial statements that comply with this FRS are authorised for issue, if the hedging relationship is to qualify for hedge accounting from the date of transition.

A first-time adopter adopting an accounting policy set out in paragraphs 11.2(b) or (c) or paragraphs 12.2(b) or (c) that has entered into a hedging relationship as described in IAS 39 or IFRS 9 in the period between the date of transition and the reporting date for the first financial statements that comply with this FRS may elect to apply hedge accounting prospectively from the date all qualifying conditions for hedge accounting in IAS 39 or IFRS 9 are met, except that an entity shall complete the formal designation and documentation of a hedging relationship no later than the date the first financial statements that comply with this FRS are authorised for issue.

Briefly, these paragraphs allow hedge accounting for a relationship that existed before the transition date (or for one that begins after the transition date but before the end of the first FRS 102 accounting period), beginning no earlier than when the conditions were met (but with no restriction on beginning later): this will require calculation of what the accounting entries would have been from the point when hedge accounting is deemed to begin, so that the relevant amounts can be recognised in equity and, where necessary, other balance sheet items adjusted at the transition balance sheet.

Entities choosing to use some combination of IAS 39 and IFRS 9 instead of Sections 11 and 12 are required to use the IFRS 1 transitional provisions rather than those from FRS 102.

7.5.4   Small entities

There is a specific transition exemption for small entities using the standard for the first time for periods beginning before 1 January 2017. They are not required to apply the fair value requirements of Sections 11 and 12 in their comparatives unless they were already using fair value measurement for financial instruments in their previous framework (which would not have been the case under the FRSSE). Instead, they would use their existing accounting policies for the comparative period (disclosing these policies) then apply the fair value rules in their first FRS 102 period, showing any necessary adjustments from the comparative balance sheet as an adjustment to opening equity in the current period.

Small entities also benefit from an exemption on transition relating to financing transactions with related parties. Paragraph 11.13 requires that financial assets and liabilities relating to a financing transaction are initially recognised at the present value of future payments, discounted at a market rate of interest for a similar debt instrument. Some entities will find this requirement means they need to restate their comparatives, changing their accounting, particularly when it comes to intercompany loans at zero or below-market interest. But the new paragraph 35.10(v) allows small entities, on first applying the standard for a period beginning before 1 January 2017, not to apply this requirement to financing transactions with related parties in the comparative period.

So, as an example, a small entity in receipt of a long-term zero coupon loan from its parent, and applying FRS 102 for the first time in its 31 December 2016 accounts, shows the loan at face value (assuming that was the old accounting) in the comparative (December 2015) balance sheet. To true up the accounting, the entity would then calculate the present value as at 1 January 2016 of the future payments and use that as the opening liability, looking only at facts and circumstances at that date rather than the date when the loan was initially taken out. The difference between the value in the December 2015 balance sheet and the newly established opening value for 2016 is adjusted through opening equity. There are no explicit disclosure requirements relating to the use of this exemption but it is to be expected that an outline of the treatment would be given in the note to the accounts covering transition to the standard, as well as an explanatory note for this line item in the statement of changes in equity, or statement of income and retained earnings, if one is presented. Small entities are not required to present either of these primary statements, but directors may well feel it necessary in order to give a full picture of any sizeable adjustments of this nature made on transition.

7.6 Disclosures

There are no disclosure requirements within Section 22, since this only deals with classification of liabilities and equity.

Those in Section 11 are extensive, because there are so many possible types of instrument and accounting choices to be covered, although they are also clearly less onerous than the comparable requirements in IFRS 7, the standard dedicated to financial instruments disclosures. The requirements are reproduced in full below, with our comments interspersed in italics.

7.6.1 Disclosure of accounting policies for financial instruments

'11.40 In accordance with paragraph 8.5, an entity shall disclose, of its significant accounting policies, the measurement basis (or bases) used for financial instruments and the other accounting policies used for financial instruments that are relevant to an understanding of the financial statements.'

7.6.2 Statement of financial position – categories of financial assets and financial liabilities

FRS 102 (2018) states:

'11.41 An entity shall disclose separately the carrying amounts at the reporting date of financial assets and financial liabilities measured at fair value through profit or loss. This disclosure may be made separately by category of financial instrument. Financial liabilities that are not held as part of a trading portfolio and are not derivatives shall be shown separately.

11.42 An entity shall disclose information that enables users of its financial statements to evaluate the significance of financial instruments for its financial position and performance. For example, for long-term debt such information would normally include the terms and conditions of the debt instrument (such as interest rate, maturity, repayment schedule, and restrictions that the debt instrument imposes on the entity).'

Note that the details in paragraph 11.42 are preceded by 'for example' – this is designed to encourage sensible judgment on which matters require disclosure.

In FRS 102 (2018) paragraph 11.42 then goes on to say: 'When the risks arising from financial instruments are particularly significant to the business (for example because they are principal risks for the entity), additional disclosure may be required. Paragraphs 34.19 to 34.30, which set out disclosure requirements for financial institutions, include examples of disclosure requirements for risks arising from financial instruments that may be relevant in such cases'. This acknowledges the simplification in 11.41 and clarifies that, where additional disclosure is material to an understanding of the financial instruments held, entities should look to Section 34 and the disclosure requirements for financial institutions as a guide to what should be disclosed.

'11.43 For all financial assets and financial liabilities measured at fair value, the entity shall disclose the basis for determining fair value, e.g. quoted market price in an active market or a valuation technique. When a valuation technique is used, the entity shall disclose the assumptions applied in determining fair value for each class of financial assets or financial liabilities. For example, if applicable, an entity discloses information about the assumptions relating to prepayment rates, rates of estimated credit losses, and interest rates or discount rates.

11.44 If a reliable measure of fair value is no longer available for any financial instruments that would otherwise be required to be measured at fair value through profit or loss in accordance with this FRS, the entity shall disclose that fact and the carrying amount of those financial instruments.

11.45 If an entity has transferred financial assets to another party in a transaction that does not qualify for derecognition (see paragraphs 11.33 to 11.35), the entity shall disclose the following for each class of such financial assets:

(a)   the nature of the assets;

(b)   the nature of the risks and rewards of ownership to which the entity remains exposed; and

(c)   the carrying amounts of the assets and of any associated liabilities that the entity continues to recognise.'

7.6.3   Collateral

'11.46 When an entity has pledged financial assets as collateral for liabilities or contingent liabilities, it shall disclose the following:

(a)   the carrying amount of the financial assets pledged as collateral; and

(b)   the terms and conditions relating to its pledge.'

7.6.4   Defaults and breaches on loans payable

'11.47 For loans payable recognised at the reporting date for which there is a breach of terms or default of principal, interest, sinking fund, or redemption terms that has not been remedied by the reporting date, an entity shall disclose the following:

(a)   details of that breach or default;

(b)   the carrying amount of the related loans payable at the reporting date; and

(c)   whether the breach or default was remedied, or the terms of the loans payable were renegotiated, before the financial statements were authorised for issue.'

It is important to note that a breach that has been remedied before the year end does not require disclosure. This may give an extra incentive for reviewing compliance with conditions and covenants in good time before the year end so that any issues can be resolved rapidly without the need for extensive disclosures.

7.6.5   Items of income, expense, gains or losses

'11.48 An entity shall disclose the following items of income, expense, gains or losses:

(a)   income, expense, net gains or net losses, including changes in fair value, recognised on:

   (i)   financial assets measured at fair value through profit or loss;

   (ii)   financial liabilities measured at fair value through profit or loss (with separate disclosure of movements on those which are not held as part of a trading portfolio and are not derivatives);

   (iii)   financial assets measured at amortised cost;

   (iv)   financial liabilities measured at amortised cost; and

   (v)   when an entity has made the accounting policy choice in paragraphs 11.2(c) and 12.2(c) to apply the recognition and measurement provisions of IFRS 9, financial instruments measured at fair value through other comprehensive income;

(b)   total interest income and total interest expense (calculated using the effective interest method) for financial assets or financial liabilities that are not measured at fair value through profit or loss; and

(c)   the amount of any impairment loss for each class of financial asset. A class of financial asset is a grouping that is appropriate to the nature of the information disclosed and that takes into account the characteristics of the financial assets. When an entity has made the accounting policy choice in paragraph 11.2(c) and 12.2(c) to apply the recognition and measurement provisions of IFRS 9, the groupings shall be based on whether the amount is equal to 12-month expected credit risk losses, equal to the lifetime expected credit losses or financial assets that are purchased or originated credit-impaired.'

7.6.6   Financial instruments at fair value through profit or loss

'11.48A The following disclosures are required only for financial instruments at fair value through profit or loss that are not held as part of a trading portfolio and are not derivatives:

(a)   The amount of change, during the period and cumulatively, in the fair value of the financial instrument that is attributable to changes in the credit risk of that instrument, determined either:

   (i)   as the amount of change in its fair value that is not attributable to changes in market conditions that give rise to market risk; or

   (ii)   using an alternative method the entity believes more faithfully represents the amount of change in its fair value that is attributable to changes in the credit risk of the instrument.

(b)   The method used to establish the amount of change attributable to changes in own credit risk, or, if the change cannot be measured reliably or is not material, that fact.

(c)   The difference between the financial liability's carrying amount and the amount the entity would be contractually required to pay at maturity to the holder of the obligation.

(d)   If an instrument contains both a liability and an equity feature, and the instrument has multiple features that substantially modify the cash flows and the values of those features are interdependent (such as a callable convertible debt instrument), the existence of those features.

(e)   Any difference between the fair value at initial recognition and the amount that would be determined at that date using a valuation technique, and the amount recognised in profit or loss.

(f)   Information that enables users of the entity's financial statements to evaluate the nature and extent of relevant risks arising from financial instruments to which the entity is exposed at the end of the reporting period. These risks typically include, but are not limited to, credit risk, liquidity risk and market risk. The disclosure should include both the entity's exposure to each type of risk and how it manages those risks.'

This requirement was inserted specifically to ensure compliance with EU/UK law, and will be of only limited relevance to most UK preparers. In general, for a financial asset or liability to qualify to be held at FVTPL, it will either be a derivative or will be part of a portfolio, meaning paragraph 11.48A will not apply.

7.6.7   Financial institutions

'11.48B A financial institution shall, in addition, apply the requirements of paragraph 34.17.

11.48C A retirement benefit plan shall, in addition, apply the requirements of paragraphs 34.39 '

7.6.8   Non-basic financial instruments

There are fewer requirements in Section 12 – again, they are reproduced in full below.

'12.26 An entity applying this Section shall make all of the disclosures required in Section 11 incorporating in those disclosures, financial instruments that are within the scope of this Section as well as those within the scope of Section 11. For financial instruments in the scope of this Section that are not held as part of a trading portfolio and are not derivative instruments, an entity shall provide additional disclosures as set out in paragraph 11.48A. In addition, if the entity uses hedge accounting, it shall make the additional disclosures in paragraphs 12.27 to 12.29.

12.27 An entity shall disclose the following separately for each type of hedging arrangement described in paragraph 12.19:

(a)   a description of the hedge;

(b) a description of the financial instruments designated as hedging instruments and their fair values at the reporting date; and

(c) the nature of the risks being hedged, including a description of the hedged item.

12.28 If an entity uses hedge accounting for a fair value hedge, it shall disclose the following:

(a) the amount of the change in fair value of the hedging instrument recognised in profit or loss for the period; and

(b) the amount of the change in fair value of the hedged item recognised in profit or loss for the period.

12.29 If an entity uses hedge accounting for a cash flow hedge it shall disclose the following:

(a) the periods when the cash flows are expected to occur and when they are expected to affect profit or loss;

(b) a description of any forecast transaction for which hedge accounting had previously been used, but which is no longer expected to occur;

(c) the amount of the change in fair value of the hedging instrument that was recognised in other comprehensive income during the period;

(d) the amount, if any that was reclassified from equity to profit or loss for the period; and

(e) the amount, if any, of any excess of the fair value of the hedging instrument over the change in the fair value of the expected cash flows that was recognised in profit or loss for the period.

12.29A If an entity uses hedge accounting for a net investment in a foreign operation it shall disclose separately the amounts recognised in other comprehensive income in accordance with paragraph 12.24(a) and the amounts recognised in profit or loss in accordance with paragraph 12.24(b).'

7.6.9 Disclosures for small entities

As might be expected, the disclosure requirements for small entities applying Section 1A of the standard are much less onerous than those for full preparers.

There is a paragraph of requirements (1AC.22) for financial instruments measured in accordance with the fair value accounting rules, asking for significant assumptions underlying the valuation techniques, fair value disaggregated by category and showing which movements were shown in the income statement and which directly in reserves. For derivatives, small entities are also required to state the nature and extent of each class including significant terms and conditions that may affect the amount, timing and certainty of future cash flows.

Details around indebtedness, guarantees and financial commitments are required by 1AC.27–31, and there is also the general catch-all requirement from company law stating that where certain financial instruments are included at fair value (for instance, investments in subsidiaries, associates and joint ventures), full IAS disclosures are made. Since these are reproduced in 11.48A, small entities will need to turn to this paragraph if relevant.

There are no disclosure requirements for small entities in respect of hedging, but for any that do choose to hedge account, it would seem likely that some disclosures would be needed for a true and fair view, notwithstanding the absence of explicit requirements.

8 Leasing

8.1 Scope of this section

This section covers Section 20 *Leases*.

A lease is an agreement whereby the lessor conveys to the lessee, in return for a payment or series of payments, the right to use an asset for an agreed period of time.

Leases are classified as operating leases or finance leases. The equivalent standard and interpretations in IFRS are currently IAS 17 *Leases* and SIC 15 *Operating Leases – Incentives.* However, for periods beginning on or after 1 January 2019, IFRS 16 *Leases* becomes effective. IFRS 16 eradicates the distinction for lessees between an operating lease and a finance lease and brings virtually all leases on to the balance sheet, with two lines charged to profit, being the asset depreciation and finance charge on the lease liability. As discussed at **1.5**, it is not yet clear when or if FRS 102 will be amended in line with IFRS 16.

Section 20 also applies to agreements that transfer the right to use assets even though they do not take the legal form of a lease. The equivalent interpretation in IFRS is IFRIC 4 *Determining whether an arrangement contains a lease*.

> **Application to micro-entities:** FRS 105 is largely consistent with FRS 102 in regards to lease accounting, although it is less specific. For example, in determining whether or not an arrangement contains a lease, FRS 105 simply says that it is necessary to consider the substance of the arrangement to assess whether there is a lease.
>
> Also, operating lease payments that have been structured to increase in line with general inflation are not specifically mentioned. In the absence of specific guidance, micro-entities should select an appropriate accounting policy in accordance with Section 8 of FRS 105.

8.2 Scope

Certain leases are scoped out of Section 20 as they are addressed elsewhere in FRS 102:

Types of lease	Section
Leases to explore for or use minerals, oil, natural gas and similar non-regenerative resources	34 *Specialised Activities*
Licensing agreements for such items as motion picture films, video recordings, plays, manuscripts, patents and copyrights	18 *Intangible Assets other than Goodwill*
Leases that could lead to a loss to the lessor or the lessee as a result of non-typical contractual terms	12 *Other Financial Instruments*

In addition the measurement of certain assets held or provided under a lease is scoped out of Section 20, although other provisions of Section 20, such as recognition of lease income and the treatment of lease incentives, continue to apply.

Types of asset	Section
Measurement of property held by lessees that is accounted for as investment property	16 *Investment Property*
Measurement of investment property provided by lessors under operating leases	16 *Investment Property*
Measurement of biological assets held by lessees under finance leases	34 *Specialised Activities*
Measurement of biological assets provided by lessors under operating leases	34 *Specialised Activities*

If an entity holds a property under an operating lease, rents it out also under an operating lease and classifies and accounts for the property as an investment property then the entity accounts for its lessee interest in the property as a finance lease even if it would normally fall to be treated as an operating lease (see **5.3.1** of this guide). [Paragraphs 16.3 and 16.6]

A lessor applies the measurement rules of Section 20 to a property that is leased to a third party under a finance lease.

Leases are agreements that transfer the right to use an asset. Some contracts may also require substantial services to be delivered by the lessor to operate or maintain the asset. An agreement that is a contract for services that does not transfer the right to use an asset is not a lease. The costs for services included within payments over the lease term are excluded from the minimum lease payments (see below).

Although this is not stated explicitly, the definition of a lease will include hire purchase contracts that convey to the hirer, in return for a payment or series of payments, the right to use an asset for an agreed period of time together with an option for the hirer to acquire legal title to the underlying asset upon the fulfilment of conditions in the contract.

8.3   Applying the requirements

8.3.1   Determining whether an arrangement contains a lease

As noted above, it is necessary to consider whether arrangements that do not take the legal form of a lease do actually convey rights to use assets. Such arrangements may include outsourcing arrangements, telecommunication contracts that provide rights to capacity, and take-or-pay contracts.

It will be necessary to consider the substance of the arrangement and assess whether (paragraph 20.3A):

- fulfilment of the arrangement is dependent on the use of a specific asset or assets. Although a specific asset may be explicitly identified in an arrangement, it is not the subject of a lease if fulfilment of the arrangement is not dependent on the use of the specified asset. An asset is implicitly specified if, for example, the supplier owns or leases only one asset with which to fulfil the obligation and it is not economically feasible or practicable for the supplier to perform its obligation through the use of alternative assets; and

- the arrangement conveys a right to use the asset. This will be the case where the arrangement conveys to the purchaser the right to control the use of the underlying asset.

This is all of the guidance within Section 20: preparers may also find it helpful to look to IFRIC 4 *Determining whether an arrangement contains a lease* as this provides further guidance.

8.5 covers the transitional provisions relating to the determination of whether an arrangement contains a lease.

8.3.2   Lease classification

Classification is determined based on whether or not the lease transfers to the lessee substantially all of the risk and rewards incidental to ownership of the asset. If it does, it is a finance lease. If it does not, it is an operating lease. This assessment is based on the substance of the transaction rather than the form of the contract.

Risks incidental to ownership of an asset include losses incurred due to idle capacity, technological obsolescence, variations in return due to changing economic conditions and variation in the value of the residual interest in the asset.

Rewards incidental to ownership of an asset include the expectation of profitable operation over the asset's life and the possible appreciation in value of the residual interest in the asset.

8.3.2.1   Finance lease or operating lease?

A number of examples are given in paragraphs 20.5–20.6 of situations that indicate that a lease is a finance lease (i.e. substantially all the risk and rewards incidental to ownership are transferred to the lessee):

- the lease transfers ownership of the asset to the lessee by the end of the lease term;

- the lessee has the option to purchase the asset at a price that is expected to be sufficiently lower than the fair value at the date the option becomes exercisable for it to be reasonably certain, at the inception of the lease, that the option will be exercised;

- the lease term is for the major part of the economic life of the asset even if title is not transferred;

- at the inception of the lease the present value of the minimum lease payments amounts to at least substantially all of the fair value of the leased asset;

- the leased assets are of such a specialised nature that only the lessee can use them without major modifications;

- if the lessee can cancel the lease, the lessor's losses associated with the cancellation are borne by the lessee;

- gains or losses from the fluctuation in the residual value of the leased asset accrue to the lessee (e.g. in the form of a rent rebate equalling most of the sales proceeds at the end of the lease); and

- the lessee has the ability to continue the lease for a secondary period at a rent that is substantially lower than market rent.

However, FRS 102 notes that the above indicators are not always conclusive – so if it is clear from other features that the lease does not transfer substantially all the risk and rewards incidental to ownership, it is classified as an operating lease. Examples where this may be the case include:

- where ownership of the asset is transferred to the lessee at the end of the lease, for a variable payment equal to the asset's then fair value; and

- the existence of contingent rents, as a result of which the lessee does not have substantially all risks and rewards incidental to ownership.

If the lease term is for the major part of the economic life of the asset, the residual value risk relating to the asset is likely to be small. In that case, whether or not ownership of the asset transfers to the lessee by the end of the lease term is less likely to be relevant to whether the lease transfers substantially all of the risk and rewards incidental to ownership to the lessee.

The present value of the minimum lease payment referred to in the finance lease indicators above is calculated using the interest rate implicit in the lease or, if that cannot be determined, the lessee's incremental borrowing rate.

There are a number of key terms that are relevant to the analysis of a lease. These are defined in the Glossary to FRS 102, but some of the key terms for lease classification are reproduced below. Note that contingent rentals are excluded from minimum lease payments.

Lease term	The non-cancellable period for which the lessee has contracted to lease the asset together with any further terms for which the lessee has the option to continue to lease the asset, with or without further payment, when at the inception of the lease it is reasonably certain that the lessee will exercise the option.

Minimum lease payments	The payments over the lease term that the lessee is or can be required to make, excluding contingent rent, costs for services and taxes to be paid by and reimbursed to the lessor, together with:
	(a) for a lessee, any amounts guaranteed by the lessee or by a party related to the lessee; or
	(b) for a lessor, any residual value guaranteed to the lessor by:
	  (i) the lessee;
	  (ii) a party related to the lessee; or
	  (iii) a third party unrelated to the lessor that is financially capable of discharging the obligations under the guarantee.
	
	However, if the lessee has an option to purchase the asset at a price that is expected to be sufficiently lower than fair value at the date the option becomes exercisable for it to be reasonably certain, at the inception of the lease, that the option will be exercised, the minimum lease payments comprise the minimum payments payable over the lease term to the expected date of exercise of this purchase option and the payment required to exercise it.

Residual value	The estimated amount that an entity would currently obtain from disposal of an asset, after deducting the estimated costs of disposal, if the asset were already of the age and in the condition expected at the end of its useful life.
Interest rate implicit in the lease	The discount rate that, at the inception of the lease, causes the aggregate present value of: (a) the minimum lease payments; and (b) the unguaranteed residual value to be equal to the sum of: (i) the fair value of the leased asset; and (ii) any initial direct costs of the lessor.
Lessee's incremental borrowing rate	The rate of interest the lessee would have to pay on a similar lease or, if that is not determinable, the rate that, at the inception of the lease, the lessee would incur to borrow over a similar term, and with a similar security, the funds necessary to purchase the asset.
Contingent rents	That portion of the lease payments that is not fixed in amount but is based on the future amount of a factor that changes other than with the passage of time (e.g. percentage of future sales, amount of future use, future price indices, and future market rates of interest).

8.3.2.2   Inception of the lease vs commencement of the lease

These terms are defined in the Glossary to FRS 102 and reproduced below.

Inception of the lease	The earlier of the date of the lease agreement and the date of commitment by the parties to the principal provisions of the lease.
Commencement of the lease term	The date from which the lessee is entitled to exercise its right to use the leased asset. It is the date of initial recognition of the lease (i.e. the recognition of the assets, liabilities, income or expenses resulting from the lease, as appropriate).

The distinction between these two terms matters because from paragraph 20.8, lease classification is made at the inception of the lease and is not changed during the term of the lease unless the lessee and the lessor agree to change the provisions of the lease (other than simply by renewing the lease), in which case the lease classification shall be re-evaluated.

A lessee holding an asset under a finance lease measures the asset and the liability based on the present value of the minimum lease payments at the inception of the lease. However, the asset and liability are not recognised in the lessee's statement of financial position until commencement of the lease term.

It is clearly possible for the inception of the lease and the commencement of the lease term to fall on different dates. It is also possible that the lease agreement may include provisions to adjust lease payments if, for example, an asset is being constructed and there are changes in price levels or financing cost between the inception of the lease and the commencement of the lease term. FRS 102 gives no guidance in this situation so preparers may choose, here, to take the option in Section 10 to look to EU-adopted IFRS. IAS 17 paragraph 5 notes that in a case such as this the effect of any changes shall be deemed to have taken place at the inception of the lease.

8.3.3   Finance leases

8.3.3.1   Accounting by lessees

A finance lease gives rise to both an asset and a liability in the lessee's statement of financial position. At the commencement of the lease, these amounts are recorded at the fair value of the leased asset or, if lower, the present value of the minimum lease payments, determined at the inception of the lease. The present value of the minimum lease payments is calculated using the interest rate implicit in the lease or, if that cannot be determined, the lessee's incremental borrowing rate (see **8.3.2**).

Any initial direct costs incurred by the lessee (incremental costs that are directly attributable to negotiating and arranging a lease) are added to the amount recognised as an asset.

The leased asset is depreciated in accordance with Section 17, discussed in **5.2.5** of this guide. The asset is depreciated over the shorter of the lease term and the asset's useful life unless there is a reasonable certainty that the lessee will obtain ownership of the asset by the end of the lease term (if the entity was reasonably certain to obtain ownership it would use the asset's useful life even though this would be longer than the lease term). The lessee should assess the asset for impairment at each reporting date.

Minimum lease payments are apportioned between the finance charge and as a reduction of the outstanding liability using the effective interest method (i.e. the method used for measuring amortised cost financial liabilities, discussed in **7.3.3**).

Any contingent rentals are expensed to profit or loss in the period in which they are incurred.

Example 8.1

On 1 January 20X1, entity X enters into an agreement with entity Y to lease an asset for six years at a rental of £50,000 per annum for the first five years and a final payment in year six of £52,500. All payments are made in arrears. At the inception of the lease the asset has a fair value of £240,000. The useful economic life of the asset is six years and it is expected to have a negligible residual value at the end of that period.

The lease is considered to be a finance lease.

The interest rate implicit in the lease is 6.999%. This is the amount that discounts the minimum lease payments plus the unguaranteed residual (nil) to the fair value of the asset (£240,000).

Time (n)	Cash flow £	$1/(1+r)^n$ Discount rate %	Discounted cash flow £
Year X1	50,000	0.9346	46,729
Year X2	50,000	0.8735	43,673
Year X3	50,000	0.8163	40,816
Year X4	50,000	0.7629	38,146
Year X5	52,500	0.7130	35,651
Present value of minimum lease payments			240,000

Initial recognition

Recognise the right to use the asset and a liability at the fair value of the leased asset or, if lower, the present value of the minimum lease payments. The asset and liability are recorded at £240,000.

Subsequent accounting

The asset will be depreciated on a straight line basis over the six years, in accordance with X's accounting policy, giving a depreciation charge of £40,000 a year.

The lease payments are apportioned between the finance charge and the reduction of the outstanding liability using the effective interest method.

Year	Opening lease liability	Finance charge	Lease payments	Closing lease liability
20X1	240,000	16,798	-50,000	206,798
20X2	206,798	14,474	-50,000	171,271
20X3	171,271	11,987	-50,000	133,259
20X4	133,259	9,327	-50,000	92,585
20X5	92,585	6,480	-50,000	49,065
20X6	49,065	3,434	-52,500	0

8.3.3.2   Accounting by lessors

Paragraphs 20.17–20.19 set out finance lease accounting by lessors:

> 'A lessor shall recognise assets held under a finance lease in its statement of financial position and present them as a receivable at an amount equal to the net investment in the lease. The net investment in a lease is the lessor's gross investment in the lease discounted at the interest rate implicit in the lease. The gross investment in the lease is the aggregate of:
>
> (a)   the minimum lease payments receivable by the lessor under a finance lease; and
>
> (b)   any unguaranteed residual value accruing to the lessor.
>
> For finance leases other than those involving manufacturer or dealer lessors, initial direct costs (costs that are incremental and directly attributable to negotiating and arranging a lease) are included in the initial measurement of the finance lease receivable and reduce the amount of income recognised over the lease term.'

Paragraph 20.19 goes on to state that:

> 'The recognition of finance income shall be based on a pattern reflecting a constant periodic rate of return on the lessor's net investment in the finance lease. Lease payments relating to the period, excluding costs for services, are applied against the gross investment in the lease to reduce both the principal and the unearned finance income. If there is an indication that the estimated unguaranteed residual value used in computing the lessor's gross investment in the lease has changed significantly, the income allocation over the lease term is revised, and any reduction in respect of amounts accrued is recognised immediately in profit or loss.'

This has the effect of recognising finance income in the same way as it would be on any loan, weighted towards the early periods when there is most capital outstanding.

8.3.3.3   Manufacturer or dealer lessor

Paragraphs 20.20–20.22, reproduced below, set out the accounting in this situation:

> 'Manufacturers or dealers often offer to customers the choice of either buying or leasing an asset. A finance lease of an asset by a manufacturer or dealer lessor gives rise to two types of income:
>
> (a)   profit or loss equivalent to the profit or loss resulting from an outright sale of the asset being leased, at normal selling prices, reflecting any applicable volume or trade discounts; and
>
> (b)   finance income over the lease term.
>
> The sales revenue recognised at the commencement of the lease term by a manufacturer or dealer lessor is the fair value of the asset or, if lower, the present value of the minimum lease payments accruing to the lessor, computed

at a market rate of interest. The cost of sale recognised at the commencement of the lease term is the cost, or carrying amount if different, of the leased asset less the present value of the unguaranteed residual value. The difference between the sales revenue and the cost of sale is the selling profit, which is recognised in accordance with the entity's policy for outright sales.

If artificially low rates of interest are quoted, selling profit shall be restricted to that which would apply if a market rate of interest were charged. Costs incurred by manufacturer or dealer lessors in connection with negotiating and arranging a lease shall be recognised as an expense when the selling profit is recognised.'

Example 8.2

This continues the example in **8.3.3** above, adding the fact that the lessor (entity Y) originally manufactured the asset at a cost of £200,000.

At the inception of the lease the asset has a fair value of £240,000. This is also the present value of the minimum lease payments accruing to the lessor calculated at a market rate of interest. The asset is leased for the period of its economic useful life (six years) and has a negligible residual value at the end of that period.

Initial recognition

The manufacturer/lessor recognises revenue at an amount of the fair value of the asset and a cost of sales of the cost of the asset.

Dr Lease receivable	240,000	
Cr Revenue		(240,000)

Dr Cost of sales	200,000	
Cr Inventories		(200,000)

Subsequent accounting

The lease payments received are apportioned between the finance charge and the reduction of the outstanding receivable to reflect a constant periodic rate of return on the lessor's net investment in the finance lease. In this example, the return is 6.999%

Year	Opening lease receivable	Finance income	Lease payments received	Closing lease receivable
20X1	240,000	16,798	-50,000	206,798
20X2	206,798	14,474	-50,000	171,271
20X3	171,271	11,987	-50,000	133,259
20X4	133,259	9,327	-50,000	92,585
20X5	92,585	6,480	-50,000	49,065
20X6	49,065	3,434	-52,500	0

8.3.4   Operating leases

8.3.4.1   Accounting by lessees

Paragraphs 20.15 and 20.15A provide that:

'A lessee shall recognise lease payments under operating leases (excluding costs for services such as insurance and maintenance) as an expense over the lease term on a straight-line basis, unless either:

(a)   another systematic basis is representative of the time pattern of the user's benefit, even if the payments are not on that basis; or

(b)   the payments to the lessor are structured to increase in line with expected general inflation (based on published indexes or statistics) to compensate for the lessor's expected inflationary cost increases. If payments to the lessor vary because of factors other than general inflation, then this condition is not met.

A lessee shall recognise the aggregate benefit of lease incentives as a reduction to the expense recognised in accordance with paragraph 20.15 over the lease term, on a straight-line basis unless another systematic basis is representative of the time pattern of the lessee's benefit from the use of the leased asset. Any costs incurred by the lessee (for example costs for termination of a pre-existing lease, relocation or leasehold improvements) shall be accounted for in accordance with the applicable Section of [FRS 102].'

The effect of the requirements in respect of inflationary cost increases is illustrated in this example, based on the example following paragraph 20.15 of FRS 102.

Example 8.3

X operates in a jurisdiction in which the consensus forecast by local banks is that the general price level index, as published by the government, will increase by an average of 10% annually over the next five years. X leases some office space from Y for five years under an operating lease commencing 01 January 20X1. The contractual lease payments are structured to reflect the expected 10% annual general inflation over the five-year term of the lease as follows:

- Year 1 CU100,000;

- Year 2 CU110,000;

- Year 3 CU121,000;

- Year 4 CU133,000; and

- Year 5 CU146,000.

Operating lease expense recognised in:	If structured to compensate the lessor for expected inflationary cost increases based on published indexes or statistics	If not so structured (recognised on a straight-line basis)
20X1	CU100,000	CU122,000
20X2	CU110,000	CU122,000
20X3	CU121,000	CU122,000
20X4	CU133,000	CU122,000
20X5	CU146,000	CU122,000

To be clear, the required accounting in this case gives the non-straight-line outcome. It is not acceptable to apply prudence and use the straight line approach to recognise a higher expense in the early years. Entities wishing to do this would need to demonstrate that the escalation of the rent expense was not based on inflation expectations (which in this case would be difficult to argue).

Paragraph 20.15B states that where an operating lease becomes an onerous contract, the lessee looks to Section 21 on provisions for guidance on how to account for it (and, indeed, on how to establish with certainty that it meets the definition).

8.3.4.2   Accounting by lessors

Paragraphs 20.24–20.29, reproduced here, set out lessor accounting for operating leases. It mirrors the lessee accounting, with the exception that lessees are not told what to do with direct costs incurred on setting up the lease.

'A lessor shall present assets subject to operating leases in its statement of financial position according to the nature of the asset. It mirrors the lessee accounting, with the exception that lessees are not told what to do with direct costs incurred on setting up the lease.

A lessor shall recognise lease income from operating leases (excluding amounts for services such as insurance and maintenance) in profit or loss on a straight-line basis over the lease term, unless either:

(a)   another systematic basis is representative of the time pattern of the lessee's benefit from the leased asset, even if the receipt of payments is not on that basis; or

(b)   the payments to the lessor are structured to increase in line with expected general inflation (based on published indexes or statistics) to compensate for the lessor's expected inflationary cost increases. If payments to the lessor vary according to factors other than inflation, then this condition is not met.

A lessor shall recognise the aggregate cost of lease incentives as a reduction to the income recognised in accordance with the above paragraph over the lease term on a straight-line basis, unless another systematic basis is representative of the time pattern over which the lessor's benefit from the leased asset is diminished.

A lessor shall recognise as an expense, costs, including depreciation, incurred in earning the lease income. The depreciation policy for depreciable leased assets shall be consistent with the lessor's normal depreciation policy for similar assets. A lessor shall add to the carrying amount of the leased asset any initial direct costs it incurs in negotiating and arranging an operating lease and shall recognise such costs as an expense over the lease term on the same basis as the lease income.

To determine whether a leased asset has become impaired, a lessor shall apply Section 27.'

A manufacturer or dealer lessor does not recognise any selling profit on entering into an operating lease because it is not the equivalent of a sale.

8.3.4.3   Sale and leaseback transactions

A sale and leaseback transaction is one where an entity (the seller-lessee) sells and leases back the same asset. These types of transaction are motivated by cash flows or, sometimes, by the desire not to show assets in the balance sheet (perhaps to improve ratios, or reduce perceived risks).

The lease payment and the sale price are usually interdependent because they are negotiated as a package. The accounting treatment of a sale and leaseback transaction by the seller-lessee depends on the type of lease, and by no means all sale and leasebacks will lead to derecognition of the asset.

If a sale and leaseback transaction results in a finance lease, the seller-lessee does not recognise any excess of sales proceeds over the carrying amount immediately as income. Instead, the excess is deferred and amortised over the lease term.

If a sale and leaseback transaction results in an operating lease, then:

- if it is clear that the transaction is at fair value, the seller-lessee recognises any profit or loss immediately;

- if the sale price is below fair value, the seller-lessee recognises any profit or loss immediately unless the loss is compensated for by future lease payments at below market price. In that case the seller-lessee defers the loss, amortising it in proportion to the lease payments over the period for which the asset is expected to be used; and

- if the sale price is above fair value, the seller-lessee defers the excess over fair value and amortises it over the period for which the asset is expected to be used.

Example 8.4

(1) A seller-lessee sells a building with a carrying amount of £280,000 to an independent third party for £350,000 (the fair value of the building). As part of the arrangement, the seller-lessee enters into a three-year operating lease arrangement to lease the same building back from the buyer. The seller-lessee would recognise a gain on disposal of £70,000.

(2) A seller-lessee sells a building with a carrying amount of £280,000 to an independent third party for £300,000. The fair value of the building is £350,000. As part of the arrangement, the seller-lessee enters into a three-year operating lease arrangement to lease the same building back from the buyer. The seller-lessee would recognise a gain on disposal of £20,000 even if subsequent rentals are below market price.

(3) A seller-lessee sells a building with a carrying amount of £280,000 to an independent third party for £260,000. The fair value of the building is £350,000. As part of the arrangement, the seller-lessee enters into a three-year operating lease arrangement to lease the same building back from the buyer and the subsequent rentals are below market price. The seller-lessee would defer and amortise the £20,000 loss in proportion to the lease payments over the period for which the asset is expected to be used.

In any case where the selling price is not equal to fair value, an auditor would be looking to test the assertion that subsequent rentals really are at market rates. This is because few businesses like to give 'something for nothing', so usually an off-market sale or purchase would be expected to be accompanied by rentals payable or receivable that are also off-market, in the opposite direction. It is always important to look at all the terms of a transaction to ensure that the accounting reflects the commercial reality of the whole arrangement.

8.4 Presentation and disclosure

8.4.1 Presentation and disclosure requirements

8.4.1.1 Lessees – finance leases (paragraphs 20.13 and 20.14)

A lessee shall make the following disclosures for finance leases:

(a) for each class of asset, the net carrying amount at the end of the reporting period;

(b) the total of future minimum lease payments at the end of the reporting period, for each of the following periods:

(i)   not later than one year;

(ii) later than one year and not later than five years;

(iii) later than five years; and

(c) a general description of the lessee's significant leasing arrangements including, for example, information about contingent rent, renewal or purchase options and escalation clauses, subleases, and restrictions imposed by lease arrangements.

In addition, the requirements for disclosure about assets in accordance with Sections 17, 18 and 27 of FRS 102 apply to lessees for assets leased under finance leases.

8.4.1.2 Lessees – operating leases (paragraph 20.16)

A lessee shall make the following disclosures for operating leases:

(a) the total of future minimum lease payments under non-cancellable operating leases for each of the following periods:

(i)   not later than one year;

(ii) later than one year and not later than five years;

(iii) later than five years; and

(b) lease payments recognised as an expense.

FRS 102 requires an aged analysis of the total future minimum lease payments under non-cancellable operating leases. This is not discounted to present value and should only include those payments that cannot be contractually avoided. For example, if a lease contains a break clause, the disclosure should only include payments up to the date of the break clause, even if the entity does not plan to exercise it.

8.4.1.3 Lessors – finance leases (paragraph 20.23)

A lessor shall make the following disclosures for finance leases:

(a) a reconciliation between the gross investment in the lease at the end of the reporting period, and the present value of minimum lease payments receivable at the end of the reporting period. In addition, a lessor shall disclose the gross investment in the lease and the present value of minimum lease payments receivable at the end of the reporting period, for each of the following periods:

(i)   not later than one year;

(ii) later than one year and not later than five years; and

(iii) later than five years;

(b) unearned finance income (i.e. the gross investment in the lease less the net investment in the lease);

(c) the unguaranteed residual values accruing to the benefit of the lessor;

(d) the accumulated allowance for uncollectible minimum lease payments receivable;

(e) contingent rents recognised as income in the period; and

(f) a general description of the lessor's significant leasing arrangements, including, for example, information about contingent rent, renewal or purchase options and escalation clauses, subleases, and restrictions imposed by lease arrangements.

8.4.1.4   Lessors – operating leases (paragraphs 20.30–20.31)

A lessor shall disclose the following for operating leases:

(a) the future minimum lease payments under non-cancellable operating leases for each of the following periods:

    (i)   not later than one year;

    (ii)   later than one year and not later than five years; and

    (iii)   later than five years;

(b) total contingent rents recognised as income; and

(c) a general description of the lessor's significant leasing arrangements, including: for example, information about contingent rent, renewal or purchase options and escalation clauses, and restrictions imposed by lease arrangements.

In addition, the requirements for disclosure about assets in accordance with Sections 17, 18 and 27 apply to lessors for assets provided under operating leases.

8.4.1.5   Sale and leaseback transactions (paragraph 20.35)

Disclosure requirements for lessees and lessors apply equally to sale and leaseback transactions. The required description of significant leasing arrangements includes description of unique or unusual provisions of the agreement or terms of the sale and leaseback transactions.

8.4.1.6   Companies Act requirements

The *Companies Act* 2006, s. 410A requires information about arrangements that are material and not reflected in the balance sheet. This includes the nature and business purpose of the arrangements and the financial affects.

The *Large and Medium-sized Companies and Groups (Accounts and Reports) Regulations* 2008 require that in relation to 'land and buildings' in the company's balance sheet, there must be stated how much of that amount is ascribable to land of freehold tenure and how much to land of leasehold tenure, and how much of the amount ascribable to land of leasehold tenure is ascribable to land held on long lease and how much to land held on short lease (Sch. 1, para. 53).

8.4.2   Example notes

8.4.2.1   Lessee's operating lease commitments

The company has entered into a number of non-cancellable operating leases as lessee for which the total of future minimum lease payments are as follows:		
	20X2	**20X1**
	£	£
Within one year	20,000	20,000
Later than one year but within five years	80,000	80,000
Later than five years	15,000	20,000
Total	115,000	120,000

A lessor is required to make the same form of aged disclosure for future minimum lease payments receivable under non-cancellable operating leases.

8.4.2.2   Lessor's reconciliation for finance leases

The receivables under finance leases are as follows:			
20X2			
	Gross investment in the lease	**Unearned finance income**	**Net investment in the lease**
	£	£	£
Within one year	600,000	39,247	560,753
Later than one year but within five years	2,400,000	500,569	1,899,431
Later than five years	600,000	200,172	399,828
Total	3,600,000	739,988	2,860,012

Note that comparatives are required for the above reconciliation.

8.4.3   Qualifying entities

There are no exemptions from the disclosures required by Section 20.

8.4.4   Disclosures for small entities

Small entities applying Section 1A of the standard have almost no disclosure requirements in respect of leases. There is only the generic requirement in 1AC.28 to state the aggregate amount of debts for which security is given, for each item shown in 'creditors', and that in 1AC.29 to state the total amount of any financial commitments, guarantees and contingencies that are not included in the balance sheet – the latter would apply to operating leases, for instance.

8.5   Transition

Section 35 includes two transition exemptions relating to leases.

First, 35.10(k) allows entities to determine whether arrangements contain a lease by looking at facts and circumstances as at the transition date, rather than at the original point that the arrangement was entered into. Note that there is no exemption around classification of a lease as finance or operating, only whether or not a lease actually exists.

Paragraph 35.10(p) then gives simplification in respect of lease incentives, by allowing, for leases that commenced before the transition date, an exemption for both lessors and lessees from the requirement to spread the effect of lease incentives.

9 Provisions and contingencies

9.1 Scope of this section

This section covers Section 21 *Provisions and Contingencies.*

Section 21 of FRS 102 is virtually identical to its IFRS counterpart, IAS 37 *Provisions, Contingent Liabilities and Contingent Assets.* The scope of FRS 102 has been extended to include financial guarantee contracts in certain situations.

Sections 19 and 21 of FRS 102 require certain provisions for contingent liabilities of an acquiree in a business combination to be recognised in the acquisition balance sheet (see **4.3.2.1** of this guide).

FRS 102 includes an appendix which provides guidance on Section 21 but is not part of Section 21. The appendix comprises nine examples which will be recognised by readers familiar with FRS 12. These are useful for a deeper understanding of the topic as applied to particular circumstances.

A provision within the scope of this section is defined as 'a liability of uncertain timing or amount'. A liability is defined in paragraph 2.15(b) of FRS 102 as 'a present obligation of the entity arising from past events, the settlement of which is expected to result in an outflow from the entity of resources embodying economic benefits'.

A contingent liability is a subset of liabilities which do not meet the criteria to be recognised in the financial statements (this is defined more fully at **9.2.4**).

A contingent asset is 'a possible asset that arises from past events and whose existence will be confirmed only by the occurrence or non-occurrence of one or more uncertain future events not wholly within the control of the entity' (see **9.2.5**).

This section applies to all provisions, contingent liabilities and contingent assets except for:

- provisions covered by other sections of FRS 102. Examples include:
    - financial instruments and loan commitments that are within the scope of Section 11 *Basic Financial Instruments* or Section 12 *Other Financial Instruments Issues*;
    - construction contracts that are within the scope of Section 23 *Revenue;*

- deferred tax liabilities covered in Section 29 *Income Tax;*

- leases covered in Section 20 *Leases* (but note that onerous contracts are covered by this section); and

- employee benefit obligations covered in Section 28 *Employee Benefits*;

- financial guarantee contracts where the entity has chosen to apply IAS 39 *Financial Instruments: Recognition and Measurement* and/or IFRS 9 *Financial Instruments* to its financial instruments (paragraphs 11.2 and 12.2 of FRS 102), or the entity has elected under FRS 103 *Insurance Contracts* to continue the application of insurance contract accounting. Otherwise financial guarantee contracts are covered by this section;

- certain contracts that are within the scope of FRS 103 *Insurance Contracts*;

- executory contracts (i.e. 'contracts under which neither party has performed any of its obligations or both parties have partially performed their obligations to an equal extent'), unless the contracts are onerous. Onerous contracts are covered at **9.2.3.1**;

- adjustments to the carrying amounts of assets, which are commonly known as provisions but are not liabilities in their own right, e.g. provisions for depreciation and impairment, bad debt provisions and stock write-downs.

It is useful to bear in mind the distinction between provisions and accruals that was noted in FRS 12: both sometimes require the use of estimates as to timings and amounts, but the uncertainties are generally much less for accruals than for provisions.

> **Application to micro-entities:** The requirements in FRS 105 are consistent with those in FRS 102.

9.2   Applying the requirements

9.2.1   Initial recognition

As will be instantly familiar to preparers of accounts, a provision is recognised in the financial statements when and only when all three of these conditions from paragraph 21.4 are met:

(a) the entity has an obligation at the reporting date as a result of a past event;

(b) it is probable that the entity will be required to transfer economic benefits in settlement; and

(c) the amount of the obligation can be estimated reliably.

9.2.1.1 Obligation

The word 'obligation' is not defined in the Glossary to FRS 102 but is clarified in 21.6 as meaning that the entity has 'no realistic alternative to settling'. This situation can arise from either a legal obligation enforceable by law as a result of a binding contract or statutory requirement, or a constructive obligation in which the entity has created sufficiently valid expectations in other parties that it accepts certain responsibilities and will discharge them.

An obligation always involves another party, and management decisions by themselves cannot create an obligation unless they have been published in such a way that backing out is not an option.

FRS 102 does not give any guidance in the situation where it is not clear whether there is an obligation at the reporting date. In this case, it is possible to use the Section 10 option to look to full IFRS, using the guidance in IAS 37 paragraphs 15 and 16:

> '… a past event is deemed to give rise to a present obligation if, taking account of all available evidence, it is more likely than not that a present obligation exists at the end of the reporting period. … for example in a lawsuit, it may be disputed either whether certain events have occurred or whether those events result in a present obligation …'

If it is more likely than not that a present obligation exists (and conditions (b) and (c) above are also met) then a provision is made; if this is not the case then the event may give rise to a contingent liability disclosure (see **9.2.4** and the example in that section). Events between the end of the reporting period and the date that the financial statements are authorised for issue are taken into account when assessing whether a present obligation existed at the balance sheet date (see **15.2** of this guide).

9.2.1.2 Past event

A provision can only be recognised if the event that creates it occurred before the reporting date. However, information obtained up to the date that the financial statements are authorised for issue should be taken into account when calculating the amount of the provision, as well as in deciding whether the obligation existed at the reporting date.

Obligations arising from future events, regardless of how likely (whether by contract or by law), must not be included as provisions, contingent liabilities or contingent assets, although they should be considered as part of the post balance sheet review. This is because the entity could choose to avoid the obligation by taking alternative action.

Example 9.1

An accountancy firm has a payroll-processing division which uses bespoke software written in-house. The firm has a 31 December 2019 reporting date. The government has announced that from April 2020 all payroll data will be required to be submitted to HMRC in an entirely new way.

The firm should not recognise a provision for the cost of rewriting its payroll software because there is no obligation at 31 December 2019 to do this. The change is in the future, and the firm could choose to deal with the change in an alternative way, for example by buying ready-made software, or by closing its payroll-processing division.

The firm may however need to make disclosures under Section 32 *Events after the End of the Reporting Period*.

9.2.1.3   Probable

'Probable' is defined in the Glossary to the standard as meaning 'more likely than not', which is a slightly lower threshold than might be implied by the word in everyday speech.

The conditions that an outflow of economic benefits is 'probable' and that the amount can be measured reliably are in fact the criteria for recognition of liabilities in general, as set out in paragraph 2.27 of the standard. Section 21 acknowledges that the measurement of the provision will often be an estimate. As paragraph 2.30 says, 'the use of reasonable estimates is an essential part of the preparation of financial statements and does not undermine their reliability.'

Similar obligations can be grouped together and considered as a class of obligations as a whole. Take, for example, warranties: the probability of an outflow of economic benefits being necessary to settle a warranty claim on any one particular individual item may be very low, but when looked at as a whole (i.e. all the products sold before the reporting date with warranties still valid, or perhaps all products within one class), the entity may know from experience that there will always be some warranty claims during any reporting period and therefore an outflow of economic benefits to settle the warranty claims as a whole is probable.

9.2.2 *Measurement*

At each reporting date, for each class of provision, the entity measures the provision as at that date, and adjusts any amounts previously provided to bring them to the latest estimate.

9.2.2.1 *Best estimate*

The main rule is that the provision is measured at the 'best estimate' of the amount required to settle the obligation at the reporting date. The best estimate is defined as 'the amount an entity would rationally pay to settle the obligation at the end of the reporting period or to transfer it to a third party at that time'. The amount to actually settle the obligation on the reporting date could be prohibitively expensive, so instead entities are required to estimate the amount they would rationally pay supposing the option to settle or transfer the obligation was available to them.

The estimate is determined by judgment and can include reports from independent experts, experience of similar transactions, knowledge of circumstances that are particularly relevant to the provision, industry benchmarks and evidence provided by events after the end of the reporting period. The effects of anticipated new technology can be taken into account, but only where there is sufficient objective evidence that the new technology will be commercially available to the entity. Similarly, cost reductions anticipated from increased experience of applying existing technology may be taken into account.

The principle of the balance between benefit and cost set out in paragraph 2.13 of the standard should always be borne in mind when gathering information to prepare an estimate.

9.2.2.2 *Single obligation*

Some provisions arise from a single obligation, for example, an event leading to a court case. In this situation, the best estimate of the amount to settle the obligation may be the individual most likely outcome. The entity should also consider other possible outcomes and where these are mostly higher or mostly lower than the most likely outcome the best estimate will be adjusted accordingly.

Example 9.2

An entity that supplies marquees for events unfortunately double-booked its facilities for one day during the reporting period and was unable to complete a contract to supply a marquee for a large society wedding. The distraught bride is suing the entity. The entity has admitted it is at fault, and there will be a court case to determine the amount of damages payable. The entity's lawyers advise that there is a 60% chance of the entity having to pay damages of £50,000, a 30% chance of the damages being £70,000 and a 10% chance of

---

the damages being £150,000. The case is not scheduled to go to court until a date after the financial statements will be authorised for issue.

The entity needs to make a provision because it has an obligation (to pay damages) as a result of a past event (failing to supply a marquee on the date during the reporting period); it is probable that the entity will be required to transfer economic benefits to settle the obligation (the entity has admitted fault and the lawyers' probabilities do not include anything for not having to make a payment); and the amount of the obligation can be estimated reliably (see below).

The individual most likely outcome, according to the independent experts, is £50,000 (a probability of 60%). However, the other outcomes should also be considered and in this example they are all higher than the most likely outcome. Therefore the best estimate used for the provision needs to be weighted higher than the most likely amount.

Using a weighted average is a reasonable method to achieve this:

Provision = (60% × £50,000) + (30% × £70,000) + (10% × £150,000) = £66,000.

The time value of money has been ignored in this example.

Supposing the court case is brought forward and is heard before the accounts are authorised for issue, then the amount of the provision would be adjusted to the actual amount of damages awarded. This is because the settlement of a court case relating to an obligation that existed at the end of the reporting period is an adjusting event as defined by Section 32 of FRS 102 (see **15.2** of this guide).

9.2.2.3   Large population of items involved

Some provisions arise from a large population of items, for example, a warranty provision. In this case the standard directs that the best estimate of the amount to settle the provision should reflect the weighting of all the possible outcomes by their associated probabilities. This statistical method is known as 'expected value'. The standard points out that where there is a continuous range of possible outcomes, and each point in the range is as likely as any other, then the mid-point of the range should be used.

Example 9.3

An entity provides online training programmes. If any learners are not 'fully delighted' with their course, they have one year to claim either a full refund or the chance to take a different course. During the reporting period, 1,500 courses were sold. The sales price of a course is £900 and the cost to the entity to provide the course materials is £200 per learner. From experience the entity expects that it is more likely than not that some claims will be made under the satisfaction guarantee, and that of the courses sold in a year, 3% of the learners will request to take a different course and 1% will request a full refund.

The entity needs to make a provision because it has an obligation (to give a refund or replacement course) as a result of a past event (selling a course); it is probable that the entity will be required to transfer economic benefits to settle the obligation (from experience the entity knows this is more likely than not, looking at the refund policy as a whole); and the amount of the obligation can be estimated reliably (see below).

The provision is made up of a large population of items (1,500 courses of which some will result in refunds), so the estimate of the provision should be calculated using the weighting of all the possible outcomes by their associated probabilities. Hence:

Provision = (96% × 1,500 × £nil) + (3% × 1,500 × £200) + (1% × 1,500 × £900) = £22,500.

The time value of money has been ignored in this example.

9.2.2.4   Discounting

Paragraph 21.7 requires that, when the effect is material, the provision is discounted to take account of the time value of money, with the discount rate being 'a pre-tax rate (or rates) that reflect(s) current market assessments of the time value of money and risks specific to the liability'. However, some preparers like to apply a separate percentage uplift to all calculations of cash outflows before discounting, to take account of the uncertainty inherent in the predicted possible outcomes. If this has been done then the discount rate must not also take into account risks specific to the liability. A risk-free rate for the time value of money can be approximated by the yield on a government bond with a maturity date close to the timing of the cash flow.

Example 9.4

An entity writes bespoke software for clients. It guarantees to correct all software faults discovered in the programs within two years of commissioning. Faults are either major faults or minor faults and the cost to rectify the software varies accordingly. During the reporting period ending 31 December 2019, the entity completed two software projects and both were commissioned on 31 December 2019. The first project was a straightforward assignment whereas the second project was considerably more complex. The project managers have provided the following information:

	Project 1	*Project 2*
Probability of major fault within first year	35%	40%
Expected cost to rectify first year major fault	£20,000	£200,000
Probability of minor fault within first year	30%	30%
Expected cost to rectify first year minor fault	£5,000	£50,000
Probability of major fault in second year	45%	55%

	Project 1	Project 2
Expected cost to rectify second year major fault	£25,000	£180,000
Probability of minor fault in second year	15%	18%
Expected cost to rectify second year minor fault	£2,000	£15,000

The entity uplifts all estimates of cash outflows by 5% to take account of the uncertainty in the estimates.

For simplicity it is assumed that faults arise and are rectified exactly 12 months or 24 months after the commissioning date. The yields on government bonds are as follows:

Bond taken out 31 Dec 2019 and expiring	Rate
31 December 2020	8% per year
31 December 2021	9% per year

The entity needs to make a provision because at the reporting date it has an obligation (to correct software) as a result of a past event (commissioning); it is probable, for both projects and for both years, that the entity will be required to incur costs to settle the obligation (by rectifying the software); and the amount of the obligation can be estimated reliably as follows (here we are assuming that the effects of discounting are material):

Date of expected outflow	Notes	£'000
31 December 2020	12 months from end of project 1: [(35% × £20,000) + (30% × £5,000)] × 1.05 × 1/1.08	8.3
31 December 2020	12 months from end of project 2: [(40% × £200,000) + (30% × £50,000)] × 1.05 × 1/1.08	92.4
31 December 2021	24 months from end of project 1: [(45% × £25,000) + (15% × £2,000)] × 1.05 × 1/1.09 × 1/1.09	10.2
31 December 2021	24 months from end of project 2: [(55% × £180,000) + (18% × £15,000)] × 1.05 × 1/1.09 × 1/1.09	89.9
Total provision at 31 December 2019:		200.8

9.2.2.5 Gains from the expected disposal of assets

Gains from the expected disposal of assets must be excluded from the calculation of a provision, even if the disposal is closely linked to the event giving rise to the provision. This is because the asset itself will already be recognised in the financial statements, and its disposal value should already have been taken into account when measuring the carrying value of the asset, in particular with regard to assessments of impairment (see **5.6** of this guide).

9.2.2.6 Reimbursements by third parties

Sometimes an entity expects to recover some or all of the cost of a provision from a third party, for example via an insurance claim. Paragraph 21.9 requires that where the entity is liable for the whole of the obligation regardless of whether or not the claim for reimbursement is successful, then the provision should be recognised in full and a related asset recognised separately only if it meets the recognition criteria for an asset (see **2.2.2** of this guide). Any expected reimbursement is disclosed, whether or not it is also recognised (see **9.3.1**). If the entity is not liable for the cost unless it is recovered from the third party, then the entity does not have a present obligation at the reporting date and so a provision is not recognised.

Where an entity is jointly and severally liable for an obligation, the amount that is expected to be settled by other parties is a contingent liability.

9.2.3 Particular types of provision

9.2.3.1 Onerous contracts

A contract is onerous if 'the unavoidable costs of meeting the obligations under the contract exceed the economic benefits expected to be received under it'. The unavoidable costs are 'the least net cost of exiting from the contract, which is the lower of the cost of fulfilling it and any compensation or penalties arising from failure to fulfil it'.

Onerous contracts are recognised and measured as provisions. If the entity has assets that are dedicated to the contract, these should be reviewed for impairment (see **5.6** of this guide).

Example 9.5

An entity has entered into a binding contract with a supplier to purchase 100 units per month of a product at £200 per unit. At the reporting date, the contract has three months left to run. The market for this particular product has completely evaporated following the entry into the market of a much superior competitor product. The entity could sell the products for scrap at £5 per unit, or cancel the contract which incurs a penalty of £20,000.

The entity needs to calculate the least net cost of the contract. If it takes delivery of the final three months' supply, and sells the products for scrap, the cost will be 100 × (£200 − £5) × 3 = £58,500. The alternative is to cancel the contract at a cost of £20,000. Being less than the cost to complete the contract, this would be the rational choice, all other things being equal.

The contract is onerous because there is an unavoidable net cash outflow. Therefore, a provision of £20,000 must be made in the financial statements.

9.2.3.2   Future operating losses

The section states specifically that provisions shall not be made for future operating losses. This is because they do not meet the definition of a liability: there is no obligation at the reporting date as a result of an event before the reporting date. The entity could make changes to the way that the loss-making business operates in order to minimise or avoid the potential losses.

The entity should consider whether any assets are impaired, as the anticipation of future losses could be an indicator of impairment.

Compare to the situation in which the entity has entered into an onerous purchase contract (as explained above). In this case the losses are unavoidable and the event giving rise to the loss occurred in the past (entering into the contract). Hence a provision is appropriate.

9.2.3.3   Restructurings

In line with all other provisions covered by this section, the costs of restructuring are recognised as a provision only when the entity has a legal or constructive obligation at the reporting date to carry out the restructuring.

A restructuring is defined in the glossary to FRS 102 as 'a programme that is planned and controlled by management and materially changes either (a) the scope of a business undertaken by an entity, or (b) the manner in which that business is conducted'.

Paragraph 21.11C gives further information on what is necessary for an entity to have created a constructive obligation relating to a restructuring. The entity must:

(a)   have a detailed formal plan for the restructuring identifying at least:

    (i)   the business or part of a business concerned;

    (ii)   the principal locations affected;

    (iii)   the location, function, and approximate number of employees who will be compensated for terminating their services;

    (iv)   the expenditures that will be undertaken; and

    (v)   when the plan will be implemented;

    and

(b)   have raised a valid expectation in those affected that it will carry out the restructuring by starting to implement that plan or announcing its main features to those affected by it.

FRS 102 does not give further information except in the examples in its appendix; however, the guidance in IAS 37 may also be helpful (even though there is no technical obligation to take it into account):

- Examples of actions that could create a valid expectation in those affected include dismantling plant, selling assets, writing to customers to advise them to find alternatives, writing to suppliers to give notice on contracts, starting redundancy procedures and announcements in the press.
- A valid expectation is likely to be created only when the timescales of the plan are sufficiently short and start to be implemented soon after the reporting date (if not already started) so that there is little chance of the entity changing its plans.
- No obligation arises for the sale of an operation until the entity is committed to the sale, i.e. there is a binding sale agreement.
- A provision for restructuring shall include only the direct expenditures arising from the restructuring, which means that they are both necessarily incurred as a result of the restructuring and not associated with the ongoing activities of the entity.
- Identifiable future operating losses up to the date of a restructuring are not included in a provision unless they relate to an onerous contract (see above).

If there is a restructuring, the preparer should also have regard to Section 5 *Statement of Comprehensive Income and Income Statement* (especially the parts relating to discontinued operations), Section 27 *Impairment of Assets* and Section 32 *Events after the End of the Reporting Period*.

9.2.3.4   Warranties

When an entity sells a product with a warranty then the action of the sale creates an event in the past obligating the entity to repair or replace the item (according to the warranty details) if it fails within a certain period after the sale. The repair or replacement cost is an outflow of economic benefits. Looking at the class of warranties, the entity assesses whether or not it is probable that there will be an outflow of economic benefits relating to the warranties as a whole, and if so it makes a reasonable estimate of the number of items still within their warranty period that are likely to require repair or replacement, and the related probabilities and costs.

If the entity expects to make corresponding claims on warranty clauses in contracts with its suppliers, these should be accounted for following the guidance for reimbursements at **9.2.2.**

Warranties are different from self-insurance for losses that have not yet occurred, because in the case of self-insurance there is usually no past event that creates an obligation at the reporting date. So even though an entity may be able to reliably estimate the probability and costs of a self-insurance policy, this does not meet the criteria to be recognised as a provision. However, once a catastrophe occurs, e.g. a fire at a warehouse, then at the end of the following reporting period the entity must review the carrying value of its assets for impairment, and consider whether a provision is required for other costs, e.g. claims from neighbours for damage to their properties.

9.2.3.5   Charities and entities with funding commitments

The Charities SORP provides detailed guidance on commitments and provisions for charities, in particular with regard to grant-making and future intentions. Paragraphs 34.57–34.63 of FRS 102 apply to funding commitments, i.e. where an entity has committed to provide resources to other entities (see **18.4** of this guide). There are some extra recognition criteria and disclosure requirements in these circumstances.

The SORP notes that funds earmarked by the trustees for a specific purpose should be accounted for via a designated fund, not by creating a provision.

9.2.4   Contingent liabilities

A contingent liability, defined in paragraph 21.12, is one of two things. Either:

- it meets condition (a) of the recognition criteria for a provision (see **9.2.1**) but does not meet either condition (b) or condition (c). In other words, there is a present obligation at the reporting date as a result of a past event but either the probability of an outflow of economic benefits is 50% or less, or the amount of the obligation cannot be estimated reliably; or

- the existence of the obligation itself is uncertain at the reporting date and will only be confirmed by an event occurring in the future. If the deciding event occurs between the reporting date and the date that the financial statements are authorised for issue, and this confirms that an obligation did exist at the reporting date, then a provision should be made in the financial statements and the event is not a contingent liability (see paragraph 32.5 in Section 32 *Events after the End of the Reporting Period*).

Contingent liabilities are not recognised in the financial statements, except in the case of provisions for contingent liabilities of an acquiree in a business combination (see **9.1** of this guide). The details of contingent liabilities have to be disclosed in the notes to the financial statements as set out at **9.3.1**.

Prior period contingent liabilities should be reviewed at subsequent reporting dates to assess whether they still meet the criteria for disclosure, or whether they have perhaps now met the criteria for recognition as a provision.

Where an entity is jointly and severally liable for an obligation, the amount that is expected to be settled by other parties is a contingent liability.

Example 9.6

An entity produces miniature thermometers that are supplied to manufacturers of industrial testing equipment. During the reporting period, one the of customers' products developed a major fault, and this is thought to be possibly due to the thermometers, or possibly due to one of several other component parts supplied by other entities. Extensive testing is being performed by independent experts, but the results of this will not be known until after the accounts have been authorised for issue. The entity disputes strongly that its thermometers have caused the problem, but has agreed to abide by the decision of the independent experts. Should the cause of the problem be attributed to the thermometers, the entity will be liable to pay damages of £25m.

This is a possible obligation as a result of a past event (i.e. the sale of the thermometers during the reporting period). The uncertainty over whether an obligation exists will only be determined by a future event outside the entity's control (the decision of the independent experts). The entity should assess the likelihood of having to pay damages. If, after taking into account all available evidence, it is more likely than not that it will have to pay damages, then a provision must be made; otherwise the obligation is only possible rather than probable, so the expected loss should be disclosed as a contingent liability in accordance with the guidance at **9.3.1**.

Suppose the management's best estimate is that there is a 65% chance that the entity will be found liable and therefore have to pay the damages of £25m. Then the obligation is more likely than not (and there will be a definite cash outflow of a known amount) so a provision is required. Using the measurement rules at **9.2.2**, the £25m must be reduced to take account of the other possible outcome (which is where nothing is payable). A weighted average is a way to do this, in which case the provision is:

(65% × £25m) + (35% × £nil) = £16.25m.

The entity may wish to adjust this amount to take account of the uncertainty of the probabilities, and also for the time value of money.

Alternatively, suppose the management's best estimate is that there is only a 25% chance that they will be found liable and therefore have to pay the damages of £25m. Then the obligation is only possible rather than probable, so it is a contingent liability instead of a provision; this is disclosed, rather than provided for. The financial effect has to be disclosed (see **9.3.1**) and is measured using the same rules as for provisions. Again using weighted average as a way of calculating the best estimate of the amount the entity would rationally pay to settle the obligation on the reporting date, the disclosed financial effect would be:

(25% × £25m) + (75% × £nil) = £6.25m.

The entity may wish to adjust this amount to take account of the uncertainty of the probabilities, and also for the time value of money.

9.2.5   Contingent assets

An asset is defined in the glossary to FRS 102 as 'a resource controlled by the entity as a result of past events and from which future economic benefits are expected to flow to the entity'. According to paragraph 2.27 of the standard, assets (and liabilities) are incorporated into the financial statements when it is probable that any future economic benefit will flow to (or from) the entity, and the amount can be measured reliably (see **2.2.2** of this guide).

A contingent asset is defined by the standard as 'a possible asset that arises from past events and whose existence will be confirmed only by the occurrence or non-occurrence of one or more uncertain future events not wholly within the control of the entity'.

Contingent assets are not recognised in the financial statements but are disclosed when an inflow of economic benefits is probable, i.e. more likely than not (see **9.3.1** for details of the disclosure). This is because of the uncertain future nature of the possible economic inflow, and the fundamental principle of prudence (see paragraph 2.9 of the standard).

If the inflow of economic benefits is virtually certain, then the existence of the event creating the asset must also be virtually certain, and so it will meet the definition and recognition criteria of an asset and must be included in the financial statements.

Paragraph 32.7 in Section 32 *Events after the End of the Reporting Period* provides some guidance on the impact of events occurring between the reporting date and the date that the financial statements are authorised for issue. For example, an amount that becomes receivable as a result of a court case in this period, relating to an event that occurred before the reporting date, would be a contingent asset at the reporting date. On the other hand, if judgment on the case was received before the reporting date and it is only the amount of damages that is decided in this period, then the entity has an asset that should be recognised in the financial statements (on the basis that there will be an inflow of economic benefits in the future arising from an event before the reporting date and the amount can be measured reliably).

Prior period contingent assets should be reviewed at subsequent reporting dates to assess whether they still meet the criteria for disclosure, or whether they have perhaps now met the criteria for recognition as an asset.

Example 9.7

During the reporting period, an entity's warehouse was destroyed by fire. The warehouse was rebuilt before the end of the reporting period and the costs of the rebuild have been included in the financial statements. The entity was insured, but the loss adjuster is disputing the claim on the grounds that the entity breached some of the terms of its insurance policy. The entity is adamant that it fully complied with all terms. The case is due to go to arbitration, but the outcome will not be decided until after the date that the financial statements are authorised for issue. The entity's advisers have indicated that it is more likely than not (but not virtually certain) that the entity will receive its full claim.

This is a contingent asset because it is a possible asset arising from a past event (i.e. the fire which took place before the reporting date), the outcome of which will be decided by an uncertain future event outside the entity's control (the arbitrator's decision).

It should be disclosed in accordance with the guidance at **9.3.1**, because the inflow of economic benefits is considered more likely than not.

9.3 Presentation and disclosure

9.3.1 *Presentation and disclosure requirements*

Instructions on the presentation of provisions and the related charges and credits are given throughout Section 21. There are also detailed disclosure requirements set out in paragraphs 21.14–21.17A.

9.3.1.1 *Income statement items*

The initial recognition of a provision is charged as an expense unless another section of FRS 102 requires that it be recognised as part of the cost of an asset. For example, paragraph 17.10(c) of the FRS requires that provisions for dismantling an item of property, plant or equipment are included within the measurement of the cost of the asset (the provision being recognised and measured in accordance with Section 21).

If a provision has been discounted, the adjustments arising from the unwinding of the discount must be calculated separately at each reporting date and shown within finance costs in the statement of comprehensive income.

Apart from unwinding of the discount, the standard does not stipulate in which section of the statement of comprehensive income the expense should be shown. It would be reasonable to assume that the expense should be shown in the same section as a similar cost would be shown had it arisen in the reporting period.

Subsequent amendments to the amount of the provision are recognised in the statement of comprehensive income (or as an adjustment to the asset value if this was the appropriate treatment on initial recognition). This is in line with the requirements of paragraphs 10.16 and 10.17 of FRS 102 relating to changes in accounting estimate.

Where an asset is recognised for an expected reimbursement (see **9.2.2)**, the asset and related liability must be shown separately on the statement of financial position; however, the expense of the provision may be offset against the amount of the reimbursement in the statement of comprehensive income.

9.3.1.2   *Balance sheet items*

Provisions are included in the statement of financial position, the location within this being set by the particular Schedule to the Regulations that has been chosen for balance sheet presentation (see **3.3** of this guide).

Where an asset is recognised for an expected reimbursement (see **9.2.2**), the asset and related liability must be shown separately on the statement of financial position.

Only expenditure which relates to the original purpose of a provision may be charged against that provision. This is in line with the general principle in paragraph 2.52 of FRS 102 that assets, liabilities, income and expenses may not be offset unless required or permitted by an FRS, and is to prevent the impact of a material item being concealed by a provision previously created for a different purpose.

9.3.1.3   *Disclosure requirements for provisions (21.14)*

For each class of provision, the following must be disclosed (comparative information is not required):

(a)   a reconciliation showing:

    (i)   the carrying amount at the beginning and end of the period;

    (ii)   additions during the period, including adjustments that result from changes in measuring the discounted amount;

    (iii)   amounts charged against the provision during the period; and

    (iv)   unused amounts reversed during the period;

(b)   a brief description of the nature of the obligation and the expected amount and timing of any resulting economic outflows;

(c)   an indication of the uncertainties about the amount or timing of those outflows; and

(d)   the amount of any expected reimbursement, stating the amount of any asset that has been recognised for that expected reimbursement.

Note that paragraphs 8.6 and 8.7 of the standard require disclosure of judgments made by management and the key assumptions concerning the future and other key sources of estimation uncertainty (see **2.3.2.6**). This is usually included in the accounting policies section of the notes to the financial statements, with the other disclosures (a)–(d) above usually given in a provisions note.

9.3.1.4   Disclosure requirements for contingent liabilities (21.15)

For each class of contingent liability, unless the possibility of an outflow of economic benefits is remote, the following must be disclosed:

(a)   a brief description of the nature of the contingent liability;

(b)   an estimate of its financial effect, measured in accordance with the guidance for measuring provisions;

(c)   an indication of the uncertainties about the amount or timing of the outflows; and

(d)   the possibility of any reimbursement. (Note that this only requires a statement of the possibility of a reimbursement, rather than the amount as required for disclosures about provisions.)

If it is impracticable to make any of the disclosures (b) to (d), then this fact must be stated. 'Impracticable' is defined in the glossary to FRS 102 as being unable to comply with a requirement 'after making every reasonable effort to do so'. The IFRS Foundation notes that 'impracticable is a high hurdle'.

The *Companies Act* 2006 also requires disclosure of the details of any valuable security provided by the entity in connection with a contingent liability.

9.3.1.5   Disclosure requirements for contingent assets (21.16)

For contingent assets the following must be disclosed:

(a)   a description of the nature of the contingent assets; and

(b)   an estimate of their financial effect measured in accordance with the guidance for measuring provisions.

If it is impracticable to make disclosure (b), then this fact must be stated.

9.3.1.6   Prejudicial disclosures (21.17)

The standard recognises that disclosing some or all of the information required by the standard could prejudice seriously the position of an entity in a dispute with other parties on the matter which has given rise to the provision, contingent liability or contingent asset, although the standard advises that such a situation will be 'extremely rare'.

In such circumstances, the entity need not disclose the particulars required above, but must still give certain information in respect of provisions:

(a) a table showing the reconciliation required by paragraph 21.14(a) in aggregate, including the source and application of any amounts transferred to or from provisions during the reporting period;

(b) particulars of each provision in any case where the amount of the provision is material; and

(c) the fact that, and reason why, the information required by paragraph 21.14 has not been disclosed.

For contingent liabilities, the minimum information is:

(a) particulars and the total amount of any contingent liabilities (excluding those which arise out of insurance contracts) that are not included in the statement of financial position;

(b) the total amount of contingent liabilities which are undertaken on behalf or for the benefit of:

(i) any parent or fellow subsidiary of the entity;

(ii) any subsidiary of the entity; or

(iii) any entity in which the reporting entity has a participating interest,

shall each be stated separately;

(c) the fact that, and reason why, the information required by paragraph 21.15 has not been disclosed.

For contingent assets, the entity shall disclose the general nature of the dispute, together with the fact that, and reason why, the information required by paragraph 21.16 has not been disclosed.

9.3.1.7   Disclosure requirements for financial guarantee contracts (21.17A)

If an entity is using Section 21 to account for financial guarantee contracts rather than the other options available (see **9.1**), then it must disclose the nature and business purpose of the financial guarantee contracts it has issued and, if applicable, the disclosures as required for provisions and/ or contingent liabilities.

9.3.1.8   Disclosure requirements for commitments

The *Companies Act* 2006 requires disclosure of the aggregate amount or estimated amount of contracts for capital expenditure not provided for, certain details in respect of pension commitments not provided for, and also the particulars of any other financial commitments that are not provided for and are relevant to assessing the state of the entity's affairs.

9.3.1.9   Disclosure requirements for small entities applying Section 1A of FRS 102

The formal requirements for small entities in this respect are minimal, with the only relevant paragraph being 1AC.29 which requires statement of the total amount of any financial commitments, guarantees and contingencies that are not included in the balance sheet. This would, obviously, not relate to provisions actually recognised on the balance sheet: there are no disclosures mandated for these.

9.4   Transition

In most cases, there will be no transitional issues on applying FRS 102 for the first time in relation to provisions, contingent assets and contingent liabilities, as Section 21 of the standard is so similar to FRS 105 and IFRS. However, the following particular situations are provided for in Section 35 *Transition to this FRS*.

9.4.1   Decommissioning liabilities

Section 17 requires that provisions for dismantling and other related costs are included within the cost of an item of property, plant or equipment. Paragraph 35.10(I) allows a first-time adopter to measure this provision at the date of transition to FRS 102, rather than on the date(s) when the obligation initially arose. However, as FRS 15 already requires recognition of such provisions within the cost of the asset, this optional transitional election is unlikely to be necessary to most preparers.

9.4.2   Business combinations

Section 21 requires that an entity makes provision for contingent liabilities of an acquiree in a business combination, in line with the requirements of Section 19. Paragraph 35.10(a) allows a first-time adopter not to apply Section 19 to pre-transition date combinations – this is discussed in more detail in **4.3.5**.

10 Revenue and government grants

10.1 Scope of this section

Accounting for revenue is one of the areas of financial reporting that seems as though it should be straightforward – recognise revenue when a sale is made – but in practice gives rise to a number of complications and difficulties.

This section covers the guidance in Section 23 *Revenue* and Section 24 *Government Grants*.

Revenue is defined in the Glossary as 'the gross inflow of economic benefits during the period arising in the course of the ordinary activities of an entity when those inflows result in increases in equity, other than increases relating to contributions from equity participants'.

Not all types of revenue are addressed by Section 23, which specifically covers income from the sale of goods, the rendering of services, execution of construction contracts, and the use by others of entity assets yielding interest, royalties or dividends.

While it is clear that income from grants is covered in the subsequent section, paragraph 23.2 also points out some other income sources where there are more specific accounting requirements given in the relevant section of FRS 102:

- lease agreements: Section 20 – see **8.3.3.2**;

- income from equity accounted investments: Section 20 – see **4.4.2** and **4.5.2**);

- changes in the fair value of financial assets or liabilities: Sections 11 and 12 – see **7.4.3**);

- changes in the fair value of investment property: Section 16 – see **5.3.3**);

- initial recognition and subsequent changes in fair value of biological assets (Section 34 – see **6.2.9**);

- initial recognition of agricultural produce (Section 34 – see **6.2.9**);

- incoming resources from non-exchange transactions for public benefit entities (Section 34); and

- insurance contracts (FRS 103).

The equivalent guidance in IFRS appears in IFRS 15 *Revenue from Contracts with Customers.* As discussed in **1.5** of this guide, it is possible that some or all of the principles in IFRS 15 will be implemented into FRS 102, but it is not yet clear when or how this will take place.

For most entities, core revenue will arise from supply of goods or services, or sometimes both. Judgments may arise in establishing the exact point of delivery, particularly where there are rights of return. There can also be difficulty, where there are multiple components, in allocating the sales price across those components.

Section 23 walks through the two key steps in accounting for revenue: measuring revenue and identifying the revenue transaction (including separating out components). A distinction is drawn between the accounting for the sale of goods and the provision of services; extra guidance is also given for construction contracts.

Application to micro-entities: Most of the principles for recognising and measuring revenue in FRS 105 are consistent with FRS 102. However, there is no mention of measuring revenue at the fair value of the amount receivable in FRS 105; instead revenue is measured at the amount receivable, net of trade discounts, prompt settlement discounts and volume rebates.

Additionally, where payment is deferred beyond normal credit terms, revenue recognised is equal to the cash price on the transaction date. Any excess payment over and above the cash price is treated as interest and spread on a straight-line basis over the life of the contract (rather than needing to apply the full amortised cost method).

Interest income is recognised in accordance with the requirements of Section 9 *Financial Instruments* except where it relates to a transaction where payment is deferred beyond normal credit terms. In this case, it is spread on a straight-line basis over the life of the contract.

10.2   Measurement

10.2.1   Measurement basics

The key requirement in respect of revenue measurement is that it is measured at the fair value of consideration received or receivable. While in many cases this will be the same as the invoice price, particularly in simple transactions, it will by no means always be true. The amount initially recorded takes account of trade discounts, prompt settlement discounts and volume discounts, and includes only amounts receivable by the entity on its own account (agent/principal issues are discussed in more detail at **10.5.1**). Based on this, VAT is excluded (since it is collected on behalf of the government not on the supplier's own account) as are any other similar sales taxes.

10.2.2   Deferred payment

In any situation where payment is deferred such that the transaction constitutes a financing transaction, the fair value of consideration is defined in paragraph 23.5 as 'the present value of all future receipts using an imputed rate of interest'. It is worth clarifying here that the description is designed to apply to transactions such as sales with extended interest-free credit terms, not to explicit loan arrangements, which would be outside the scope of the section, and are instead addressed by Sections 11 and 12 of FRS 102 (see **7.3.2** and **7.4.2** of this guide).

Example 10.1

Supplier S sells goods with a list price of £100,000 to purchaser P. Instead of its normal 30 days' credit terms, S offers P one year of interest-free credit, motivated by the intention of building a strong customer relationship.

Assuming that the appropriate imputed interest rate is 10%, the sale will originally be recorded at £90,900 (£100,000/1.1), with the difference of £9,100 between this and the face value being recognised as interest income, rather than sales revenue, over the year up to settlement.

The requirement to discount deferred payments to reach the value to be recognised for revenue is not a new one, but still may require careful explanation to stakeholders, since it means that the amount ultimately recognised in revenue is not equal to the invoiced value. It is also not always straightforward to determine the interest rate to use in the discounting. Paragraph 23.5 requires the imputed rate to be:

'The more clearly determinable of either:

(a)   the prevailing rate for a similar instrument of an issuer with a similar credit rating; or

(b)   a rate of interest that discounts the nominal value of the instrument to the current cash sales price of the goods or services.'

These two approaches are quite different. The first is not particularly likely to be clearly determinable, as it appears to require that the interest rate is based on that which would normally apply to the buyer (the issuer of debt is usually the party which has the liability). Depending on the nature of the customer (for instance, whether it is a public or private company), and its size, there may not be sufficient information in the public domain to allow the vendor to make an assessment of the customer's typical borrowing rate. The second approach may therefore be simpler to apply, if there is a comparable cash price.

If all of a company's sales are on an extended interest-free credit basis, then there will be no comparable cash price for an immediate payment, but evidence may still be available of a proxy figure if, for instance, the company is in the habit of granting a discount to those that choose to settle early (even if this is only a matter of practice rather than a formal policy). It may, on the other hand, be argued that if this is standard practice in the seller's industry, then sales with long credit terms do not represent financing transactions at all, but instead reflect a typical vendor/customer relationship for this kind of transaction.

10.2.3   *Exchange transactions*

Also known as 'barter' transactions, it is common for companies to exchange goods and/or services. For example, a magazine might offer an events company a free advertisement in return for promoting the magazine at a relevant event. FRS 102 sets out clear requirements for these kinds of transaction, stating that revenue can only be recognised if the goods and/or services exchanged are dissimilar from one another in nature and value and the transaction has commercial substance. In the example of the magazine and the events company, the services are similar in nature, both being promotional, and are also likely to be similar in value. Accordingly, no revenue should be recognised.

If it is appropriate to recognise revenue on an exchange transaction, FRS 102 states that revenue should be measured according to the following hierarchy:

(a)   at the fair value of the goods or services received, adjusted by the amount of any cash or cash equivalents transferred;

(b)   if the amount under (a) cannot be measured reliably, then at the fair value of the goods or services given up adjusted by the amount of any cash or cash equivalents transferred; or

(c)   if the fair value of neither can be measured reliably, at the carrying amount of the goods or services given up adjusted by the amount of any cash or cash equivalents transferred.

10.3   Identifying revenue transactions

The first stage in recognising revenue is determining exactly which transactions give rise to revenue, and whether they should be separated or accounted for together. A single transaction, in commercial terms, may still need to be disaggregated for accounting purposes, and paragraphs 23.8–23.9 expand on this a little.

Simply put, if a single transaction contains two or more separable components, then each of these components is assessed in its own right for the purposes of revenue recognition. The standard example is a piece of software sold with a maintenance package: this has an element which relates to the sale of goods, and an element which is the provision of services.

Conversely, if two items are technically sold in distinct transactions but are inextricably linked, they are treated as one item for revenue recognition purposes. This might apply where a customer pays separately for an asset and a maintenance package covering that asset, which is only available when an asset is purchased, and which gives the purchaser a right to a nominal 'discount' on the asset's purchase cost.

Example 10.2

Company W sells a piece of machinery to customer Z for £48,000. This represents a discount from the list price of £70,000, because the customer also signed up for a (separately invoiced) three-year maintenance agreement, for £30,000.

These transactions appear to be linked, so it seems that the best accounting treatment would be to view them together when determining the values to be attributed to each component.

This example shows that an attempt to manipulate revenue (in this case, by allocating an excessive value to the part that will be deferred) is unlikely to be successful.

The guidance is brief, and has no real information on how to apply it. However, preparers will generally be able to apply their own knowledge of their business in order to identify whether they are providing a single good or service or a number bundled together.

10.3.1 *Evidence of price of components when sold or provided separately*

If goods and services are being sold bundled together but can also be purchased as individual items, the list prices for the separate items may provide a good indicator of their standalone fair values. It may be the case that when they are bundled together the sales price is below that for the purchase of each item separately, in which case their relative individual selling prices would typically be the most acceptable approach to dividing and apportioning the actual proceeds, although it would also be acceptable to use other reasonable methods.

Example 10.3

Company B sells software, technical support, and packages combining the two.

Its list prices are £800 for the software, £200 for one year of technical support, and £900 for the software with one year of technical support.

Where a customer purchases only the software, B has no ongoing obligations. This means it recognises the revenue of £800 immediately on sales.

For the telephone support, an indeterminate number of acts will be needed to provide the service, so the £200 is recognised evenly over the year.

When customers buy the bundle, they are effectively receiving a discount. Unless there is evidence that it relates only to one of the elements, the special £900 price can be allocated 80% to the software sale, and 20% to the services – that is, £720 recognised immediately, and the remaining £180 spread over the year of the service contract.

10.3.2   Evidence of price of only one of the components

The use of vendor-specific evidence for components' separate prices is harder to apply when only one of the components is sold separately. In the example above, if B did not sell a separate support package then there would be more judgment involved in deciding whether to allocate the whole £800 software list price to the software, and only the balance of £100 to the support element. While this may well still be the most appropriate allocation, it would be necessary to perform a very basic 'sense check', for example by ascertaining the costs to B of providing the support element. If this part clearly costs more than £100, so that allocating only the balance of £100 to this element renders that part of the contract loss-making, this would suggest it is necessary to revisit the allocation, as on the face of it, it is not commercial to undertake loss-making services. Of course losses do arise in reality, but only in certain industries are prices routinely set in order to be loss-making. This consideration is only one of the judgmental factors to be weighed up in allocating revenue between components – there is not a single objective method.

10.3.3   No element-specific evidence available

Where a vendor sells packages that include both goods and services, but does not sell any of the elements separately, it is more difficult to allocate the sales price between the two (or more) elements.

In this case, it will be necessary to look at a wider range of evidence, which may include typical prices charged by other vendors for items the same as or similar to the individual elements. This will work better for some lines of business than others: a vendor selling a highly bespoke product or service is unlikely to be able to find comparable sales by competitors, whereas one selling a generic item that is widely available should be able to perform enough research to establish separate values.

If this does not give a reliable measure, other means must be used. It would probably not be appropriate to attempt an allocation based on the relative cost to the vendor of providing each element of the contract, as this basis relies on an assumption of constant margins across the board, which are not often achieved in practice.

10.3.4 'Free' items

Where an entity provides 'free gifts' to customers when they make a purchase, the substance of the transaction needs to be considered very carefully. A decision is needed on whether any of the item's price should be allocated to the apparently free component: factors to consider might include:

- whether the entity normally sells the 'free' component (compare a free DVD player sold with a television set to a free branded pen for every washing machine purchased);

- whether the price that the main item is being sold for reflects its usual list price (if the television set in the example above previously retailed at £200 and is now being sold at £250 including the free DVD player, this suggests that the consideration needs to be allocated more reasonably between the two); and

- whether the offer looks set to continue indefinitely (if it does, this might suggest that two items are being sold together, rather than one being issued for free).

It is important to distinguish between gifts that represent promotional or marketing activity (such as the example of the branded pen) from those where the substance is that both products are sold at a discounted price. As with most areas addressed in this section, the appropriate accounting treatment depends on the detailed facts and circumstances, and there are few 'if-then' rules. It should also be noted that it often does not matter how revenue is allocated between components, if both are the sale of goods (and recognised immediately).

10.4   Timing of revenue recognition

The point for revenue recognition depends on whether the revenue is earned through the sale of goods, the provision of services, or a construction contract.

10.4.1   Sale of goods

Revenue is recognised from selling goods when all the following conditions are satisfied (paragraph paragraph 23.10):

'(a)   the entity has transferred to the buyer the significant risks and rewards of ownership of the goods;

(b)   the entity retains neither continuing managerial involvement to the degree usually associated with ownership nor effective control over the goods sold;

(c)   the amount of revenue can be measured reliably;

(d)   it is probable that the economic benefits associated with the transaction will flow to the entity; and

(e)   the costs incurred or to be incurred in respect of the transaction can be measured reliably.'

The most significant point to emphasise here is that revenue recognition has no link to the timing of consideration, but instead is triggered by the transfer of risks and rewards relating to the goods, and the timing of this transfer will depend on the type and detail of the transaction. This will not always occur at the same point. In a typical retail sale, risks and rewards are transferred as the goods are handed over (see below for more discussion of warranties and rights to return), but wholesalers, for instance, will often provide goods to their customers on a sale or return basis. Where this happens, the wholesaler retains the inventory risk, as it can be obliged to repurchase the goods (usually within a finite period). It would not be appropriate, in this case, to recognise a sale.

10.4.2   Rendering of services

Revenue for the rendering of services is recognised with reference to the stage of completion of the transaction, if the outcome can be measured reliably. The following conditions from paragraph paragraph 23.14 must be met:

'(a)   the amount of the revenue can be measured reliably;

(b)   it is probable that the economic benefits associated with the transaction will flow to the entity;

(c)   the stage of completion of the transaction at the end of the reporting period can be measured reliably; and

(d)   the costs incurred for the transaction and the costs to complete the transaction can be measured reliably.'

In general, it will be necessary to use the percentage of completion method (see below): the exception is where the services are 'an indeterminate number of acts over a specified period of time', where the contract value is recognised on a straight line basis over its life unless there is evidence of a better method. Even using this simplified straight line approach, it is still necessary to adjust this recognition if there is a specific act much more significant than any others: in this case, revenue recognition does not start until that significant act has been executed.

Example 10.4

Entity T provides technical support to its customers via a phone line. The commitment made to each customer is to answer all of that customer's calls for the duration of the contract life: at the outset, the call volume cannot be predicted.

For each customer contract, T recognises the revenue evenly over the contract life.

Entity Q also provides technical support, but in some of its contracts it offers an intensive three-day training course to its client's staff near to the beginning of the support period. This would be likely to qualify as a significant event which would act as the starting point for the recognition of revenue (which would then be spread evenly over the life).

For a service contract, if the outcome of the transaction cannot be measured reliably (perhaps because of variable pricing that depends on yet-to-be-determined performance volumes), revenue is recognised only to the level of recoverable expenses – that is, to make a zero margin. In other words, if an outcome is not reliably determinable, a contract is not forced to be accounted for as loss making, but nor can a profit be recognised.

10.4.3   Percentage of completion method

To recognise revenue from providing services, it is necessary to estimate the stage of completion of these services. Paragraph 23.22 specifies three possible methods, though it does not prohibit the use of other methods:

(a)   costs incurred to date (excluding items purchased for future use) as a proportion of total costs;

(b)   surveys that estimate the value of work performed; and

(c)   completion of a physical proportion of the contract work or a proportion of the service contract.

The choice of which method to use will depend on the information available, the type of work being performed, and the stated accounting policy. Method (b) is relevant to construction contracts (see **10.4.4**), where it may be relatively easy to obtain survey information, and this may be part of the contract terms anyway – the customer may wish for a regular check on progress through agreed valuation certificates.

It should be noted, though, that payment schedules often do not have a particularly close relationship with the progress of work performed, and cannot themselves be used as a proxy in establishing percentage completion. A seller in a strong negotiating position is likely to have arranged for payments to be front loaded, or at the very least balanced such that it is always in a favourable cash flow position, but this may not be reflected in the profile of the work, which is the factor that must drive the revenue recognition.

Where costs have been incurred on a services contract that relate to future activity, such as purchase of materials that have not yet been used, these are recognised as an asset if it is probable that they will be recovered, following the general guidance for assets.

No comment is made on the presentation of balance sheet amounts relating to revenues recognised on contracts that have not yet been invoiced. The most reasonable position seems to be within accrued income, assuming that it passes the tests to qualify as an asset. Conversely, where cash payments have been received that add to a higher value than the cumulative revenue recognised, this gives rise to deferred income.

10.4.4   *Construction contracts*

Construction contracts merit their own special treatment because they fall between two stools, being neither straightforward contracts for the delivery of goods nor for the provision of services. The provider undertakes to perform a service of constructing a property, and at the end of this time title will pass to the buyer. An accounting treatment that deferred all revenue until this end point where title passes would seem to be too prudent, as it does not reflect the extended period over which the work is performed.

This means that specific requirements are given for construction contracts, defined as '[contracts] specifically negotiated for the construction of an asset or a combination of assets that are closely interrelated or interdependent in terms of their design, technology and function or their ultimate purpose or use'. While the most obvious, and typical, examples are contracts for the construction of properties or bespoke large scale machinery, the definition is not limited to the construction of PPE items so could also include a project to create an intangible asset such as a technical database.

The basic principle for recognition of revenue on a construction contract is as for a service contract: revenue is recognised based on the stage of completion, if the outcome can be reliably measured. Where the treatment diverges, though, is in respect of cost: in a construction contract, the recognition of contract costs, too, is based on the percentage of completion, with the likely effect of a reasonably smooth margin across the contract life.

If the outcome cannot be measured reliably then contract costs are expensed as incurred, and revenue is recognised only to the extent of those costs (meaning that no profit will be recognised). If the contract as a whole is expected to be loss-making, then the whole expected loss is recognised immediately, with the liability being included as a provision for an onerous contract. To be clear, this does not mean that only the costs are accelerated, but rather that the total anticipated loss is recognised early: in the absence of guidance to the contrary, it seems reasonable to assume that this would be gross in revenue and expenses.

Paragraph 23.17A explains how costs incurred in relation to securing a construction contract should be dealt with. Costs that relate directly to a contract and are incurred in securing the contract are also included as part of the contract costs if they can be separately identified and measured reliably and it is probable that the contract will be obtained. When costs incurred in securing a contract are recognised as an expense in the period in which they are incurred, they are not included in contract costs if the contract is obtained in a subsequent period.

10.5 Other issues and areas to consider

10.5.1 The agent-principal problem

As mentioned briefly above, revenue only includes amounts that an entity receives from sales made on its own account, and paragraph 23.4 clarifies that 'in an agency relationship, an entity (the agent) shall include in revenue only the amount of its commission. The amounts collected on behalf of the principal are not revenue of the entity', with an agent defined in the Glossary as being an entity that does not have exposure to the risks and rewards typically associated with its transactions, with an indicative feature being 'that the amount the entity earns is predetermined, being either a fixed fee per transaction or a stated percentage of the amount billed to the customer'. Example 27 in the Appendix to Section 23 provides guidance on establishing whether preparers are acting as agent or principal:

'Determining whether an entity is acting as a principal or as an agent requires judgement and consideration of all relevant facts and circumstances.

An entity is acting as a principal when it has exposure to the significant risks and rewards associated with the sale of goods or the rendering of services. Features that indicate that an entity is acting as principal include:

(a) the entity has the primary responsibility for providing the goods or services to the customer or for fulfilling the order, for example by being responsible for the acceptability of the products or services ordered or purchased by the customer;

(b)   the entity has inventory risk before or after the customer order, during shipping or on return;

(c)   the entity has latitude in establishing prices, either directly or indirectly, for example by providing additional goods or services; and

(d)   the entity bears the customer's credit risk for the amount receivable from the customer.

An entity is acting as an agent when it does not have exposure to the significant risks and rewards associated with the sale of goods or the rendering of services.

One feature indicating that an entity is acting as agent is that the amount the entity earns is predetermined, being either a fixed fee per transaction or a stated percentage of the amount billed to the customer.

When an entity has entered into a contract as an undisclosed agent, it is normally acting as principal.

The amounts collected by an agent on behalf of a principal are not revenue. Instead, revenue is the amount of commission.'

Example 10.5

(1)   Company P has a formal agreement to act, and describe itself, as a selling agent for company Q. P receives commission of 5% of the value of any products it sells: it normally collects cash then passes this on to Q net of its commission charge, though it can also bill Q for commission on amounts that have not been settled by customers within an agreed period.

P is acting as an agent and therefore will show only the commissions as revenue in its own accounts.

(2)   Company R sells Company S's products in a similar way, but customers do not know that it is acting as an agent, and have no awareness of cash being passed on or of a commission charge. Company R has the risks associated with being the primary responsible party in the eyes of the customer and, in the event of a dispute, the customer would have recourse to Company R, not Company S. Accordingly, Company R is considered to be holding itself out as principal and should account as such.

10.5.2   Interest, royalties and dividends

The general principles behind the recognition of interest, royalties and dividends are unsurprising: they are recognised when it is probable that the relevant economic benefits will flow to the entity, and the amount of revenue can be measured reliably.

Paragraph 23.29 then gives a specific basis for each of these three revenue types.

10.5.2.1   Interest income

Interest income is measured using the effective interest method, as set out in Section 11 of FRS 102 (and discussed in **7.6.5** of this guide). In performing this calculation, account is taken of fees, finance charges, transaction costs and other premiums or discounts.

Example 10.6

Company C effectively lends £250,000 to one of its customers by granting it one year extended payment terms at a market rate (for the business) of 7%. It also charges a fee of £5,000 for this extended credit.

The total amount recognised as income over the year will be £22,500, being one year of interest at 7% plus the fee. This will be recognised so as to give a constant rate of return over the life of the loan, under the effective interest method.

10.5.2.2   Royalty income

Royalties are recognised on an accrual basis in accordance with the substance of the agreement. This wording is quite vague, because royalty agreements are so variable in practice so it would be impossible to give more detailed guidance that would be sufficiently broadly applicable. The key point, though, is that it would not be acceptable to defer the recognition of royalties until cash was received, or until the amount was formally agreed.

This latter point is particularly pertinent, since there are often considerable delays in confirming exact amounts due for royalties, for example in arrangements between retailers and their suppliers. In the meantime, trade will continue, and royalties may be invoiced some months after the sales which gave rise to them. This late invoicing should not lead to late recognition, unless it is really the case that the amounts cannot be measured reliably. Small uncertainties about the precise value, based on the detail of the agreements, would not necessarily render the whole amount 'not reliably measurable' – clearly judgment will be needed, but care should be taken to avoid what might be called excessive prudence.

10.5.2.3   Dividend income

Dividends are recognised when the shareholder's right to receive payment is established. Again this may well be earlier than the point when the cash is received.

10.5.3   Customer loyalty awards

The issue when accounting for customer loyalty programmes, such as those that award points for each purchase which can then be redeemed against future purchases, is whether a portion of the original revenue should be allocated to the points, effectively as if the sale was of a combination of goods and points.

In situations (such as typical supermarket reward schemes) where clear value has been given away, then it appears necessary to account for this at the outset, thus reducing the amount of the original transaction that is allocated to the sale of goods. In particular, if one point is granted per pound spent, and each point allows the shopper a 1p discount from a future spend, then it may be that only 99p is allocated to the sale, with the remainder recognised as deferred income and not reaching revenue until the points are used.

This is not set out clearly in the standard, which instead provides, in the Appendix to Section 23, the more complex Example 13. This example sets out a situation where product A is sold for 100, and purchasers thereby have the right to purchase product B for a discount of 8 to the normal price. In this fact pattern, the vendor estimates that only 40% of the purchasers of product A will make use of the discount; we are also told that the normal selling price of A is 95.

This allows allocation of the 100 proceeds based on the relative fair values of the two elements, using the assumption that the fair value of the voucher is 40% × 8 = 3.2, and the fair value of A is its normal selling price, 95.

The example is mainly helpful in its illustration of the need to take into account the probability that customer awards will be used. If points are granted but are hard to use, or expire very quickly, or require extensive further purchases to make them useful, then this will affect the likelihood that they are used, and thus will reduce the fair value of the award. So, in the supermarket example above, experience may show that only 70% of points issued are used before they expire (most have long lives), so in this case the fair value of the award would at most be only 0.7p. The fair value of the sold item is, in the absence of further information, £1, since customers not participating in the scheme cannot buy it any cheaper. This means that the proceeds would be apportioned based on the relative proportions of 1.007 (being the sum of the fair values of the two components).

10.5.4   Membership fees

Another specific application that is illustrated in the appendix to the standard is membership fees for entities such as gyms, which may charge a theoretically non-refundable joining fee and then an annual membership.

The basic principle of revenue recognition would suggest that in this situation the whole membership fee should be recognised immediately, and the annual fee over the course of the year, based on the idea that offering gym membership is providing a service but that the one-off joining fee is a discrete event which is more akin to the provision of goods.

The treatment becomes a little more challenging when we consider areas such as lifetime memberships, where a member pays once and has access to the facilities, for no further charge, for the rest of their lives. If the provider has no obligations to repay the fee, and in practice not even any obligations to continue operating for the whole of the member's life, then some might argue for immediate recognition of the whole amount, perhaps supported by the observation that there is no clear contract life over which it could be spread.

Paragraph 23A.24 states that where a fee relates only to membership (e.g. where there is a separate annual subscription, and all other goods and services are charged separately) 'the fee is recognised as revenue when no significant uncertainty about its collectability exists'. This represents a decoupling from the principles set out in the main part of Section 23, which do not link revenue recognition to collectability at all.

This example illustrates the difficulty in practice of applying the revenue recognition conditions in Section 23. Preparers trying to develop a suitable policy will need to balance carefully the basic principles with the specific examples in the appendix, as well as bearing in mind the overall aim of giving a true and fair view. In this area, though, as with all others, it should be borne in mind that unwelcome accounting consequences can always be mitigated with disclosure (although disclosure can never compensate for inaccurate or non-compliant accounting).

10.5.5   *Other specific application guidance*

As well as the areas discussed in this section, there are a considerable number of examples of revenue recognition included in the Appendix to Section 23, which accompanies, but is not part of, Section 23.

The broad areas covered are as follows:

- sales of goods where the buyer has some kind of rights of return, e.g. bill and hold sales, goods shipped subject to approval;
- sales of subscriptions;
- instalment sales;
- agreements for construction of real estate;
- sales with customer loyalty awards (see **10.5.3**);

- installation and servicing fees;
- commissions;
- financial services fees;
- admission fees;
- initiation, entrance and membership fees (see **10.5.4**);
- franchise fees; and
- licence fees and royalties.

10.6   Disclosures

Paragraph 23.30 requires disclosure of:

(a) the accounting policies adopted for the recognition of revenue, including the methods adopted to determine the stage of completion of transactions involving the rendering of services; and

(b) the amount of each category of revenue recognised during the period, showing separately, at a minimum, revenue arising from:

   (i)   the sale of goods;

   (ii)   the rendering of services;

   (iii)   interest;

   (iv)   royalties;

   (v)   dividends;

   (vi)   commissions;

   (vii)   grants; and

   (viii) any other significant types of revenue.

Because construction contracts are particularly complicated, paragraphs 23.31–23.32 add further requirements, being disclosure of:

(a) the amount of contract revenue recognised as revenue in the period;

(b) the methods used to determine the contract revenue recognised in the period; and

(c) the methods used to determine the stage of completion of contracts in progress.

and separate presentation of:

(a) the gross amount due from customers for contract work, as an asset; and

(b) the gross amount due to customers for contract work, as a liability.

Paragraphs 23.33–35 further assist with this disclosure:

'The gross amount due from customers for contract work is the net amount of:

(a)   costs recognised as contract expenses plus recognised profits; less

(b)   the sum of recognised losses and progress billings,

for all contracts in progress for which contract expenses plus recognised profits (less recognised losses) exceeds progress billings.

The gross amount due to customers for contract work is the net amount of:

(a)   costs recognised as contract expenses plus recognised profits; less

(b)   the sum of recognised losses and progress billings,

for all contracts in progress for which progress billings exceed contract expenses plus recognised profits (less recognised losses).

Costs incurred less costs recognised as contract expenses shall be presented as contract work in progress within inventories, unless an entity has chosen to adapt its statement of financial position in accordance with paragraph 4.2A.'

10.6.1   Disclosures for small entities applying Section 1A of FRS 102

Small entities are exempt from the disclosure requirements in Sections 8–35 of the standard. Although an Appendix to Section 1A gives certain minimum requirements that replace these, there are no explicit requirements in respect of revenue. As ever, directors must still consider the overriding requirement to ensure the accounts contain the right amount of information to give a true and fair view.

10.7   Government grants

The accounting for government grants, which are a source of income for some entities, is addressed in Section 24, and is discussed in this section for completeness.

> **Application to micro-entities:** Micro-entities with government grants can only apply the accrual model under FRS 105.

10.7.1   Definition

A government grant is defined in the Glossary to FRS 102 as 'assistance by government in the form of a transfer of resources to an entity in return for past or future compliance with specified conditions relating to the operating activities of the entity. Government refers to government, government agencies and similar bodies whether local, national or international'.

There are two important aspects of the definition. The first may seem quite obvious, namely that the section only applies to grants from governmental bodies. The second is more subtle in that it only applies to grants related to an entity's operating activities. Operating activities are defined as 'the principal revenue-producing activities of the entity and other activities that are not investing or financing activities'.

10.7.2   Scope

Following the definition of government grants, it seems that if the government assistance is related to conditions associated with the entity's financing or investing activities (as opposed to its operating activities), then the transaction is not within the scope of Section 24.

Note that the definition of a government grant would not seem to exclude assistance in the form of financing (say a loan provided by government at less than commercial rates), as long as any conditions of such assistance relate to the operating activities of the entity. However, assistance which is only contingent on conditions relating to the entity's financing or investment activities are met would be outside the scope. An example might be a below-market loan from government where the cheap rate is only available as long as the entity has no other borrowings.

That said, if such forms of government assistance do exist, it is difficult to see how else they should be accounted for other than in accordance with the requirements of Section 24. One could point to the requirements of Section 34 on non-exchange transactions; however those are explicitly reserved for entities meeting the definition of a public benefit entity. As such it is not clear why the definition of a government grant needs to specifically relate the conditionality of receipt back to an entity's operating activities. It may simply be that grants relating purely to financing give rise to another accounting item – in this case a loan – so are in the scope of Sections 11 or 12 and need no special treatment by virtue of being from the government.

As well as government grants which stipulate conditions attaching to an entity's financing or investing activities, the following are explicitly excluded from the scope of Section 24:

- those forms of government assistance that cannot reasonably have a value placed upon them. No examples are given in FRS 102 but this exclusion may be intended to cover less tangible forms of assistance such as negotiations entered into by a national government to support the bid of a significant employer in that country to win overseas contracts;

- transactions with government that cannot be distinguished from the normal trading transactions of the entity. In such circumstances, it may be expected that the entity in question had negotiated the terms of a contract on normal arm's-length, commercial terms; and

- government assistance that is provided for an entity in the form of benefits that are available in determining taxable profit (tax loss), or are determined or limited on the basis of income tax liability. Examples of such benefits given in FRS 102 are income tax holidays, investment tax credits, accelerated depreciation allowances and reduced income tax rates. Such benefits are accounted for in accordance with Section 29 *Income Tax*.

10.7.3 Accounting requirements

10.7.3.1 Initial recognition

Paragraph 24.3A states that government grants, including non-monetary grants shall not be recognised until there is reasonable assurance that:

- the entity will comply with the conditions attaching to them; and

- the grants will be received.

Judgment is therefore required to determine when an entity is reasonably assured that the conditions will be met. In the case of a government grant that is to be received in cash, an entity might on some occasions be reasonably assured that these two criteria are satisfied some time before the cash is actually received and hence might recognise a debtor. Where the grant is of a non-monetary nature (such as an item of property, plant and equipment), it is not clear which asset category in the balance sheet should be debited once there is reasonable assurance of its receipt but it has not actually been received, though there is no rule stating that debtors can only be recognised for expected cash inflows.

The credit entry on initial recognition of a government grant is determined by whether the entity chooses to apply the performance model or the accrual model. Note that this is an accounting policy to be applied consistently on a 'class-by-class' basis as opposed to an accounting policy to be applied consistently to all government grants. However, FRS 102 is not clear what is meant by a class-by-class basis, i.e. whether a class is to be interpreted by reference to:

- the grantor (e.g. local v central v international government);

- the nature of the asset (e.g. monetary v non-monetary, current v non-current); or

- the class of non-monetary asset as the term 'class' is used in the context of a revaluation policy (i.e. land and buildings v fixtures and fittings v plant and machinery v motor vehicles, etc.).

In seeking to develop a reasonable interpretation, preparers may find it helpful to look at the glossary definition of a class of assets, 'a grouping of assets of a similar nature and use in an entity's operations', although this does not address the question of whether the grouping by class in this case should look internally to the receiver or externally to the grantor.

10.7.3.2   Measurement

Government grants are measured at the fair value of the asset received or receivable. It is unclear why the standard refers to 'received or receivable' as opposed to 'recognised', although this may perhaps allow some re-measurement of the amount of the grant where it is recognised prior to actually being received. This may be necessary where there is certainty of receipt of (say a monetary grant) but insufficient certainty as to the precise amount (but not so much uncertainty as to preclude recognition). Alternatively the asset which being granted has the capacity to vary (say land and buildings) between the date the grant falls for recognition and the actual value on receipt, in which case it is unclear whether FRS 102 allows for the measurement of the asset to be based on the date of actual receipt rather than its value on the date of initial recognition of the grant.

10.7.4   **The two models**

10.7.4.1   *Performance model*

Under the performance model, grants are recognised as income if all performance conditions have been met in full. This means that to the extent there are no performance-related conditions attaching to a grant it is recognised as income immediately. This is true even if the grant received is in respect of a capital asset such as property, plant and equipment.

A performance-related condition is defined in the glossary as 'a condition that requires the performance of a particular level of service or units of output to be delivered, with payment of, or entitlement to, the resources conditional on that performance'.

Where the only condition attaching to a government grant is that the asset received is used, or money received is spent, on a particular purpose (i.e. the grant is subject to a restriction) then the grant would still be accounted for in full as income when the recognition conditions (above) are met. In other words, a restriction on the use of a government grant funding does not constitute a performance-related condition and therefore does not preclude it being recognised as income in full under the performance model.

Under this model, where government grants are received subject to performance-related conditions they are not recognised in profit and loss as income until the performance-related conditions have been met.

Again, though, it is important to note that this will not necessarily mean that the government grant is recognised as income to match with the expenditure to which it may relate. It might, of course, happen to coincide with the timing of the meeting of performance conditions, for instance if the performance condition is the ongoing employment of a specific worker, in which case the payment of his salary (and its recognition as an expense) will be what meets the performance obligation.

Realistically, it is not uncommon to see government grants where the performance that triggers payment is not a one-off event but either a sequence of events or a sustained period of performance, such as keeping a facility open for three years. In this case, to judge the appropriate accounting it will be necessary to look carefully at the terms of the grant. 'Performance' may mean opening for the full three years, or there may be three separate year-long periods, each of which triggers an entitlement to another third of the income.

Example 10.7

Entity W receives a grant from its local government to run an education centre on the site of its established tourist facility.

Scenario A

The grant is for £600,000 and is all paid up front but if the centre does not run for at least three years, it will be repayable in full.

In this case, no income can be recognised until the end of the critical three year period, and the grant received will remain in deferred income on the balance sheet until then.

Scenario B

The grant still requires three years of operation, but only two-thirds is repayable if the centre closes after one year, or one-third if it remains open for two.

In this case, one-third of the income is recognised each year.

10.7.4.2 Accrual model

The accrual model begins with an assessment of whether government grants relate to revenue or capital expenditure.

Under this model, government grants relating to revenue expenditure are recognised in income on a systematic basis over the periods in which the entity recognises the related costs for which the grant is intended to compensate. In other words, grant income is matched with the related expenditure. Grants related to the purchase of assets are recognised on a systematic basis over the useful economic life of the underlying asset that was acquired with the grant. In the case of grants used to purchase items of property, plant and equipment, it is difficult to see that the systematic basis referred to would ever be anything other than to match the pattern of depreciation. The only case where a divergence might arise is if there is a very clear weighting of benefits from the asset, perhaps where revenue is much higher in the very early years (e.g. film rights). Revenue-based depreciation methods are not usually acceptable for assets, but there might be an argument for matching the grant income to the revenue pattern even if this exacerbates lumpiness of profits.

Example 10.8 – grant relating to revenue

Using the same facts as in the example above, W receives a government grant to operate a facility for three years, but this time chooses to account for it using the accrual model.

Costs in the first year are higher because of staff training and additional marketing (all covered by the grant) so instead of recognising £200,000 each year, W reviews its budgets and recognises £300,000 in the first year and £150,000 for each of the other two, based on expecting twice the level of costs in year one.

Recognising income more quickly than the right to the grant accrues means there is a risk of overstating an asset since accrued income appears on the balance sheet. This would be subject to the usual review for recoverability.

Example 10.9 – grant relating to an asset

Entity Z receives a £50,000 government grant towards the building of a series of birdwatching hides on local wetlands that it owns and maintains as Sites of Special Scientific Interest.

The hides cost £5,000 each to construct, with a ten year life, and Z will build 20 in total, 10 in 2018 and 10 in 2019.

If the grant is worded as relating to 20 hides, then Z will allocate £25,000 to the 2018 tranche, recognising £2,500 each in 2018 and each subsequent year to match the depreciation. Then in 2019, when the other hides are built, it can start to recognise the other half of the grant.

The combined effect is £2,500 of grant income in 2018, £5,000 in each of the following nine years, and £2,500 in 2028 when the first set have been fully depreciated and the second set are in their final year.

Alternatively, if the grant application and documents referred only to 'hides', with no floor or cap on numbers, Z might argue that £50,000 relates solely to the first ten hides, thus recognising £5,000 per year from the outset.

Note the difference in outcome through using the accrual model – if the performance model had been applied instead in this case, then conditions would have been met as soon as the hides were constructed, so all of the grant income would have been recognised at that point, rather than being spread over the lives of the hides.

10.7.5   Presentation and disclosure

10.7.5.1   Presentation

Where government grants are received prior to being eligible to be recognised as income, they should be included within deferred income on the balance sheet. If it becomes apparent that, for whatever reason, the grant needs to be repaid, then the amount repayable should be presented as a liability with a profit and loss account charge arising to the extent that any amount received has previously been recognised as income.

Note there is no option to offset the grant value against the carrying value of the asset.

10.7.5.2   Disclosure

Paragraphs 24.6–24.7 require an entity to disclose the following:

- the accounting policy adopted for grants;
- the nature and amounts of grants recognised in the financial statements;
- unfulfilled conditions and other contingencies attaching to grants that have been recognised in income; and
- an indication of other forms of government assistance from which the entity has directly benefited.

10.7.5.3   Disclosures for small entities applying Section 1A of FRS 102

As described above, small entities are exempt from the main disclosure requirements of FRS 102, and there are no explicit requirements for them in respect of government grants. As with all other areas, entities for whom government grants are significant will nonetheless need to consider carefully whether they need to give more information than the bare minimum, in order to be confident the accounts give a true and fair view.

11 Income tax

11.1 Scope of this section

This section covers Section 29 *Income Tax*. The equivalent standard in IFRS is IAS 12 *Income Taxes*.

Section 29 covers accounting for income taxes, being 'all domestic and foreign taxes that are based on taxable profit', and taxes that are payable by a subsidiary, associate or joint venture on distributions to the reporting entity. It deals with both current and deferred tax.

VAT is also addressed even though it is outside the above definition, being levied on individual transactions regardless of profits.

Other charges with 'tax' in their name may well be excluded from the scope if they relate to something other than profits, for instance stamp duty land tax (SDLT) which is paid on individual property purchases. The treatment of SDLT would be governed by the property-related Sections 16 *Investment property* and 17 *Property, plant and equipment*.

A *timing difference* arises when profits or losses are recognised in the financial statements in a different period from that in which they are assessed for tax.

A *permanent difference* arises when there are differences between accounting and taxable profits that will never reverse, for instance relating to an item of expenditure which is disallowed for tax purposes.

> **Application to micro-entities:** The requirements for accounting for current tax and VAT are set out in Section 24 of FRS 105 and are consistent with the requirements in FRS 102. However, micro-entities are not permitted to account for deferred tax.

11.2 Recognition of current tax

Current tax is recognised for actual tax payable, whether relating to the current or previous periods. Given the way the tax system in the UK functions, this will usually be only an estimate, and is based on the amounts expected to be paid or recovered, using tax rates and laws that have been enacted or substantively enacted at the reporting date (see **11.2.3**).

FRS 102 (2018) incorporates new requirements in relation to Gift Aid payments made by charitable subsidiaries. Paragraph 29.14A says that when:

(a)   an entity is wholly-owned by one or more charitable entities;

(b)   it is probable that a Gift Aid payment will be made to a member of the same charitable group, or a charitable venturer, within nine months of the reporting date; and

(c)   that payment will qualify to be set against profits for tax purposes,

the income tax effects of that Gift Aid payment are recognised at the reporting date. The income tax effects are measured consistently with the tax treatment planned to be used in the entity's income tax filings. A deferred tax liability is not recognised in relation to such a Gift Aid payment.

In this context, 'charitable' refers to an entity that has been recognised by HMRC as being eligible for certain tax reliefs because of its charitable purposes.

11.3   Recognition of deferred tax

The basic principle for recognition is that a deferred tax asset or liability is recognised in respect of all timing differences, and never recognised in respect of permanent differences. The only explicit modification of the requirement to recognise deferred tax on timing differences is in respect of some deferred tax assets (discussed further below).

The standard gives very little guidance on identifying timing differences and permanent differences: perhaps this is because they are assumed to be concepts that are already familiar to UK preparers.

Where an item affects profits in several years, the calculation of the timing difference is based on the comparison between cumulative effects on accounting and taxable profits, as illustrated in the first example below.

Example 11.1

An entity purchases a piece of equipment on 1 January 2015 for £60,000, and assesses its useful life as six years and residual value as nil, so for accounting purposes the annual straight-line depreciation charge will be £10,000.

Suppose for tax purposes a short life asset election is made, so the capital allowances would be £25,000 in the first year, 18% reducing balance in years 2–5 and a balancing allowance in the final year.

A timing difference arises in each year of the asset's life because the accounting depreciation always differs from the tax depreciation even though the ultimate total for each will be the same – the difference is only in allocation between periods.

The depreciated cost, tax written down value, difference between cumulative write-downs and consequent timing difference for each period are shown below.

	Accounting depreciation current (cumulative)	Tax depreciation current (cumulative)	Timing difference	Deferred tax liability at 19%
2015	10,000 (10,000)	25,000 (25,000)	15,000	2,850
2016	10,000 (20,000)	6,300 (31,300)	11,300	2,147
2017	10,000 (30,000)	5,166 (36,466)	6,466	1,229
2018	10,000 (40,000)	4,236 (40,702)	702	133
2019	10,000 (50,000)	3,474 (44,176)	(4,176)	(793)
2020	10,000 (60,000)	15,824 (60,000)	–	–

So, a deferred tax liability is set up in the first year, via a debit to the P&L, and then released over the asset's life, as the cumulative difference between depreciation and capital allowances lessens.

Example 11.2

An entity has a particularly generous year, and spends £100,000 on client entertaining, which is recognised as an expense in the accounts.

Client entertaining is not deductible for tax purposes, and hence a permanent difference arises. There are no entries for deferred tax relating to this expenditure.

The approach adopted by Section 29 is often described as a 'timing differences plus' approach, and care is needed by UK preparers who will find a small number of areas where they did not previously need to account for deferred tax, but now need to.

11.3.1 Revaluation of assets (paragraph 29.15)

Where a freehold property (for instance) is revalued upward for accounting purposes, a revaluation gain is recognised through other comprehensive income (see **5.2.4.4**). For tax purposes (ignoring indexation), the asset stays at its original value, with the gain not being taxed until the asset is disposed of (and perhaps not then, if rollover relief is available). So a timing difference arises, and a deferred tax liability is recognised.

Example 11.3

A property asset with a 20-year life, an original cost of £200,000 and a depreciated cost of £150,000 is revalued to £250,000 when it has 15 years of useful life remaining. As the asset is land and buildings, it is not eligible for capital allowances. The applicable tax rate is expected to remain at 19% for both income and capital gains for the whole of the asset's life.

The revaluation gain of £100,000 gives rise to a timing difference because the accounting gain recognised in other comprehensive income is not matched with an immediate increase in taxable profits (instead, the gain will be taxed when the asset's additional value is realised, whether through sale at a higher price or through higher reported profits during its useful life). Accordingly a deferred tax liability of £19,000 (£100,000 at 19%) is recognised, with the charge going through other comprehensive income as required by paragraph 29.22.

Note that where tax rates vary depending on profit levels, the company would use the rate applicable to the most likely outcome. It would assess its predicted profit levels at the point when the asset's value was expected to be recovered, and choose a tax rate accordingly (paragraph 29.13). The timing of recovery may also affect the chosen rate, based on whether the value is to be recovered through extra profits, or on disposal of the asset.

Queries might arise with respect to the treatment of a difference arising from a revaluation gain where it is expected that the revaluation uplift will never itself be taxed, as a result of factors such as indexation, the ability to use capital losses brought forward, and so on. This expectation of the future is not, however, particularly relevant to the question of whether to recognise a deferred tax liability.

The only way in which non-recognition would be justified would be if the revaluation gain gave rise to a permanent difference, but this is not the case here, because a permanent difference would only arise where the gain is 'non-taxable', that is not taxable by virtue of its very nature, rather than incidentally likely not to be taxed because of tax planning opportunities such as the use of losses.

Expected indexation would be taken account of in establishing the rate applied to measure the deferred tax balance, based on when the timing differences will reverse; accumulated capital losses would be assessed as distinct items which may give rise to deferred tax assets in their own right.

11.3.2   Unremitted earnings

FRS 102 adopts the principle of IAS 12, and requires that:

'Deferred tax shall be recognised when income or expenses from a subsidiary, associate, branch, or interest in a joint venture have been recognised in the financial statements, and will be assessed to or allowed for tax in a future period, except where:

(a)   The reporting entity is able to control the reversal of the timing difference; and

(b)   It is probable that the timing difference will not reverse in the foreseeable future.'

[paragraph 29.9]

This means that additional deferred tax may need to be recognised under FRS 102 in relation to certain investments. This is because the value at which the investment is recorded in the financial statements may reflect earnings which have not yet been remitted to the reporting entity. These typically arise in consolidated financial statements, because the profits of the investment have been recorded in the accounts but are not yet liable to tax because they have not been remitted to the investor. However, this situation could also arise in individual financial statements where an investment is carried at fair value.

In most cases, an investor in a subsidiary will be able to meet the two criteria above and therefore no deferred tax would need to be recognised. However, for other types of interest deferred tax may need to be recorded.

11.3.3   Business combinations and goodwill (paragraph 29.10)

Where an entity acquires a subsidiary, it performs an exercise to assess the fair value of the assets in the acquired business, which will often give rise to an uplift for the purpose of the group accounts. The difference between the consideration paid for the investment, and the fair value of the net assets acquired, is goodwill, also recognised on the consolidated balance sheet (see **4.2**).

Paragraph 29.11 requires that:

'When the amount that can be deducted for tax for an asset (other than goodwill) that is recognised in a business combination accounted for by applying the purchase method is less (more) than the value at which it is recognised, a deferred tax liability (asset) shall be recognised for the additional tax that will be paid (avoided) in respect of that difference. Similarly, a deferred tax asset (liability) shall be recognised for the additional tax that will be avoided (paid) because of a difference between the value at which a liability is recognised in a business combination accounted for by applying the purchase method and the amount that will be assessed for tax. The amount attributed to goodwill (or negative goodwill) shall be adjusted by the amount of deferred tax recognised.'

FRS 102 (2018) includes a new paragraph 29.11A:

'In applying paragraph 29.11 and determining the amount that can be deducted for tax an entity shall consider the manner in which the entity expects, at the end of the reporting period, to recover or settle the carrying amount of the asset or liability.'

Under IFRS, the recognition of this fair value uplift on the acquisition balance sheet would give rise to a difference between the carrying amount and the tax base, and it would be clear how to calculate deferred tax – it would be based on this new temporary difference. This effectively is a combination of any pre-existing temporary difference (upon which deferred tax was already recognised) and the additional temporary difference arising from the fair value uplift. It seems that because this requirement has been transplanted in from IFRS, the same approach should be applied, without an attempt to squeeze the description into a vocabulary of timing differences.

Example 11.4

Parent P acquires subsidiary S, which has assets with book value £1m and fair value £1.2m, for consideration of £2m. In P's group accounts, S's assets are brought in at £1.2m. An additional deferred tax liability is recognised at £38,000, being 19% of the £200,000 uplift. Goodwill is therefore £838,000: £800,000 difference between the fair value of assets acquired and the consideration, plus the £38,000 deferred tax adjustment.

This new deferred tax provision is in addition to any deferred tax already included on S's balance sheet, for instance, in relation to properties where capital allowances have been received in excess of depreciation. The extra part recognised here relates to the fair value uplift.

The subsequent treatment of the £38k liability will depend on how the underlying asset value is recovered. If it is recovered through sale, then the liability will be released to profit at the point of disposal. In the subsidiary, there will be a book profit with a corresponding tax charge; in the group, the book profit will be lower because the fair value uplift had already been recognised, and the tax charge is then made correspondingly lower by this release of the deferred tax liability. If, on the other hand, the asset value is deemed to be recovered through higher future profits, it is theoretically possible to argue that the timing difference reverses (and hence the liability is released) over the asset's life. This might, however, be difficult to support given that the initial recognition of the deferred tax liability is based on a special provision in the standard, rather than on the definition of a timing difference.

11.3.4   Share-based payments

A prima facie timing difference arises in respect of share-based payment charges because in general a tax deduction will not be available until any options are exercised, meaning it may be that an expense is recognised some years before the deduction.

Example 11.5

A company grants share options with a grant date fair value of £200,000 in total and a five year vesting period, meaning it expects to recognise a charge of £40,000 in profit each year.

It anticipates that the tax deduction available on exercise will be £300,000 (this is based on the expected intrinsic value at exercise date).

A timing difference arises because the accounting charges are recognised over the vesting period, but the tax deduction is recognised in a different accounting period, at the point when the options are exercised.

Because the future tax deduction is greater than the total accounting charge, the timing difference in each of the five years is equal to the accounting expense, i.e. £40,000 per year. A deferred tax asset will be built up at £7,600 (19% of £40,000) each year, credited to profit (to match the accounting charge) and then on exercise an additional credit of £19,000 will be recognised in profit, being 19% of the value by which the tax deduction exceeds the accounting charge.

11.3.5   Deferred tax assets

A timing difference will give rise to a deferred tax asset when income is taxed before it is recognised in the accounts, or when expenses are recognised in the accounts before a tax deduction is available.

Unrelieved losses also give rise to deferred tax assets because they represent a future tax benefit. Intuitively, though, some restriction should be applied to recognising such assets. Consider, for instance, a start-up business which has yet to make a profit, and is forecast not to break even until its fifth year of trading. It will accumulate large volumes of unrelieved losses, but a deferred tax asset based on these would not seem to meet the definition of an asset in paragraph 2.15, 'a resource controlled by the entity as a result of past events and from which future economic benefits are expected to flow to the entity'. The losses will give rise to a benefit via a reduction in the future tax charge only when – and if – the business becomes profitable, and it could not be reasonably predicted at this early stage when or whether this move to profitability might happen.

Section 29 deals with this by stating that:

> 'Unrelieved tax losses and other deferred tax assets shall be recognised only to the extent that it is probable that they will be recovered against the reversal of deferred tax liabilities or other future taxable profits (29.7)'

It continues by pointing out that:

> 'The very existence of unrelieved tax losses is strong evidence that there may not be "other future taxable profits" against which losses will be relieved (29.7).'

In other words, a loss-making company usually continues to be loss-making.

'Probable' is defined in the Glossary to the standard as meaning 'more likely than not', which is a slightly lower threshold than might be implied by the word in everyday speech.

There are no bright lines or fixed rules here, and it is certainly not the case that a deferred tax asset can never be recognised in respect of tax losses. Management judgment will be necessary in looking at forecasts and determining the level of confidence in future profits. Examples of situations where it might be reasonable to recognise a deferred tax asset in respect of losses include:

- an entity has one loss making line of business which has now been disposed of, and all its remaining business areas have been, and are forecast to continue being, profitable (but of sufficiently similar trades that offset of the tax losses against their profits will be permissible);

- a major reorganisation has taken place in the year which will give rise immediately to quantifiable reductions in overheads so that a previously loss-making trade will now be profitable;

- past years have seen capital losses on asset disposals which have not yet been used, but a large disposal is planned for the coming year where the expected gain (based on a steady second hand market) will be sufficient to absorb the previous capital losses, and it is not expected that rollover relief would be claimed (if rollover relief was taken then the gain arising would be rolled into an new asset purchase, so it would not be available for absorbing capital losses).

The ability to recover a deferred tax asset will also depend on local tax legislation, which may (as in the UK) include rules on the circumstances under which brought forward trading losses may be offset against capital gains or against current profits.

A question also arises around how far it is reasonable to look into the future when establishing whether a deferred tax asset can be recovered. For instance, a business may have accumulated losses of £800,000 and have moved into profitability, with forecast future profits (based on committed sales orders) of £250,000 each year for the next five years. This would mean it would take a little over three years for the accumulated losses to be used (and for the company to start paying any tax on its profits) but many would baulk at recognising, based only on forecasts, an asset relating to the whole balance of losses.

Under old UK GAAP, there was an acceptance that looking further out than 12 months would be imprudent, so in this example an asset would only be recognised in respect of the first £250,000 of losses, with the remainder drip-fed into the income statement as each new year end allows another year of looking forward. This 12-month period, though, is not specified in FRS 102 and appears somewhat arbitrary. Management should, therefore, use judgment based on the company's particular circumstances, which may lead to the recognition of a higher value of assets as the fairest representation of the situation.

11.4   Measurement of current and deferred tax

11.4.1   *Identifying the appropriate tax rate*

Current and deferred tax must be measured with reference to the rates and laws that have been enacted or substantively enacted by the reporting date.

This requirement means, in the UK, that a law needs at least to have passed its final reading in the House of Commons.

The *Finance Act* 2016 included a reduction in the main rate of corporation tax to 17% from 1 April 2020 from 19%.

In the case of deferred tax, the rate to be used may be affected not just by enacted or substantively enacted future changes, but also by the nature of the timing difference and the way in which it is expected to reverse. Once a timing difference has been calculated, the deferred tax asset or liability is recognised by multiplying this difference by the enacted or substantively enacted tax rate that is expected to apply when the difference reverses.

To illustrate this, an entity has a year end of 31 March. The entity is based in a jurisdiction where a change in tax rate from 26% to 23% is substantively enacted on 1 April 20X1. The 23% rate will apply to taxable profits arising on or after 1 April 20X1. The tax rate of 26% will apply to taxable profit for the year ended 31 March 20X1. Even though the new tax rate of

23% is known before the financial statements are authorised for issue, it has not been substantively enacted by 31 March 20X1. Therefore, any deferred tax assets and liabilities at 31 March 20X1 should continue to be measured using the tax rate of 26%. If the effect is significant, disclosures will be required in accordance with Section 32.

Although in this section, the tax rate at reversal has, for convenience, been assumed to be 19% in all cases, in practice preparers need to look at future expectations, based on legislation already enacted or substantively enacted, and, sometimes, at the expected manner of recovery.

11.4.2   Discounting tax balances

Consistent with IAS 12, discounting is prohibited under Section 29 for both current and deferred tax balances.

11.4.3   Measuring deferred tax on non-depreciable assets

Paragraphs 29.15 and 29.16 give two situations where companies are required to use the rates and allowances applicable to the sale of an asset (rather than the realisation of its value through use) – when a non-depreciable asset has been revalued, and when an investment property is measured at fair value. This is unlikely to cause issues for UK preparers under current tax law, since the same rate is applied to capital and revenue gains.

11.5   Value added tax (VAT)

The treatment for VAT is set out in paragraph 29.20 which is relatively straightforward:

> 'Turnover shown in profit or loss shall exclude VAT and other similar sales taxes on taxable outputs and VAT imputed under the flat rate VAT scheme. Expenses shall exclude recoverable VAT and other similar recoverable sales taxes. Irrecoverable VAT allocable to fixed assets and to other items disclosed separately in the financial statements shall be included in their cost where practicable and material.'

The standard does not specify whether VAT should be included in the cash flow statement. Under old UK GAAP, cash flows were required to be presented net of VAT and it is probable that this practice will continue to be followed under FRS 102.

11.6   Presentation and disclosure

Section 29 contains guidance on presentation of tax charges and credits, and the corresponding balances. There are also detailed disclosure requirements.

11.6.1   Income statement items

Changes in current and deferred tax assets and liabilities are recognised as an expense, in the same component of total comprehensive income or equity as the transaction or event that had the tax effect. A 'component' for this purpose means the matching goes down to the level of whether the item is in continuing operations, discontinued operations or other comprehensive income.

FRS 102 (2018) includes a new paragraph 29.22A which states that as an exception to the above, the tax effects of distributions to owners must be shown in profit or loss.

Example 11.6

Company M, which has only continuing operations, recognises deferred tax in respect of accelerated capital allowances on its machinery, and revaluation of its properties.

Depreciation is an income statement item so the charge to set up a deferred tax liability arising from accelerated capital allowances is also recognised in income from continuing operations.

Property revaluations are recognised in other comprehensive income, so the charge to set up the associated liability is also recognised in other comprehensive income.

11.6.2   Balance sheet items

No explicit guidance is given on the presentation of current tax assets and liabilities, but paragraph 29.23 is clear on deferred tax balances:

'An entity shall present deferred tax liabilities within provisions for liabilities and deferred tax assets within debtors unless it has chosen to adapt its statement of financial position in accordance with paragraph 4.2A.'

Where separately presented, deferred tax assets shall be presented within debtors falling due after more than one year.

The guidance on offsetting assets and liabilities in paragraph 29.24 is also not entirely clear in its wording, but seems to be bringing in the same requirements as IAS 12: current tax assets and liabilities, or deferred tax assets and liabilities, may and must only be offset if there is a legally enforceable right to offset them and the entity intends either to settle them net or to realise the asset and settle the liability simultaneously.

Example 11.7

Company Q has unused tax losses of £1m arising from trading, in respect of which it has established it should recognise a deferred tax asset of £300,000 (there is strong evidence of the availability of future profits). It also has revalued a property in the year, giving rise to a deferred tax liability of £200,000.

The asset and liability must not be netted off on the balance sheet, because tax law does not allow the use of capital losses against trading gains, so there is no legally enforceable right to offset them.

11.6.3   Disclosure requirements

The major components of tax expense or income must be disclosed, which may include:

(a) current tax expense or income;

(b) adjustments recognised in the period for current tax of prior periods;

(c) the amount of deferred tax expense or income relating to the origination and reversal of timing differences;

(d) the amount of deferred tax expense or income relating to changes in tax rates or the imposition of new taxes;

(e) adjustments to deferred tax expense arising from a change in the tax status of an entity or its shareholders; and

(f) the amount of tax expense relating to changes in accounting policies or errors.

Note that this requirement allows for the possibility that there are other major components. Judgment is needed on whether a particular component is major, qualitatively or quantitatively.

A number of specific details are also required, if they are material (it is not clear why this is stated, since paragraph 3.16B is already perfectly explicit that 'an entity need not provide a specific disclosure required by this FRS if the information is not material'):

(a) the aggregate current and deferred tax relating to items that are included in other comprehensive income;

(b) a reconciliation between the total expense or income reported in profit and the product of profits and the applicable tax rate;

(c) the quantum of net reversals of deferred tax balances expected in the following year;

(d) an explanation of changes in the applicable tax rates from the previous period;

(e) the amount of deferred tax liabilities and deferred tax assets at the end of the reporting period for each type of timing difference and each type of unused tax losses and tax credits;

(f) the expiry date, if any, of timing differences, unused tax losses and unused tax credits; and

(g) an explanation of the potential income tax consequences that would result from the payment of dividends to shareholders.

Most of these requirements are fairly self-explanatory. Point (g) only becomes relevant in situations where the payment out of dividends to shareholders triggers the application of a different tax rate from the retention of profits in the company, which is not relevant under current UK tax legislation.

11.6.4   Disclosure requirements for small entities

The only tax-related disclosure included in the minimum requirements for small entities in Appendix C to Section 1A of the standard actually appears in the fixed assets section. Paragraph 1AC.18 states that 'the treatment for taxation purposes of amounts credited or debited to the revaluation reserve must be disclosed in a note to the financial statements'.

12 Foreign currency issues

12.1 Scope of this section

This section covers Section 30 *Foreign currency translation* and Section 31 *Hyperinflation.*

The equivalent standards in IFRS are IAS 21 *The Effects of Changes in Foreign Exchange Rates* and IAS 29 *Financial Reporting in Hyperinflationary Economies.*

> **Application to micro-entities:** Section 25 of FRS 105 appears to assume that micro-entities will use pounds sterling; it does not talk in detail about functional currency and there is no concept of a presentation currency. It does note, though, that where a micro-entity has a foreign branch it should refer to Section 30 of FRS 102 to determine that branch's functional currency.
>
> In general, the requirements for translation of foreign currency transactions are the same as FRS 102. However, there is an exception where a transaction is to be settled at a contracted rate or is covered by a related forward contract. In these cases, the contracted rate must be used (note this is a requirement, not an option).
>
> FRS 105 does not address the accounting for a net investment in a foreign operation. This is because FRS 105 may only be applied in company-only accounts, where the accounting treatment is the same as for all other monetary items.

12.2 Functional currency

The core concept that Section 30 relies on for its requirements on foreign currency translation is that of the functional currency. This is defined in paragraph 30.2 as 'the currency of the primary economic environment in which the entity operates'.

12.2.1 Establishing the functional currency

Although many companies will find determining the functional currency to be straightforward, detailed guidance is needed for those with significant overseas transactions or interests.

Section 12 gives the general note that usually an entity's primary economic environment is the one in which it generates and expends cash, and then gives a set of factors to consider. These should usually be sufficient

361

to establish the functional currency: it is only where they do not give a conclusive answer that the secondary factors are necessary.

12.2.1.1   Primary indicators (30.3)

(a) The currency:

  (i)   that mainly influences sales prices for goods and services (this will often be the currency in which sales prices for its goods and services are denominated and settled); and

  (ii) of the country whose competitive forces and regulations mainly determine the sales price of its goods and services.

(b) The currency that mainly influences labour, material and other costs of providing goods or services (this will often be the currency in which such costs are denominated and settled).

12.2.1.2   Secondary indicators (30.4)

(a) The currency in which funds from financing activities (issuing debt and equity instruments) are generated; and

(b) The currency in which receipts from operating activities are usually retained.

The best way to understand the application of these indicators is to look at practical examples.

Example 12.1

(1) Company A is based in the UK. All of its costs and most of its revenues are also UK-based, although it has a small number of customers around Europe.

  A has a GBP functional currency as this is the main influence on its sales prices and its costs.

(2) Company B is an oil producer. Although it has a small head office presence in the UK, its operations are mainly in Africa. Sales are in US dollars, as this is the standard currency for oil sales.

  B has at least three candidates for its functional currency, but the most likely is US dollars, since this determines the selling price of oil (and prices are denominated in USD).

(3) Company C makes sales all around the globe, but its production facilities are in China.

  It is likely that its functional currency will be determined to be Renminbi, as this is the currency that influences labour, materials and other costs, and there is no single other currency that has a significant overall influence on sales prices.

---

(4) Company D has its head office and all of its cost-incurring activities in the UK, but all of its customers are in India. Its bank accounts are held in sterling, which is also the currency of its share capital and its bank loans.

Here, there are two contrary indications, because looking at sales suggests Rupee as the functional currency, but looking at costs suggests that sterling would be more appropriate. So, D would turn to the supplementary indicators, which would lead to a conclusion that the functional currency is sterling because this is the currency in which cash is retained and funds are raised.

Several points can be drawn out from these examples. First, the presence of a UK head office by no means guarantees that sterling is the appropriate functional currency: it is more important to look at sales and costs. Second, the currency of share issues and loan financing is not accorded as much weight as considerations relating to trading: in fact it would not even be considered if the output from looking at sales and costs appeared to be clear-cut.

The wording of the indicators, looking at the currency that influences sales prices rather than in which sales are determined, draws a distinction which will often have no effect, since in many regions and industries these will be one and the same. Areas in which to be careful include industries where there is a standard currency that influences the sales price but where, for convenience, sales might still be invoiced in the local currency.

12.2.1.3 Functional currency of a foreign operation

When a company has an investment in a foreign operation, establishing that operation's functional currency is a crucial first part of including it in the consolidation. Four factors are given to be considered in determining whether the foreign operation has its own functional currency or the functional currency of the parent (30.5):

(a) whether the activities of the foreign operation are carried out as an extension of the reporting entity, rather than being carried out with a significant degree of autonomy;

(b) whether transactions with the reporting entity are a high or a low proportion of the foreign operation's activities;

(c) whether cash flows from the activities of the foreign operation directly affect the cash flows of the reporting entity and are readily available for remittance to it;

(d) Whether cash flows from the activities of the foreign operation are sufficient to service existing and normally expected debt obligations without funds being made available by the reporting entity.

Effectively, each of these points is trying to get to the core of whether the operation functions as a branch of the parent or as a distinct operation in its own right. In many cases this will be very clear cut, but where there is doubt these indications can be used to structure the decision-making process.

Example 12.2

Company Q, a GBP functional currency entity, has two subsidiaries, R and S.

R is based in the US and has its own management team, supplier contracts etc. It both buys and sells in USD, acting autonomously (although Q does still have enough control to qualify as its parent).

S, on the other hand, is based in France and effectively acts as a distribution agent for Q. It purchases inventories from Q rather than directly from suppliers, and most of its logistical decisions and its selling prices are centrally determined by Q.

Where R's functional currency is likely to be USD, based on analysis of its operations, S's functional currency is probably sterling, i.e. that of its parent company, as this is the currency with the key influence on S's revenues and costs.

12.2.2   *Reporting transactions outside the functional currency*

When an entity has transactions in a currency other than its functional currency, it needs a way of recording these in the functional currency.

The requirements for initial recognition are straightforward, with each transaction being translated at the spot rate on the transaction date. Since this could be onerous in practical terms, it is acceptable to use an average rate for the week or month, providing this is a reasonable approximation of the daily rate. This allows for weekly batch processing of invoices, for instance, rather than having a system which uses a different exchange rate for each date.

Subsequent reporting depends on the nature of the item:

- monetary assets and liabilities are retranslated using the exchange rate at the reporting date, with exchange differences recognised in the income statement;

- non-monetary items measured at cost are left at their historical cost, translated at the rate that was originally used (i.e. spot rate at transaction date);

- non-monetary items measured at fair value first have their fair value redetermined in the foreign currency, then this is retranslated using the rate when fair value was determined.

Again, this is best explained through illustrative examples.

Example 12.3

Company G, with a GBP functional currency, makes a $100 purchase two months before its year end, which is initially recorded at £70, using the average rate in the week of purchase.

At the year end, the $100 liability is still outstanding, so this is retranslated using the year end rate, at which point it has a value of £65.

The remeasurement gain of £5 is included in profit for the year.

Company H purchases a piece of plant at the beginning of its reporting period, with a cost of €2m. Its cost is initially recorded based on that month's average rate, at £1.8m. At the year end, the amount shown as historic cost is not retranslated.

Company I purchases an investment property for $2m and elects to measure it at fair value. At initial recognition, this is translated to £1.2m (rate is 0.6). At the year end, the fair value has increased to $2.2m – this is translated using the year end rate of 0.7, so the value included in the balance sheet is £1.54m. The revaluation gain of £340,000 does not split the 'true' revaluation gain from the effects of currency movement.

While this guidance seems straightforward, there are some nuances where no guidance is given and where, therefore, preparers may need to seek guidance from outside Section 30.

12.2.2.1 Definition of monetary and non-monetary

The standard defines monetary items as 'units of currency held and assets and liabilities to be received or paid in a fixed or determinable number of units of currency'. In practice this will cover items expected to be settled ore realised in cash, and will have a significant overlap with items defined as financial asset and liabilities, though some items qualifying as financial instruments – for instance investments in equity – do not meet the definition of monetary assets.

12.2.2.2 Revaluation of non-monetary assets

Paragraph 30.11 requires that if a gain or loss on a non-monetary item is recognised in other comprehensive income, the related exchange movement is also recognised in OCI. A common example is the revaluation of property.

Example 12.4

Company H in the examples above purchased an asset for €2m which was initially recorded at £1.8m.

One year later, the asset is revalued to €2.5m, while the exchange rate has moved from 0.9–0.8.

The gain reported in OCI is the difference between the previous cost at the old rate (€2m at 0.9 = £1.8m) and the new revalued amount at the new year end rate (€2.5m at 0.8 = £2m), i.e. £200,000.

This is the net of two amounts:

Revaluation gain [€500,000 at 0.8]	£400,000
Forex loss [€2m at (0.9−0.8)]	(£200,000)
Net gain	£200,000

12.2.3   Changing functional currency

There are two aspects to changing functional currency: determining that a change is necessary, and accounting for that change.

Changes should not be common, as most entities have a reasonably stable structure which means their economic environment would not be expected to undergo significant changes. Typical exceptions might include an oil company moving from the exploration phase to the production phase, where the functional currency might originally have been the currency local to its operations (or perhaps even to its head office), but this moves to being US dollars once it begins to generate revenues. Aside from such early stage changes, which effectively just relate to a company settling into its mature structure, it might also happen that a company shifts production to a new geographical area, or curtails sales to somewhere that was previously a key market. What is clear is that there would usually be a distinct trigger event to suggest that a review of the appropriate functional currency was necessary – it would be unlikely to arise without this type of discrete event or very clear change in circumstances.

When a change does take place, the accounting is straightforward: the change operates prospectively, so all items at the date of change are translated at the exchange rate on that date, with the resulting value used as their historic cost.

In practice, there is an interaction between this and the choice of presentation currency, discussed further below and illustrated in a fuller example.

12.3   Presentation currency

12.3.1   Selecting and using a presentation currency

The presentation currency is, unsurprisingly, the currency in which the financial statements are presented. There is a free choice of presentation currency, and there are no restrictions on changing it, so in theory a different currency could be chosen each year, though it would be hard to see how directors could justify this on the basis of providing more relevant information.

To translate a set of results from the functional currency into the chosen presentation currency, the following steps are followed (summarised from paragraph 30.18):

(a)   translate the assets and liabilities for the current year and comparative balance sheets at the relevant exchange rate for each date (i.e. a different rate for the two balance sheets);

(b)   translate income and expenses for each period presented using the actual transaction date rates (or an average for each period if rates have not fluctuated significantly in the year);

(c)   include the balancing figure in other comprehensive income.

To understand how the balancing figure referred to above arises, consider a company with a USD functional currency that reports in GBP, with December 2018 net assets of $3m, profits for the year of $800k and therefore closing (December 2019) net assets of $3.8m. Now, if the December 2018 exchange rate is 0.62, and the December 2019 rate 0.75, with an average rate of 0.65, the translation process as described above will result in:

GBP opening net assets	£1,860,000
GBP profit	£520,000
GBP closing net assets (sum)	£2,380,000
GBP closing net assets (translated)	£2,850,000

The difference between the 'sum' and 'translated' amounts above is the amount to be shown in other comprehensive income with the closing balance sheet using the 'translated' amount. As explained in paragraph 30.20, there are two components to this movement, which in this example is a gain: first, the effect of the difference between the actual or average rates used for transactions in the year and the closing rates used for the two balance sheets, and second, the effect of the difference between opening and closing rates (if in the example above there had been no profit for the year, so that net assets had remained at $3m throughout, an exchange difference would still arise between £1,860,000 and £2,250,000, being the balance sheet totals at the opening and closing rates respectively).

Example 12.5

Company D has a GBP functional currency in its early years, but has recently developed a massive market in the US due to one particular product. It presents its accounts in GBP.

It concludes that from 1 January 2019 its functional currency has changed from GBP to USD, but it will still continue to present its financial statements in GBP.

The exchange rate at 31/12/2018 is 0.62; the average in the year is 0.7, and the closing rate is 0.85.

In the 2019 accounts, the comparatives will be unchanged from those previously reported, since the presentation currency is unchanged and the functional currency change only has prospective effects. At 1 January 2019, the GPB functional currency balance sheet is retranslated into USD in the accounting records, using the spot rate, so the opening net assets are $3.333m in the records. Profit for the year is $800,000, so closing net assets are $4.133m. When these amounts are reported in the GBP presentation currency, profit is £560,000 for 2019, and closing net assets £3.513m. The difference between this closing figure and the sum of £2m opening net assets and £560,000 reported profits (total £2.56m) is a gain of £953,000, reported in OCI.

Note that if the functional currency had remained unchanged, the reported figures would have been different, since it would be the USD transactions and balances giving rise to exchange differences, rather than the GBP transactions and balances.

12.3.2   Group issues

The process of incorporating the results of a foreign subsidiary into a consolidation involves the same steps as for any translation to a different presentation currency, meaning again that a balancing gain or loss will always need to be recognised in other comprehensive income. This section covers some detailed application points.

12.3.2.1   Determining the foreign operation's functional currency

As described at **12.2.1**, the starting point must be to establish the functional currency of the overseas operation, which is affected by its interactions with the parent, looking at the extent to which it operates as an independent entity as opposed to running more like a branch or extension of the parent's activities. If it is determined that the operation's functional currency is the same as the parent's, then the inclusion in the consolidation is straightforward, although it will be important to check that the translation of balances and transactions outside that functional currency has been correctly dealt with in the subsidiary's results included in the consolidation (as part of a general review to ensure the subsidiary's account policies are consistent with FRS 102 and with those of the parent).

12.3.2.2 Intragroup loans

For any entity with a monetary item payable or receivable, retranslation at the year end will give rise to an exchange gain or loss, being the difference between the amount at which it was initially recorded and its subsequent year end value based on the closing rate.

In the particular case of intercompany balances where the balance is, for at least one of the entities, in a foreign currency, this is slightly problematic because usually the consolidation process eliminates intercompany balances and any intragroup gains or losses. Here, though, paragraph 30.22 makes it clear that after elimination of such balances a gain or loss will remain and will be included in the consolidation. As it explains, 'the monetary item represents a commitment to convert one currency into another and exposes the reporting entity to a gain or loss through currency fluctuations'.

Example 12.6

Parent P has a GBP functional currency and has lent £1m to its subsidiary S, which has a USD functional currency. S translated the liability at the spot rate when it initially received the loan, recording it at $1.4m, but in its year end accounts it must retranslate at the new spot rate, giving a new liability value of $1.5m and loss of $100,000 (assuming no extra accounting for interest, because the interest charge is settled in cash each month).

For inclusion in the consolidation, the year end balance is translated back to £1m and cancels with the receivable in P; the exchange loss in S's income statement is translated into GBP at an average rate for the period, and is included in group profits.

12.3.2.3 Goodwill

Goodwill often arises on the acquisition of subsidiaries, and foreign subsidiaries are no exception. Paragraph 30.23 states that it is treated as an asset of the foreign operation, as are any further fair value adjustments that originally arose on acquisition and continue to have an effect on the consolidation journals in subsequent periods. This means that the relevant adjustments are determined at the acquisition date, in the foreign currency, and then when the consolidation is prepared each reporting date they are translated at the closing rate, in the same way as all of the other assets and liabilities of the subsidiary. It can be seen that this will give a different effect from the alternative of translating the adjustments just once, when they are originally calculated, and then viewing goodwill and the fair value adjustments as being an asset of the parent and therefore remaining unchanged (excepting amortisation) year on year.

Example 12.7

When Parent Q buys Subsidiary R in 2018, it pays £2.33m and R has net assets with a fair value of $1.8m. Goodwill calculated at the point of the purchase is calculated by translating the consideration into USD (£2.33m at 1.5 = $3.5m), leaving a balance of $1.7m as goodwill.

At the end of the following year, R has net assets of $2.4m, which are translated at a rate of 1.6 and therefore give £1.5m to be included in the consolidation. The goodwill balance is also retranslated using the same rate, so is shown as £1.06m.

If Q had incorrectly treated the goodwill as a GBP asset of the parent, it would have been initially recorded at £1.1m (£2.3m less $1.8m at 1.5) and not retranslated at subsequent reporting dates.

12.3.2.4 'Group functional currency'

It is a common misconception that a group can have a functional currency of its own – there is nothing in the standard to support this. Functional currency should be assessed by individual reporting entity and then when the parent prepares group accounts, these accounts will be based on its own functional currency. This could lead to some questionable consequences – for instance where the parent is a virtually empty company without sales or costs, so appears to have its currency set by the currency of its shares and debt, but it has a subsidiary with a clear, and different, functional currency. If the group accounts include mainly the results of this foreign subsidiary, it seems counter intuitive that these will all be translated as if they were foreign, even where they are in the economy that drives the group.

There are two possible approaches to this issue. First is simply to ensure that sufficient information is given in the accounts to explain the situation and allow users to draw their own conclusions. Second, it might be possible to argue that for a parent with literally no trade of its own, taking its only income from current or future dividend streams of the subsidiary, the primary economic environment affecting it is that of the subsidiary, even though it has no direct engagement with that environment as an independent entity itself. While this may seem a slightly tortuous argument, it is not prohibited by the standard, and preparers seeking to develop this idea may find precedents under currently accepted readings of IFRS.

12.4   Hyperinflation

Section 31 covers the special case of an entity whose functional currency is the currency of a hyperinflationary economy.

The standard accounting from Section 30 would not be appropriate because of the rapid loss of purchasing power of the currency in this type of economy, which means that two transactions at opposite ends of the reporting period might have the same value in a second currency but would be reported at vastly different amounts in the financial statements, making it difficult for users to understand the economic substance.

12.4.1   Definition

Section 31 does not provide a precise definition of a hyperinflationary economy. Instead, it states that an entity should consider all available information including the following typical indicators of hyperinflation (summarised from paragraph 31.2):

(a) the population prefers to keep its wealth in non-monetary assets or in a relatively stable foreign currency;

(b) the population views monetary amounts (e.g. by quoting prices) in a relatively stable foreign currency;

(c) sales and purchases on credit take places at prices designed to allow for an expected loss in purchasing power, even when the credit period is short;

(d) costs such as interest rates, wages and prices are linked to a price index;

(e) the cumulative inflation rate over three years is approaching, or exceeds, 100%.

12.4.2   Accounting procedures

The key to the accounting in this situation is that all amounts in the financial statements, including comparatives, are stated in terms of the measuring unit current at the end of the reporting period. To achieve this, amounts are restated using a general price index that reflects changes in general purchasing power.

The following guidance sets out how this is achieved:

•   monetary items (explained in paragraph 31.6 as items to be received or paid in money, but more fully defined in the glossary and discussed at **12.2.2** above) are not restated because they are already expressed in terms of the measuring unit that is current;

- assets and liabilities that are linked, by agreement, to changes in prices are adjusted in accordance with the agreement and included at this restated amount;

- non-monetary items that are already carried at amounts current at the end of the reporting period (e.g. at net realisable value or fair value) are not restated;

- for non-monetary items carried at cost less depreciation, the relevant amount is based on the change in general price index from the acquisition date to the end of the reporting period;

- when Section 31 is applied for the first time, all components of equity except retained earnings are restated by applying a general price index from the date they first arose. The entry to retained earnings is a balancing figure after all other balance sheet values are determined; and

- income statement and statement of comprehensive income items are all restated based on the change in general price index between the transaction date and the reporting date. If inflation has been reasonably smooth over the period, an average rate may be used.

These steps can be followed reasonably mechanically if the preparer possesses a spreadsheet with enough information on the dates of transactions and movements in the general price index.

On examination, it is clear that a loss or gain will arise relating to the net monetary position, that is the excess or deficit of monetary assets over monetary liabilities, since this changes reflects a real loss in purchasing power (hence the desire of the general population to keep its wealth away from monetary assets). This loss or gain is included in profit or loss.

Example 12.8

Dreamland has the currency DR, and its economy has been determined to be hyperinflationary.

Its RPI was at 100 at the beginning of the financial year, 128 in the middle, and 156 at the end.

When preparing the year end accounts, a transaction that cost DR100,000 at the beginning of the year will be reported at DR156,000, and one that cost DR100,000 in the middle of the year will be reported at 121,875 (100,000 × 156/128).

A fixed asset purchased in the previous year for DR50,000 when the price index was at 85 will be restated to DR91,765, being 50,000 × 156/85.

12.4.3 Economies ceasing to be hyperinflationary

When an economy moves out of being hyperinflationary, a starting point is needed for the ongoing accounting. This is based on the carrying amount at the end of the previous reporting period, in the presentation currency.

12.5 Other foreign currency issues

12.5.1 Hedging

When an entity has a monetary item that is receivable from or payable to a foreign operation, the treatment depends on expectations of that balance. If it is expected to be settled similarly to any other balance, it is dealt with accordingly (retranslated each period end with a gain or loss in the income statement). If, however, settlement 'is neither planned nor likely to occur' (paragraph 30.12) which is reasonably common with intercompany loans, the balance is included within the entity's net investment in the foreign operation.

This means that while exchange differences on the whole net investment arising in the reporting entity or the investee's individual accounts are recognised in profit, on consolidation they are adjusted into other comprehensive income and accumulated in equity. They are then not recycled on disposal.

FRS 102 (2018) clarifies that a gain on foreign exchange arising on a monetary item that forms part of a reporting entity's net investment in a foreign operation is only recognised in profit or loss in the separate financial statements of the reporting entity to the extent that the gain is realised. Any unrealised gain should be recorded in OCI.

Example 12.9

Parent P, which has a GBP functional currency, has an investment in French subsidiary F. The cost of the investment was €500,000 and P has made a further €200,000 long term loan to F.

In P's individual accounts, the €200,000 loan receivable is retranslated at the year end and a gain is recognised in profit (the investment balance, which is not a monetary item, is not retranslated).

Because the loan is in F's currency, F does not have a gain or loss on retranslation, but when F's accounts are translated into GBP (the presentational currency used in the consolidation) the carrying value of the payable and the receivable cancel out, leaving only the gain or loss in P's books.

This gain or loss is reclassified to other comprehensive income as a consolidation adjustment. (Note: there will be other foreign currency related items in OCI arising from the consolidation, as set out at **12.3.2**.)

12.6   Disclosures

Paragraph 30.25 requires disclosure of:

(a) the amount of exchange differences recognised in profit or loss during the period, except for those arising on financial instruments measured at fair value through profit or loss in accordance with Sections 11 *Basic Financial Instruments* and Section 12 *Other Financial Instruments Issues*; and

(b) the amount of exchange differences arising during the period and classified in equity at the end of the period.

The currency in which the financial statements are presented must be disclosed, as must the functional currency if it is different, with an explanation for the difference. (paragraph 30.26)

If the functional currency changes, the fact of the change and the reasons for it must be disclosed (paragraph 30.27).

For hyperinflationary economies, paragraph 31.15 requires disclosure of:

(a) the fact that financial statements and other prior period data have been restated for changes in the general purchasing power of the functional currency;

(b) the identity and level of the price index at the reporting date and changes during the current reporting period and the previous reporting period; and

(c) the amount of gain or loss on monetary items.

12.6.1   Disclosures for small entities applying Section 1A

Small entities applying Section 1A of the standard are exempt from the disclosure requirements of Section 30, and there are no explicit foreign currency disclosure requirements replacing these. As usual, directors will need to use their judgment in determining what, if any, disclosures are needed in this area in order to ensure the accounts give a true and fair view.

13 Borrowing costs

13.1 Scope of this section

This section covers Section 25 *Borrowing Costs*.

The equivalent standard in IFRS is IAS 23 *Borrowing Costs*.

Borrowing costs are defined in the Glossary as 'interest and other costs incurred by an entity in connection with the borrowing of funds'. These include (but are not explicitly limited to) (Paragraph 25.1):

(a) interest expense calculated using the effective interest method (Section 11 of FRS 102 and **7.6.5** of this guide);

(b) finance charges in respect of finance leases (Section 20 of FRS 102 and **8.3** of this guide); and

(c) exchange differences arising from foreign currency borrowings to the extent that they are regarded as an adjustment to interest costs.

The final one of these scoping points bears a little expansion. Typically, a foreign currency loan would be held at amortised cost with the calculations performed in the currency in which the loan is denominated (since the final capital amount has to be the final foreign currency amount payable). The interest charge for each period would then be translated at the average rate for inclusion in the year end accounts, and the closing balance at the closing rate. An exchange difference would usually arise and be included within the interest charge for the period, and this type of movement is scoped into Section 25.

Examples that would fall outside the scope are less common – the main target of the exclusion seems to be exchange differences on foreign currency borrowings that are for some reason recognised outside profit (where they arise as a result of a translation into a different presentation currency, or relate to a net investment hedge).

Application to micro-entities: Micro-entities must expense borrowing costs as incurred; there is no option to capitalise them.

13.2 Accounting requirements

There is an accounting policy choice for borrowing costs:

(1) capitalise those that are directly attributable to the acquisition, construction or production of a qualifying asset as part of the cost of that asset; or

(2) expense them as incurred.

The selected policy must be applied consistently to a class of qualifying assets, with a class of assets being defined in the Glossary as 'a grouping of assets of a similar nature and use in an entity's operations'.

13.2.1 Directly attributable borrowing costs

Paragraph 25.2A defines directly attributable borrowing costs as 'those borrowing costs that would have been avoided if the expenditure on the qualifying asset had not been made'.

It is easy to see how this applies where a specific loan has been taken out to finance the purchase of an asset, because the loan would not otherwise have been needed; this also has the effect of automatically bringing in all finance charges on finance leases of qualifying assets, since this type of liability always comes with an asset. The greater difficulty comes when an entity only has general borrowings, because it can be hard to discern whether interest costs would have been lower had the asset in question not been acquired, constructed or produced.

Entities are, however, permitted to assume that a proportion of finance costs on general borrowings can be attributed to a qualifying asset, presumably based on the idea that most entities do not choose to borrow beyond their needs, so their general borrowings would, over time, be lower if they were not undertaking the construction. To achieve this, a 'capitalisation rate' is applied to the average carrying amount of the asset in the period – this rate is 'the weighted average of rates applicable to the entity's general borrowings that are outstanding during the period'.

Example 13.1

Entity F begins constructing a new property at the start of 2019. It spends £10,000 per month in the first half of the year and £20,000 per month in the second half, so that at the end of the year £180,000 is on the balance sheet relating to construction costs.

F has a bank loan of £300,000 to finance its day to day operations: it bears interest at a fixed rate of 7%. It also has a further £200,000 of general borrowings at a variable rate of base plus 5 points: the base rate was 1% for the first three months of 2019, and 1.25% for the remaining nine months.

> The weighted average rate applicable to the general borrowings is calculated as
>
> [(7% × £300,000) + (6% × 3/12 × £200,000) + (6.25% × 9/12 × £200,000)]/ (£300,000 + £200,000) = 6.675%
>
> The average carrying value of the asset during the year is the sum of each month end value, divided by 12, i.e. (£10,000 + £20,000 + ... + £160,000 + £180,000)/12 = £82,500 (note this is higher than the value as at the middle of the year, since spending accelerated after this point).
>
> The amount of interest to capitalise is therefore 6.675% × £82,500 = £5,507.

Paragraph 25.2C also includes a cap on the borrowing costs capitalised in a period, restricting them to the actual borrowing costs incurred. While this seems to be common sense, it needs to be stated explicitly to ensure the requirements are not thoughtlessly applied.

> **Example 13.2**
>
> Assume the same fact pattern as above for Entity S, with the same general borrowings at the same rates, but with expenditure on the construction of the asset increased tenfold (that is, £100,000 per month in the first half of the year and £200,000 per month in the second half, adding to £1.8m).
>
> Applying the weighted average borrowing rate of 6.675% to the average carrying value of £825,000 would lead to capitalising £55,000 of borrowing costs, but this value is higher than the total actually incurred in the year, so the amount capitalised would be capped at £33,000.

This example shows an area where there may be a need for entities to work on policies of their own. If Entity S also undertook another project to construct a qualifying asset, then it would need to decide which of two paths to pursue:

(1) do not capitalise any costs on the second asset, since the total costs incurred have already been 'used up' on the first project; or

(2) calculate what the total amount would have been for each project, ignoring the cap, then allocate the total actual costs between the two pro rata.

There may also be other approaches available: what is crucial is to have a stated policy for such situations, and to be able to justify it.

13.2.2 Ending or suspending capitalisation

The clear intention of the Section 25 permission to capitalise borrowing costs is to recognise that one of the true costs of constructing an asset (as opposed to purchasing it in a condition ready to use) is having money tied up in the construction process, which could otherwise have been used elsewhere and gives rise to a real cash cost. The corollary is that when construction ends, so does capitalisation – it would never be acceptable to continued capitalising costs on an asset that had already been brought into use, or was fully available for use. It also follows that capitalisation should be suspended during extended periods when no construction is taking place: if this rule (in paragraph 25.2D(b)) was not in place, entities could store up interest costs on the balance sheet for protracted periods simply by beginning construction of an asset, even where it was growing increasingly unlikely that economic benefits would flow in the foreseeable future.

13.2.3   Amounts to be capitalised

Note that the 'capitalisation rate' applied is based on the effective interest rate calculation performed for the loan under Section 11, not on the cash interest cost. If a loan has a period of low interest followed by a period of high interest, this will not give a capitalisation rate that begins low then increases, but will reduce the overall effective interest rate applied each period.

In the example above, the capitalisation rate takes account of actual costs on the variable rate loan because this reflects the accounting under Section 11.

13.2.4   Qualifying assets

The definition of a qualifying asset in the Glossary is very specific:

'An asset that necessarily takes a substantial period of time to get ready for its intended use or sale. Depending on the circumstances any of the following may be qualifying assets:

(a)   Inventories;

(b)   Manufacturing plants;

(c)   Power generation facilities;

(d)   Intangible assets; and

(e)   Investment properties.

Financial assets, and inventories that are produced over a short period of time, are not qualifying assets.

Assets that are ready for their intended use or sale when acquired are not qualifying assets.'

It should be clear from this definition that belonging to one of the above groups does not automatically lead an item into being a qualifying asset. Inventories, in particular, do not usually take a substantial period of time to get ready for use, though there are some well-known counterexamples: whisky, for instance, needs to mature before it is complete and ready to be sold.

There is no definition of a substantial period of time, and judgment will be needed: there may be a vague intuition that assets taking over a year to complete meet the condition, but this can only be judged on the individual facts. As always, materiality should be considered: some entities may view a period of a few months as a substantial period of time, but if the resulting value of borrowing costs to be capitalised is of a very small value, this might indicate that the construction period is actually not substantial enough to have an effect on the accounts.

13.2.5   *Timing of capitalisation*

Again the provisions here, in paragraph 25.2D, are not unexpected. Capitalisation of borrowing costs for a qualifying asset begins when the entity first incurs both expenditure on the asset and borrowing costs, and 'undertakes activities necessary to prepare the asset for its intended use or sale'. This appears to have the effect of requiring capitalisation to start from the later of the point when activities begin, and the point when the loan is advanced.

Example 13.3

Entity T plans to construct a qualifying asset, and obtains a bank loan of £200,000 specifically for its construction. Although the loan finance is received in May, asset construction does not start until September.

The loan interest between May and September is expensed as normal; only from September is it capitalised within the cost of the asset. There is no provision in the standard to back date the capitalisation even though the loan was specifically for the asset.

Entity V has a long term project constructing a large property, expected to take three years in total. When construction begins, V has no borrowings, but one year in it takes out a £2m bank loan to provide general finance.

An appropriate portion of the finance costs on the new loan can be capitalised as part of the ongoing cost of construction, from the point when the loan starts to incur interest.

13.3   Disclosures

The disclosure requirements are not onerous. If an entity has an accounting policy of expensing borrowing costs, no additional disclosures are required (beyond the standard disclosures with respect to interest expense from paragraphs 5.5 and 11.48).

If the policy is to capitalise borrowing costs, this policy should be disclosed with a note of which classes of assets it applies to; paragraph 25.3A also requires disclosure of:

(a) the amount of borrowing costs capitalised in the period; and

(b) the capitalisation rate used.

13.3.1   Disclosure requirements for small entities

The only requirement for small entities applying Section 1A of the standard is one reproduced from company law in paragraph 1AC.19: 'when a small entity adopts a policy of capitalising borrowing costs, the inclusion of interest in determining the cost of the asset and the amount of the interest so included is disclosed in a note to the financial statements'.

13.4   Transition

Paragraph 35.10(o) allows that the date of transition to FRS 102 can be treated as the date capitalisation of borrowing costs commences. This takes away the burden of looking back to earlier dates to determine relevant borrowing costs from the very beginning of a project, although the exemption is not compulsory so entities that wish to perform a thorough process (and thus to capitalise the highest possible value of borrowing costs) will also be permitted to do so.

Example 13.4

Company W previously applied FRS 105, under which it was not permitted to capitalise borrowing costs. It began constructing a manufacturing complex in May 2015, and took out a £1m loan to finance this.

When it applies FRS 102 for the first time, 1 January 2017 is its transition date. It elects to begin capitalising borrowing costs from this point on, so the transition date balance sheet is not restated, but the 2017 statement of comprehensive income shows a lower interest charge than the previously reported 2017 profit and loss account, and the restated 31 December 2017 statement of financial position reports a correspondingly higher value for the asset in the course of construction.

If it had so wished, W could alternatively have revisited all of its calculations from the outset and restated the 1 January 2017 balance sheet accordingly: if, for instance, £50,000 of interest had been incurred on the loan between May 2015 and December 2016, then a transition adjustment could have been posted to assets under the course of construction, with the corresponding credit entry recognised as an adjustment to opening reserves.

---

14 Employee benefits and share-based payments

14.1 Scope of this section

This section brings together the two most significant areas of FRS 102 which deal with employee remuneration: Section 26 on share-based payments, and Section 28 on employee benefits. They are grouped together because of this commonality, and because some entities may, when selecting how best to reward and motivate their employees, take into account the financial reporting consequences of the schemes that they have in place.

Section 26 does not solely cover share-based payments to employees, though this is its most common application; its other applications are also discussed below.

14.1.1 Share-based payments

Like IFRS 2 *Share-based Payment*, FRS 102 requires a charge where an entity provides some form of benefit under a share-based payment transaction. This applies whether the benefits provided are in the form of equity, or in cash at an amount that is based upon equity.

The treatment of cash-settled share-based payment transactions has never been very contentious. Whilst there may be more than one way of allocating the total costs, ultimately cash resources will leave the business. Applying the most basic of accruals principles, it is clear that there must be a charge to profits, by the time that the payment needs to be made, that is equal to the amount of the liability. There are far more disagreements concerning the treatment of equity-settled share-based payment transactions. Despite attempts by the IASB, not everyone has been persuaded that it is appropriate that there should be a charge when an entity provides equity, whether directly or indirectly, and where in some cases the only transaction that affects net assets involves an inflow of resources, for example where an option is exercised.

FRS 102 does not alter the principles that apply in this area, but contains less guidance than the equivalent IFRS standard, IFRS 2. This is intended to simplify the application of the requirements, but in practice may lead to greater flexibility and recording the effects of an entity being a party to a share-based payment transaction.

> **Application to micro-entities:** Under Section 21 of FRS 102, micro-entities do not have to account for equity-settled share-based payments other than for the actual issue of the shares, once this takes place. The accounting for cash-settled share-based payments is consistent with that in FRS 102.

14.1.2   Employee benefits

Section 28 sets out the required accounting for long and short-term employee benefits, including holiday pay, termination pay and long-term incentives. It also covers the accounting for defined benefit and defined contribution pension schemes.

> **Application to micro-entities:** Accounting for short-term employee benefits, defined contribution plans, other long-term benefits and termination benefits is consistent in Section 23 of FRS 105 with FRS 102. The primary difference lies in the treatment of defined benefit schemes.
>
> Micro-entities are able to account for defined benefit schemes in the same way as defined contribution schemes, i.e. recognising the contributions paid in the year rather than the full defined benefit obligation or surplus and related requirements.
>
> However, if the entity has entered into an agreement to fund a deficit, such as a schedule of contributions, a liability is recognised for the present value of the total contributions payable under that agreement. The discount rate is determined by reference to the yield on high quality corporate bonds as at the reporting date.
>
> There is no specific guidance for multi-employer plans in FRS 105; they are treated in the same way as other plans.
>
> If a micro-entity participates in a defined benefit plan where the risks are shared between entities under common control, it recognises a liability and expense for its contributions payable for the period.

14.2   Share-based payments – scope and definitions

The Glossary to FRS 102 defines a share-based payment transaction as:

'A transaction in which the entity:

(a)   receives goods or services from the supplier of those goods or services (including employee services) in a share-based payment arrangement; or

(b)   incurs an obligation to settle the transaction with the supplier in a share-based payment arrangement when another group entity receives those goods or services.'

FRS 102 (2018) adds that 'In the absence of specifically identifiable goods or services, other circumstances may indicate that goods or services have been (or will be) received, in which case this section applies'.

The simplest example is where an entity receives goods or services, for example work undertaken by directors or employees, and all or part of the consideration is in the form of the issue of shares. However, this Section of the standard also applies where the consideration is:

- in the form of another type of equity instrument, such as a share option; or

- in the form of cash (or other assets), but where the value of that consideration is based on the price of the company's shares or the price of other equity instruments of the entity or of another entity which forms part of the same group.

It is the second of these situations which really justifies the description of 'share-based' payment, since the requirement covers any transactions which are based on the value of shares, even if that consideration will be paid in another form. Such arrangements are referred to as cash-settled share-based payment transactions. A simple example would be a bonus which is paid to staff in cash but where the amount paid is dependent on the increase in the company's share price (usually referred to as share appreciation rights). While it is cash that the company will actually pay, the amount of cash will depend on the change in the share price of the company and such an arrangement would, therefore, fall within the scope of this Section of FRS 102.

The Glossary to the standard defines both equity-settled and cash-settled share-based payment transactions. However, the definitions are simply derived from the definition of a share-based payment transaction in general. A transaction is deemed to be equity-settled if it falls within (a) or (b) in the general definition, and cash-settled if it falls within (c).

In most cases, it will be clear how the transaction should be classified, but the section also deals with cases where the consideration could be in the form of either equity instruments or cash. The wording in the original standard caused some concerns, so in 2015, the FRC issued an amendment to clarify the wording. The requirements are set out in paragraphs 26.15, 26.15A and 26.15B:

'Some share-based payment transactions give either the entity or the counterparty a choice of settling the transaction in cash (or other assets) or by the transfer of equity instruments.

When the entity has a choice of settlement of the transaction in cash (or other assets) or by the transfer of equity instruments, the entity shall account for the transaction as a wholly equity-settled share-based payment transaction... unless:

(a) The choice of settlement in equity instruments has no commercial substance (eg because the entity is legally prohibited from issuing shares); or

(b) The entity has a past practice or a stated policy of settling in cash, or generally settles in cash whenever the counterparty asks for cash settlement.

In circumstances (a) and (b) the entity shall account for the transaction as a wholly cash-settled transaction in accordance with paragraph 26.14.

Except as set out in paragraph 26.15C, when the counterparty has a choice of settlement of the transaction in cash (or other assets) or by the transfer of equity instruments, the entity shall account for the transaction as a wholly cash-settled share-based payment transaction in accordance with paragraph 26.14.

26.15C: If the choice of settlement in cash (or other assets) has no commercial substance because the cash settlement amount (or value of the other assets) bears no relationship to, and is likely to be lower in value than, the fair value of the equity instruments.

The entity shall account for the transaction as a wholly equity-settled transaction in accordance with paragraphs 26.7 to 26.13.'

So, where the counterparty has a choice of settlement options, the share-based payment will usually be accounted for as cash-settled (even if similar options have in the past always been settled in equity). This will also apply where the entity, not the counterparty, has the choice but usually settles in cash.

Considerable care needs to be applied in determining whether some arrangements should be treated as equity-settled or cash-settled. As noted above, where no equity instruments will be passed on to the recipient and instead they will receive cash or other assets then the assessment will be straightforward. This applies to arrangements such as the granting of share appreciation rights. Where instruments which appear to be equity will be passed on to the recipient it might appear that this will necessarily mean that the scheme is equity-settled, but this is not always the case. Consideration needs to be given to the arrangement as a whole and not just the initial transfer. For example, paragraph 26.2 includes the following when dealing with transactions that fall to be treated as cash-settled:

'... an entity might grant to its employees a right to receive a future cash payment by granting to them a right to shares (including shares to be issued upon the exercise of share options) that are redeemable, either mandatorily (e.g. upon cessation of employment) or at the employee's option.'

Whilst in the first instance the employees might be given shares or share options at some point in the future, the entity will have an obligation to transfer cash. This needs to be reflected in the initial accounting treatment. Where redemption of the shares (whether those shares have been granted to the employees or whether they have arisen as a result of the exercise of share options) is mandatory the situation is fairly clear. This situation is also fairly common. Many private companies which issue shares or share options to staff may wish shares to be held only by individuals in current employment. As a result, such a company might agree to buy back the shares when the employee resigns or retires, often with an agreed valuation basis. Whilst the cash flow may take place a considerable time after the grant of the options it nonetheless renders the scheme cash-settled.

Where the shares are not subject to mandatory redemption, but such redemption is at the employee's option this will also make the scheme cash-settled. There is no certainty that any payment will need to be made in the future, but the company has an obligation to make such payment if requested. It is worth noting that if redemption is solely at the option of the company then this will not necessarily mean that the scheme must be treated as cash-settled. In this case some consideration would need to be given to past practice and any statements of intent, to avoid the situation where a company treats a share-based payment scheme as being equity-settled whilst in reality a future cash payment is certain to be made.

It is extremely common for share-based payment transactions to involve employees of entities other than the entity whose shares are involved. The simplest example is where there is a share option scheme for all of the employees of a group but the rights are in all cases over the shares of the parent. As a result, and as is made clear in paragraph 26.1A, this section of FRS 102 applies to transactions where other group entities are involved:

> 'A share-based payment transaction may be settled by another group entity (or a shareholder of any group entity) on behalf of the entity receiving or acquiring the goods or services. Paragraph 26.1 also applies to an entity that:
>
> (a) receives goods or services when another entity in the same group (or shareholder of any group entity) has the obligation to settle the share-based payment transaction; or
>
> (b) has an obligation to settle a share-based payment transaction when another entity in the same group receives the goods or services,
>
> unless the transaction is clearly for a purpose other than payment for goods or services supplied to the entity receiving them.'

It is implicit in Section 19 of the standard that shares or other equity instruments which are issued directly as part of a business combination are outside the scope of share-based payment transactions and should be dealt with using the normal rules for a business combination. However, arrangements which are affected by a business combination, but where the issue does not form part of the consideration for the acquisition or merger, are within the scope of share-based payment transactions as is noted in paragraph 19.15C. This paragraph is extremely short and simply states that share-based payment transactions should be recognised and measured in accordance with the rules that would apply in the absence of a business combination. An example of such a situation might be where shares are issued to employees on a business combination, or where the terms of an existing arrangement are altered as a result of a business combination, such as where rights crystallise when a company is taken over. In this case, there is no specific guidance given within the standard.

Whilst FRS 102 does not make it explicit, it can also be safely assumed that the rules on share-based payment transactions do not apply to transactions with employees who are also holders of equity instruments, where the transaction is in that latter capacity. For example, a company might make a rights issue at below fair value. The requirements in relation to share-based payment transactions would not apply where an employee, who is also a shareholder, takes up the rights issue in his or her capacity as shareholder. This would be the case even if the employee's share interest had originally arisen as a result of a share-based payment transaction.

14.3   Share-based payments – accounting

14.3.1   Recognition

The basic principle of the standard is set out in paragraph 26.3:

'An entity shall recognise the goods or services received or acquired in a share-based payment transaction when it obtains the goods or as the services are received. The entity shall recognise a corresponding increase in equity if the goods or services were received in an equity-settled share-based payment transaction, or a liability if the goods or services were acquired in a cash-settled share-based payment transaction.'

For the avoidance of doubt, the standard then goes on to point out that if the goods and services received do not qualify for recognition as assets then they will need to be recognised as expenses.

Put simply, this usually means that where a share-based payment transaction involves parties other than employees the recognition of the asset or expense will take place at the same time for a share-based payment transaction as if it were a normal cash-based transaction, unconnected with shares. Similarly, the rules on whether an item is an asset or an expense are not affected by the fact that a share-based payment transaction was involved. As a general rule, goods will be treated as assets and services as expenses, but there are exceptions in both cases. The impact of the standard is more likely, in general, to be upon the amount that is recognised rather than the timing of the recognition.

Where a share-based payment transaction involves employees, the situation will often be more complex. In some cases, rights may be granted immediately, which effectively means that the rights are being provided as a bonus for past performance, but in many cases the rights are intended to create an incentive for individuals and as a result will have a vesting period. FRS 102 deals with both situations. In the absence of a vesting period, in accordance with paragraph 26.5, a charge will arise at the date on which the rights are granted.

> 'If the share-based payments vest immediately, the counterparty is not required to complete a specified period of service before becoming unconditionally entitled to those share-based payments. In the absence of evidence to the contrary, the entity shall presume that services rendered by the counterparty as consideration for the share-based payments have been received. In this case, on grant date the entity shall recognise the services received in full, with a corresponding increase in equity or liabilities.'

Whilst the grant date is often clear, the standard includes a lengthy definition in order to ensure that the date is certain.

> 'The date at which the entity and another party (including an employee) agree to a share-based payment arrangement, being when the entity and the counterparty have a shared understanding of the terms and conditions of the arrangement. At grant date, the entity confers on the counterparty the right to cash, other assets, or equity instruments of the entity, provided the specified vesting conditions, if any, are met. If that agreement is subject to an approval process (for example, by shareholders), grant date is the date when that approval is obtained.'

It is notable that this definition makes reference to a shared understanding, which may arise prior to the completion of any legal formalities. This is little different from the general use of constructive as well as legal obligations. At the same time where there is a condition which is more than a formality, with shareholder approval been the example provided within the standard, then the grant date is deferred until that condition is met.

Where there is a vesting period, the accounting treatment required differs. Any charge is not recognised in full at the date of grant, but under 26.6 is spread over the period from the grant date to the date of vesting.

> 'If the share-based payments do not vest until the counterparty completes a specified period of service, the entity shall presume that the services to be rendered by the counterparty as consideration for those share-based payments will be received in the future, during the vesting period. The entity shall account for those services, as they are rendered by the counterparty during the vesting period, with a corresponding increase in equity or liabilities.'

14.3.2   Measurement principle for equity-settled transactions

In a sense, an equity-settled share-based payment transaction is simply an alternative to the payment of cash. For example, a recently formed company may have little cash resources but be able to obtain the services it requires in order to expand through providing shares or rights based on shares to third parties. As a result, where it is possible, then the share-based payment transaction should be recorded at the fair value of the goods or services received. This seems entirely reasonable. If the cash cost of an asset would have been £1,000, but instead of paying cash, a company grants shares to the provider of the asset, and assuming that the transaction is on an arm's length basis, the shares should be worth £1,000.

FRS 102 therefore requires equity-settled share-based payment transactions involving the receipt of goods or services to be recorded at the fair value of the goods or services received, unless fair value cannot be estimated reliably.

Unfortunately, the situation is not always so simple. It may not be possible to determine the fair value of the goods or services that have been received. FRS 102 also presumes that is not possible to measure the value of the services that have been provided by employees or similar (such as non-executive directors). Therefore, when the fair value of the goods or services received cannot be valued reliably or in all cases where services have been provided by employees or similar, then the transaction is recorded at the fair value of the equity instruments that have been granted.

Given that values can change, FRS 102 also specifies the date that should be used for the purposes of measuring the value of the equity instruments that have been granted. Where the transaction involves a party other than an employee, the value should be measured at the date the entity obtains the goods or the other party provides the service. Where the transaction is with an employee, or similar, then the fair value of the equity instruments is measured as at the grant date.

14.3.3   Vesting and other conditions

As noted above, it is common, particularly in relation to arrangements with employees, that there are conditions associated with the grant of rights based on shares. FRS 102 divides such conditions into vesting conditions and others, in paragraph 26.9:

A grant of equity instruments might be conditional upon satisfying specified **vesting conditions** related to service or performance. An example of a **service condition** is when a grant of shares or share options is conditional on the employee remaining in the entity's employ for a specified period of time. Examples of **performance conditions** are when a grant of shares or share options is conditional on the entity achieving a specified growth in profit (a non-market vesting condition) or a specified increase in the entity's share price (a **market condition**). Vesting conditions and conditions that are not vesting conditions (such as a condition that an employee contributes to a savings plan) are accounted for as follows:

(a) Vesting conditions, other than market conditions, shall not be taken into account when estimating the fair value of the shares or share options at the measurement date. Instead, such vesting conditions shall be taken into account in estimating the number of equity instruments expected to vest. Subsequently, the entity shall revise that estimate, if new information indicates that the number of equity instruments expected to vest differs from previous estimates. On the vesting date, the entity shall revise the estimate to equal the number of equity instruments that ultimately vested.

(b) All **market vesting conditions** and conditions that are not vesting conditions shall be taken into account when estimating the fair value of the equity instruments granted at the measurement date, with no subsequent adjustment to the estimated fair value, irrespective of the outcome of the market condition or condition that is not a vesting condition, provided that all other vesting conditions are satisfied.

As the standard says, the most common vesting condition is likely to be continuous service. It is very common that share options are granted to staff which will vest only if they remain within the employment of the granting entity for a specified period, for example three or five years. This has no impact on the valuation of the rights have been granted, at an individual level, but is taken into account in determining the number of rights that fall to be accounted for.

Example 14.1

Continued employment

A company grants 100,000 share options to its employees. The value of each share option is established at £2. The options vest only if employees remain within the service of the company for a period of five years.

The theoretical maximum value of the options that have been granted is therefore £200,000. If spread over the vesting period this would give rise to a charge of £40,000 per annum.

This assumes that none of the employees will leave over a five-year period. Such an assumption is unlikely to be realistic. As a result the company, taking account of previous experience, estimates that 20% of employees will leave over the period.

The total expected charge in respect of the options will now be 80% of £200,000, or £160,000. This will give rise to an annual charge of £32,000.

Each year the company is required to reconsider the assumption that it has made in respect of employee retention. It should be adjusted if it becomes clear that more or fewer employees are likely to leave than was originally assumed.

After one year, and in the light of its recent experience, the company continues to consider that 20% is a reasonable estimate. As a result the company will charge £32,000.

The same applies in the second year. The company has seen no reason to amend its estimate, and they will therefore be a further charge of £32,000 giving a cumulative of £64,000.

In the third year, it is becoming apparent that more employees are leaving than had originally been assumed, and the company revises its estimate to 25%.

By this stage the cumulative charge should be equal to £200,000 × 75% × 3/5, or £90,000. Given that the previous cumulative was £64,000, the charge for the year will be £26,000.

In the fourth year, the assumption at 25% appears to continue to be valid, and there will therefore be a further charge of £30,000, giving a total of £120,000.

In the final year, no assumption is required. At this point the options have either vested or they have not and the company will adjust the cumulative charge to arrive at the actual. So, if the actual number of options vested is 76% or 76,000 the cumulative charge must be £152,000. To arrive at this, the charge in the final year must be £32,000.

When dealing with non-market conditions, exactly the same principle is applied. Again, the conditions are ignored in valuing the individual rights that been granted, so for example, an option is worth no more nor less if there is a non-market condition attached but that condition will be reflected in deciding how many of the options fall to be included. One of the implications of this is that if rights are granted which depend upon the fulfilment of a condition which is not market-based then if the condition is ultimately never fulfilled there will be no cumulative charge, although a charge may have been made and then reversed in previous accounting periods.

A market condition is defined in the Glossary as:

'A condition upon which the exercise price, vesting or exercisability of an equity instrument depends that is related to the market price of the entity's equity instruments, such as attaining a specified share price or a specified amount of **intrinsic value** of a **share option**, or achieving a specified target that is based on the market price of the entity's equity instruments relative to an index of market prices of equity instruments of other entities.'

Such conditions, even where they are vesting conditions, are taken into account in determining the value of the rights that have been granted, rather than in the estimate of the number of such rights that are likely to vest. The same applies to any conditions which are non-vesting. The implication of this is that the ultimate charge will depend upon the assessment of the condition which is made at the measurement date it is ultimately not affected by whether or not the condition is met. This in turn implies that there may be cases where there is a cumulative charge for share-based payments even though there are ultimately no vested rights.

More complex schemes may include a combination of vesting conditions, both market-based and otherwise, and other conditions. Care needs to be taken in ensuring that each condition is dealt with in the appropriate manner.

Apart from providing details of the conditions that need to be taken into account in valuing share-based payment transactions, FRS 102 also provides specific guidance in relation to the valuation of the equity instruments that may be issued.

Paragraph 26.10 provides guidance in relation to the valuation of shares:

'An entity shall measure the fair value of shares (and the related goods or services received) using the following three-tier measurement hierarchy:

(a) If an observable market price is available for the equity instruments granted, use that price.

(b) If an observable market price is not available, measure the fair value of equity instruments granted using entity-specific observable market data such as:

(i) a recent transaction in the entity's shares; or

(ii) a recent independent fair valuation of the entity or its principal assets.

(c) If an observable market price is not available and obtaining a reliable measurement of fair value under (b) is impracticable, indirectly measure the fair value of the shares using a valuation method that uses market data to the greatest extent practicable to estimate what the price of those equity instruments would be on the grant date in an arm's length transaction between knowledgeable, willing parties. The entity's directors shall use their judgement to apply a generally accepted valuation methodology for valuing equity instruments that is appropriate to the circumstances of the entity.'

This is broadly analogous to the fair value hierarchy that is included within Section 11 and covered in **7.3.4** of this guide.

Share valuation is outside the scope of this section, but all of these methods are trying to ensure that the shares are stated at a reasonable approximation of their fair value at the measurement date.

FRS 102 also provides guidance on the valuation of share options and equity settled share appreciation rights in paragraph 26.11:

'An entity shall measure the fair value of share options and equity-settled share appreciation rights (and the related goods or services received) using the following three-tier measurement hierarchy:

(a) If an observable market price is available for the equity instruments granted, use that price.

(b) If an observable market price is not available, measure the fair value of share options and share appreciation rights granted using entity-specific observable market data such as for a recent transaction in the share options.

(c) If an observable market price is not available and obtaining a reliable measurement of fair value under (b) is impracticable, indirectly measure the fair value of share options or share appreciation rights using an alternative valuation methodology such as an option pricing model. The inputs for an option pricing model (such as the weighted average share price, exercise price, expected volatility, option life, expected dividends and the risk-free interest rate) shall use market data to the greatest extent possible. Paragraph 26.10 provides guidance on determining the fair value of the shares used in determining the weighted average share price. The entity shall derive an estimate of expected volatility consistent with the valuation methodology used to determine the fair value of the shares.'

This clearly has many similarities, in principle, to the requirements that apply to shares. This is hardly surprising given that in both cases the intention is to determine the fair value of what has been granted. Again, option valuation is outside the scope of this section but it is noteworthy that FRS 102 does not strictly require the use of an option pricing model, in cases where market prices are not available, and certainly does not specify any particular models that can be applied. In practice, it is likely that the Black Scholes option pricing model will continue to be used in many cases. It is long established and extremely simple to apply, given that it is basically a formula. The most common problem that actually arises is not the application of the model but the determination of the inputs that need to be used. As FRS 102 implies, where an option pricing model needs to be used this often also means that the share price is not known, since the company may be unquoted. In addition, without a share price record, the volatility will need to be estimated, often done on the basis of the closest equivalent quoted entities. There is, inevitably, subjectivity involved in determining the value of an option in such circumstances.

As noted above, and in the example, where there is a vesting period FRS 102 requires that any charge that arises is spread over that period. It is worth noting that this applies to each grant. This may be relevant where an entity complying with FRS 102 has overseas connections and is party to an arrangement whereby rights vest over a number of periods. For example, an entity may issue 3,000 options of which 1,000 vest after one year, 1,000 after two years, and 1,000 after three years. Some GAAPs, primarily US GAAP, would allow the options to be valued as a package and spread evenly over three years. FRS 102 does not allow this. Each grant is separate, so if the options were issued on the first day of the accounting year, the first year charge would be 100% of the value of the first tranche, 50% of the value of the second and 33.3% of the third. The charge would then reduce significantly in each of the next two years. This is very front-loaded.

14.3.4   Modifications

Where there are no changes to the terms associated with a share-based payment scheme, the theoretical amount that will be charged is known in advance, and the variation in the actual charge will be affected only by non-market conditions and service conditions and the extent to which this varies the number of rights which vest.

However, entities may vary the terms and conditions on which equity instruments are granted. For example, some companies will reduce the exercise price of an option if the value of shares falls and the option ceases to have any incentive effect.

Paragraph 26.12 deals with modifications in the following way.

An entity might modify the terms and conditions on which equity instruments are granted in a manner that is beneficial to the employee, for example, by reducing the exercise price of an option or reducing the vesting period or by modifying or eliminating a performance condition. Alternatively, an entity might modify the terms and conditions in a manner that is not beneficial to the employee, for example, by increasing the vesting period or adding a performance condition. The entity shall take the modified vesting conditions into account in accounting for the share-based payment transaction, as follows:

(a) If the modification increases the fair value of the equity instruments granted (or increases the number of equity instruments granted) measured immediately before and after the modification, the entity shall include the incremental fair value granted in the measurement of the amount recognised for services received as consideration for the equity instruments granted. The incremental fair value granted is the difference between the fair value of the modified equity instrument and that of the original equity instrument, both estimated as at the date of the modification. If the modification occurs during the vesting period, the incremental fair value granted is included in the measurement of the amount recognised for services received over the period from the modification date until the date when the modified equity instruments vest, in addition to the amount based on the grant date fair value of the original equity instruments, which is recognised over the remainder of the original vesting period.

(b)   If the modification reduces the total fair value of the **share-based payment arrangement**, or apparently is not otherwise beneficial to the employee, the entity shall nevertheless continue to account for the services received as consideration for the equity instruments granted as if that modification had not occurred.

The requirements in this paragraph are expressed in the context of share-based payment transactions with employees. The requirements also apply to share-based payment transactions with parties other than employees if these transactions are measured by reference to their fair value of the equity instruments granted, but reference to the grant date refers to the date that the entity obtains the goods or the counterparty renders service.

This means that whenever there is a modification to the terms of a share-based payment scheme, two valuations are required. The first involves valuation of the existing rights at the current date, immediately prior to the modification. The second involves valuation of the amended rights immediately after the modification. If the new rights have a lower value than the current value of the previous rights, then this is ignored and the accounting entries proceed as if no change had ever taken place. In the more likely scenario where the value of the rights has increased this will give rise to an additional charge which will be calculated as the difference between the two values.

Example 14.2

A company issues 10,000 share options to staff. The terms of the options include an exercise price of £1, which is equal to the company's current share price, and have a vesting period of four years. All of the options are expected to vest. An option valuation model is applied and the value of a single option at the grant date is determined to be £2.

The total charge which would arise under the scheme would be £20,000, which would be spread over the four years at a rate of £5,000 per annum.

However, after two years the company's share price has fallen to 50p and the company decides to improve the terms of the share option scheme. The exercise price is amended to 50p.

The first thing that needs to be done is to value the options immediately prior to the amendment. The option valuation model is run again based on the current position. The exercise price will still be £1, but the life of the options will now be only two years, the share value will be 50p, and there may be changes to other variables such as volatility. Once this has been done the value of the options is determined to be 75p.

The second thing is to value the options immediately after the amendment. The inputs be used will be the same as those used in the previous model, that is, the model that has just been run to value the options prior to the change. The difference will be that the exercise price will now be set at 50p and not £1. Once the model has been run, the option value is determined to be £1.20.

The final stage is to value the increment. The increment in respect of each option is 45p, which when applied to the number of options granted gives £4,500.

The charge for the first two years of the scheme will have been £5,000 per annum as set out above. The new charge will be £7,250 per annum the remaining two years, being the £5,000 originally calculated plus the incremental value that has been granted, spread over the remaining period.

14.3.5 Cancellations and settlements

In some cases, all or part of an equity-settled share-based payment scheme may not run its full course. The scheme may be cancelled or a settlement may be reached.

In both cases, FRS 102 requires that the previous charges are not reversed. Instead all of the charges that would otherwise have been spread over future accounting periods are made immediately.

This requirement has been carried over from FRS 20, and IFRS 2 on which that standard was based. It was not in the original version of either standard but there had been cases where schemes were cancelled or settled deliberately in order to allow the reversal of charges that had previously been made, particularly where the scheme had not worked as originally intended, for example where the options were not going to be exercised as the share price had fallen. To avoid this, the IASB amended the standard so that far from reversing a charge such a change created an acceleration of that charge.

It is important to distinguish a cancellation or settlement from a failure to meet a vesting condition. Where a vesting condition, such as a service condition, has not been met then this does lead to the reversal of charges that had previously been made, unless the condition that has not been met is a market condition.

FRS 102 says very little about the accounting treatment of settlements, other than that they give rise to an acceleration of charge. The accounting treatments that are specified in IFRS 2 may be helpful in applying FRS 102 in this case:

- any payment made on cancellation or settlement is treated as a repurchase of an equity instrument, up to the fair value of the equity instruments at the repurchase date. Any amounts over and above this must be treated as an expense;

- if new equity instruments are granted at the same time, and the company identified them as replacement instruments, then the issue of those new instruments is treated as a modification of the conditions associated with the existing instruments. The incremental fair value is then calculated as the difference at the date of replacement between the fair value of the new instruments and the fair value of the old, less any amounts that have been treated as a deduction from equity; and

- where new equity instruments are granted at the same time, but are not identified as replacement instruments then the two transactions are treated separately.

However, this is not mandatory.

14.3.6   *Cash-settled share-based payments*

Cash-settled share-based payments are more straightforward than equity-settled ones. The basic requirements are set out very clearly in paragraph 26.14:

'For cash-settled share-based payment transactions, an entity shall measure the goods or services acquired and the liability incurred at the fair value of the liability. Until the liability is settled, the entity shall remeasure the fair value of the liability at each reporting date and at the date of settlement, with any changes in fair value recognised in profit or loss for the period.'

In effect, with a cash-settled scheme there will ultimately be a payment made by the entity. The transaction is initially recorded at the best estimate of the amount that will be payable, subject to any conditions, and this amount is then adjusted to take account of all changes in that estimate. The ultimate charge is the amount paid.

Where the rights are granted retrospectively, such as where a bonus is based on the share price over a year and determined at the end of that year, and there is no future service requirement, then the services are presumed to have been received and a liability is therefore recognised immediately.

Where the terms of the grant contain conditions related to the future, such as a continuing period of service, then the services received and the liability are recognised over the service period. So for example where a company provides employees with a bonus payable in two years' time, so long as they remain in the company's employ, and based on the company's share price at that time, then the amount recorded will reflect the expected staff retention as well as the estimated future share price. The total expected charge will be spread over the two years.

As noted above, the main problem with cash-settled share-based payment schemes is not the accounting treatment that needs to be applied to them, but their identification. Where a scheme will ultimately give rise to an outflow of cash it is cash-settled, even if that outflow is long delayed, such as where shares are granted but the company is required to repurchase those shares when the individual leaves the company's employment.

14.3.7 Group plans

There is nothing to stop all of the members of the group where there is a share-based payment plan which is common to them from allocating the total charge in a manner that is consistent with all of the requirements that have been set out above.

However, FRS 102 also allows a simplified treatment to be adopted by each of the members of the group. This will have no impact on any amount shown in the group accounts, but will affect the individual components. The simplification is set out in paragraph 26.16:

> 'If a share-based payment award is granted by an entity to the employees of one or more members in the group, the members are permitted, as an alternative to the treatment set out in paragraphs 26.3–26.15, to recognise and measure the share-based payment expense on the basis of a reasonable allocation of the expense for the group.'

This is intended to be a reasonably permissive option. It allows, for example, the total cost of a group scheme to be allocated across components without needing to consider whether or not different vesting assumptions might be appropriate for each entity.

FRS 102 (2018) in paragraph 26.2A states:

> 'The entity settling a share-based payment transaction when another entity in the group receives the goods or services shall recognise the transaction as an equity-settled share-based payment transaction only if it is settled in its own equity instruments. Otherwise, the transaction shall be recognised as a cash-settled share-based payment transaction.'

In other words, where the parent issues the shares but a subsidiary receives the service, the parent should treat the transaction as an equity-settled share-based payment. An example is where share options are granted to employees across a group, but the options all relate to shares in the parent.

However, this paragraph does not clarify the treatment by the entity receiving the service. Following current practice, there are two possibilities. Firstly, and most commonly, the parent may grant share rights to the subsidiary's employees directly. In this situation, the subsidiary does not have an obligation to provide shares to its employees – the obligation sits with the parent company. As such the share-based payment should be treated as equity-settled in the accounts of the subsidiary as well as the parent. The subsidiary should record a charge, and the equity element should be treated as a capital contribution from the parent. The parent should record an increase in investment in subsidiary and an increase in equity. In the group accounts, the charge and equity will remain after consolidation adjustments.

In the case where the subsidiary grants the rights to its parent's shares to its own employees, the obligation to obtain and deliver the shares sits with the subsidiary. In other words, the subsidiary has incurred a liability to pay cash or other assets to acquire shares from the parent. In this situation, the transaction is treated as cash settled in the subsidiary, creating a liability to the parent, whilst the parent records an increase in its own equity and an amount receivable from its subsidiary. Note that in practice there are legal restrictions on a subsidiary purchasing shares from its parent and these types of arrangement typically involve the use of an intermediary such as an employee benefit trust (EBT) or employee share ownership (ESOP) trust.

The two different approaches can be illustrated by the following example.

Example 14.3

(a) Parent issues options directly to employees

Parent X grants options over its own shares directly to 100 employees of Subsidiary Y. Each employee receives 30 share options. The only condition is that the employees must remain in employment for three years. Subsidiary Y does not need to pay Parent X for the shares. The fair value of each option on the grant date is £10. All employees remain in employment over the three-year period.

Subsidiary Y accounts for this arrangement as an equity-settled share-based payment, recognising a charge of £10,000 (((100 × 30) × £10)/3) per annum in profit or loss and a corresponding credit to retained earnings (essentially representing the capital contribution received from the parent company).

(b) Subsidiary grants rights to parent's shares

Assume the facts are the same as in (a) above, except that in this case, Subsidiary Y grants the rights to Parent X's shares directly to the employees. This means that the arrangement is treated as cash-settled in Subsidiary Y's financial statements.

Subsidiary Y therefore recognises a liability for the fair value of the options as service is rendered. If the fair value of each option is £10 at the end of year 1, £12 at the end of year 2 and £15 at the end of year 3, the liability will be recorded at the following amounts each year:

Year 1: 100 employees × 30 share options × £10 × 1/3 = £10,000

Dr P&L £10,000

Cr Liability £10,000

Year 2: 100 employees × 30 share options × £12 × 2/3 - £10,000 = £14,000

Dr P&L £4,000

Cr Liability £4,000

Year 3: 100 employees × 30 share options × £15 × 3/3 - £10,000 – £14,000 = £21,000

Dr P&L £7,000

Cr Liability £7,000

If, at the end of the three years, the parent gifts the shares to the subsidiary for distribution to its employees, the liability will be removed and a credit recognised in equity to reflect the capital contribution from the parent. Likewise, if the parent sells the shares to the subsidiary at an under-value, the difference between the sale price and the fair value is recognised as a capital contribution in the subsidiary's financial statements.

14.3.8   Government-mandated plans

FRS 102 notes that some jurisdictions have regulations under which equity investors, which may include employees for this purpose, can acquire equity without providing specific goods or services, or where the value of goods and services they are required to provide is clearly less than the value of the instruments they are granted. The standard includes such transactions within the scope of equity-settled share-based payment transactions. The transaction is valued at the difference between the fair value of the share-based payment and the fair value of the identifiable goods or services received or receivable, if any, measured as at the grant date.

This is unlikely to apply within the UK, but of course it could still affect a UK entity with an overseas interest.

14.4   Share-based payments – disclosure

FRS 102 contains a number of disclosure requirements relating to share-based payment arrangements. In all cases, an entity must disclose the following in respect of all arrangements that were in place during the period:

- a description of each type of arrangement that was in place during the period, including the general terms and conditions of each arrangement, such as vesting requirements, the maximum term of options granted, and the method of settlement (e.g. whether cash or equity). This information may be aggregated where an entity has a number of such arrangements;

- the number and weighted average exercise prices of share options for each of the following groups of options:

    - outstanding at the beginning of the period;

    - granted during the period;

    - forfeited during the period;

    - exercised during the period;

    - expired during the period;

    - outstanding at the end of the period; and

    - exercisable at the end of the period.

- the total expense that has been recognised in profit or loss for the period in respect of share-based payment transactions; and

- the total carrying amount at the end of the period for liabilities arising from share-based payment transactions.

Where an entity has modified any of its share-based payment arrangements during the period, it has to provide an explanation of the modification.

Where an entity has equity-settled share-based payment arrangements, it must disclose information about how it measured the fair value of the goods or services received or the value of the equity instruments which were granted, as appropriate. Where valuation methodology has been used the entity shall disclose the method and the reasons why that methodology was adopted.

Where an entity has cash-settled share-based payment arrangements, it needs to provide information about how the liability has been measured.

Where the entity is a member of a group share-based payment plan, and has taken advantage of the option to measure its share-based payment expense of the basis of a reasonable allocation of the group expense than that fact needs to be disclosed together with the basis on which the expense has been allocated.

14.4.1 Share-based payment disclosures for small entities

There are no explicit requirements for disclosures relating to share-based payments, for entities applying Section 1A of the standard. However, caution is advised where small entities make use of the transitional provision permitting them to avoid having to account for equity-settled share-based payment accounting for arrangements granted before the start of the first FRS 102 reporting period (assuming they did not previously apply FRS 20 or IFRS 2 – see **14.5**). Where this is the case, the general disclosure requirement in paragraph 1AC.31 regarding off-balance sheet arrangements means that disclosure may need to be given about any material share-based payment transactions that are not accounted for.

14.5 Share-based payments – transition

There is one transition exemption relevant to share-based payments, in paragraph 35.10(b). This allows a first time adopter not to apply Section 26 to equity instruments (including the equity component of share-based payment transactions previously treated as compound instruments) granted before the transition date (in other words, to open equity-settled share based payment arrangements), or to liabilities from share based payment transactions that were already settled before the transition date.

Unusually, there is an exception to this exception, which is that an entity that previously applied FRS 20 or IFRS 2 to its equity-settled transactions must keep applying that accounting – in other words, it is not permitted to undo the previous accounting for arrangements still open at the transition date.

A small entity applying FRS 102 for the first time for a period beginning before 1 January 2017 can also take this exemption for equity instruments granted before the start of its first period reported in accordance with FRS 102, as long as it was not previously applying FRS 20 or IFRS 2. Effectively, this gives FRSSE preparers the chance to keep using the FRSSE for the last time in 2015 then move in 2016 without restating their 2015 comparatives in relation to this area (unlike a non-small entity which can only apply the exemption to instruments granted before the transition date, i.e. usually one year earlier).

14.6   Employee benefits – scope and definitions

FRS 102 defines employee benefits in paragraph 28.1 as:

'... all forms of consideration given by an entity in exchange for service rendered by employees, including directors and management.'

Whilst this definition includes amounts which are payable to directors or other management, disclosure in respect of such transactions is not dealt with in this section but when dealing with related party transactions.

Section 28 of FRS 102 applies to all employee benefits other than those that arise as a result of share-based payment transactions, which are dealt with separately.

The Section divides all other employee benefits into four categories:

- short-term employee benefits – those benefits (other than termination benefits) which are expected to be settled wholly within 12 months of the end of the reporting period in which the services have been provided by the employees;

- post-employment benefits – those benefits (other than termination and short-term benefits) which are payable after the completion of employment. This will primarily relate to pensions, but may cover other benefits such as post-retirement healthcare;

- other long-term employee benefits – all benefits other than short-term, post-employment or termination. This would include longer term incentive schemes; and

- termination benefits – those benefits provided in exchange for the termination of an employee's employment, whether this arises from a decision to terminate an employee's employment before the normal retirement date or an employee's decision to accept voluntary redundancy in exchange for those benefits.

The intention of this list is that it is comprehensive, particularly as a result of the definition of other long-term employee benefits.

14.7   Employee benefits – accounting

14.7.1   General recognition principle

Apart from dealing with specific accounting treatments, FRS 102 also includes a general recognition principle which can be applied to all employee benefits. This has two main functions. First, it underpins the accounting treatments that are required in the remainder of the Section, perhaps in some cases clarifying the principles and making application easier. Second, it means that the standard can be applied to any benefits to which no specific reference has been made by directly applying the general principle for recognition.

The overall principle is that entities should recognise the cost of all employee benefits to which their employees have become entitled as a result of the services that they have rendered to the entity during the accounting period.

This is then dealt with in two parts.

A liability should be recorded after the deduction of any amounts that have been paid either directly to the employees or as a contribution to an employee benefit fund. In any case where the amount that has been paid exceeds the obligation that has arisen from the services provided by the employees prior to the reporting date then the excess should be recorded as an asset, so long as that prepayment will lead to a reduction in future payments or is available as a cash refund.

Although the standard refers to amounts being paid to the employee directly this should also be taken to cover amounts which are paid to third parties but on behalf of the employees, for example, amounts which are paid over to HMRC in respect of income taxes and employees' National Insurance contributions. (This is made clear in the list of examples of short-term employee benefits where social security contributions are included. This also means that employers' National Insurance contributions will form part of employee benefits for the purposes of standard, notwithstanding that strictly they are not paid on behalf of the employees but are an additional cost to the employer.)

The second part requires that the cost be treated as an expense, unless it has to be recognised in the cost of another asset in accordance with another Section of FRS 102. The specific examples provided in the standard that such costs may, in certain circumstances, be treated as part of the cost of inventories or property, plant and equipment, but there are others, for example, where staff have been involved in the creation of intangible assets such as development costs.

The standard points out that where contributions have been made to an employee benefit fund that falls within the definition of an intermediate payment arrangement, then those contributions should be accounted for in accordance with the requirements set out in Section 9 of the standard. If the employer is a sponsoring entity in respect of that arrangement this means that the assets and liabilities of the intermediary will be accounted for as an extension of its own business. In such a case the contribution that has been made by the entity will also give rise to an asset that falls to be recorded. As a result, the entity will also have to continue to record a liability in respect of the amount to be received by the employee. Intermediate payment arrangements are covered in greater depth in **4.2.8** of this guide.

14.7.2   Short-term employee benefits

In addition to the definition of short-term employee benefits included with the list of categories of such benefit, FRS 102 also provides a list of examples of typical short-term employee benefits, in all cases with the caveat that the amounts are expected to be settled within 12 months of the end of the year in which the services were provided by the employees:

- wages, salaries and social security contributions;

- paid annual leave and paid sick leave;

- profit-sharing and bonuses;

- non-monetary benefits, such as medical care, housing, cars, free or subsidised goods or services, which are provided for current employees.

The standard does not just rely on the general principle in relation to the measurement of short-term benefits in general. Instead, it makes this a little more specific.

Paragraph 28.5 states:

'When an employee has rendered service to an entity during the reporting period, the entity shall measure the amounts recognised ... at the undiscounted amount of short-term employee benefits expected to be paid in exchange for that service.'

This is an example of the application of the general principle, but adds the clarification that the amounts involved should not be discounted. In many cases the amounts that will be payable will be extremely clear. For example, the payment of basic salaries is unlikely to give rise to any accounting issues. The simplicity of the accounting treatment required means that FRS 102 makes no further comment on basic wages, salaries and social security contributions as the general principle is clearly considered to be sufficient.

14.7.3   Short-term compensated absences

Slightly more complex considerations may arise in relation to other matters that still fall within the definition of short-term employee benefits.

One of the areas that is dealt with in the standard is that of short-term compensated absences. The most common examples will be paid annual leave and sick leave.

The simplest situation is where such compensated absences are non-accumulating. What this means is that the arrangement does not give rise to an entitlement which can be carried forward into a future accounting period. For example, if a company provides five weeks of annual leave for its employees and that leave must be taken in the company's accounting year, and cannot be carried forward into subsequent years, then the accounting treatment will be extremely straightforward. The cost of the annual leave will be charged in full in the year. The standard notes that this will be at the undiscounted amount of the salaries and wages that are paid or payable for the period of absence.

Of course, in practice this actually means doing little else than ignoring the fact there was an absence and simply treating the salary in the same way as for periods when the employee was actually working. The situation is not much more complex if employees are able to increase the total payments made to them by reducing the annual leave that they take (that is, 'cashing in' unused holiday for additional pay), as long as this all takes place in a single accounting period. The employee benefit for the year would simply be increased by the amount of the additional payment.

The situation can be a little more complex where compensated absences may accumulate, for example where staff are allowed to carry forward unused annual leave entitlements into future accounting periods, or where the accounting year does not coincide with the holiday year.

In this case, FRS 102 requires that the employer recognise the expected cost of such accumulating compensated absences at the time that the employees render the services that create or increase the future entitlement. The amount should be measured at the additional amount that the entity expects to pay as a result of the entitlement that has been built up but has not been used at the end of the accounting year. Given that this Section of the standard is dealing solely with short-term employee benefits, it specifically states that the amount accumulated must be presented as falling due within one year of the reporting date.

For example, an employee has a salary of £52,000 per annum. The employee is entitled to four weeks of annual leave, but actually takes only three. The leave entitlement is accumulating, so can be carried forward into the next accounting year. No future salary increase is known.

The employer would need to reflect the cost of providing the future annual leave in the current accounting period. As a result, the charge in respect of the employee for the year would be £53,000, being the annual salary plus the amount expected to be payable in respect of the leave entitlement that has been created. In the following year, and on the assumption that the additional week is taken and not carried forward, the charge for the employee services would be £51,000. It should be noted that a more accurate result would be obtained by using the rate per working day, given that employees do not work whilst on annual leave. The calculation, however, becomes a little circular for those on fixed salaries since the daily rate itself depends on the number of days worked and the leave carried forward.

14.7.4   *Profit-sharing and bonuses*

The guidance in FRS 102 dealing with profit-sharing and bonus arrangements as part of short-term employee benefits is very short. Unlike such arrangements which may form part of long-term benefits there may be few accounting issues that arise, particularly in relation to measurement.

The guidance does not really deal with measurement at all, but instead with the issue of recognition.

Under FRS 102, entities must recognise the expected cost of any profit-sharing bonus payments only when:

- the entity has a present legal or constructive obligation to make the payments at a result of past events, which the standard notes means that the entity has no realistic alternative but to do so; and

- a reliable estimate of the obligation can be made.

It is very noticeable that these requirements do little more than state the general requirements that apply to all types of provision, not just those that arise in relation to profit sharing and bonuses.

There is some background to this. It has long been common for some companies to pay bonuses to staff in respect of a period, although the payment is actually determined and made in the following accounting period, often once the profits have been determined. In principle, if bonuses are paid to staff in respect of a period, they should be shown as part of the cost of that period, even if they are not actually paid until the next. But care also needs to be taken to ensure that such bonuses are allocated to accounting periods in an appropriate way, and that no provision is made for such bonuses where there is no obligation to pay them at the balance sheet date. Bonuses may be accrued only where there is a legal or constructive obligation for their payment. Legal obligation normally means that it is a term of the employee's contract of employment, and perhaps there is a specific formula which is used in order to calculate the bonus or profit share.

This does not generally give rise to many accounting problems as a contractual entitlement is normally clear. The more complicated question is where there is no contractual entitlement and the issue of whether there is a constructive obligation arises. A constructive obligation may arise through, say, a specific statement. So, for example, a company might make a statement that it expects to pay bonuses, in respect of a year, before the end of that year. Even though the actual amounts to be paid will probably be determined after the end of the year; in such a case an accrual may still be made. Similarly, where a company has a previous practice of paying bonuses, then this might give rise to a constructive obligation, that is, staff are expecting to receive them, even if there is no contractual entitlement and the company has made no specific statement that bonuses will be paid for the year.

The most complex problems often arise where bonuses were paid, say, for the first time in the previous year. Is there an expectation that bonuses will be paid in the current year? This will always depend on the specific circumstances and some care will need to be taken in determining whether or not the bonuses or profit shares fall to be recorded in accordance with FRS 102.

One thing that is not unclear is that in quantifying a profit-sharing or bonus payment arrangement, account can be taken of amounts which have been determined after the end of the year, so long as there was a legal or constructive obligation at the end of that year. This is because such a determination is provided as an example of an adjusting event in Section 32 of the standard (discussed in **15.2**).

14.7.5   Post-employment benefit plans

The first section of FRS 102 dealing with post-employment benefits distinguishes between defined contribution plans and defined benefit plans, as well as introducing some of the other terminology that is relevant and covering some of the types of plan that may be available.

Post-employment benefits are defined in the list of employee benefits within FRS 102, which are dealt with above. The standard goes on to define a post-employment benefit plan as any arrangement which an entity uses to provide post-employment benefits. The most common, of course, is a pension plan, although FRS 102 also notes that post-employment benefits are not restricted to retirement benefits such as pensions, but can also cover other benefits such as life insurance or medical care which is provided after an employee has retired.

The scope of post-employment benefit plans is deliberately wide. The standard makes clear that the requirements must be applied to all such arrangements even where they do not involve the establishment of a separate entity, such as a separate pension scheme, to receive the contributions and to pay the benefits. Similarly, the requirements must be applied both to arrangements which are imposed by law and to those which arise as a result of action by the entity. Finally, the standard makes clear that actions by the entity can also give rise to such arrangements even where there is no formal documented plan. Taken together, this means that entities may need to deal with the implications of the requirements in relation to post-employment benefit plans that they have deliberately set up, that they have in fact set up as a result of the obligations they have taken on in relation to employees, and those that are imposed upon them by law.

One of the implications of this is that an employer who has created obligations to employees which will be met after retirement must account for a post-employment benefit plan even where no separate plan has been created. For example, a post-employment benefit plan liability would include any obligations to pay pensions even where no pension scheme has been set up, often referred to as unfunded schemes.

FRS 102 divides post-employment benefit plans between defined contribution plans and defined benefit plans. The distinction needs to be drawn based on the principal terms and conditions of the plan.

They are defined in paragraph 28.10 in the following terms:

(a) Defined contribution plans are post-employment benefit plans under which an entity pays fixed contributions into a separate entity (a fund) and has no legal or constructive obligation to pay further contributions or to make direct benefit payments to employees if the fund does not hold sufficient assets to pay all employee benefits relating to employee service in the current and prior periods. Thus, the amount of the post-employment benefits received by the employee is determined by the amount of contributions paid by an entity (and perhaps also the employee) to a post-employment benefit plan or to an insurer, together with investment returns arising from the contributions.

(b) Defined benefit plans are post-employment benefit plans other than defined contribution plans. Under defined benefit plans, the entity's obligation is to provide the agreed benefits to current and former employees, and actuarial risk (that benefits will cost more or less than expected) and investment risk (that returns on assets set aside to fund the benefits will differ from expectations) are borne, in substance, by the entity. If actuarial or investment experience is worse than expected, the entity's obligation may be increased, and vice versa if actuarial or investment experience is better than expected.

The intention behind the distinction is very clear, and in practice most plans will unambiguously fall into one category or the other. Under a defined contribution plan, some of which are often referred to as money purchase plans, the cost to the employer to date is known with certainty and the performance risk has been passed onto the employee. As the name rather implies, the amount that needs to be contributed is known whilst the amount that will be paid out is not. Under a defined benefit plan it is the benefits that are known (although in practice it is usually only the formula that is known with certainty and the benefits themselves arise as a result of actuarial estimates) and what is not known is the amount that will be needed in order to be able to provide those benefits.

However, there are borderline cases. Problems have sometimes arisen where documents produced within a plan have appeared to give rise to obligations which may not have been intended by the entity. In some cases, legal advice has been required in order to establish the nature of the plan, or even a decision of the court.

Such issues might arise, for example, where there is or appears to be a guarantee of the returns that will be obtained on the contributions.

14.7.6   Defined contribution plans

Defined contribution plans have never caused many accounting problems. By definition, the contributions that are payable are known and the accounting charge simply needs to reflect this.

The accounting treatment for defined contribution plans, in most cases, is set out in paragraph 28.13. This is little more than a restatement of the general principle for employee benefits with specific reference to the type of benefit involved:

> 'An entity shall recognise the contribution payable for a period:
>
> (a) as a liability, after deducting any amount already paid. If contribution payments exceed the contribution due for service before the reporting date, an entity shall recognise that excess as an asset to the extent that the prepayment will lead to a reduction in future payments or a cash refund; and
>
> (b) as an expense, unless another Section of this FRS requires the cost to be recognised as part of the cost of an asset such as inventories or property, plant and equipment.'

The same treatment is applied where a defined benefit plan is treated as a defined contribution plan by one or more of the participants, as dealt with below.

The normal accounting treatment assumes that all contributions are to be settled within 12 months of the end of the accounting period in which the employees provide the services.

There is one slight complication dealt with in the standard.

Where this is not the case the liability should be measured at the present value of the contributions payable calculated using a discount rate based on the market yield at the reporting date on high-quality corporate bonds (with limited exceptions). The unwinding of the discount is recognised as a finance cost in profit or loss in the period in which it arises and not as an employee benefit.

14.7.7   *Defined benefit plans – valuation*

Defined benefit plans give rise to far more accounting issues than defined contribution plans.

The determination of both the position of the plan at the end of the accounting year and of the movements in that plan over the year involve the use of actuarial estimates.

FRS 102 stresses that the recognition principle to be applied to defined benefit plan is just a specific example of the general recognition principle in Section 28.

Specifically, under paragraph 28.14, an entity must recognise:

(a) a liability for its obligations under defined benefit plans net of plan assets – its 'net defined benefit liability' ...; and

(b) the net change in that liability during the period as the cost of its defined benefit plans during the period ...

The problem with defined benefit plans is not that is difficult to determine the principles that should be applied to their recognition, but that it can be difficult to determine the amounts involved.

The net defined benefit liability has to be measured at the net total of:

- the present value of its obligations under defined benefit plans, referred to as its defined benefit obligation, at the reporting date. This then needs to be measured using the guidance included within the standard; minus

- the fair value of the reporting date of plan assets (if there are any) out of which the obligations are to be settled.

For entities already recognising assets or liabilities for defined benefit plans in accordance with FRS 102, no additional liabilities need be recognised in respect of a 'schedule of contributions', even if such an agreement would otherwise be considered onerous.

The standard also provides guidance on the bases on which fair value of the assets held within the plan should be determined. This is not specific, and instead reference is made to the requirements in Section 11 that deal with fair values in general. Those rules are dealt with in **7.3.4** of this publication.

However, there is one exception to this. Where the asset is an insurance policy which exactly matches the amount and timing of some or all of the benefits that are payable under the plan then the fair value of the asset is deemed to be exactly equal to the present value of the related obligation.

The inclusion of this requirement avoids having rather spurious assets and liabilities in respect of obligations which will in fact be met by insurance.

FRS 102 is very clear on the nature of the obligations that are covered within the measurement of a defined benefit plan. As paragraph 28.16 states:

'The present value of an entity's obligations under defined benefit plans at the reporting date shall reflect the estimated amount of benefit that employees have earned in return for their service in the current and prior periods, including benefits that are not yet vested (…) and including the effects of benefit formulas that give employees greater benefits for later years of service. This requires the entity to determine how much benefit is attributable to the current and prior periods on the basis of the plan's benefit formula and to make estimates (actuarial assumptions) about demographic variables (such as employee turnover and mortality) and financial variables (such as future increases in salaries and medical costs) that influence the cost of the benefit. The actuarial assumptions shall be unbiased (neither imprudent nor excessively conservative), mutually compatible, and selected to lead to the best estimate of the future cash flows that will arise under the plan.'

Whilst this description is included within an accounting standard, some of its relevance will be greatest to actuaries in their determination of the liability. One of the changes introduced by the standard is presaged in this paragraph, since it makes clear that the obligation reflects estimates of the benefits earned to date even where those benefits have not yet vested. Whilst this applies generally it also applies most specifically to past service costs which, under FRS 102 but not FRS 17, are accounted for as an immediate obligation and not spread over any vesting period.

FRS 102 justifies its treatment of vesting in the following terms in paragraph 28.26:

'Employee service gives rise to an obligation under a defined benefit plan even if the benefits are conditional on future employment (in other words, they are not yet vested). Employee service before the vesting date gives rise to a constructive obligation because, at each successive reporting date, the amount of future service that an employee will have to render before becoming entitled to the benefit is reduced. In measuring its defined benefit obligation, an entity considers the probability that some employees may not satisfy vesting requirements. Similarly, although some post-employment benefits (such as post-employment medical benefits) become payable only if a specified event occurs when an employee is no longer employed (such as an illness), an obligation is created when the employee renders service that will provide entitlement to the benefit if the specified event occurs. The probability that the specified event will occur affects the measurement of the obligation, but does not determine whether the obligation exists.'

The obligation must be calculated on a discounted present value basis. The discount rate that must be used is determined by reference to market yields at the reporting date on high-quality corporate bonds. The currency and term of the bonds should be consistent with the currency and estimated periods in which payments under the plan will be made.

There is an exception to this. For a plan in a country which has no deep market in such bonds, then a government bond should be used in its place. This is unlikely to be very relevant to many entities falling within the scope of FRS 102, since such a situation does not obtain in the UK. Nonetheless, it is always possible that a UK entity may have operations, whether directly or through a subsidiary, in countries where the bond market is limited. This exception would then need to be applied. The same requirement, to ensure that the currency and term of the bond and the obligation are the same, applies where the exception has been applied.

The defined benefit obligation, and the consequent expense, must be calculated using the projected unit credit method. Under this method if the benefits are based on future salaries than this requires the entity to estimate future salary increases, although in practice such estimates will normally be made by or in conjunction with the actuary. It also requires a number of other actuarial assumptions to be made including discount rates employee turnover and mortality. If the plan is not a pension plan, for example deals with post-retirement medical benefits, then other assumptions may be required such as those applicable to medical cost trends.

The standard makes it clear that:

- it does not require an entity to engage an independent actuary to perform the comprehensive actuarial valuation that is required to calculate the defined benefit obligation; and

- it does not require a comprehensive actuarial valuation to be undertaken on an annual basis.

This might be considered a little disingenuous. For many UK pension plans, it is of little relevance whether FRS 102 requires an actuarial valuation for the purposes of recognition in the financial statements of a sponsoring employer since the plan itself will normally require such a valuation. Similarly, whilst it does not require an independent actuary to perform a comprehensive actuarial valuation, a comprehensive actuarial valuation still needs to be performed. There are few who are not actuaries who would be competent to undertake such a task. Perhaps it is only the reference to independence that has much substance. Similarly, whilst there is a slightly higher likelihood that entities may make adjustments to previous valuations between full valuations this again assumes a fairly high level of technical knowledge on the part of those undertaking this task. It is perhaps worth noting that in the course of the development of FRS 102 proposals to allow a simplified valuation method for measuring the liability were removed. This means that the FRS 102 requirements are, quite deliberately, more onerous than the requirements in the IFRS for SMEs.

In some cases the fair value of the plan assets at the reporting date may be in excess of the present value of the defined benefit obligation at the same date. In principle, this gives rise to a surplus. However, such a surplus can be recognised as an asset only to the extent that the entity can recover that surplus either through a reduction in its contribution to the future or through being able to obtain refunds from the plan. This principle has not changed from previous accounting practice. What has changed is that the previous standard gave considerable guidance on how it could be demonstrated that these conditions have been met. FRS 102 provides no such detail. For example, this means that there is no specific guidance dealing with the progress that needs to have been made in order to determine that a refund is available. While such a situation is comparatively rare, this does mean that in such cases there may be less consistency than in the past on the point of recognition, since this will need to be determined on the basis of the general principles set out in FRS 102 rather than specific targeted guidance.

The standard also deals with the situation where the defined benefits that will be paid to employees are reduced as a result of amounts that will be payable under government-sponsored plans. This would apply where, for example, the terms of the plan take account of the level of state benefits payable in retirement. The entity is allowed to measure its defined benefit obligations taking account of the benefits payable under the government plans if and only if:

- those plans were enacted before the reporting date; or

- there is reliable evidence, such as past history, that indicates the state benefits will change in a predictable manner such as where they are increased in line with future changes in price levels or salary levels.

Entities can also record a right to reimbursement in relation to defined benefit obligations if they are virtually certain that another party will reimburse some or all of the expenditure required. In such a case, the right to reimbursement is recognised as a separate asset but is treated in the same way as plan assets. Such a situation is likely to be relatively rare but is most likely to arise within a group.

FRS 102 (2018) clarifies that where there is a right to reimbursement, the cost of the defined benefit plan can (but does not have to) be presented net of the amounts relating to changes in the carrying amount of the right to reimbursement.

14.7.8   Defined benefit plan costs

FRS 102 is very specific on the way in which the costs of a defined benefit plan should be recognised. Other than where another Section of the FRS requires all or part of that cost to be recognised within an asset, the cost should be recognised in the following way:

- the change in the net defined benefit liability that arises from the employee service rendered during the reporting period should be recognised in profit or loss;

- net interest in net defined benefit liability that arises due to reporting period should be recognised in profit or loss;

- the costs (or reduction in costs) associated with any plan that has been introduced, changes in benefit, curtailment or settlements should be recognised in profit or loss; and

- the remeasurement of the net defined benefit liability should be recognised in other comprehensive income.

The cost is reduced by any contribution that has been made by or on behalf of the employees who are covered by the plan.

The net interest on the net defined benefit liability is calculated by multiplying that net defined benefit liability by the discount rate determined as discussed above. The net defined benefit liability used for this purpose should take account of the amount calculated at the start of the year and then any changes that have taken place during the year as a result of any contributions or benefit payments. Whether or not this equates to the average balance will depend upon the pattern of contributions, benefit payments or any other changes within the plan.

A similar calculation is required when applying the discount rate to plan assets. This again needs to take account of the opening position and of any changes that have taken place to those assets during the year as a result of contributions and benefit payments.

The net interest on the net defined benefit liability is explained as comprising an interest cost of the defined benefit obligation and interest income on the plan assets, ignoring the effect of any surplus which has not been accounted for as recoverable. This is consistent with the approach in IAS 19 as revised in 2011.

The amount of the remeasurement of the net defined benefit liability, which is included within other comprehensive income, comprises three elements:

- actuarial gains and losses, which arise as a result of changes in actuarial assumptions or where actuary assumptions have not been met;

- the difference between the actual return on plan assets and the amount that has been included in respect of such assets in net interest on the net defined benefit liability; and

- any change in the amount of a defined benefit plan surplus that is not recoverable, excluding amounts included in net interest on the net defined benefit liability.

For the avoidance of doubt, FRS 102 makes clear that any remeasurement of the net defined benefit liability that has been recognised in other comprehensive income is never reclassified to profit or loss in a subsequent accounting period.

14.7.9   Defined benefit plan changes

Where a defined benefit plan has been introduced in the period, or the benefits have been changed, the entity is required to increase or decrease its net defined benefit liability to reflect that change. The resulting increase or decrease is recognised as an expense or income in measuring profit or loss of the current period. This is a change from previous accounting practice, and was referred to briefly above. One of the implications of this is that no account is taken of whether or not a change has vested, it is simply treated as a current year item.

A similar accounting treatment is applied where a defined benefit plan has been curtailed or settled. A curtailment applies where benefits are reduced or the coverage of employees is reduced. A settlement is where the obligation in respect of all or part of the plan is completely discharged. Where either of these events has taken place the defined benefit obligation is decreased or eliminated, as appropriate, and the resulting gain or loss is recognised in profit or loss in the current period.

As mentioned in 1.5 the FRC exposure draft, FRED 71 *Draft amendments to FRS 102 – Multi-employer defined benefit plans (January 2019)*, proposes new requirements in FRS 102 for presenting the impact of transition from defined contribution accounting to defined benefit accounting for affected pensions.

14.7.10   Multi-employer and state plans

Multi-employer benefit plans are defined in the Glossary to FRS 102 as:

'Defined contribution plans (other than state plans) or defined benefit plans (other than state plans) that:

(a) pool the assets contributed by various entities that are not under common control, and

(b) use those assets to provide benefits to employees of more than one entity, on the basis that contribution and benefit levels are determined without regard to the identity of the entity that employs the employees concerned.'

This definition excludes any plans which cover entities under common control, such as a pension plan that has been set up in respect of a group – these 'group plans' are treated separately (see **14.7.11**). However, it does not exclude plans which may have been set up in the past when the entities were under common control, but where common control no longer exists, for example, where a pension plan was set up for companies in a group but where the group has subsequently been broken up.

State plans are defined in the Glossary as:

'Employee benefit plans established by legislation to cover all entities (or all entities in a particular category, for example a specific industry) and operated by national or local government or by another body (for example an autonomous agency created specifically for this purpose) which is not subject to control or influence by the reporting entity.'

Despite having drawn the distinction, FRS 102 does little with it. One of the requirements of the standard is that an entity shall account for a state plan in the same way as for a multi-employer plan.

Multi-employer and state plans need to be classified as defined contribution or defined benefit plans on the basis of their terms, which again includes any constructive obligation which goes beyond the formal terms set out for the plan. In that sense, this is no different to any other type of plan.

Nonetheless, the standard deals with these separately because there is an increased likelihood that full information in respect of the implications of the plan may not be available. A multi-employer plan may be a defined benefit plan but it may be impossible to obtain sufficient information to account for it in the same way as for other types of defined benefit plan, normally because the overall liability cannot be appropriately allocated to the participants. In this case, the employer will account for the plan as if it were a defined contribution plan and provide additional disclosure.

Sometimes an entity may account for its involvement with a multi-employer plan as if it were a defined contribution plan, even though it is a defined benefit plan, as covered in more detail below. Despite this, if there is a deficit in respect of the plan as a whole, an agreement may have been reached with each of the participants dealing with how that deficit may be funded, in whole or in part. Where such an agreement has been entered into, the participant is required under FRS 102 to recognise a liability for the contributions payable that arise from the agreement, to the extent that they relate specifically to the deficit and not the ongoing position of the plan, and to recognise the resulting expense in profit or loss. This liability is measured at the present value of the future contributions payable under the agreement.

14.7.11 Group plans

Group plans are structurally the same as multi-employer plans, but with the key difference that they involve the sharing of risk between entities which are under common control.

Each entity that participates in the plan must obtain information about the plan as a whole that has been measured in accordance with FRS 102 on the basis of the assumptions that apply to the whole plan.

Where there is a contractual agreement or stated policy for charging the total cost to each of the individual group entities then that basis should be used for the entity's individual financial statements.

FRS 102 (2018) adds that 'As the net defined benefit cost is calculated by reference to both the defined benefit obligation and the fair value of plan assets, recognising a net defined benefit cost requires the recognition of a corresponding net defined benefit asset or liability in the individual financial statements of any group entity recognising a net defined benefit cost'.

In the absence of an agreement or policy, the whole of the net defined benefit cost must be recognised in the individual financial statements of whichever group entity is legally responsible for the plan.

Where the cost has been recognised in the books of just one entity the other group entities, in their individual financial statements, will recognise a cost that is equal to their contribution payable for the period. In effect, this means that they are treating the plan as though it were a defined benefit plan.

14.7.12 Insured benefits

As an alternative to a conventional pension plan, an entity may pay insurance premiums in order to fund post-employment benefits.

In most cases, such an arrangement should be accounted for as a defined contribution plan. This is on the basis that the insurance premiums which have been paid are the equivalent of making contributions to a defined contribution plan.

There may, however, be exceptions. This normal accounting treatment should only be applied where the entity does not have a legal or constructive obligation either:

- to pay the employee benefits directly at the time they fall due; or
- to pay further amounts if the insurer does not pay all of the future employee benefits that relate to the employee service in the current in prior periods.

The standard notes that there are various ways in which such an obligation might arise. This might arise as a result of the terms of the plan, or through a related party relationship with the insurer. Where such a legal or constructive obligation is retained, the plan should be accounted for as a defined benefit plan.

Care may also need to be taken with the basis on which future premiums are determined. If future premiums are likely to be affected by the ability of the insurer to meet the obligations out of the funds that have already been provided, then the plan is akin to a defined benefit plan, and should be accounted for as such.

14.7.13   *Other long-term employee benefits*

Apart from the definition of other long-term employee benefits, the standard also provides a list of examples of items that might fall within this definition. In all cases, this will also require that the amount is not expected to be settled wholly within 12 months of the end of the accounting period in which the employee renders the service:

- long-term paid absences, for example long service or sabbatical leave;
- other long service benefits;
- long-term disability benefits;
- profit-sharing and bonuses; and
- deferred remuneration.

The liability for other long-term employee benefits is measured at the net total of:

- the present value of the benefit obligation at the reporting date, calculated using the discount rate on high-quality corporate bonds; minus
- the fair value at the reporting date of plan assets (if there are any) out of which the obligations are to be directly settled.

FRS 102 states that the change in the liability is recognised in profit or loss except to the extent that the FRS requires or permits their inclusion in the cost of asset. This is the one case where the standard refers to being permitted to include costs within an asset. In all other cases, the standard refers to a requirement to include such costs. It is not clear if this is an intended difference, since it is not obvious that long-term employee benefits, other than post-retirement benefits, should be treated in a different way to others in this respect.

It is perhaps surprising that FRS 102 says so little about long-term benefits, given that in practice they may be far more complex than short-term benefits. For example, if a profit-sharing scheme is based on the results for a number of accounting periods, including future periods, it would be useful to have guidance on how the obligation might be determined. The absence of such guidance is likely to lead to divergent accounting practices being applied.

14.7.14 Termination benefits

By way of background, FRS 102 notes that an entity may be committed, whether by legislation, contract or otherwise, and whether directly with employees or other representatives, to make payments or provide other benefits to employees when it terminates their employment. This may also cover constructive obligations, such as those derived from business practice or custom, to make such payments. These payments are referred to as termination benefits.

As made clear in the definitions, termination benefits also cover amounts which are payable where employees are offered redundancy on a voluntary basis.

In terms of recognition, the standard notes that since termination benefits do not provide the entity with any future economic benefits they need to be recognised as an expense in profit or loss immediately. At the same time, the standard also points out that when termination benefits are recognised this will also have an impact upon other benefits, such as retirement benefits. Nonetheless, the need to work through the implications of voluntary redundancy or other termination would arise independently without the standard having to recognise that fact in the Section dealing with termination benefits.

Termination benefits are recognised as a liability, and an expense, only once the entity is demonstrably committed either to:

- terminate the employment of an employee or group of employees before their normal retirement date; or

- provide termination benefits as a result of an offer made to encourage voluntary redundancy.

Such demonstrable commitment can only be in place once the entity has a detailed formal plan for the termination and there is no realistic possibility that it can withdraw from that plan. The standard cross refers to the guidance in paragraph 21.11C which deals with restructuring provisions. That guidance states that a constructive obligation in relation to restructuring arises only when the entity:

(a)   has a detailed formal plan for the restructuring identifying at least:

    (i)   the business or part of a business concerned;

    (ii)   the principal locations affected;

    (iii)   the location, function, and approximate number of employees who will be compensated for terminating their services;

    (iv)   the expenditures that will be undertaken; and

    (v)   when the plan will be implemented; and

(b)   has raised a valid expectation in those affected that it will carry out the restructuring by starting to implement that plan or announcing its main features to those affected by it.

These conditions should therefore be applied in determining whether or not provision may be made for termination benefits.

Where it is determined that termination benefits may be recorded, they must be measured at the best estimate of the expenditure that would be required to settle the obligation at the reporting date. Where an offer has been made to employees to encourage voluntary redundancy, the measurement should be based on the number of employees who are expected to accept the offer.

Most termination benefits will probably be short-term, that is, payable within twelve months of the reporting date. Where this is not the case, the amount expected to be payable should be discounted using the discount rate on high-quality corporate bonds at the reporting date.

14.8   Employee benefits – disclosure

FRS 102 contains no specific disclosure requirements in relation to short-term employee benefits.

However, where the entity is a company (or an LLP or qualifying partnership) it will still be required to comply with the disclosures in company law, the extent of which will depend upon the size of the company. The statutory disclosures in this area are not generally onerous, with a requirement to analyse the staff costs between wages and salaries, social security costs and other pension costs, and to provide details of staff numbers analysed by category. There are additional disclosures in respect of the remuneration of directors, and connected matters, which are outside the scope of this section.

Where an entity has a defined contribution plan, the only disclosure that always arises is the requirement to show the amount recognised in profit or loss as an expense in respect of the plan.

There are additional disclosures where an entity treats a defined benefit multi-employer plan as though it were a defined contribution plan on the basis that it has insufficient information to enable it to apply defined benefit accounting. In this case, the entity must also disclose:

- the fact that it is a defined benefit plan;

- the reason why the plan has been accounted for as defined contribution plan;

- any available information about the surplus or deficit in the plan as a whole and the implications, if any, that this has for the entity;

- a description of the extent to which the entity can be liable to the plan for other entities' obligations under the terms and conditions of the plan; and

- how any liability recognised in respect of a funding arrangement to deal with a deficit has been determined.

There are far more disclosures where an entity has a defined benefit plan, other than a multi-employer defined benefit plan which is treated as a defined contribution plan. Where an entity has more than one plan the disclosures can be made in aggregate, separately for each plan, or in groupings where the groupings are based on those that are considered to be the most useful.

The disclosures required are:

- a general description of the type of plan, including the funding policy;

- the date of the most recent comprehensive actuarial valuation;

- if the most recent comprehensive actuarial valuation was not undertaken as at the reporting date then a description of the adjustments that have been made to measure the defined benefit obligation at the current reporting date;

- a reconciliation of the opening closing balances for each of the following;

- – the defined benefit obligation;

- – the fair value of plan assets; and

- – any reimbursement right which has been recognised as an asset;

- in each of the relevant reconciliations as set out above:

  - – the change in the defined benefit liability that arises from employee service rendered during the period and that has been recorded in profit or loss;

  - – interest income or expense;

  - – remeasurement of the defined benefit liability, showing separately the actuarial gains and losses and the return on plan assets less amounts included within interest income or expense;

  - – plan introductions, changes, curtailments or settlements;

- the total cost of defined benefit plans in the period, split between:

  - – the amounts recognised in profit or loss as an expense; and

  - – the amounts that have been included in the cost of an asset;

- for each major class of plan assets the percentage or amount that each major class constitutes of the fair value of the total plan assets at the reporting date. This analysis must include, but is not limited to, an analysis between equity instruments, debt instruments, property and all other assets;

- the amounts, if any, that have been included in the fair value of plan assets for:

  - – each class of the entity's own financial instruments; and

  - – any property occupied by, or other assets used by, the entity;

- the return on plan assets;

- the principal actuarial assumptions used, including where appropriate:

  - – the discount rates applied;

  - – the expected rates of salary increases;

  - – medical cost trends rates; and

  - – any other material actuarial assumptions which have been used.

Comparatives are not required for the reconciliations.

Where an entity participates in a defined benefit plan that shares risk between entities under common control it has to disclose the following:

- the contractual agreement or details of the stated policy for charging the cost of a defined benefit plan, or a statement that there is no such agreement or policy;

- the policy for determining the contribution that has to be paid by the entity;

- if the entity accounts for an allocation of the net defined benefit cost then the information that would normally be required for any other type of defined benefit plan; and

- if the entity accounts the contributions payable for the period then the following information about the plan as a whole:

  - a general description of the type of plan, including the funding policy;

  - the date of the most recent comprehensive actuarial valuation;

  - if the most recent comprehensive actuarial valuation was not undertaken as at the reporting date then a description of the adjustments that have been made to measure the defined benefit obligation at the current reporting date;

  - for each major class of plan assets the percentage or amount that each major class constitutes of the fair value of the total plan assets at the reporting date. This analysis must include, but is not limited to, an analysis between equity instruments, debt instruments, property and all other assets; and

  - the amounts, if any, that have been included in the fair value of plan assets for:

    (i) each class of the entity's own financial instruments; and

    (ii) any property occupied by, or other assets used by, the entity.

This information does not always have to be provided in the financial statements of the individual entity. It can be included by cross-reference to disclosures that are provided in the financial statements of another group entity if:

- that group entity's financial statements separately identify and disclose the information required about the plan; and

- that group entity's financial statements are available to users of financial statements and the same as those for the entity and at the same time or earlier.

Where an entity has provided any other long-term benefits to its employees it must disclose:

- the nature of the benefits;
- the amount of its obligation; and
- the extent of funding at the reporting date.

Where an entity has provided termination benefits to its employees it must disclose:

- the nature of the benefits;
- the accounting policy that has been applied;
- the amount of its obligation at the reporting date; and
- the extent of funding at the reporting date.

Section 28 points out that where there is an uncertainty about the number of employees who might accept an offer of termination benefits then this means that the liability is a contingent liability. In such a case, all of the disclosures which are normally required in relation to a contingent liability must also be provided.

14.8.1   Retirement benefits disclosures for small entities

For small entities applying Section 1A of the standard, there are no explicit disclosure requirements relating to retirement benefits. As in all other areas, directors will need to form a judgment on whether some disclosures are nonetheless needed to give a true and fair view. For instance, a small entity operating a defined benefit scheme with a considerable deficit may view it as necessary to provide the supporting notes so that users can properly understand the assumptions and entries that have led to the figures on the balance sheet.

15 Events after the end of the reporting period

15.1 Scope of this section

This chapter addresses the requirements of Section 32 in respect of events after the reporting period, or 'post balance sheet events' as they are commonly known.

Paragraph 32.2 defines events after the end of the reporting period as:

'... those events, favourable and unfavourable, that occur between the end of the reporting period and the date when the financial statements are authorised for issue. There are two types of events:

(a) those that provide evidence of conditions that existed at the end of the reporting period (adjusting events after the end of the reporting period); and

(b) those that are indicative of conditions that arose after the end of the reporting period (non-adjusting events after the end of the reporting period).'

Importantly, the reporting period is clearly delimited: it ends at the point that the financial statements are authorised for issue, not when they are approved by shareholders, when public announcements of results are made, or any other date. This can be critical when it comes to assessing the effect of a discrete event occurring close to the point of issue of the financial statements (and is helpful for auditors planning their final procedures, which must include a discussion of relevant post balance sheet events with management).

The comparable standard in IFRS is IAS 10 *Events After the Reporting Period*. Both standards are consistent with one another.

Application to micro-entities: The requirements in FRS 105 are consistent with those in FRS 102.

15.2 Adjusting events

An adjusting event, defined above, is one that reflects conditions that were already in place at the balance sheet date, and therefore needs to be reflected in the accounts by recognition of any relevant assets or liabilities, income or expense, or by alterations to the measurement of amounts already recognised.

15 Events after the end of the reporting period

Paragraph 32.5 gives five examples of typical adjusting events:

(1) The settlement, post year-end, of a court case that confirms that the entity had a present obligation at the end of the reporting period. So if, for instance, a customer has made a claim against the entity for damage caused by one of its products that was supplied in the year, then when it prepared its accounts the entity would consider whether to make a provision in respect of this claim. Its initial assessment would be based on information available during the accounts preparation process, and might lead to the conclusion that there was only a contingent liability to disclose, because of uncertainty. If, however, the case was then settled close to the date the financial statements were to be issued, this would need to be reflected in the accounting, meaning that a provision would be recognised in place of a disclosure of a contingent liability.

(2) 'The receipt of information after the end of the reporting period indicating that an asset was impaired at the end of the reporting period, or that the amount of a previously recognised impairment loss for that asset needs to be adjusted.' At the unsubtle end of the spectrum, this would include events such as selling a property shortly after the balance sheet date for considerably less than its carrying value.

In some cases, this will also apply to inventory, although as the time between the balance sheet date and the inventory sale date increases, the correlation falls. A clothing retailer with a January year end may already have stocked up on certain of its spring/summer lines, and not written these down in January because there was no reason to suppose them impaired; by August, when the accounts are being pulled together at the last minute, it may turn out to have been a rainy summer, with sale prices slashed, but this does not of itself indicate that the items should have been written down as at the year end (it might be argued that a rainy summer is a discrete event taking place after the reporting date). It is also noted in paragraph 32.5(b) that often, the bankruptcy of a customer after the balance sheet date indicates that the customer was already unstable at that date, so that this bankruptcy is an adjusting event and receivables from the customer need to be written down.

Again, though, judgment is needed in such areas: while most bankruptcies are the result of a long decline, some can occur with no previous warning, as a result of a discrete event (perhaps a customer falls victim to an uninsured natural disaster after the year end, and is forced to close its business with immediate effect). In this case, the bankruptcy would be a non-adjusting event.

(3) 'The determination after the end of the reporting period of the cost of assets purchased, or the proceeds from assets sold, before the

end of the reporting period.' This may, at first glance, appear a little odd, since it raises the possibility of making sales or purchases of unknown value, but will be particularly relevant to entities transacting in foreign currencies, to those making acquisitions or disposals of businesses where the final price is based on post-transaction agreed asset values, and other similar cases.

(4) 'The determination after the end of the reporting period of the amount of profit-sharing or bonus payments, if the entity had a legal or constructive obligation at the end of the reporting period to make such payments as a result of events before that date.' So, if there is, for instance, a directors' bonus scheme that promises each director 1% of the year's profits, then this needs to be recognised as a liability at the year end, but the precise amount will not be settled until profits have been finalised, and at that point the estimate is updated, as an adjusting event.

Similarly, if there is a generally held, and precedent-supported, expectation among employees that a certain level of bonuses will be paid, then this may give rise to a constructive obligation that merits the recognition of a provision based on the amount that is eventually determined. In contrast, if the board reviews the year's results after the year end and finds them surprisingly positive, such that it decides on a windfall bonus for everyone, this cannot be backed into the reporting year (that is, it is only a non-adjusting event) because the condition, the obligation to pay a bonus, only arose after the year end.

(5) 'The discovery of fraud or errors that show that the financial statements are incorrect.' This is a very broad-brush final example. A systematic data entry error that had been overstating each transaction by a factor of 10 would fit into this category, as would the discovery that a reported bank account containing millions was in fact empty as a result of an employee fraud. Care is needed, though, because as with all of these examples, it is necessary that the fraud or error had already occurred (or was in progress) as at the reporting date, for an adjustment to be needed to the financial statements.

15.3   Non-adjusting events

Non-adjusting events are not recognised in the financial statements, although disclosures will often still be necessary (see **15.5**).

The standard gives just two examples of non-adjusting events, in paragraph 32.7, although clearly an almost infinite list could be compiled, since most events after the reporting date are non-adjusting. The two highlighted cases, though, are:

(1) 'A decline in market value of investments between the end of the reporting period and the date when the financial statements are authorised for issue.' This seems reasonably obvious, and it seems the main reason for its inclusion is as a contrast to the situation above where an impairment is noted after the year end in circumstances which would give rise to an adjustment. The standard points out that a decline in an investment's value is usually unrelated to its previous value, so does not reflect conditions that were already in place at the year end.

(2) 'An amount that becomes receivable as a result of a favourable judgement or settlement of a court case after the reporting date but before the financial statements are authorised for issue.' Again this is a counterpoint to the example above of an adjusting event where an entity has a court case, that had been in progress at the year end, subsequently settled against it. This highlights the fundamental difference in approach between the recognition of assets and of liabilities – a positive result after the year end does not confirm that an asset existed as at the year end in the same way that a negative result would confirm that a liability existed.

The standard also provides further examples in paragraph 32.11 of non-adjusting events after the end of the reporting period that would generally result in disclosure, see **15.5**.

15.4 Other issues

15.4.1 Going concern

Going concern is afforded its own special section because it is so important to make the right decision on whether a set of accounts is prepared on the going concern basis. Crucially, and set out in paragraph 32.7A, if management decides after the year end to terminate the business, even if this has not even been considered to be an option as at the year end, this must be reflected in the accounts by use of a basis other than going concern. In other words, the decision (or realisation of the inevitability) to terminate the business is always an adjusting event.

15.4.2 Dividends

Even where shareholders expect dividends, and a company has a habit of paying them each year, if they are not declared until after the year end they are a non-adjusting event, and as such may not be recognised as a liability in the accounts.

Interestingly, paragraph 32.8 does permit the amount of the dividend to be presented 'as a segregation of retained earnings' (so, presumably as a separate line item within equity) in the balance sheet, so preparers can choose to show readers which of their reserves have subsequently been committed to dividends, but there is no requirement for this segregation, so where entities do not show this separate component, users will need to look to the notes for information on dividends subsequently declared.

Although this is not explored in Section 32, it is important to note that in effect this ruling on dividends applies only to shares classified as equity (this is noted briefly in paragraph 32.8's reference to 'dividends to holders of [an entity's] equity instruments'). Where there are, for instance, preference shares in issue, which have been classified as a liability under Section 22, this classification is because of an unavoidable obligation on the entity's part to pay out cash. So, whether or not a preference dividend has been formally declared, a liability does exist as at the balance sheet date.

Some ambiguity may be observed relating to the best treatment for shares classified as compound instruments, for instance, redeemable ordinary shares which have debt features (the obligation to redeem) and equity features (the right to a residual share of profits). Since these are not pure equity instruments, it might be argued that paragraph 32.8 does not apply and the accounts can be adjusted for dividends declared on such shares after the year end; this would, however, seem to be a stretch of the words in the standard, which clearly has the intention of distinguishing between cases where an obligation exists at the year end and those where one does not, and uses the term 'equity instruments' because it usually captures this distinction sufficiently.

15.5   Disclosure

The disclosure requirements in Section 32 are not detailed, since the information needed will depend on the precise nature of the event. So paragraph 32.10 merely requires, for non-adjusting events, disclosure of the nature of the event, and either an estimate of its financial effect or a statement that such an estimated cannot be made.

By their nature, adjusting events will have been fully reflected in the accounts, so disclosures relating to them will be included within the notes for the relevant line item. To give complete clarity, though, the date on which the financial statements were authorised for issue must be disclosed (because this defines the period in which adjusting events may arise). In the reasonably rare circumstances in which the entity's owners or others have the power to amend the financial statements after issue, this must also be disclosed.

Although those are the only formal disclosure requirements, the final paragraph of the section does then give a list of examples of non-adjusting events 'that would generally result in disclosure'. While this is not the same as a statement that such events must always be disclosed, it is a strong indicator that good reasons would be needed not to disclose them. The full list from paragraph 32.11 is as follows:

(a)   a major business combination or disposal of a major subsidiary;

(b)   announcement of a plan to discontinue an operation;

(c)   major purchases of assets, disposals or plans to dispose of assets, or expropriation of major assets by government;

(d)   the destruction of a major production plant by fire;

(e)   announcement, or commencement of the implementation, of a major restructuring;

(f)   issues or repurchases of an entity's debt or equity instruments;

(g)   abnormally large changes in asset prices or foreign exchange rates;

(h)   changes in tax rates or tax laws enacted or announced that have a significant effect on current and deferred tax assets and liabilities;

(i)   entering into significant commitments or contingent liabilities, for example, by issuing significant guarantees; and

(j)   commencement of major litigation arising solely out of events that occurred after the end of the reporting period.

15.5.1   *Disclosures for small entities*

For small entities applying Section 1A of FRS 102, there are no explicit disclosure requirements relating to events after the balance sheet date.

16 Related parties

16.1 Scope of this section

16.1.1 Scope and exemptions

This section covers Section 33 which addresses disclosure requirements for an entity's transactions with related parties, so that a user can understand the effect on position and performance of the existence of these related parties, and any transactions and balances with them.

There are two exemptions from the application of the Section's requirements. First, disclosures are not required of transactions between two parties which are only classified as related by virtue of both being state-controlled. Second, disclosures are also not required of transactions between group members, as long as any subsidiary involved is wholly owned.

The equivalent standard in IFRS is IAS 24 *Related Party Disclosures*. UK company law also includes disclosure requirements in relation to directors' remuneration and a company's ultimate parent company, and these requirements apply to entities using FRS 102. The company law requirements are discussed in detail at **16.3**.

> **Application to micro-entities:** FRS 105 does not contain a section on related party disclosures. This is because the only related party disclosure required is set out in Section 6 of the standard, and relates to loans, credits and advances made to directors.

16.1.2 Definitions

The definition of a related party is in paragraph 33.2, and is reproduced here in full:

> 'A related party is a person or entity that is related to the entity that is preparing its financial statements (the reporting entity).
>
> (a) A person or a **close member of that person's family** is related to a reporting entity if that person:
>
>   (i)   has **control** or **joint control** over the reporting entity;
>
>   (ii) has **significant influence** over the reporting entity; or
>
>   (iii) is a member of the **key management personnel** of the reporting entity or of a **parent** of the reporting entity.

(b)   An entity is related to a reporting entity if any of the following conditions applies:

(i)   the entity and the reporting entity are members of the same group (which means that each parent, subsidiary and fellow subsidiary is related to the others);

(ii)   one entity is an **associate** or **joint venture** of the other entity (or of a member of a group of which the other entity is a member);

(iii)   both entities are joint ventures of the same third party;

(iv)   one entity is a joint venture of a third entity and the other entity is an associate of the third entity;

(v)   the entity is a **post-employment benefit plan** for the benefit of employees of either the reporting entity or an entity related to the reporting entity. If the reporting entity is itself such a plan, the sponsoring employers are also related to the reporting entity;

(vi)   the entity is controlled or jointly controlled by a person identified in (a); and

(vii)   a person identified in (a)(i) has significant influence over the entity or is a member of the key management personnel of the entity (or of a parent of the entity).'

16.1.2.1   Close family members

The piece in paragraph 33.2(a) about close family members means that if an individual has any of the listed direct relationships to the reporting entity, then he and all of his close family are related parties of the entity.

The phrase 'close member of that person's family' is not explained within Section 33, but does appear in the Glossary – the relevant people are:

'... those family members who may be expected to influence, or be influenced by, that person in their dealings with the entity and include:

(a)   that person's children and spouse or domestic partner;

(b)   children of that person's spouse or domestic partner; and

(c)   dependants of that person or that person's spouse or domestic partner.'

So, a director's close family would include his wife, civil partner or cohabiting partner; all of his children regardless of their ages and whether they live with him; his stepchildren through his current partner (it would seem that stepchildren would cease to be close family if the domestic relationship ends); and any other dependants either of him or of his partner. The term 'dependants' is not defined, but would certainly include those who were living with the director and financially dependent on him, but probably not self-sufficient siblings, parents, and so on.

It can be seen that this is a broad definition which could capture several people with each director; these people are all then invoked in paragraph 33.2(b)(vi) and (vii). Company B would be a related party of company A if Mr X was a director of company A and Mr X's adult stepson was a director of company B, although the converse would not hold, since although the stepson is, by this definition, a close member of Mr X's family, Mr X is not a close member of the stepson's family. The breadth of the definition does not necessarily mean voluminous disclosures, though, as in most cases the close families of investors or directors will have no dealings with the company in question.

Example 16.1 – Identification of related parties

1. Parent, subsidiaries, and associates

    A parent company P has two subsidiaries, S and R, and an associate, A. S has an associate, B, and R has a subsidiary, Q.

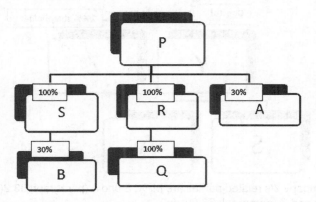

    In this situation, all of the parties are related to all of the others, with the exception of A and B, which are not related to each other. These relations are all by virtue of 33.2(b)(i) and (ii).

    A and B are not related because for an associate to be brought into a related party relationship though (b)(ii), the relationship needs either to be direct or through a group member, so since associates are not members of a group (being less than 50% owned) then by definition they are not related to each other.

2. Associates and joint ventures

    Parent P has a subsidiary, S, an associate, A, and two joint ventures, J and K.

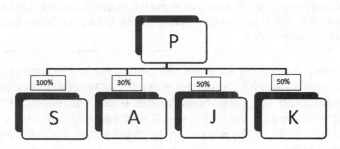

433

All of these entities are related parties of each other. Most of S's relations are by virtue of paragraph 33.2(b)(ii) (since A, J and K are associates and joint ventures of a group of which S is a member). J and K are related to each other by virtue of paragraph 33.2(b)(iii), and A is related to both of J and K (and vice versa) through paragraph 33.2(b)(iv).

3.   Shared directors/shareholders

Mr X is a director of company Y, and owns 90% of the shares of company Z. Company Y has a subsidiary, S, and an associate, A.

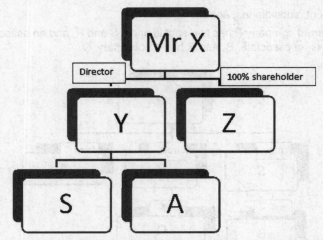

Company Y's related parties are Mr X; S and A (paragraph 33.2(b)(i) and (ii)); and Z (paragraph 33.2(b)(vi)).

Similarly, company Z's related parties are Mr X, Y and S – this is the effect of the shared link through Mr X, as in paragraph 33.2(b)(vii). A, though, is not a related party of Z, because Y is only an investor in A, rather than a parent.

Company S's related parties are A, Y, Mr X and Z.

One of the difficulties that these examples serve to illustrate is that identifying the relevant relationships for these purposes is not as simple as drawing a ring on a group structure within which all entities are related to each other. In each of the three examples, there is at least one entity for which all the others in the diagram are related parties, but also at least one for which they are not. Put another way, the relation of 'being a related party of' is not transitive: in the final example above, A is a related party of Y and Y is a related party of Z, but it does not follow that A is a related party of Z.

Unfortunately, Section 33 does not include any worked examples, and the wording in paragraph 33.2 does not make for easy reading (for instance, in sub paragraph (b), references to 'the entity', as distinct from 'the reporting entity' mean 'the entity which might or might not be a related party', except in (ii) to (iv) where 'entity' might mean the reporting entity or the other entity.

Careful reading can assist with the application to a practical situation, but the examples published in IAS 24 may also be helpful, as it has the same definition of a related party, so this appears to be a valid source of guidance.

16.1.2.2   State-controlled entities

Special rules regarding state-controlled entities have been imported from the most recent version of IAS 24, to address a problem that arose in some jurisdictions but is less common in the UK. In summary (from paragraph 33.11), if an entity is controlled by the government it need not disclose transactions or balances with that government (in other words, it does not treat it as a related party apart from the disclosure of the basic relationship) and it also does not classify as related parties any other entities which would be related to it only by virtue of also being government-controlled.

16.2   Disclosure requirements

16.2.1   Key management personnel

The requirements in Section 33 regarding key management personnel are exceedingly brief.

Only one line of disclosure is required, being total key management personnel compensation. This is based on the definition of key management personnel as 'those persons having authority and responsibility for planning, directing and controlling the activities of the entity, directly or indirectly, including any director (whether executive or otherwise) of that entity' (paragraph 33.6). The standard also explains that compensation includes all employee benefits (as per Section 28) including share based payments. Perhaps the biggest challenge in making this disclosure is in establishing whether there are any other key management personnel apart from the board of directors (many UK companies applying IFRS have taken the view that the terms are synonymous, but this is not always the case). Other challenges, though, come with reconciling the requirements of this note with the more onerous requirements in company law, as discussed further at **16.3**. In particular, share based payment expense is excluded from the legal definition of directors' remuneration, so this total will often be different from the total for 'key management personnel compensation'.

There is an exemption in FRS 102 (2018) paragraph 33.7A acknowledging that in many cases key management personnel may be the same as the directors. Accordingly, where an entity is required by law or regulation to disclose directors' remuneration and the directors are the same as key management personnel, there is no need to disclose key management personnel compensation. When this exemption is used, the standard also clarifies that it is not necessary to provide additional disclosure about directors' share-based payment arrangements. This mirrors what was frequently already occurring in practice.

16.2.2   Related party transactions

16.2.2.1   Basic disclosure requirements

A related party transaction is defined in paragraph 33.8 as 'a transfer of resources, services or obligations between a reporting entity and a related party, regardless of whether a price is charged'. This includes, but is not limited to, normal sales and purchases, transfers of fixed assets, payments for services, lease arrangements and the resulting transactions, financing transactions such as the issue of loans, payment of dividends, and the taking on of commitments such as guarantees.

The minimum information to be disclosed about related party transactions is set out in paragraph 33.9:

(a)   the amount of the transactions;

(b)   the amount of outstanding balances; and

   (i)   their terms and conditions, including whether they are secured, and the nature of the consideration to be provided in settlement; and

   (ii)   details of any guarantees given or received;

(c)   provisions for uncollectible receivables related to the amount of outstanding balances; and

(d)   the expense recognised during the period in respect of bad or doubtful debts due from related parties.

This is quite a level of detail, meaning that any users of the accounts should be able to form a full picture of the transactions' true nature and whether it appears that the related party relationship seems to have made its terms different from normal.

16.2.2.2   Relationships that change during the period

The standard is silent on the situation where relationships change, such that another entity is a related party of the reporting entity for only part of the year. On the face of it, several different policy decisions would be compatible with this lack of guidance:

(1)   Disclose transactions and year end balances only with entities which are related parties as at the reporting date.

(2) Disclose transactions and year end balances with all entities which were related parties at any point during the year.

(3) Disclose transactions with all entities which were related parties as at the date of the transaction, and outstanding balances relating to those transactions.

(4) As per (3) above, but also disclose outstanding balances with parties which were not related parties at the time of the transaction but have subsequently become related parties.

The argument supporting approach 1 is that the definitions in paragraph 33.2 are all in the present tense, which might be read as implying that related party status is assessed at a single point in time, being the reporting date. The wording in paragraph 33.9 is compatible with this, beginning as it does with 'If an entity has related party transactions' – one might suggest that if the standard setters meant any of approaches 2–4 to be used, then they would have used language such as 'if an entity had transactions with related parties during the year' or similar.

If, however, we look back to the goal of this section, it pushes towards a broader reading. The underlying reason for disclosing related party transactions is to allow users to make their own assessments of whether and how this type of relationship may have affected the pricing, terms or any other aspect of the transaction. In other words, the relationship that was in place at the point when the transaction happened is the critical one, effectively ruling out approaches 1 and 2 (approach 2, in failing to discriminate between transactions when the counterparty was related and those when it was not, risks obscuring the information that is most relevant). Any balances still outstanding at the year end which relate to these transactions are likely still to be of interest, even if the counterparty has subsequently ceased to be related (in particular, it may cast an interesting light on this judgment, if there is theoretically no longer a close link between the companies but balances have nonetheless been able to remain outstanding for longer than would be normal or expected). Finally, if a transaction's counterparty was not related as at the time of the transaction but has subsequently become so, the outstanding balance becomes interesting, since the new relationship may have altered the repayment terms.

Thus, approach 4 seems to be the one most in line with the aim of Section 33, although there are no clear statements in the standard explicitly prohibiting any of the other approaches.

In any event, the accounting policy note should make it clear how such a situation is treated. Also, if there are significant transactions or balances with parties whose status changed during the year, additional narrative disclosure would be helpful. An example would be a statement such as

'Included within sales to group companies in the table above is £150,000 of sales to a company that ceased to be a subsidiary part way through the year. There were no outstanding balances with this company at the reporting date'.

These considerations apply equally to disclosure of any parent or ultimate controlling party (see **16.2.3**).

16.2.2.3   Aggregation of transactions

It is clearly not expected that each transaction with each related party is disclosed separately in the accounts, and nor would it be reasonable to be required to disclose total transactions for each counterparty: this would be unwieldy, and would not take enough account of the ways in which such information is commercially sensitive. Aggregation is therefore permitted, into four categories:

- investors in the entity (those which have control, joint control or significant influence);
- investees of the entity (subsidiaries, joint ventures or associates);
- key management personnel (see **16.2.1**); and
- other related parties (this would include, among others, fellow subsidiaries in a group, close family of key management personnel, and pension schemes).

Along with this grouping into four categories, 'items of a similar nature' may also be aggregated, so there might be a grouping of 'sales of goods to subsidiaries and associates' or 'loans owed to investors with significant influence'.

The exception to this permission to aggregate is in paragraph 33.14, which requires separate disclosure where this is necessary for a full understanding of the effects of related party transactions on the financial statements. For example, a company that guarantees the debts both of one of its fellow subsidiaries and of the adult stepdaughter of one of its directors would, in theory, be able to aggregate the disclosures of these items, as they are 'items of a similar nature' transacted with entities in the category 'other related parties'. This aggregation, though, would obscure the uncommon nature of one of the transactions (the guarantee for the family members) and as such this seems to be a case for further disaggregation under paragraph 33.14.

16.2.2.4   Materiality

Section 33 does not make any explicit reference to the concept of materiality. As such, it must be assumed that materiality is as relevant a concept as it is everywhere else in the standard, so related party relationships and transactions should be disclosed if '[their] omission or misstatement could influence the economic decisions of users made on the basis of the financial statements' (paragraph 2.6). Some of this phrasing is picked up in paragraph 33.9, which requires the disclosure of transactions and the nature of the related party relationship so far as is 'necessary for an understanding of the potential effect of the relationship on the financial statements'.

It seems best to err on the side of caution in making materiality judgments in such a sensitive area. It may be, in the board's view, irrelevant that transactions took place with a company majority-owned by one of the directors, perhaps because the financial value is low, or because the board are confident that the transaction was on commercial terms and was unaffected by the position of the director. This is not, though, entirely the board's judgment to make: users may quite reasonably be interested in such transactions even when they are of low value, and should where possible be enabled to make that judgment of interest for themselves. In borderline cases, therefore, where the monetary value of related party transactions is a little below the materiality threshold used for preparing the remainder of the accounts, it may still be most appropriate to disclose the transactions anyway. There may well also be occasions where very low-value items should be disclosed, such as assets or services sold at artificially low prices to related parties, or loans provided at zero interest. In these cases, the absolute value is not a material number, but the absence of charge of a proper price may be a material fact (depending partly on the true value of the items or services which are being given away or undercharged for).

16.2.2.5   Practical presentation

Depending on the volume and diversity of an entity's related parties and its transactions with them, the most efficient and readable way of providing the required disclosures will vary. For entities with a small number of simple arrangements, a few lines of narrative with figures may be sufficient; if the situation is more complex, though, a matrix presentation is easier to read at a glance, and can be augmented if necessary with additional narrative.

Example 16.2

A company has drafted the following narrative note for its parent-only accounts:

During 2019, the company made sales of £145,000 and purchases of £215,000 respectively to and from its fellow subsidiaries (2018: £138,000 and £190,000). The related balances receivable and payable at the year-end were £35,000 and £51,000 (2018: £12,000 and £nil). It provided management services valued and charged at £200,000 (2018: £200,000) to its subsidiary companies, relating to which £400,000 (2018: £200,000) was outstanding at the year end.

> *The company was also in receipt of loans for the first time this year from some members of its key management personnel. £150,000 was advanced during the year, of which the whole balance remained outstanding at the year-end; interest charges of £1,200 were accrued within the year and have been added to the outstanding loan balance.*
>
> *The company's office is leased from its parent, at a rent of £120,000 per year (2018: £120,000) all of which was paid during the year.*
>
> This could, as an alternative, be summarised in a table:
>
> | | **2019** | | **2018** | |
> |---|---|---|---|---|
> | | Income/ (expense) | Year end debtor/ (creditor) | Income/ (expense) | Year end debtor / (creditor) |
> | | £ | £ | £ | £ |
> | Sales to fellow subsidiaries | 145,000 | 35,000 | 138,000 | 12,000 |
> | Purchases from fellow subsidiaries | (215,000) | (51,000) | (190,000) | - |
> | Management services charged to subsidiaries | 200,000 | 400,000 | 200,000 | 200,000 |
> | Loans from key management personnel | (1,200) | (151,200) | - | - |
> | Operating lease payments to parent company | (120,000) | - | (120,000) | - |

The only point to be careful with in this note is the implication in the comment about management charges being 'valued and charged at £200,000'. Paragraph 33.13 forbids claims that transactions are made on an arm's length basis 'unless such terms can be substantiated' and so it is important to avoid using language that suggests there is an objective value to a transaction if this is not really the case.

Since some of the transaction types required to be disclosed are also covered by other Sections of the standard (for instance, lease arrangements, directors' remuneration, and financial instruments), additional information may be required. The simplest approach seems to be to include all of the information required by Section 33 in one self-contained 'related party transactions' note, with cross references to where more details about certain transactions can be found. An alternative, though, is to include the Section 33 disclosures in each relevant note (e.g. a section on loans from related parties within the financial instruments note) with an additional related parties note in place only to 'mop up' those which are not disclosed elsewhere. This may be preferred by some preparers, and arguably has the effect of being more informative to users by helping them to understand related party transactions in the context of the entity's operations, rather than as if they were a distinct group, disclosed on their own at the very back of the accounts.

16.2.3 Parent-subsidiary relationships

The standard includes some minimum disclosure requirements in respect of groups, even where there are no intragroup transactions. Paragraph 33.5 requires the disclosure of the name of the parent company and, if different, of the ultimate controlling party. If neither of these higher companies produces publicly available financial statements, then the name of the highest company in the chain that does produce them must be disclosed. This does not seem to be affected by whether or not the relevant parent company prepares consolidated accounts. In addition, though, there is the requirement from paragraphs 8 and 9 of Schedule 4 to the Regulations, which asks for details of 'the parent undertaking of the largest group of undertakings for which group financial statements are drawn up and of which the reporting company is a member, and also the parent undertaking of the smallest such group' (see **16.3**).

It is important to note that the disclosure refers to the 'ultimate controlling party', not the ultimate controlling parent. Although FRS 102 does not define this term, FRS 8 was clear that the definition of a 'party' encompassed both individuals and entities and this intention seems to be present in FRS 102 also. Therefore, it is necessary to look beyond the ultimate parent company to identify whether there is an individual – or two closely related individuals (e.g. a husband and wife) with overall control. If so, the name of the individual should be disclosed as the ultimate controlling party.

Example 16.3

S is a subsidiary of immediate parent P1, which is itself a subsidiary of P2, which is wholly owned by P3. P3 is the only company in the chain which prepares consolidated financial statements, but these are not publicly available.

Assuming that there are no individuals with overall control of P3, S will meet the FRS 102 requirements by disclosing the names of P1 (immediate parent) and P3 (ultimate controlling parent). In addition, the name of P3 will need to be disclosed to meet the Company law requirements.

16.2.4 Disclosures for small entities

Related parties are one of the few areas where significant disclosure requirements remain for small entities applying Section 1A of FRS 102. These appear in paragraphs 1AC.34–1AC.36 and are reproduced in full here – it can be seen that they are similar to the requirements for other entities, but are somewhat briefer even though they cover both transactions with directors and with other related parties.

'1AC.34 Where the small entity is a subsidiary, the following information must be given in respect of the parent of the smallest group for which consolidated financial statements are drawn up of which the small entity is a member:

(a) The name of the parent which draws up the consolidated financial statements;

(b) The address of the parent's registered office (whether in or outside the UK); or

(c) If it is unincorporated, the address of its principal place of business (Schedule 1, paragraph 65)

1AC.35 Particulars must be given of material transactions the small entity has entered into that have not been concluded under normal market conditions with:

(a) Owners holding a participating interest in the small entity;

(b) Companies in which the small entity itself has a participating interest; and

(c) The small entity's directors [or members of its governing body].

Particulars must include:

(a) The amount of such transactions;

(b) The nature of the related party relationship; and

(c) Other information about the transactions necessary for an understanding of the financial position of the small entity.

Information about individual transactions may be aggregated according to their nature, except where separate information is necessary for an understanding of the effects of the related party transactions on the financial position of the small entity.

Particulars need not be given of transactions entered into between two or more members of a group, provided that any subsidiary which is a party to the transaction is wholly-owned by such a member. (Schedule 1, para 66)

Although disclosure is only required of material transactions with the specified related parties that have not been concluded under normal market conditions, small entities disclosing all transactions with such related parties would still be compliant with company law.

Transactions with directors, or members of an entity's governing body, include directors' remuneration and dividends paid to directors.

1AC.36 Details of advances and credits granted by the small entity to its directors and guarantees of any kind entered into by the small entity on behalf of its directors must be shown in the notes to the financial statements.

The details required of an advance or credit are:

(a)   Its amount;

(b)   An indication of the interest rate;

(c)   Its main conditions;

(d)   Any amounts repaid;

(e)   Any amounts written off; and

(f)   Any amounts waived.

There must also be stated in the notes to the financial statements the totals of amounts stated under (a), (d), (e) and (f).

The details required of a guarantee are:

(a)   Its main terms;

(b)   The amounts of the maximum liability that may be incurred by the small entity; and

(c)   Any amount paid and any liability incurred by the small entity for the purpose of fulfilling the guarantee (including any loss incurred by reason of enforcement of the guarantee).

There must also be stated in the notes to the financial statements the totals of amounts stated under (b) and (c). (Section 413 of the Act)'

The question arises, particularly in the case of directors' remuneration and dividends, as to whether such transactions are concluded under normal market conditions. Small companies, especially those which are owner-managed, often make decisions about remuneration based on factors such as how profitable a company is and the tax impact of the different methods of profit extraction.

At the current time, there is no clear guidance on whether or not such a situation might constitute an off-market transaction. In practice, though, it seems increasingly common that, for a small company, this is viewed as a common approach and is therefore concluded under normal market conditions. However, there is scope for further guidance to be issued by the FRC or other authoritative bodies clarifying what is meant by normal market conditions.

16.3   Related party disclosures required by company law

In addition to the requirements set out in the *Companies Act* 2006, s. 33 and the Accounting Regulations (SI 2008/410) contain further disclosures to be given to comply with company law.

16.3.1   Disclosures about related undertakings

All large and medium-sized parent companies need to include details of all related undertakings in the notes to their accounts.

The detailed disclosure requirements are set out in SI 2008/410, Sch. 4, which is divided into three Parts:

- Part 1 contains provisions applying to all companies, whether group accounts are prepared or not;
- Part 2 contains provisions that apply where group accounts are not prepared; and
- Part 3 contains provisions that apply where group accounts are prepared.

Schedule 4 requires detailed disclosures around investments in subsidiaries, associates, joint ventures and other 'significant holdings' (i.e. any investment of 20% of more, or where the carrying value of the holding exceeds 20% of the holding company's net assets). Generally speaking, the name, registered address (regardless of whether it is in the UK or elsewhere) and proportion of shares held are disclosed whether or not group accounts are prepared. Information about the underlying profit or loss and capital and reserves of related undertakings is also required in certain circumstances.

Where the company is a subsidiary undertaking, paragraph 8 of Schedule 4 to SI 2008/410 requires the following information to be given with respect to the parent undertaking of the largest group of undertakings for which group accounts are drawn up and of which the company is a member, and the smallest such group of undertakings.

- The name of the parent undertaking must be stated.
- There must also be stated:
  - the address of the undertaking's registered office (whether in or outside the United Kingdom); or
  - if it is unincorporated, the address of its principal place of business.
- If copies of the group accounts referred to above are available to the public, there must also be stated the addresses from which copies of the accounts can be obtained.

Where the company is a subsidiary undertaking, paragraph 9 of Schedule 4 to SI 2008/410 requires the following information to be given with respect to the company (if any) regarded by the directors as being the company's ultimate parent company.

- The name of that company must be stated.

- If that company is incorporated outside the United Kingdom, the country in which it is incorporated must be stated (if known to the directors).

- In this paragraph 'company' includes any body corporate.

16.3.2 Information about directors' benefits

CA 2006, s. 413 also requires disclosures relating to advances and credits granted by the company (or its subsidiaries) to its directors and guarantees of any kind entered into by the company (or its subsidiaries) on behalf of its directors.

The details required of an advance or credit are:

- its amount (and total);

- an indication of the interest rate;

- its main conditions; and

- any amounts (and total) repaid.

The details required of a guarantee are:

- its main terms;

- the amount of the maximum liability (and total maximum liability) that may be incurred by the company (or its subsidiary); and

- any amount (and total amount) paid and any liabilities incurred by the company (or its subsidiary) for the purpose of fulfilling the guarantee (including any loss incurred by reason of enforcement of the guarantee).

These disclosures are required for any person who was a director at any time in the financial year to which the accounts relate.

The disclosures also relate to every advance, credit or guarantee subsisting at any time in the financial year to which the accounts relate: whenever it was entered into, whether or not the person concerned was a director of the company in question at the time it was entered into, and in the case of an advance, credit or guarantee involving a subsidiary undertaking of that company, whether or not that undertaking was such a subsidiary undertaking at the time it was entered into.

These requirements are not covered by the FRS 102 principle of materiality as they arise from CA 2006 and the wording of the legislation would suggest disclosure of every single advance and repayment thereof. In larger organisations this may be possible as advances to directors are not commonplace. However in smaller, owner managed companies there may be a significant number of advances and repayments between a company and a director and therefore general consensus is that the disclosure requirements are satisfied on an aggregated basis which might also coincide with the FRS 102 Section 33 disclosure requirements.

16.4   Directors' remuneration disclosures in company law

As described at **16.2.1**, the requirements in FRS 102 do not explicitly address disclosure of directors' remuneration, being based instead on the concept of key management personnel. However, UK preparers subject to company law will still need to comply with all of the company law requirements discussed in this section. Additional requirements apply to quoted companies; these are outside the scope of this guide.

16.4.1   Definition

Before dealing with directors' remuneration, or transactions with directors, it is first necessary to provide definitions of a director, a shadow director and a connected person. The Companies Act definition of a director is not quite as enlightening as one might desire:

> '"director" includes any person occupying the position of director, by whatever name called. (CA 2006, s. 250)'

This does, however, make it clear that 'director' is a function and not a job title. This has two implications:

(1)   A person can be a director, for the purposes of company law, even though he or she has a different title within the company.

(2)   A person can have director within his or her job title yet not fall within the *Companies Act* definition, for example, if he or she is described as a regional director but is not involved in the overall running of the business.

There are some dangers associated with the second situation, primarily those of holding out.

For some purposes a 'shadow director' is also treated as a director. A shadow director is defined as:

> '... a person in accordance with whose directions or instructions the directors of the company are accustomed to act.'

A person is not to be regarded as a shadow director by reason only that the directors act on advice given by him in a professional capacity. (CA 2006, s. 251(1) and (2))

This means that professional advisers, such as accounting firms or stockbrokers, will not normally be treated as shadow directors. The key point behind this exemption is that such persons only provide suggestions, they cannot force the company to act in accordance with this advice. While they may provide advice to the managers of the company, they are not involved in the company's management.

The main purposes for which shadow directors are treated as directors are:

- directors' duty to have regard to interests of employees;

- directors' long-term contracts of employment;

- substantial property transactions involving directors; and

- requirements concerning companies making loans, or similar, to directors and connected persons.

An exception is made in group situations.

A body corporate is not to be regarded as a shadow director of any of its subsidiary companies for the purposes of:

– Chapter 2 (general duties of directors);

– Chapter 4 (transactions requiring members' approval); or

– Chapter 6 (contract with sole member who is also a director) by reason only that the directors of the subsidiary are accustomed to act in accordance with its directions or instructions (CA 2006, s. 251(3)).

The provisions that apply to directors also usually apply to persons connected with a director. The basic rules on identifying a connected person under the *Companies Act* 2006 are:

'The following persons (and only those persons) are connected with a director of a company:

(a) members of the director's family (see s. 253);

(b) a body corporate with which the director is connected (as defined in s. 254);

(c) a person acting in his capacity as trustee of a trust:

(i) the beneficiaries of which include the director or a person who by virtue of paragraph (a) or (b) is connected with him; or

(ii) the terms of which confer a power on the trustees that may be exercised for the benefit of the director or any such person, other than a trust for the purposes of an employees' share scheme or a pension scheme;

(d) a person acting in his capacity as partner:

(i) of the director, or

(ii) of a person who, by virtue of paragraph paragraph (a), (b) or (c), is connected with that director;

(e) a firm that is a legal person under the law by which it is governed and in which:

(i) the director is a partner,

(ii) a partner is a person who, by virtue of paragraph (a), (b) or (c) is connected with the director, or

(iii) a partner is a firm in which the director is a partner or in which there is a partner who, by virtue of paragraph paragraph (a), (b) or (c), is connected with the director. (CA 2006, s. 252 (2))'

There is an exclusion where a person falls within the definition above, but is also a director in his or her own right.

As well as the very obvious relationships, this definition of a connected person covers all of the following:

- spouse or civil partner;
- any other person (whether of a different sex or the same sex) with whom the director lives as partner in an enduring family relationship;
- children or stepchildren;
- parents; and
- children or stepchildren of any other person with whom the director lives as partner in an enduring family relationship (and who are not children or stepchildren of the director), and who are under 18.

For the avoidance of doubt, the *Companies Act* 2006 notes that living in an 'enduring family relationship' does not apply to someone who lives with a director who is that director's grandparent, grandchild, sister, brother, aunt or uncle, nephew or niece.

It should be noted how close in practice this definition is to that of 'close family members' in Section 33, as discussed at **16.1.2.1**; care is needed, though, to ensure that the right version of the definition is used, depending on the purpose of the determination (i.e. is it for directors' remuneration disclosures, or disclosures of transactions with related parties).

In addition, the references to the beneficiaries of a trust in determining whether or not a trustee is a connected person also refer to the wider definition of family members. Directors are connected with a body corporate if they and any connected persons:

- are interested in shares which comprise 20% of the nominal value of the issued share capital of that body; or
- can exercise or control 20% or more of the votes at any general meeting of that body.

Directors control a body corporate if they and any connected persons:

- are interested in any equity shares of the body and can exercise or control any part of the voting power at any general meeting of that body; and

- together with the other directors of their company are interested in more than 50% of the share capital, or are entitled to exercise or control the exercise of more than 50% of the voting power at a general meeting.

Solely for the purposes of determining if a company is connected with the director, any other body corporate with which the director is associated is only deemed to be connected with him or her if it is connected under CA 2006, s. 252(2)(c) or (d) quoted earlier. A trustee of a trust, of which a beneficiary is a body corporate with which the director is connected, is not to be treated as a connected person.

Where the provisions refer to voting power controlled by a director this includes voting power controlled by a body corporate which he or she controls.

The most complicated part of these provisions is that dealing with shares or voting rights held by companies with which a director might be deemed to be connected. Three examples will give some idea of the impact of the provisions.

Example 16.4

A director owns 15% of the shares and voting rights in company A. He also owns 25% of the shares and voting rights in company B, and a further 10% of the shares and voting rights of company B are held by his wife. Company B owns 10% of the shares in company A. There are no other relevant connections.

The director is clearly connected with company B. Even ignoring his wife's holding, he controls 25% of the voting rights and shares in that company. However, he is not connected with company A. Although he owns 15% of the votes and shares, no control is considered to be exercised through company B, since only 35% of shares are held. A 15% holding is not sufficient to establish a connection.

Example 16.5

A director owns 15% of the shares and voting rights in company A. She also owns 45% of the shares and voting rights in company B, and a further 10% of the shares and voting rights of company B are held by her husband. Company B owns 10% of the shares in company A. There are no other relevant connections.

The director is clearly connected with company B. Even ignoring her husband's holding, she controls 45% of the voting rights and shares in that company. She is also connected with company A. The direct holding of 15% is added to the 10% of shares held by company B, since she controls company B, having a total of 55% of the shares and votes in issue. The total holding is then 25%, which is above the 20% threshold.

Example 16.6

A director owns 51% of company A. Company A owns 51% of company B. Company B owns 51% of company C. Company C owns 51% of company D. In all cases, the proportions apply to both shares and voting rights. The director is connected with companies A, B, C and D. This is despite the fact that the effective interest in company D is only 6.77% of the share capital. This arises because there is control throughout the chain. This can be seen as being very similar to the rules for inclusion of subsidiaries in group accounts; where there is a chain of control it is the extent of this chain and not the effective interest that determines the accounting treatment and disclosure.

16.4.2   *Aggregate remuneration*

Companies, other than small companies, are required to disclose various aggregate amounts in respect of directors:

(a) the aggregate amount of remuneration paid to or receivable by directors in respect of qualifying services;

    ...

(b) the aggregate of the amount of money paid to or receivable by directors, and the net value of assets (other than money and share options) received or receivable by directors under long term incentive schemes in respect of qualifying services; and

(c) the aggregate value of any company contributions:

   (i) paid, or treated as paid, to a pension scheme in respect of directors' qualifying services, and

   (ii) by reference to which the rate or amount of any money purchase benefits that may become payable will be calculated; ... (The *Large and Medium-sized Companies and Groups (Accounts and Reports) Regulations* 2008 (SI 2008/410), Sch. 5, para. 1)

Small companies are only required to disclose the total of these three amounts.

16.4.3   *Emoluments and remuneration*

Under the *Companies Act* 2006 'remuneration' is the term used when dealing with aggregate disclosures, i.e. for all directors, while 'emoluments' is used when referring to individual directors. 'Emoluments' are defined fairly widely to include salaries, fees and bonuses, expense allowances subject to income tax, and the estimated money value of any non-cash benefits. However, they exclude items which fall within any of the other categories that need to be disclosed. As a result, emoluments do not include:

- the value of share options granted to directors;

- the value of share options exercised by directors;

- pension contributions;

- pensions received; or

- amounts received under long-term incentive schemes.

'Qualifying services' are defined as:

> '... services as a director of the company, and his services while director of the company:
>
> (a)   as a director of any of its subsidiary undertakings; or
>
> (b)   otherwise in connection with the management of the affairs of the company or any of its subsidiary undertakings.' (The *Large and Medium-sized Companies and Groups (Accounts and Reports) Regulations* 2008 (SI 2008/410), Sch. 5, para. 15)

A special extended definition of a subsidiary is used for this purpose, and no other. Apart from normal subsidiary undertakings:

> 'Any reference in this Schedule to a subsidiary undertaking of the company, in relation to a person who is or was, while a director of the company, a director also, by virtue of the company's nomination (direct or indirect) of any other undertaking, includes that undertaking, whether or not it is or was in fact a subsidiary undertaking of the company.' (The *Large and Medium-sized Companies and Groups (Accounts and Reports) Regulations* 2008 (SI 2008/410), Sch. 5, para. 14(1))

Probably as a result of this wider definition, there is an exemption from disclosure if a company cannot obtain the necessary information from its 'subsidiaries':

> 'This Schedule requires information to be given only so far as it is contained in the company's books and papers or the company has the right to obtain it from the persons concerned.' (The *Large and Medium-sized Companies and Groups (Accounts and Reports) Regulations* 2008 (SI 2008/410), Sch. 5, para. 6)

The amount to be shown includes amounts paid by:

- the company;

- any of the company's subsidiary undertakings (using the wider definition included above); and

- any other person.

This also applies to all other disclosure requirements connected with directors' emoluments. The financial statements no longer need to distinguish between such amounts.

It does not include amounts which the director must pay over, or pay back, to the company or any of its subsidiary undertakings or to past or present members of the company or any of its subsidiaries. However, if such an amount is subsequently waived, then the amount should be shown as part of the directors' emoluments in the year in which the waiver takes place. They should be shown separately from emoluments earned during the year.

Disclosure is also required where such a balance has not been enforced after a period of two years.

Amounts paid to a person connected with a director are treated as if they had been paid to the director, but not if this would cause them to be treated twice.

The emoluments include all amounts receivable in respect of the year in question, whether or not they were actually received in that year. Where a sum is not receivable in respect of any particular period then it should be accounted for when received by the director.

It is notable that the definition of emoluments does not, at least theoretically, include *all* amounts paid to directors. Where part of a director's income from the company derives from work undertaken for the company, but not in connection with their duties as director or in connection with management, then that part of the income would not strictly fall within the definition. Nonetheless, the drawing of such a distinction is likely to be extremely difficult, if not impossible, in practice, and such amounts are almost universally included under directors' emoluments.

Direct payments to directors cause very few accounting problems. The more difficult areas are those of expense allowances and benefits in kind. Expense allowances are disclosable only in so far as they are subject to UK income tax. The reasoning behind this rule is presumably that amounts which are allowed for tax purposes do not usually provide anything other than an incidental benefit to the director. Their inclusion in the amount of directors' emoluments would mean that this figure would be overstated, by including business costs which should be treated elsewhere. Where an amount is charged to tax after the end of the relevant financial year then it should be disclosed as directors' emoluments in the earliest financial statements in which this is practicable, and should be disclosed separately.

Although CA 2006 requires disclosure of benefits other than cash at their 'estimated money value' this is not always a straightforward assessment. It would appear that the following procedures would arrive at a result consistent with the aims of the legislation:

- where the company has incurred a direct and identifiable cost in providing a benefit to a director, such as the hire of a motor car or the purchase of directors' indemnity insurance, this cost should be included within directors' emoluments;

- where there is no identifiable cost, for example where the company owns an asset that is used by a director, an estimate should be made of the market value of the benefit, and this should be included as part of directors' emoluments;

- only where neither of the methods above can be used should the taxable value of the benefit be used; and

- where there is no reasonable method of valuation, disclosure of the facts should be given, together with a statement explaining why such a valuation is not possible.

The amount of the taxable benefit is the least satisfactory of the possible methods, since tax rules are written for a specific purpose unconnected with accounting.

It should be noted that, since in some cases the market value of a benefit will be disclosed in the financial statements instead of the amount of any cost to the company, the directors' emoluments will not necessarily agree with the amount of directors' emoluments included in the company's accounting records. Similarly, where all of the employees of a company are directors the amount shown as directors' emoluments may be higher than the total staff costs.

16.4.4   Long-term incentive schemes

There is a requirement to provide separate disclosure of the aggregate amounts paid under long-term incentive schemes. A long-term incentive scheme is defined as:

'(1) ... an agreement or arrangement:

   (a)   under which money or other assets may become receivable by a director, and

   (b)   which includes one or more qualifying conditions with respect to service or performance which cannot be fulfilled within a single financial year.

(2)   For this purpose the following must be disregarded:

(a)   bonuses the amount of which falls to be determined by reference to service or performance within a single financial year;

(b)   compensation for loss of office, payments for breach of contract and other termination payments; and

(c)   retirement benefits.' (The *Large and Medium-sized Companies and Groups (Accounts and Reports) Regulations* 2008 (SI 2008/410), Sch. 5, para. 11)

The amount which needs to be disclosed includes both cash and the value of any non-cash assets. For this purpose non-cash assets always exclude share options and, in the case of companies other than listed companies, also exclude shares.

16.4.5   Pension contributions

There is a requirement for accounts to disclose the aggregate of the amounts paid to (or accrued in respect of) money purchase pension schemes for directors.

Where a scheme pays the higher of money purchase benefits or a defined benefit, the assessment of the nature of the scheme should be based on which seems most likely to apply, as judged at the end of the financial year.

Companies are also required to disclose:

- the number of directors who are accruing benefits under money purchase pension schemes; and

- the number of directors who are accruing benefits under defined benefit schemes.

There is no requirement to state the amounts attributable to directors under defined benefit schemes (although, as noted at **16.4.8**, there is additional disclosure required for excess retirement benefits).

16.4.6   Shares and share options

Unlisted companies are required to disclose:
- the number of directors who exercised share options; and

- the number of directors who received (or became entitled to) shares under long-term incentive schemes.

For these purposes, 'shares' include shares in the company or any group undertakings, and share warrants.

16.4.7   Highest-paid director

Disclosure of details of the emoluments of the highest-paid director is required only where the total directors' remuneration (excluding pension contributions) equals or exceeds £200,000. The information is never required for a small company.

Where the disclosure is needed, the following information must be given:

- the total emoluments, excluding pension contributions, of the highest-paid director;
- the amount of contributions to pension schemes attributable to the highest paid director's qualifying services in respect of which money purchase benefits may be payable;
- if the highest paid director exercised any share options, that fact should be disclosed;
- if any shares were received or receivable by that director in respect of qualifying services under a long-term incentive scheme, that fact should be disclosed; and
- if the highest paid director has performed qualifying services during the financial year by reference to which the rate or amount of any defined benefits that may become payable will be calculated, there must also be shown:
  - the amount at the end of the year of his accrued pension; and
  - where applicable, the amount at the end of the year of his accrued lump sum.

The accrued pension and accrued lump sum are based on the amounts payable to the director on reaching normal retirement age. They are to be calculated on the assumption that:

- the director left at the end of the year;
- there is no inflation from the end of the year to the director's retirement date;
- there is no commutation of the pension or inverse commutation of the lump sum; and
- there are no voluntary contributions from the director.

16.4.8   Excess retirement benefits

Companies, other than small companies, are required to disclose:

- the benefits paid to or receivable by directors under pension schemes; and

- the benefits paid to or receivable by past directors under pension schemes,

to the extent that these amounts are in excess of the benefits to which they were entitled on the date they first became eligible for benefits, or 31 March 1997, whichever is the later.

This disclosure is not required if the payments are made from a pension scheme which does not require additional funding as a result of the additional benefit, and where the additional amounts are available to all pensioner members of the schemes on the same basis.

If any amount needs to be disclosed, then any amounts paid other than in cash need to be shown separately.

16.4.9 Compensation for loss of office

All companies are required to show the aggregate amount of compensation to directors or past directors for loss of office. This includes all amounts in respect of loss of office as a director of the company, or any of its subsidiaries, and loss of any other office connected with the management of the company or any of its subsidiary undertakings. It includes amounts which are not paid in cash, which must be disclosed separately.

The amount also includes compensation for retirement, and any payments made which result from a breach of the person's contract with the company, whether as damages or in settlement or compromise of a claim for breach.

16.4.10 Sums paid to third parties

The aggregate amount of sums paid to third parties in respect of making the services of a director available should be disclosed. This applies whether the third party has made the director's services available as director, or otherwise in connection with management, and whether this is for the company or one of its subsidiaries. It includes amounts other than in cash, when the nature of the consideration needs to be disclosed. 'Third party' excludes the director himself, or a person connected with him or her, and the company or any of its subsidiaries.

16.4.11 Reconciling directors' remuneration with amounts paid to key management personnel

A set of accounts prepared under FRS 102 and UK company law currently needs to include totals for both 'key management personnel compensation in total' (paragraph 33.6) and aggregate directors' remuneration (although as noted at **16.2.1**, there is an exemption from disclosing key management personnel compensation where the directors and key management personnel are the same and directors' remuneration is required to be disclosed).

As can be seen from the discussions above, there could be several differences between these figures, either from the definitions of the individuals involved (statutory directors who are not key management personnel, and vice versa) or from amounts which are attributed value in one grouping and not in the other (Section 33, for instance, makes no mention of attributing a value to a reward to a director which has no incremental cost to the company, whereas as discussed at **16.4.3**, company law would seem to expect some attempt at valuing this).

A satisfactory note will reconcile the two as cleanly as possible. One attempt is shown below, though this would need to be tailored for particular circumstances, and the reconciliation would be much cleaner if the differences were only in the people included, or only in the amounts included.

	Directors	Other key management personnel	Adjustment for directors who are not key management personnel	Total key management personnel
Salary	X	X	(X)	X
Bonuses	X	X	(X)	X
Total compensation	**X**	**X**		**X**
Value of other benefits with no cost to the company	X			
Total directors' remuneration	**X**			

17 Public benefit entities

17.1 Scope of this section

As described in **1.2**, FRS 102 has a very broad scope. It is intended for all financial statements that are intended to give a true and fair view and do not apply IFRS, FRS 101 or FRS 105, not just those of limited companies.

Public benefit entities (PBEs) have some features or types of transaction that are particular to their nature and require special accounting treatment. To make it possible for such entities to use FRS 102, a small amount of additional guidance has been included, spread through the standard. All such paragraphs are prefixed 'PBE' and may only be used by entities that meet the definition:

> 'An entity whose primary objective is to provide goods or services for the general public, community or social benefit and where any **equity** is provided with a view to supporting the entity's primary objectives rather than with a view to providing a financial return to equity providers, shareholders or members.'

A footnote to the definition expands on this slightly, pointing out that to qualify as a PBE, an entity does not need to have activities that benefit the public as a whole, but may exist instead for the direct benefit of a particular group of people, although this may not be in the form of economic benefits to investors.

Paragraph PBE3.3A requires that a PBE may only apply the 'PBE' paragraphs if it makes an explicit and unreserved statement that it is a public benefit entity. Small PBEs applying Section 1A are encouraged to make this statement.

> **Application to micro-entities:** FRS 105 does not contain any provisions for PBEs as such entities would not qualify for the regime.

17.1.1 Charities

The most significant group of PBEs is charities, which by their nature will meet the definition.

Those charities that prepare accounts on an accruals (rather than cash) basis are also required to apply the FRS 102 Charities SORP. The SORP includes wide-ranging guidance on a large number of charity-specific accounting areas, and is beyond the scope of this guide.

In October 2018, the Charity Commission released Update Bulletin 2 to the Charities (FRS 102) SORP, which implements the changes proposed by the FRC in the Triennial Review of FRS 102 in Sections 4 and 5 of the Bulletin, together with a handful of other clarifications.

The FRS 102 Charities SORP requires charities to present a Statement of Financial Activities (SoFA) in place of the statement of comprehensive income required by FRS 102 (charitable companies need to present a statement of income and expenditure, which may be incorporated into the SoFA). There is no exception from the requirement in Section 5 of FRS 102 to produce a statement of comprehensive income, so care will be needed to ensure that sufficient headings and subtotals from the SORP format are used to comply with Section 5 too.

The FRS 102 Charities SORP applies to charities of all sizes. Whilst there is no mention of it in FRS 102, small charities will not in practice be able to make use of Section 1A as Bulletin 1 to the Charity SORP requires all charities to follow the FRS 102 SORP. The disclosure requirements in this generally exceed those in Section 1A, although there is an exemption from preparing a cash flow statement for charities whose gross income does not exceed £500k. Those wishing to prepare charity accounts should refer to *Preparing Charity Accounts*.

17.1.2 PBE groups

The concept of a 'public benefit entity group', defined in the Glossary as 'a public benefit entity parent and all of its wholly-owned subsidiaries' matters because in certain situations entities within a PBE group may apply the PBE-prefixed paragraphs even where they are not PBEs themselves. One example is at **17.2.3**, where all entities within a PBE group can apply the special accounting for concessionary loans, even if they are not PBEs themselves, providing the other conditions are met.

17.2 Areas of specific guidance in FRS 102

17.2.1 Incoming resources in non-exchange transactions

This accounting issue is addressed by paragraphs 34.64–34.74.

The transactions scoped in are those where the PBE receives something of value but does not pay for it with valuable consideration, with typical examples being the receipt of donations for sale by a charity shop, and the use by many charities of volunteers, who provide their time but are not remunerated. Paragraph PBE34.66 gives the examples of donations (of cash, goods and services) and legacies, but allows that other non-exchange transactions may also be in scope.

Government grants, although they do not involve an exchange transaction, are not in the scope of this section, since they are addressed separately by Section 24.

The basic accounting depends on whether the transaction imposes a performance condition on the recipient:

- if there are no performance conditions, the transaction is recognised in income when the resources are received or receivable;

- if there are performance conditions, the transaction is recognised in income when the performance conditions are met; and

- if resources are received before the criteria are met, the credit entry is to liabilities.

To value the resources, there are two possibilities set out in paragraph PBE34.73:

(a) donated services and facilities, that would otherwise have been purchased, are measured at the value to the entity;

(b) all other incoming resources are measured at the fair value of resources received or receivable.

To make sure these requirement are not too onerous for charities, the Appendix to Section 34, clarifies that:

- it may be impracticable, in some cases, to recognise incoming resources, and in these cases the income may instead be recognised when the resources are sold or redistributed. This means that charity shops, for instance, do not have to value bin bags full of donated clothes, but instead can recognise the donation as the clothes are sold on;

- if donated services come from a professional with clear normal charging structures, it would be expected that these are recognised as received as an expense or, if they relate to construction for instance, as an asset. However, paragraph PBE34B.11 states 'It is expected that contributions made by volunteers cannot be reasonably quantified and therefore these services shall not be recognised', though they must be disclosed.

The appendix also gives a little more guidance on measurement, and on the treatment of legacies.

17.2.2   PBE combinations

The guidance on PBE combinations appears in paragraphs 34.75–34.86.

While at first glance it may not be clear why PBEs need specific guidance on this issue, queries arose during the drafting of FRS 102, over the common situation where PBE combinations take place with no consideration changing hands, either because a business is received as a gift or donation, or because two smaller entities are genuinely merged.

In the first case, where the combination is in substance a gift, the accounting is as for a business combination, but with some alterations. If positive goodwill appears to arise (that is, where the fair value of the assets received is lower than the fair value of liabilities assumed), a loss is recognised immediately (rather than an asset on the balance sheet). Conversely, if the fair value of assets received is higher than the fair value of liabilities taken on, the resulting credit is all recognised immediately rather than being released based on the consumption of non-monetary assets, as would normally be the case for negative goodwill.

This guidance makes sense because there does appear to be a genuine difference between this type of combination and a typical commercial combination – entities that are not PBEs are unlikely to engage in zero-consideration combinations (apart from occasionally where the acquired business has significant liabilities and the consideration is zero or a nominal sum).

For merger accounting, the need for guidance is less obvious, since Section 19 of FRS 102 already sets out a merger accounting method, albeit only for group reconstructions. A merger is defined in the Glossary as follows:

> 'An **entity combination** that results in the creation of a new reporting entity formed from the combining parties, in which the controlling parties of the combining entities come together in a partnership for the mutual sharing of risks and benefits of the newly formed entity and in which no party to the combination in substance obtains **control** over any other, or is otherwise seen to be dominant.

> All of the following criteria must be met for an entity combination to meet the definition of a merger:

> (a)   no party to the combination is portrayed as either acquirer or acquiree, either by its own board or management or by that of another party to the combination;

> (b)   there is no significant change to the classes of beneficiaries of the combining entities or the purpose of the benefits provided as a result of the combination; and

all parties to the combination, as represented by the members of the board, participate in establishing the management structure of the combined entity and in selecting the management personnel, and such decisions are made on the basis of a consensus between the parties to the combination rather than purely by exercise of voting rights.'

The version of merger accounting for PBEs has no substantive differences from that in Section 19, although the language used is slightly different, referring for instance to the 'results' rather than 'total comprehensive income' of the combining parties, presumably in recognition of the differing captions in some PBE primary statements. The PBE guidance also omits any comment on the accounting for share capital, presumably because it is irrelevant to many PBEs. If two combining PBEs do have share capital and need to account for a merger, there is nothing prohibiting them from looking to the guidance in Section 19 by analogy.

17.2.2.1 Disclosures

Where a PBE combination is accounted for as a merger, the newly formed entity's financial statements must disclose the following information (paragraph PBE34.86):

(a) the names and descriptions of the combining entities or businesses;

(b) the date of the merger; and

(c) an analysis of the principal components of the current year's total comprehensive income to indicate:

  (i)   the amounts relating to the newly formed merged entity for the period after the date of the merger; and

  (ii) the amounts relating to each party to the merger up to the date of the merger.

(d) an analysis of the previous year's total comprehensive income between each party to the merger;

(e) the aggregate carrying value of the net assets of each party to the merger at the date of the merger; and

(f)   the nature and amount of any significant adjustments required to align accounting policies and an explanation of any further adjustments made to net assets as a result of the merger.

17.2.2.2 Transition

Paragraph 35.10(q) sets out a transition exemption allowing PBEs not to apply the above requirements for PBE combinations that were effected before the transition date. As with the main business combinations exemption, though, if a PBE chooses to apply the accounting to any combination before the transition date, it must apply it to all combinations that took place after that date.

17.2.3   PBE concessionary loans

The guidance on concessionary loans is very carefully delimited so it only applies to arrangements that explicitly meet the definition of a concessionary loan, being:

'A loan made or received between a public benefit entity or an entity within a public benefit entity group and another party:

(a)   at below the prevailing market rate of interest;

(b)   that is not repayable on demand; and

(c)   is for the purposes of furthering the objectives of the public benefit entity or public benefit entity parent.'

Note that the definition includes loans made or received by a member of a PBE group, so its scope is wider than it may initially appear. In a very large group that includes just one PBE, if any group entity makes or receives a loan meeting the above conditions then the special accounting is available. This may apply in groups where one entity is used for most financing arrangements, including those relating to the activities of the PBE.

For loans in the scope of this definition, paragraph PBE34.89 allows entities two choices: apply Section 11 or 12 of FRS 102 as appropriate (that is, follow normal financial instrument accounting), or follow a special concessionary loan treatment as follows:

- measure the loan initially at the amount paid or received;

- adjust the carrying amount in subsequent periods to reflect any accrued interest payable or receivable;

- recognise an impairment loss where a loan made is irrecoverable;

- present concessionary loans made and those received as separate line items on the statement of financial position or in the notes;

- split these amounts between those repayable or receivable within one year and after more than one year;

- disclose the measurement basis used, and any other relevant accounting policies; and

- disclose the terms and conditions, and the value of concessionary loans committed but not taken up at the year end.

Example 17.1

This example illustrates the different accounting outcomes depending on whether a recipient of a concessionary loan chooses to account for it under Section 11 or under the special provisions of Section 34.

Charity C receives a loan of £50,000 from a supporter. The loan has a three year life, and bears no interest.

Option 1 – use Section 11

The loan is a basic financial instrument in the scope of Section 11.

Accordingly it is initially measured at the present value of future payments (as it constitutes a financing transaction). Applying a market rate of interest for similar debt of 8%, the loan would be recorded at £39,683 (£50,000 payable in three years' time, discounted at 8%) and the discount will then be unwound over the loan life, giving an interest charge each year.

This would lead to the following balances and charges over the life, which without rounding's would lead to the settlement amount of £50,000 after three years.

Year	Opening carrying value	Interest charge	Closing carrying value
1	39,683	3,175	42,858
2	42,858	3,429	46,287
3	46,287	3,703	49,990

Option 2 – use Section 34

Under this option, the loan is initially recorded at £50,000, the amount received.

Because no interest is payable or receivable, and the loan is a liability and therefore cannot be impaired, no accounting entries are made during the loan's life, until it is settled after three years.

The above example has a notable omission – in 'option 1' the initial double entry is not clarified. Since the cash amount received is fixed, and the initially recorded amount is lower than this, there is a balancing credit to be recognised somewhere. The most appropriate treatment would be recognition of this credit immediately in income, representing the value transferred by the lender's having agreed an interest-free loan. This is consistent with the accounting for non-exchange transactions where there is no performance condition: the resources (the loan) are received immediately, and there are no performance conditions, so the income arising is also recognised immediately.

17.3   Other areas of concern for PBEs

There was considerable debate, in the drafting process for FRS 102, about the scope of any additional guidance for PBEs. The areas covered by Section 34 are those where there was a broad consensus; however for some PBEs there will be accounting issues that are not covered here. It may be the case that other areas of the standard provide sufficient guidance (for instance, PBEs in receipt of government grants should find them adequately covered in Section 24). If this is not the case, though, they will need to use the provisions in paragraph 10.5 requiring that they first look to elsewhere in the standard, then to any relevant SORP, and then to the recognition and measurement criteria and concepts and the pervasive principles in Section 10.

18 Other guidance

Here we look at some of the other specialised areas for which FRS 102 provides guidance.

> **Application to micro-entities:** There is no guidance in FRS 105 for specialised activities other than agriculture as micro-entities are unlikely to enter into these kinds of activities. In rare cases where they do, they should select an appropriate accounting policy in accordance with Section 8 of FRS 105.

18.1 Service concession arrangements

18.1.1 Definitions

Paragraph 34.12 defines a service concession arrangement as:

> 'An arrangement whereby a public sector body, or a public benefit entity (the grantor) contracts with a private sector entity (the operator) to construct (or upgrade), operate and maintain infrastructure assets for a specified period of time (concession period). The operator is paid for its services over the period of the arrangement. A common feature of a service concession arrangement is the public service nature of the obligation undertaken by the operator, whereby the arrangement contractually obliges the operator to provide services to, or on behalf of, the grantor for the benefit of the public.'

A typical example of a service concession arrangement is the construction of a section of motorway where the operator has the right to charge a toll for use of the road; another example is the construction of public use properties such as hospitals where the operator hands over the property for the duration of the contract, and interest reverts to the grantor at the end.

Paragraph 34.12A adds two further conditions: first that the grantor must control or regulate the services provided by the operator using the infrastructure, to whom, and at what price, and also that the grantor must control any significant residual interest at the end of the term. In the special case where there is no residual value, then all focus is on control or regulation of services.

If a service concession arrangement contains a group of contracts, then these are reviewed to determine whether they should be accounted for together or separately, based on whether they are linked together in such a way that 'the commercial effect cannot be understood without reference to them as a whole'.

Example 18.1

The Government enters into contracts with companies Q and R to build two sections of motorway at opposite ends of the country.

Company Q has an agreed payment scheme relating to the construction, and then has the right to charge a fixed toll per vehicle, increasing each year with inflation as specified in the agreement.

Company R is to be less well remunerated at the outset but has the right to set its own tolls, and intends to analyse the pricing carefully to maximise revenues over the contract life, through the combination of price and volume.

It is likely that the arrangement with Q will be accounted for as a service concession arrangement, but the arrangement with R will not, because R has the discretion to set prices.

For R, the arrangement will fall into the scope of Section 23, probably accounted for as a construction contract.

18.1.2   Accounting by operators

Arrangements that meet the definition of a service concession arrangement merit special treatment because, unlike with a normal construction contract, there is not a clear cut point when risks pass, nor does the operator have proper control of the asset, either during or subsequent to construction.

The guidance focuses on how to account for the infrastructure asset, to which one of two models will be applied.

18.1.2.1   Financial asset model

This model applies where the operator receives a financial asset – 'an unconditional contractual right to receive a specified or determinable amount of cash or another financial asset from, or at the direction of, the grantor in return for constructing (or upgrading) the infrastructure assets, and then operating and maintaining the asset for a specified period of time'.

The operator initially recognises a financial asset measured at the fair value of the consideration received or receivable, based on the fair value of construction services provided. After this, the financial asset is accounted for under Sections 11 or 12, the parts of the standard that cover financial instruments.

When classifying the financial asset as basic or other, any payment that is contingent on the operator ensuring that the infrastructure meets specified quality or efficiency requirements does not in itself prevent its classification as basic.

18.1.2.2   Intangible asset model

This model is used where the operator receives an intangible asset, being the right to charge for use of the infrastructure asset (though note that, in order to meet the definition of a service concession arrangement, this must be on the grantor's terms). This cannot be a financial asset because there is no unconditional right to receive any cash at all, if no one uses the asset.

Under this model, the operator recognises an intangible asset to the extent that it has the right to charge users for the use of the infrastructure asset, again initially recognised at the fair value of consideration received or receivable based on the fair value of the construction services provided. This is then subsequently accounted for (including amortisation and impairment) in accordance with Section 18.

Note that for both models, the initial valuation of the asset does not take account of expected future cash flows, except in so far as their nature (contractually committed or otherwise) affects the classification. Instead, it is based on the costs to date: the future cash flows are mainly relevant for testing the resulting asset for impairment based on the guidance in either Section 11 or Section 18, for financial assets and intangible assets, respectively.

In the real world, contracts may not be simple to classify as one or the other of these types. Paragraph 34.13 deals with this possibility, stating that 'to the extent that the grantor has given an unconditional guarantee of payment for the construction (or upgrade) of the infrastructure assets, the operator has a financial asset; to the extent that the operator receives a right to charge the public for using the service the operator has an intangible asset'. This would apply where, for instance, the operator's risk was managed somewhat by its receiving guaranteed payment from the grantor, but it was incentivised to provide the best possible asset and service by having the right to increase its profits by charging the public for usage too.

18.1.2.3   Revenue

There is no guidance for revenue specific to service concession arrangements. Instead operators are directed to Section 23 (discussed in **10.4.2** of this guide).

18.1.2.4   Borrowing costs

The default position for borrowing costs incurred by operators of service concession arrangements will be to expense these costs. If, however, the operator has the right to charge for use of the asset, such that the intangible asset model applies, then the option in Section 25 to capitalise borrowing costs may be taken.

18.1.3   Accounting by grantors

The accounting for grantors is simpler than that for operators – in particular, there is no choice of models, as the grantor is always required to treat the arrangements as if it were the lessee in a finance lease.

So, it will recognise an asset, being the infrastructure asset, and an associated liability, valued initially in the same way as any finance lease liability (Section 20 of the standard, and **8.3.3.2** of this guide). The subsequent accounting for the lease liability also follows this model, and the infrastructure asset is recognised as property, plant and equipment or an intangible asset, as appropriate, and then accounted for under the relevant section of the standard.

18.1.4   Transition

Paragraph 35.10(i) allows a significant exemption for operators in service concession arrangements. For any such arrangements that were already in place at the transition date, an operator need not apply Section 34, and may continue with the accounting that it was already using.

This will have a greater impact for some preparers than others, but could prove very welcome for those with a significant number of such arrangements.

18.1.5   Disclosures

There are specific disclosures operators and grantors need to make, which are as follows:

'An operator and a grantor shall disclose information that enables users of the entity's financial statements to evaluate the nature and extent of relevant risks arising from service concession arrangements. This information shall typically include, but is not limited to, a description of the arrangement, including any rights, obligations or options arising, and any significant terms of the arrangement that may affect the amount, timing and certainty of future cash flows.

An operator shall disclose the amount of revenue, profits or losses and other income recognised in the period on exchanging construction services for a financial asset or an intangible asset.'

Preparers should also consider if they need to include the disclosure requirements in the relevant sections of FRS 102 (PPE, intangible assets, financial assets, leases) for their particular situation.

18.2 Financial institutions

Because the scope of FRS 102 is so wide, it allows in some financial institutions, for instance unlisted building societies. There was some concern during the process of establishing this scope, over how to ensure that these specialist, perhaps higher-risk, entities could be required to do enough in their accounts: the FRC did not wish to include large quantities of niche content within the standard, but it still needed to be suited to all entities that might be required or choose to apply it.

This has been dealt with by providing a substantial number of additional disclosure requirements, which financial institutions other than retirement benefit plans (see **18.3**) must comply with on top of the requirements of Sections 11 and 12. The requirements apply to the individual accounts of a financial institution and to the consolidated accounts of any group containing a financial institution, if the financial instruments that financial institution holds are material to the group.

Clearly, the precise definition of a financial institution is vital since being scoped into these paragraphs of Section 34 will lead to substantially more disclosures. The definition, reproduced in full here, reflects some very careful work on behalf of the FRC in its attempt to capture precisely the types of entity that have exposure to additional risks from financial instruments and are, in some sense, responsible for looking after others' money (this obviously excludes the general obligations of company directors to fulfil fiduciary duties in respect of their shareholders' funds).

From the Glossary, a financial institution is any of the following:

'(a) a bank which is:

  (i) a firm with a Part A permission which includes accepting deposits and:

    (a) which is a credit institution; or

    (b) whose Part A permission includes a requirement that it complies with the rules in the General Prudential sourcebook and the Prudential sourcebook for Banks, Building Societies and Investment Firms relating to banks, but which is not a building society, a friendly society or a credit union;

  (ii) an EEA bank which is a full credit institution;

(b) a building society which is defined in section 119(1) of the Building Societies Act 1986 as a building society incorporated (or deemed to be incorporated) under that act;

(c)   a credit union, being a body corporate registered under the Industrial and Provident Societies Act 1986 as a building society incorporated (or deemed to be incorporated) under that act;

(d)   custodian bank or broker-dealer;

(e)   an entity that undertakes the business of effecting or carrying out **insurance contracts**, including general and life assurance entities;

(f)   an incorporated friendly society incorporated under the Friendly Societies Act 1992 or a registered friendly society registered under section 7(1)(a) of the Friendly Societies Act 1974 or any enactment which it replaced, including any registered branches;

(g)   an investment trust, Irish Investment Company, venture capital trust, mutual fund, exchange traded fund, unit trust, open-ended investment company (OEIC); or

(h)   [deleted];

(i)   any other entity whose principal activity is similar to those listed above but is not specifically included in that list.

A **parent** whose sole activity is to hold investment in other group entities is not a financial institution.'

The disclosure requirements are too extensive to reproduce in full here, but cover the following areas:

- significance of financial instruments for financial position and performance;
- impairment;
- fair value;
- nature and extent of risks arising from financial instruments;
- credit risk;
- liquidity risk;
- market risk; and
- capital.

When a financial institution has made the accounting policy choice to apply the recognition and measurement provisions of IFRS 9, it shall disclose information that enables users of its financial statements to understand the effect of credit risk on the amount, timing and uncertainty of future cash flows.

18.3   Retirement benefit plans

This part of the section deals with the requirements set out in FRS 102 in relation to retirement benefit plans.

With two basic exceptions, FRS 102 deals with retirement benefit plans in relation to presentation and disclosure. Most of the requirements in relation to such plans consist of references to other parts of the standard in relation to items that are likely to be of relevance to retirement benefit plans or deal with the disclosure requirements with which they should comply.

The first exception is that the financial statements of retirement benefit plans are not required to recognise any liability in respect of the obligation to provide retirement benefits. Such obligations are dealt with in the actuarial information that is provided along with the financial statements.

Because of this omission, a retirement benefit plan does not provide a statement of financial position, but a statement of net assets available for benefits. This is very clearly not the same thing.

The second exception is that there is wider use of fair value than would often be applied for other types of entity.

This guide is not intended to provide comprehensive coverage of the accounting issues that face retirement benefit plans that prepare financial statements in accordance with FRS 102. It is intended solely to provide a brief summary of the applicable requirements included within the standard.

18.3.1   Scope

In principle, all of the requirements that apply to any entity which prepares financial statements in accordance with FRS 102 also apply to a retirement benefit plan, except where the standard says otherwise.

Of course in practice, most retirement benefit plans will find that many of the requirements of the standard do not apply to them. This is not because they are strictly outside the scope of those requirements, just that they do not do, or have, the things with which the standard deals.

The special requirements of the standard apply to retirement benefit plans as defined. The Glossary describes these as:

'Arrangements whereby an entity provides benefits for employees on or after termination of service (either in the form of an annual **income** or as a lump sum) when such benefits, or the contributions towards them, can be determined or estimated in advance of retirement from the provisions of a document or from the entity's practice.'

It is not to be expected that this definition will cause many problems in practice, although it is based wholly on the perspective of the employer, and not on the perspective of the arrangement that is being considered as a plan. It has clearly been drafted for the purposes of dealing with the accounting consequences for an employer of being a party to a retirement benefit arrangement, and not for the purposes of the accounting consequences for the plan.

The requirements cover both defined benefit and defined contribution plans, as well as those which have elements of both. Paragraph 34.34 states:

'An entity applying this FRS that is a **retirement benefit plan** shall also apply the requirements of paragraphs 34.35 to 34.48. A retirement benefit plan may be a **defined benefit plan**, a **defined contribution plan**, or have both defined benefit and defined contribution elements. The **financial statements** shall distinguish between defined benefit and defined contribution elements, where **material**.'

For most purposes, and other than the separate disclosure required in the paragraph above, the standard does not distinguish between defined benefit and defined contribution plans for the purposes of accounting by the plan itself. There are exceptions to this which are dealt with in the notes below.

18.3.2   Accounting requirements

18.3.2.1   Primary statements

The primary statements prepared by a retirement benefit plan are not the same as those that are required for the majority of entities that fall within the scope of FRS 102.

Retirement benefit plans are exempted in full from the requirements for a complete set of financial statements that apply to other entities. Under paragraph 34.35 instead:

'… The financial statements of a retirement benefit plan shall contain as part of the financial statements:

(a)   a statement of changes in **net assets available for benefits** (which can also be called a Fund Account) …;

(b)   a statement of net assets available for benefits …; and

(c)   **notes**, comprising its significant **accounting policies** and other explanatory information.'

These statements are quite different from those required for other entities. The statement of changes in net assets available for benefits contains elements that are analogous to both a statement of comprehensive income and a statement of changes in equity, but in neither case is the analogy that close.

The statement of net assets available for benefits has elements in common with a statement of financial position or balance sheet, but omits the single largest liability of the plan; the liability to pay retirement benefits in the future. There is no real equivalent of equity. Net assets available for benefits are defined in the Glossary as:

> 'The **assets** of a plan less **liabilities** other than the actuarial **present value** of promised retirement benefits.'

This paragraph also reimposes the requirement for notes, which was automatically removed by exempting retirement benefit plans from the normal requirements for a complete set of financial statements.

18.3.2.2   Basic accounting treatments

The basic accounting treatments that apply to retirement benefit plans are set out very briefly and simply in paragraph 34.36:

> 'At each **reporting date**, the net assets available for benefits shall be measured in accordance with paragraph 28.15(b). Changes in fair value shall be recognised in the statements of changes in net assets available for benefits.'

Paragraph 28.15(b), which is drafted by reference to the employer, states:

> 'the **fair value** at the reporting date of plan assets (if any) out of which the obligations are to be settled. Paragraphs 11.27 to 11.32 establish requirements for determining the fair values of those plan assets, except that, if the asset is an insurance policy that exactly matches the amount and timing of some or all of the benefits payable under the plan, the fair value of the asset is deemed to be the present value of the related obligation.'

The reference to paragraphs 11.27–11.32 is to the guidance on the determination of fair value, in the context of financial instruments. This guidance is covered in **7.3.4** of this guide.

This paragraph requires retirement benefit plans to record an asset in respect of an insurance policy that exactly matches some or all of the retirement benefits payable under the plan. These are recorded at fair value, being the present value of the related obligation. This requirement is further clarified in the FRS 102 Pensions SORP, which explains that although the policies may be intended to match certain obligations, the trustees are not legally discharged of their obligations in these circumstances and the asset must therefore be recorded.

The exception to this is where trustees purchase individual insurance policies in the name of individual beneficiaries. In these circumstances the intention is usually to discharge the trustees of their legal obligations in respect of those individual beneficiaries. Accordingly, no asset would be recognised as the legal transfer of obligations has taken place.

In other words, it is essential to identify whether or not the trustees remain legally responsible for the discharge of retirement benefits.

18.3.2.3   Statement of changes in net assets available for benefits

Paragraph 34.37 sets out very clearly the items that must be included in a statement of changes in net assets available for benefits, which may also be called a fund account:

'The financial statements of a retirement benefit plan, whether defined contribution or defined benefit, shall present the following in the statement of changes in net assets available for benefits:

(a)   employer contributions;

(b)   employee contributions;

(c)   investment income such as interest and dividends;

(d)   other income;

(e)   benefits paid or payable (analysed, for example, as retirement, death and disability benefits, and lump sum payments);

(f)   administrative expenses;

(g)   other expenses;

(h)   taxes on income;

(i)   profits and losses on disposal of investments and changes in value of investments; and

(j)   transfers in; and

(k)   payments to and on account of leaver.'

While this does not quite amount to a format, it comes fairly close.

18.3.2.4   Statement of net assets available for benefits

The requirements in relation to the statement of net assets available for benefits, set out in paragraph 34.38 are even shorter, and on the face of it provide considerable flexibility on format:

'The financial statements of a retirement benefit plan, whether defined contribution or defined benefit, shall present the following in the statement of net assets available for benefits:

(a)   **assets** at the end of the period suitably classified; and

(b)   **liabilities** other than the actuarial **present value** of promised retirement benefits.'

Retirement benefit plans do not tend to hold the variety of assets that may be held by trading entities, and a requirement that they be 'suitably classified' is probably sufficient. Similarly, the lack of detail on liabilities cause few issues since retirement benefit plans are unlikely to have many major liabilities which fall to be recorded.

There is also a requirement that the basis of valuation of assets has to be included in the notes to the financial statements.

18.3.3 Disclosures

18.3.3.1 General disclosure requirements

FRS 102 notes that where a retirement benefit plan has assets which are not financial instruments held at fair value then the disclosure requirements normally applicable to assets of that type will also apply to the retirement benefit plan. It gives the example of an investment property where a plan would need to give the details normally required for such properties. This is a slightly odd requirement, which it can only be assumed was included for the avoidance of doubt. Given that, as noted above, retirement benefits plans are theoretically subject to all of the requirements of FRS 102, except where specifically excluded or outside the scope, then the same result would have been reached had this paragraph not been included.

Many of the assets likely to be held by retirement benefit plans are financial instruments and, as noted above, these are required to be stated at fair value even where that would not always be the case were such items held by other entities. Because of the importance of financial instruments, it is not surprising that FRS 102 contains in paragraph 34.40 a requirement that:

> 'A retirement benefit plan shall disclose information that enables users of its financial statements to evaluate the significance of financial instruments for its **financial position** and **performance**.'

The exact import of this requirement is not made clear in the standard. It is very similar to paragraphs in IFRS 7. This paragraph is assumed to be intended to be more than an introduction to the paragraphs that follow. As such, it must impose an overarching requirement to disclose relevant information, even where this goes beyond the specific examples that appear in the paragraphs that follow. (This is consistent with the intent behind the similar paragraphs in IFRS 7.) This does not mean that there will be many cases where additional information is required – the FRC has populated the following paragraphs with the matters that it considers to be adequate to meet such overarching requirements in the majority of cases – but the possibility needs to be borne in mind. In rare cases, it might be considered that there is relevant information that has not been captured by the provision of the specific disclosures in the standard and in such cases this paragraph would require its inclusion.

18.3.3.2 Categories

FRS 102 contains a general requirement, in paragraph 34.41, for an analysis of the financial instruments held by the plan:

'A retirement benefit plan shall disclose a disaggregation of the statement of net assets available for benefits by class of financial instrument. A class is a grouping of financial instruments that is appropriate to the nature of the information disclosed and that takes into account the characteristics of those financial instruments.'

The requirement is deliberately set at a level that allows flexibility in determining the categories that are to be used. This allows each plan to provide the information in a way that is appropriate to the holdings of the plan.

18.3.3.3   Fair value

There is also a requirement for details of the basis on which the fair value of financial instruments which are held at fair value has been determined. Paragraph 34.42 states:

'For financial instruments held at fair value in the statement of net assets available for benefits, a retirement benefit plan shall disclose for each class of financial instrument, an analysis of the level in the following fair value hierarchy into which the fair value measurements are categorised. A fair value measurement is categorised in its entirety on the basis of the lowest level input that is significant to the fair value measurement in its entirety.

–   Level 1: The unadjusted quoted price in an active market for identical assets or liabilities that the entity can access at the measurement date.

–   Level 2: Inputs other than quoted prices included within Level 1 that are observable (ie developed using market data) for the asset or liability, either directly or indirectly.

–   Level 3: Inputs are unobservable (ie for which market data is unavailable) for the asset or liability.'

This means that fair value disclosures made by retirement benefit schemes and financial institutions are aligned with those in IFRS 13. However, the FRC has acknowledged that there is something of a mismatch, since other entities look to the hierarchy in Section 11.

18.3.3.4   Risks

As with both the general disclosure requirement and categorisation, FRS 102 deliberately provides high-level guidance on disclosure of risk. The disclosures required include both quantitative and qualitative information. The basic requirement is set out in paragraph 34.43:

'A retirement benefit plan shall disclose information that enables users of its financial statements to evaluate the nature and extent of **credit risk** and **market risk** arising from financial instruments to which the retirement benefit plan is exposed at the end of the **reporting period**.'

This is then made more specific in relation to credit and market risk in paragraph 34.44:

'For each type of credit and market risk arising from financial instruments, a retirement benefit plan shall disclose:

(a)   the exposures to risk and how they arise;

(b)   its objectives, policies and processes for managing the risk and the methods used to measure the risk; and

(c)   any changes in (a) or (b) from the previous period.'

Such disclosure will be primarily descriptive.

Paragraph 34.45 then provides more detailed requirements in relation to credit risk.

'A retirement benefit plan shall disclose by class of financial instrument:

(a)   The amount that best represents its maximum exposure to credit risk at the end of the reporting period. This disclosure is not required for financial instruments whose **carrying amount** best represents the maximum exposure to credit risk.

(b)   A description of collateral held as security and of other credit enhancements, and the extent to which these mitigate credit risk.

(c)   The amount by which any related credit **derivatives** or similar instruments mitigate that maximum exposure to credit risk.

(d)   Information about the credit quality of financial assets that are neither past due nor impaired.'

Whilst the disclosure requirements may appear onerous, there will be many cases where the level of information that actually needs to be provided is not as excessive as it might first appear. The modification in the first point is important, as in many cases the maximum exposure to credit risk will be the same as the carrying amount of the asset. As the standard says, in such a situation no further disclosure is required.

Similarly, many retirement benefit plans may have no collateral held as security nor credit derivatives, or similar, that have been used to mitigate the maximum exposure to credit risk.

The one disclosure that will be required in virtually all cases is information concerning the credit quality of financial assets which are neither past due nor impaired. This will apply, for example, where a retirement benefit plan has a holding of corporate bonds. In this case, the credit ratings applicable to the bond portfolio would need to be disclosed.

FRS 102 also requires disclosure in the relatively uncommon situation where a retirement benefit plan obtains financial or non-financial assets during the period by either taking possession of the collateral that it holds or calling on any other credit enhancements, such as guarantees, which may have. If the assets which are obtained in this manner meet the recognition criteria, which will be derived from the relevant section of FRS 102 applying to assets of that type, then the plan will be required to disclose:

- the nature and the carrying amount of the assets that have been obtained; and

- its policies for disposing of or retaining such assets, if the assets are not of a kind that is readily convertible into cash.

18.3.3.5   Actuarial liabilities in defined benefit plans

Whilst defined benefit plans are not required to account for any liability in respect of the retirement benefits that are offered under the plan, they are required to provide some actuarial information, as indeed they long have. Under paragraph 34.48:

> 'A defined benefit plan shall disclose, in a report alongside the financial statements, information regarding the actuarial present value of promised retirement benefits including:
>
> (a)   a statement of the actuarial present value of promised retirement benefits, based on the most recent valuation of the scheme;
>
> (b)   the date of the most recent valuation of the scheme; and
>
> (c)   the significant actuarial assumptions made and the method used to calculate the actuarial present value of promised retirement benefits.'

As it is made clear, this report does not form part of the financial statements.

18.4   Funding commitments

The guidance on funding commitments is set out in paragraphs 34.57–34.63, with compulsory additional guidance in Appendix A to Section 34.

There is no formal definition of a funding commitment, with 34.57 only saying that it applies to 'an entity that commits to provide resources to other entities', except for commitments to provide a loan, which are dealt with in Section 11 (**see 7.3**).

18.4.1   Accounting

The broad principle for accounting for a funding commitment is that an entity recognises a liability and a corresponding expense if and only if (paragraph 34.59):

> '(a)   the definition and recognition criteria for a liability have been satisfied;

(b)   the obligation (which may be a constructive obligation) is such that the entity cannot realistically withdraw from it; and

(c)   the entitlement of the other party to the resources does not depend on the satisfaction of performance-related conditions.'

With reference to the final point, any commitments that are performance-related are recognised when the performance-related conditions are met.

Unsurprisingly, the liability (if recognised) is measured at the present value of the resources committed – this reflects the general point in the Section that the requirements of Section 21 *Provisions and contingencies* are taken into account.

There are no surprises in this accounting, which seems to add little to the requirements already in Section 2 (in respect of the definition of liabilities) and Section 21 (in respect of provisions). In practice, the intention seems to be to capture situations where an entity is unavoidably committed to making future payments but might, without this part of the standard, avoid recognising a liability on the grounds that the obligation does not quite meet the definition either of a financial liability or of a provision.

The appendix provides a little further guidance, noting that a general statement of intent to provide resources to certain classes of potential beneficiaries does not give rise to a liability – this would apply where, for instance, a charity had as one of its stated goals the provisions of bursaries to a certain category of deserving candidate. The appendix also notes that the intended recipient of funding must be aware of the commitment, in order for a liability to arise. Finally, the appendix notes that some conditions within a commitment will not constitute performance conditions (and hence, will not prevent immediate recognition of an expense and liability). This might apply, for instance, when the condition is a purely administrative one, such as 'a requirement to provide an annual financial report to the grantor' (34A.5), though this same paragraph is careful to distinguish this from a more substantive requirement such as a the need to provide a statement to the grantor of how funds will be used, without which those funds will not be provided.

18.4.2   Disclosures

The disclosure requirements in respect of funding commitments are set out in paragraphs 34.62–34.63:

'An entity that has made a commitment shall disclose the following:

(a)   the commitment made;

(b)   the time-frame of that commitment;

(c)   any performance-related conditions attached to that commitment; and

(d)   details of how that commitment will be funded.

The above disclosures may be made in aggregate, providing that such aggregation does not obscure significant information. However, separate disclosure shall be made for recognised and unrecognised commitments.'

19   Transition to FRS 102

19.1   Scope of this section

This section covers Section 35 *Transition to this FRS*.

Section 35 applies to a first-time adopter of FRS 102; that is an entity preparing its first set of financial statements that conform to the FRS. These are defined as 'the first financial statements in which the entity makes an explicit and unreserved statement in those financial statements of compliance with this FRS'.

An entity's date of transition to FRS 102 is defined as the beginning of the earliest period for which it presents full comparative information. By now, companies will have transitioned to FRS 102 from either old UK GAAP or the FRSSE, but Section 35 still applies where a company adopts FRS 102 having previously applied FRS 105 or IFRS.

Section 35 can also be applied where an entity previously applied FRS 102 then changed to another GAAP. Paragraph 35.2 states that '... an entity that has applied FRS 102 in a previous reporting period, but whose most recent previous annual financial statements did not contain an explicit and unreserved statement of compliance with this FRS, must either apply this section or else apply FRS 102 retrospectively ... as if the entity had never stopped applying this FRS'. In other words, on re-adoption of FRS 102, an entity can either use Section 35 again or restate fully, as if FRS 102 had never ceased to be used.

Under IFRS, IFRS 1 sets out transition procedures and a list of exemptions.

More detailed guidance on transition to FRS 102 and FRS 105, including a step-by-step checklist and worked examples, can be found in *Transition Guide: FRS 102 and FRS 105*.

> **Application to micro-entities:** Transition to FRS 105 is dealt with in Section 28 of FRS 105. The overall principles are identical to FRS 102, i.e. full retrospective restatement is the 'norm' but there are some mandatory exceptions and optional exemptions. The key differences are as follows:
>
> (1)   FRS 105 only identifies two areas where the accounting is not retrospectively restated: derecognition of financial assets and liabilities and accounting estimates. The other compulsory exceptions are not relevant under FRS 105.

> (2)   Many of the transitional provisions are the same as under FRS 102, to the extent that they are relevant; any differences are noted at **19.4**.

19.2   Basic procedures for preparing the first set of FRS 102 accounts

The basic procedures a company should follow in drawing up the opening balance sheet are set out in paragraph 35.7:

'(a)   recognise all assets and liabilities whose recognition is required by this FRS;

(b)   not recognise items as assets or liabilities if this FRS does not permit such recognition;

(c)   reclassify items that it recognised under its previous financial reporting framework as one type of asset, liability or component of equity, but are a different type of asset, liability or component of equity under this FRS; and

(d)   apply this FRS in measuring all recognised assets and liabilities.'

In summary, the general approach required by FRS 102 (and FRS 105) is to restate the balance sheet at the date of transition as it would have been had the new standard been applied at the time the balance sheet was prepared. The basic principle is of full retrospective application.

All of these steps are subject to the compulsory exceptions and voluntary exemptions discussed at **19.3** and **19.4** of this section respectively. In summary, though, the opening (transition date) balance sheet is prepared using a set of policies which complies with FRS 102, and any necessary adjustments to previously reported amounts are put through equity.

19.3   Compulsory exceptions

There are four areas in relation to which it is not permitted to make retrospective changes, so the position as at the transition date is carried over from the previous GAAP accounting, and any adjustments for compliance with FRS 102 are made only from that point onwards.

> **Application to micro-entities:** FRS 105 only identifies two areas where the accounting is not retrospectively restated: derecognition of financial assets and liabilities and accounting estimates. The other compulsory exceptions are not relevant to FRS 105.

19.3.1 *Derecognition of financial assets and liabilities*

If financial assets or financial liabilities were derecognised before the transition date then they may not be 're-recognised' on the transition date balance sheet, even if their derecognition would not have been permitted under the new standard.

If, however, the opposite applies and there are financial assets and liabilities on the balance sheet at transition which would have been derecognised before that point had FRS 102 always been in place, then there is a choice over whether to keep them on the opening balance sheet (that is, acting as if the derecognition event had not happened) or to remove them (that is, retrospectively applying the derecognition criteria in paragraphs 11.33–11.38).

19.3.2 *Accounting estimates*

Adoption of a new standard is not an opportunity to revisit accounting estimates retrospectively (thereby pushing changes through reserves rather than recognising them in profit). As set out in Section 10, and discussed at **2.5.1**, changes in estimates are dealt with prospectively by including the effect in profit or loss in the period of the change and, if relevant, future periods.

It would have been helpful if the standard could have been more explicit in these areas, as no explanation at all is given, only the phrase 'accounting estimates'. The best assumption seems to be that the intention is that transition date accounting estimates may not be revised, but those in the comparative period could be. If this is the case, entities wishing to push bad news out of the prior period and into the current period would theoretically be able to do so, though only if they could justify the change in estimate based on a substantive difference in FRS 102 (that is, so it could properly be classified as a transition adjustment). This does not seem likely to occur often, as FRS 102 has little content that would change accounting estimates.

19.3.3 *Measuring non-controlling interests*

Paragraph 5.6 requires profits and other comprehensive income to be split between non-controlling interests and owners of the parent, and paragraph 35.9 requires that this split is established only prospectively from the date of transition. For preparers that previously applied IFRS, though, the balance sheet will already contain a non-controlling interest balance representing the minority's initial share of the fair value of assets acquired plus its subsequent share of profits less distributions received, so the requirement at paragraph 5.6 is not new. It seems clear that this exclusion does not mean that an entity which already accounts for a non-controlling interest should actually stop doing so.

19.4   Optional exemptions

Paragraph 35.10 (and paragraph 28.10) permit, but do not require, entities to use the following exemptions on transition.

19.4.1   Business combinations

Business combinations taking place after the transition date must be accounted for under FRS 102.

An entity may elect not to apply FRS 102 to business combinations before the date of transition. However, if it elects to apply FRS 102 to any business combination before the transition date, it must apply it to all subsequent business combinations (paragraph 35.10(a)). If the exemption is taken, no adjustment may be made to the transition-date goodwill value. Conversely, if the exemption is not taken, and previous business combinations are restated, all of the requirements of FRS 102 need to be applied fully retrospectively as if the standard had been in place at the acquisition date.

> **Application to micro-entities**: This exemption is also included in FRS 105.28.10(a) but would only be applicable to trade and asset acquisitions in individual accounts, since FRS 105 cannot be applied to group accounts. FRS 105 does not permit the separation of intangible assets from goodwill, so if the exemption is not taken, it would be necessary to recombine goodwill and any separated intangible assets on transition. No deferred tax is required in micro-entity accounts.

19.4.2   Share-based payments

A first-time adopter is not required to apply Section 26 *Share-based Payment* to equity instruments, including the equity component of share-based payment transactions previously treated as compound instruments that were granted before the date of transition, or to liabilities that were settled before the date of transition. However, if the first time adopter had previously followed FRS 20, no amendment can be made on transition (paragraph 35.10(b)).

> **Application to micro-entities**: FRS 105.28.10(b) does include an exemption allowing that micro-entities do not have to apply Section 21 *Share-based Payment* to obligations arising from share-based payment transactions that were settled before the date of transition. However, micro-entities do not have

> to account for equity-settled share-based payments anyway so this exemption is relevant only to cash-settled share-based payments.

19.4.3 Fair value as deemed cost

A first-time adopter can elect to measure an item of property, plant or equipment, investment property or intangible asset at the date of transition at its fair value and use that fair value as its deemed cost at the date of transition (paragraph 35.10(c)). This exemption is available on an asset by asset basis.

> **Application to micro-entities**: Fair values and revaluations are prohibited under FRS 105 so this exemption is not available. Any assets that were measured at a valuation prior to adoption must revert to depreciated historical cost at the transition date (i.e. what the carrying value would have been had historic cost always been used).

19.4.4 Previous revaluation as deemed cost

On a similar basis to **19.4.3**, a previous revaluation may be used as deemed cost (paragraph 35.10(d)). This may be of interest to an entity which has previously revalued property but has not kept the valuations up to date, and does not wish to keep valuations up to date. The revaluation does need to have taken place on or prior to the transition date, though.

> **Application to micro-entities**: As with the exemption at **19.4.3**, this is not available to micro-entities.

19.4.5 Individual and separate financial statements

Paragraph 9.26, 14.4 and 15.9 require an entity to account for its investments in a subsidiary, associate or joint venture on of the following bases (as an accounting policy choice by class of investment):

(a) cost less impairment;

(b) at fair value with gains recognised in other comprehensive income (unless reversing a loss recognised in profit and loss); or

(c) at fair value with gains recognised in profit or loss (unless reversing a loss recognised in OCI).

If a first time adopter opts to use cost, it has a choice between:

(a) cost under FRS 102;

(b) carrying amount under previous GAAP as deemed cost (paragraph 35.10(f)).

In most cases cost as determined under FRS 102 will be the same as under FRS 105 or IFRS.

> **Application to micro-entities**: There is no equivalent exemption in FRS 105 because all micro-entities would need to account for these at cost less impairment.

19.4.6   Compound financial instruments

Section 22 of FRS 102 requires a compound financial instrument to be split into liability and equity elements at the date of issue. Where the liability component is not outstanding at the date of transition, a first-time adopter need not separate the elements (paragraph 35.10(g)).

> **Application to micro-entities**: The exemption is identical in FRS 105.28.10(d).

19.4.7   Service concession arrangements – operators

There is no requirement to apply the requirements of FRS 102 to service concession arrangements entered into before the date of transition. Such concession can continue to be accounted for under previous GAAP (paragraph 35.10(i)). This exemption is only available for operators, not grantors.

> **Application to micro-entities**: There is no equivalent exemption in FRS 105 as it is unlikely to be relevant.

19.4.8   Extractive industries

Special transitional rules may apply. Given the limited application of this area, it is not considered further (paragraph 35.10(j)).

> **Application to micro-entities**: There is no equivalent exemption in FRS 105 as it is unlikely to be relevant.

19.4.9   Determining whether an arrangement contains a lease

A first-time adopter can determine whether an arrangement constitutes or contains a lease at the date of transition, rather than when the arrangement was entered into (paragraph 35.10(k)). Note that there is no exemption around classification of a lease as finance or operating, only whether or not a lease actually exists.

> **Application to micro-entities**: The exemption is identical in FRS 105.28.10(e).

19.4.10 Decommissioning liabilities included in the cost of property, plant and equipment

A first-time adopter can measure the component of cost relating to decommissioning property, plant and equipment at the date of transition, rather than at the date the asset was acquired or the obligation arose (paragraph 35.10(l)).

> **Application to micro-entities**: The exemption is identical in FRS 105.28.10(f).

19.4.11 Dormant companies

A dormant company may elect to retain its accounting policies for measurement until there is any change to the balances or the company undertakes any new transactions (paragraph 35.10(m)).

This ensures that the adoption of FRS 102 does not of itself trigger a transaction which needs to be recorded and therefore causes the company to cease to be dormant. If such companies were required to restate the financial statements on transition to FRS 102, they would in many cases cease to be dormant.

> **Application to micro-entities**: The exemption is identical in FRS 105.28.10(g).

19.4.12 Borrowing costs

The date of transition may be the date on which capitalisation of borrowing costs commences (paragraph 35.10(o)). In other words, where a policy of capitalisation is adopted for the first time on transition to FRS 102, it only needs to start from the transition date rather than attempting to retrospectively restate the transition-date balance sheet.

> **Application to micro-entities**: There is no equivalent exemption in FRS 105 because borrowing costs must be expensed as incurred under that standard.

19.4.13 Lease incentives

A first-time adopter may elect not to apply the requirements of paragraph 20.15 where the lease term commenced before date of transition. This means that having started to recognise lease incentives over the period to the next on-market rent review, the entity may continue to do so on that basis (paragraph 35.10(p)).

The usual retrospective treatment would be to restate the incentive over the terms of the lease.

> **Application to micro-entities**: The exemption is identical in FRS 105.28.10(h).

19.4.14   Public benefit entity combinations

Public benefit entities adopting FRS 102 for the first time may elect not to apply Section 34 of FRS 102 where a business combination occurred before date of transition (paragraph 35.10(q)).

> **Application to micro-entities**: There is no equivalent exemption in FRS 105 because most public benefit entities will not qualify as micro-entities.

19.4.15   Assets and liabilities of subsidiaries, associates or joint ventures

This exemption relates to subsidiaries, joint ventures and associates which become first-time adopters later than the parent entity, and allows them to use the amounts that would be included in the parent's consolidated accounts, based on the parent's transition date, in its own financial statements.

> **Application to micro-entities**: There is no equivalent exemption in FRS 105.

19.4.16   Designation of previously recognised financial instruments

Certain debt instruments may be designated as at fair value through profit or loss provided that this results in more relevant information, because either:

(a) it eliminates or significantly reduces a measurement or recognition inconsistency (sometimes referred to as 'an accounting mismatch' that would otherwise arise from measuring assets or debt instruments or recognising gains and losses on them on different bases (paragraph 11.14(b)(i)); or

(b) a group of debt instruments or financial assets and debt instruments is managed and its performance evaluated on a fair value basis, in accordance with a documented risk management or investment strategy, and information about that group of instruments is provided internally on that basis to key management personnel (paragraph 11.14(b)(ii)).

The treatment usually is allowed only if it meets the conditions on initial recognition. The exemption allows the treatment if it meets the conditions outlined above at the date of transition.

> **Application to micro-entities**: There is no equivalent exemption in FRS 105.

19.4.17   Hedge accounting

There are three generous exemptions around application of hedge accounting:

(1) where a hedging relationship existed at the transition date, first-time adopters can still apply hedge accounting even if it was not formally designated and documented at that point, as long as this is done prior to the date of approval of the accounts;

(2) where a hedging relationship ceased to exist before the transition date because the hedging instrument was sold, terminated, or exercised pre-transition, first-time adopters can elect not to adjust the carrying amount of an asset or liability for previous GAAP accounting effects of a hedging relationship that has ceased to exist;

(3) where a hedging relationship commenced post-transition, first-time adopters can still apply hedge accounting even if it was not formally designated and documented at that point, as long as this is done prior to the date of approval of the accounts.

> **Application to micro-entities**: There is no equivalent exemption in FRS 105 as micro-entities cannot apply hedge accounting.

19.4.18   FRS 105 – investment property exemption

In addition to those highlighted above, FRS 105 contains a specific transitional exemption which is not included in FRS 102 in relation to investment property. On adoption of FRS 105 investment property must be retrospectively restated at depreciated historical cost.

There is no exemption from full retrospective restatement, but there is some relief in how it is applied. If the exemption is taken a micro-entity can apply depreciation to an investment property based on the useful life of the most significant component of the investment property, rather than having to identify useful lives for separate major components (which would normally be required). To apply this exemption, the micro-entity would apply the following procedure:

(1) Determine the total cost of the investment property including all of its components. Where no depreciation had been charged under the micro-entity's previous financial reporting framework, this can be calculated by reversing any revaluation gains or losses previously recorded in equity reserves.

491

(2) Separate the cost of land from buildings.

(3) Estimate the total depreciated cost of the investment property (excluding land) at the date of transition to FRS 105 by recognising accumulated depreciation since the date of initial acquisition calculated on the basis of the useful life of the most significant component of the item of investment property (e.g. the main structural elements of the building).

(4) Allocate a portion of the estimated total depreciated cost calculated in paragraph (3) to each of the other major components (i.e. excluding the most significant component identified above) to determine their depreciated cost. The allocation should be made on a reasonable and consistent basis. For example, a possible basis of allocation is to multiply the current cost to replace the component by the ratio of its remaining useful life to the expected useful life of a replacement component.

(5) Allocate any amount of the total depreciated cost not allocated under (4) to the most significant component of the investment property.

19.5   General impracticability clause

Paragraph 35.11 contains a very theoretically broad exemption from making restatements of the opening balance sheet where it is 'impracticable'. This term is defined in the Glossary as meaning that the entity cannot apply a requirement 'after making every reasonable effort to do so'.

Where this is the case, instead of restating the transition date balance sheet, the relevant requirement is applied from the earliest point possible after this date, with disclosures of which data has not been restated.

In practice, there will only be rare circumstances in which it is necessary to take this general exemption, because of the large number of specific exemptions discussed above.

19.6   Disclosures

Section 35 requires an explanation of how the transition from the old to the new financial reporting framework has affected an entity's financial position, financial performance and cash flows. Paragraph 35.13 then explains what constitutes such an explanation:

(a) a description of the nature of each change in accounting policy;

(b) reconciliations of [the entity's] equity determined in accordance with its previous financial reporting framework to its equity determined in accordance with this FRS for both of the following dates:

   (i)   the date of transition to this FRS; and

   (ii) the end of the latest period presented in the entity's most recent annual financial statements determined in accordance with its previous financial reporting framework;

(c) a reconciliation of the profit or loss determined in accordance with its previous financial reporting framework for the latest period in the entity's most recent annual financial statements to its profit or loss determined in accordance with this FRS for the same period.

In the reconciliations, the effect of changing accounting policies on adoption of FRS 102 should, where practicable, be distinguished from any restatements of errors picked up as part of the transition process.

Where an entity has applied FRS 102 in a previous reporting period but not in its most recent annual financial statements, paragraph 35.12A requires the following disclosures are made:

(a) the reason the entity stopped applying FRS 102;

(b) the reason for resuming the application of FRS 102; and

(c) whether the entity has applied Section 35 or has applied FRS 102 fully retrospectively.

Small entities are not required to give this disclosure, but it is encouraged by Appendix D to Section 1A and should be considered in the context of ensuring the accounts give a true and fair view. In practice, where a small entity has material adjustments to make on transition, it would be difficult to justify making no disclosure about them.

Application to micro-entities: Micro-entities are not required to make any disclosures about transition to FRS 105.

Example 19.1

This example sets out two possible formats for the required transition disclosures, for the December 2019 accounts of a company adopting FRS 102 for the first time, having previously applied FRS 105, with a transition date of 1 January 2019.

Illustrative examples – option 1

Reconciliation of equity

	Note	At 1 Jan 2019			At 31 Dec 2019		
		Previous GAAP	Effect of transition	FRS 102	Previous GAAP	Effect of transition	FRS 102
		£'000	£'000	£'000	£'000	£'000	£'000
Fixed assets		14,083	-	14,083	12,998	-	12,998
Current assets	(i) (ii)	5,940	36	5,976	6,048	41	6,089
Creditors: amounts falling due within one year	(i)	(5,652)	(38)	(5,690)	(4,378)	(48)	(4,426)
Net current assets		288	(2)	286	1,670	(7)	1,663
Total assets less current liabilities		14,371	(2)	14,369	14,668	(7)	14,661
Creditors: amounts falling due after more than one year	(i)	(6,960)	(15)	(6,975)	(6,816)	(7)	(6,823)
Provisions for liabilities		(984)	-	(984)	(1,116)	-	(1,116)
Net assets		6,427	(17)	6,410	6,736	(14)	6,722
Capital and reserves		6,427	(17)	6,410	6,736	(14)	6,722

Reconciliation of profit or loss for the year

	Note	Year ended 31 Dec 2019		
		Previous GAAP	Effect of transition	FRS 102
		£'000	£'000	£'000
Turnover		1,997	-	1,997
Cost of sales	(i) (ii)	(1,248)	(7)	(1,255)
Gross profit		749	(7)	742
Administrative expenses	(i) (ii)	(156)	10	(146)
Other operating income		101	-	101
Operating profit		694	3	697
Interest receivable and similar income		12	-	12
Interest payable and similar charges		(312)	-	(312)
Taxation		(84)	-	(84)
Profit on ordinary activities after taxation and for the financial year		310	3	313

Illustrative examples – option 2

Reconciliation of equity

	Note	At 1 Jan 2019	At 31 Dec 2019
		£'000	£'000
Capital and reserves (as previously stated)		6,427	6,736
Recognition of derivative financial instruments	(i)	(17)	(12)
Re-measurement of stock using spot exchange rate	(ii)	-	(2)
Capital and reserves (as restated)		6,410	6,722

Reconciliation of profit or loss for the year

	Note	Year ended 31 Dec 2019
		£'000
Profit for the year (as previously stated)		310
Recognition of derivative financial instruments	(i)	5
Re-measurement of stock using spot exchange rate	(ii)	(2)
Profit for the year (as restated)		313

Notes to the reconciliations

The following notes are applicable to both options set out above.

Financial instruments

(i)   Brit Ltd previously applied FRS 105 and was not previously required to recognise derivative financial instruments on the balance sheet as a result. Instead the effects of the derivative financial instruments were recognised in profit or loss when the instruments were settled. Derivative financial instruments are classified as 'other financial instruments' in FRS 102 and are recognised as a financial asset or a financial liability, at fair value, when an entity becomes party to the contractual provisions of the instrument. Consequently, financial assets of £36,000 and financial liabilities of £38,000 have been recognised in the opening balance sheet at 1 January 2019. Financial assets of £43,000 and financial liabilities of £48,000 have been recognised in the balance sheet as at 31 December 2019. Derivatives are measured at fair value with gains (losses) from changes in fair value recognised in profit or loss. The effect on profit for the year ended 31 December 2019 is an increase of £5,000.

(ii)   The derivative financial instruments are foreign exchange forward contracts. In applying FRS 105, Brit Ltd was required to translate purchases in foreign currencies at the rate of exchange specified in a matching forward contract. This is not permitted by FRS 102, which requires purchases to be translated using the spot exchange rate on the date of the transaction. FRS 102 does not provide an exemption from measuring stock bought in a foreign currency and paid for before the transition date in accordance with its required accounting policies, but the difference is not material and accordingly no adjustment has been made. Items purchased since the transition date have been re-measured based on spot exchange rate. Consequently, stock at 31 December 2019 has been reduced and cost of sales for the year then ended has been increased by £2,000 and costs of £5,000 have been reclassified as administrative expenses rather than cost of sales.

19.7   Practical tips

In this section, we suggest some practical tips for applying the requirements of Section 35 and anticipating issues as soon as possible.

> **Application to micro-entities**: These tips and suggestions generally apply equally to micro-entity accounts, although some specific areas (such as defined benefit scheme accounting) are not relevant to micro-entity accounts because the underlying requirements differ.

19.7.1   Plan ahead

FRS 102 generally requires retrospective application so it is important to identify those areas most likely to have a significant impact on your financial statements and actions which might be taken to ease the burden, for example deciding which exemptions to take. In particular, you need to identify those actions which are time-critical. Particular care will need to be taken by entities that engage in hedging activities or that have defined benefit pension schemes.

19.7.2   Review accounting policies

At an early stage entities should perform a detailed review of whether their current accounting policies meet the requirements of FRS 102 and whether change is necessary or desirable. In some cases the requirements under FRS 102 will be different from previous GAAP and changes in accounting policy will be inevitable. However, transition to FRS 102 can also provide an opportunity to look again at current accounting policies and reconsider their appropriateness to the business. In some cases there will also be accounting options that were not previously available.

19.7.3   Gather information for the restatement of comparatives

Do not underestimate the challenge of restating comparative information, including numerical and narrative disclosures, on adoption of FRS 102. There may be disclosures which were not required previously or which are now required in greater depth. This information will generally be easier to gather at the time a transaction takes place or on or near the date a particular balance arises, rather than when the first FRS 102 financial statements are being prepared.

19.7.4   Establish fair values at the appropriate time

Although usually it will be possible to obtain fair values at a later date, it will involve more effort and research than if the valuations are done as close as possible to the date to be reflected in the valuation.

19.7.5   Determine priorities

Some areas of the financial statements will be more specifically affected than others by the changes in accounting policies. As part of the planning process it may be useful to produce a table of the items in the financial statements and identify the extent to which these will be affected by moving to FRS 102 using an 'ABC' (or similar) grading, where:

- 'A' represents items likely to have major issues or impact on conversion to FRS 102;

- 'B' represents modest impact or issues; and

- 'C' represents items that are unlikely to be significantly affected.

Such an approach is designed to focus attention at an early stage on the key areas in which additional resource or expertise may be required.

19.7.6   Identify financial instruments

Make sure that contracts and agreements are reviewed to identify all financial instruments within your business at the earliest possible stage, including contracts such as derivatives that may not have previously been recognised on the balance sheet (this is discussed further in **7.3**). Some accounting options will be available only when the necessary steps have been taken by the transition date. Fair values are used extensively in the measurement of certain financial instruments and this information is gathered more easily at the time of transition than at a later date.

19.7.7   Keep contract terms basic wherever possible

Make sure all staff with responsibilities for negotiating contracts on behalf of the organisation, from sales and trade purchases to financing arrangements, are aware of the potential pitfalls associated with any unusual contract terms. It may be helpful to draw up a list of issues that need consideration or ensure prior approval before contracts are completed.

19.7.8   Consider the effects of foreign exchange transactions

When the entity has entered into a forward currency contract to hedge the risk of a recognised debtor or creditor balance (e.g. arising from a sale or purchase) at the date the debtor or creditor is first recognised, the standard accounting treatment under FRS 102 will usually ensure no accounting mismatch arises. The debtor or creditor will be translated at the closing rate with any exchange difference recognised in profit or loss, and the related forward currency contract will be measured at FVTPL.

Therefore, there is no need to designate or document the hedging relationship as the treatment of the hedging instrument and the hedged item are already matched.

19.7.9 *Assess the impact on employment costs and profit-related bonuses*

FRS 102 introduces guidance on the treatment of employment costs requiring, for example, the inclusion of accrued holiday pay where material. They also include guidance on the other areas of remuneration such as profit-related pay and bonuses and the treatment of termination payments such as redundancy pay. For companies transitioning from FRS 105, FRS 102 also introduces a requirement to account fully for equity-settled share-based payment schemes. Previously, these would not have been accounted for but would only require disclosure.

Many companies also have profit-related pay or bonus arrangements. These will typically be based on profit before tax in the published financial statements. As a new accounting standard could change that profit figure, the bonus will also change unless the basis of calculation changes. The question for the entity is whether such changes should be rewarded by inclusion in the bonus or whether changes should be made to the basis of any profit-related pay agreement or bonus scheme. Such changes do not need to be in place by the date of transition, but should have been made by the beginning of the first reporting period under the new GAAP.

19.7.10 *Review group defined benefit plans*

As discussed in **14.7.11**, when there is a contractual agreement or stated policy in place for charging the net benefit cost of a group defined benefit plan to individual group entities, the accounting treatment will follow the terms of the contractual agreement or policy. When no such agreement exists, the net defined benefit cost will be recognised in the individual financial statements of the group entity that is legally responsible for the plan, usually the parent. The other group entities will recognise a cost equal to their contribution payable for the period in their individual financial statements. Putting an agreement in place by the transition date will therefore have a direct impact on how the net defined benefit cost is allocated between the individual entities in the group.

Additionally, if there is an agreement to fund a deficit in a multi-employer plan (such as a schedule of contributions), the entity will need to calculate and recognise the net present value of the committed payment.

19.7.11   Consider taxation

Accounting profit is the starting point for taxable profit. Adjustments are required to reflect alternative treatments imposed by tax law. As accounting profit changes, so does taxable profit – unless overridden by tax law.

Where accounting policy or exemption choices result in differing accounting profits – and, as a result, differing taxable profits – an entity may wish to choose the option which gives the lower taxable profit – unless the adverse effect on balance sheet outweighs the tax advantage.

Index

Index